GLOBAL ISSUES

WORLD POVERTY

Sylvia Whitman

Foreword by Steven N. Durlauf

University of Wisconsin at Madison

Viva Books

New Delhi | Mumbai | Chennai | Kolkata | Bangalore | Hyderabad | Kochi | Guwahati

First Indian Edition 2010

VIVA BOOKS PRIVATE LIMITED

- 4737/23 Ansari Road, Daryaganj, New Delhi 110 002
  E-mail: vivadelhi@vivagroupindia.net, Tel. 42242200
- 76, Service Industries, Shirvane, Sector 1, Nerul, Navi Mumbai 400 706
  E-mail: vivamumbai@vivagroupindia.net, Tel. 27721273, 27721274
- Jamals Fazal Chambers, 26 Greams Road, Chennai 600 006
  E-mail: vivachennai@vivagroupindia.net, Tel. 28290304, 28294241
- B-103, Jindal Towers, 21/1A/3 Darga Road, Kolkata 700 017
  E-mail: vivakolkata@vivagroupindia.net, Tel. 22836381, 22816713
- 7, Sovereign Park Apartments, 56-58, K. R. Road, Basavanagudi, Bangalore 560 004
  E-mail: vivabangalore@vivagroupindia.net, Tel. 26607409, 26607410
- 101-102 Mughal Marc Apartments, 3-4-637 to 641, Narayanguda, Hyderabad 500 029
  E-mail: vivahyderabad@vivagroupindia.net. Tel. 27564481, 27564482
- First Floor, Beevi Towers, SRM Road, Kaloor, Kochi 682 018, Kerala
  E-mail: vivakochi@vivagroupindia.net, Tel: 0484-2403055, 2403056
- 232, GNB Road, Beside UCO Bank, Silpukhuri, Guwahati 781 003
  E-mail: vivaguwahati@vivagroupindia.net, Tel: 0361-2666386

www.vivagroupindia.com

Published by arrangement with

Facts on File, Inc.
132 West 31st Street
New York 10001
USA

ISBN 978-81-309-1427-5

Published by Vinod Vasishtha for Viva Books Private Limited, 4737/23, Ansari Road, Daryaganj, New Delhi-110 002. Printed and bound by Anand Sons, Delhi - 110 092.

CONTENTS

Foreword

Not only arbitrariness, however, but also contingent physical factors and circumstances based on external conditions . . . may reduce individuals to poverty. In this condition, they are left with the needs of civil society and yet since society has at the same time taken from them the natural means of acquisition . . . and also dissolves . . . the bonds of the family in its wider sense as a kinship group . . . they are more or less deprived of all advantages of society, such as the ability to acquire skills and education, in general, as well as of the administration of justice, health care, or even of the consolation of religion.

—G. W. F. Hegel, *Elements of the Philosophy of Right* § 241

It is both a pleasure and a source of envy to introduce Sylvia Whitman's *Global Issues: World Poverty* to high school and general readers. The pleasure stems from the comprehensiveness of the material and the clarity of the writing. The envy applies to a reader who may for the first time be exposed to the ways in which social science can illuminate the most difficult questions. The problem of world poverty is both so serious and so complex that it is easy to despair of its reduction. The optimistic message of *World Poverty* is that progress is possible both in understanding the causes of poverty and in its amelioration. The pessimistic message is that it is far from obvious how changes in the level of poverty, as it currently exists, can be achieved.

An important theme in *Global Issues: World Poverty* is the recognition that the term *poverty*, as a general catchall phrase, embodies very different phenomena. For the United States, poverty is a condition that affects a fraction of the population, whereas in places like sub-Saharan Africa, poverty is endemic. Further, the consequences of economic deprivation are very different for the citizen of an affluent society than they are for the citizen of a poor one. As Nobel Laureate in Economics Friedrich Hayek wrote in *The Constitution of Liberty,*

> *In a progressive society . . . poverty has . . . become a relative, rather than an absolute, concept. This does not make it less bitter. Although in an advanced society the unsatisfied wants are usually no longer physical needs, but the results of civilization, it is still true at each stage some of the things most people desire can be provided only for a few and can be made accessible to all only by further progress.*

The heterogeneity of poverty does not invalidate its usefulness as a concept, but rather means that one should be sensitive to the extent to which one is concerned with an absolute set of living standards or about the degree of inequality between the most and least affluent. The distinctions among various types of poverty have obvious implications for the ethical justification of foreign aid versus domestic poverty amelioration, as well as for the ethical justification of possible policy interventions when considered in isolation. And Hayek's remarks hint at the importance of economic growth in reducing poverty. For the developing countries, most would agree that policies that improve growth performance would be far more important in reducing poverty than policies that engage in redistribution.

Another important theme of *World Poverty* is that poverty derives from a range of social, political, and economic factors and these factors can vary widely in relative importance, depending on context. This is most obvious when one compares the determinants of poverty in different countries. Arguments that geography contributes to low levels of economic development have little to do with the American experience. The claim also applies to time. The poverty of Victorian England derives from factors very different from the poverty of contemporary London.

It is easy to study the basic facts of poverty and feel a profound need for government to act aggressively to combat it. The scholarly study of poverty is important partially because it makes clear that this impulse must be assessed with respect to what is in fact feasible. The presence of poverty does not speak to the lack of effectiveness of any particular government policy. Although the moral importance of aiding poor countries is not in dispute, there are deep disagreements about whether specific policies have succeeded in stimulating economic development. The magnitude of Third World poverty does not diminish the problems of governmental corruption, lack of well-defined property rights, or, for that matter, limits to the ability of an outside agency to make economically efficient judgments at a local level.

In the case of American poverty, decades of research have failed to identify a magic bullet, although one can point to policies that have made a change. For example, John Donohue and James Heckman in their paper, "Continuous Versus Episodic Change: The Impact of Civil Rights Policy on the Economic Status of Blacks," show how civil rights legislation had a massive effect on the economic status of blacks. Their findings are in fact a hint as to why policy solutions to contemporaneous poverty are less evident than was the case 50 years ago. The lifting of barriers to economic participation of the type faced by blacks for much of American history allowed the private economy to "do the work" of increasing affluence among those who had been the victims of the barriers. Contemporary poverty has elements that are self-perpetuating because of peers, role models, or social norms. These factors are exacerbated by the economic stratification that occurs, for example in housing patterns, when individuals choose neighborhoods. Put differently, to the extent that high poverty neighborhoods constitute poverty traps, in which low education, single parenthood, drug use, etc., become self-perpetuating via social influences, it is less obvious how policy can break these factors.

Analyzing the correlation between neighborhoods and levels of poverty is useful as it illustrates an important point about the relationship between positive claims about the determinants of poverty and normative claims about the obligations of society toward the poor. The argument that certain behaviors are self-perpetuating via social factors is often criticized as "blaming the poor." Such a claim is confused. Children do not choose the neighborhoods in which they grow up, and their parents often make these choices because of financial constraints. Similarly, the suggestion that there are cultural determinants to levels of economic growth does not make sense. Glenn Loury has argued in the *Anatomy of Racial Inequality* that African-American economic opportunities are now more impeded by stigma than overt racism, by which he means that there are perceptions that blacks are less able than whites. Stigma is a social influence just as role models are. Another example of the difficulties in designing effective antipoverty policies concerns the question of timing. Should efforts be made to improve the environments of the very young or should efforts be focused on adolescence? There are good reasons to think that interventions may not be effective if they do not occur early in life. James Heckman has argued, I believe persuasively, that resources spent on improving the environment of the very young versus other ages are strongly justified by cost benefit calculations. Yet Heckman's research and that of others means that effective government policies may take a very long time before being effective. And effective interventions may be quite expensive.

My emphasis on the limits to what may be done to reduce poverty is not meant to suggest that poverty is intractable, but rather to indicate why a book of this type is so important. Public policy debates all too often degenerate into advocacy based on utopian considerations, whether one considers the suggestion that poverty will naturally disappear if the economy is unencumbered by government interventions or the claim that poverty among minorities is largely due to overt discrimination. Poverty is far too complex a phenomenon for simple solutions. Much of the virtue of *World Poverty* derives from the richness of its analyses. It is inevitable for such a wide-ranging endeavor that one comes across claims with which one disagrees; but it is hard to imagine a better introduction than *World Poverty* to this profoundly difficult subject.

—Steven N. Durlauf
Department of Economics
University of Wisconsin at Madison

List of Acronyms

ADB	Asian Development Bank
ADC	Aid to Dependent Children
AFDC	Aid to Families with Dependent Children
AIDS	acquired immunodeficiency syndrome
ARV	antiretroviral
BIA	Bureau of Indian Affairs
CAFTA	Central American Free Trade Agreement
CCC	Civilian Conservation Corps
CEDAW	Convention on the Elimination of All Forms of Discrimination Against Women
CEO	chief executive officer
CIA	Central Intelligence Agency
CODISRA	Commission on Discrimination and Racism against Indigenous Peoples
CSSM	Child Survival and Safe Motherhood
DFI	direct foreign investment
DOCS	Doctors on Call for Service
DRC	Democratic Republic of the Congo
ESL	English as a Second Language
EU	European Union
FAO	Food and Agriculture Organization
FDA	Food and Drug Administration
FEMA	Federal Emergency Management Agency
FERA	Federal Emergency Relief Administration
FHA	Federal Housing Administration
FSA	Farm Security Administration
GATT	General Agreement on Tariffs and Trade
GDP	gross domestic product
GED	general equivalency diploma

GMO	genetically modified organism
GNP	gross national product
HDI	Human Development Index
HIPC	Heavily Indebted Poor Countries
HIV	human immunodeficiency virus
HPI	human poverty index
HUD	U.S. Department of Housing and Urban Development
IBRD	International Bank for Reconstruction and Development
ICFTU	International Confederation of Free Trade Unions
IDA	International Development Association
IDP	internally displaced person
ILO	International Labour Organization
IMF	International Monetary Fund
I-PRSP	Interim Poverty Reduction Strategy Paper
ISC	Institute for Sustainable Communities
ISP	Internet service provider
MDB	Multilateral Development Bank
MDG	Millennium Development Goal
MDRI	multilateral debt relief initiative
MENA	Middle East and North Africa
NGO	nongovernmental organization
OECD	Organisation for Economic Co-operation and Development
OVC	orphans and vulnerable children
PRONADE	National Program for Community Management of Educational Development
PRSP	Poverty Reduction Strategy Paper
PRWORA	Personal Responsibility and Work Opportunity Reconcilation Act
SAP	structural adjustment program
SCHIP	State Children's Health Insurance Program
SCLC	Southern Christian Leadership Conference
SEBC	Syrian-European Business Centre
SMES	small and medium enterprises
SSI	Supplemental Security Income
TANF	Temporary Assistance for Needy Families
TVA	Tennessee Valley Authority
UNDAF	United Nations Development Assistance Framework
UNDP	United Nations Development Programme
UNESCO	United Nations Educational, Scientific and Cultural Organization
UNFPA	United Nations Population Fund

List of Acronyms

UNHCR	United Nations High Commissioner for Refugees
UNICEF	United Nations Children's Fund
UNRWA	United Nations Relief and Works Agency
USAID	United States Agency for International Development
USDA	United States Department of Agriculture
USSR	Union of Soviet Socialist Republics
VA	United States Department of Veterans Affairs
WFP	World Food Programme
WHO	World Health Organization
WIC	Women, Infants, and Children Program
WID/GAD	Women in Development/Gender and Development
WPA	Works Progress Administration
WTO	World Trade Organization

PART I

At Issue

1

Introduction

Poverty is the worst form of violence.
—Mohandas Gandhi (1869–1948)

To be poor is to struggle. About 40 percent of the world's population lives on less than $2 per day according to 2004 World Bank estimates. Roughly one in seven people—just under a billion—subsist on less than $1.[1] These numbers only hint at human misery. In Albania, more than a third of children under 14 work—cleaning shoes, picking crops, running drugs, but especially begging.[2] In Pakistan, laborers sell their kidneys to transplant clinics to pay debts.[3] In Niger, one of Africa's poorest countries, aid workers reported that desperate parents were feeding starving children grass and leaves in summer 2005 after drought and locusts had destroyed food crops.[4] Even in years without famine, a quarter of Niger's children die before the age of five.[5]

The good news is that poverty has decreased over the past two centuries. In 1820, most people lived and died in extreme poverty. By 1950, just over half did. Worldwide, the average life expectancy jumped from 27 to 50 years over that same time period, and by 1992, it had climbed to 62.[6] Improvement accelerated at the end of the 20th century, thanks in part to China's economic leap forward.[7] Between 1981 and 2001, the percentage of the extremely poor fell from 53 to 8 percent of the Chinese population—a sign of progress for 400 million people.[8]

Poverty has retreated, but it has not disappeared. Since 1820, the number of poor people in Africa has almost doubled.[9] While poverty exists everywhere, it is not evenly distributed. Most extreme poverty—survival on less than $1 a day—surfaces in the least developed countries, particularly in heavily populated South Asia and sub-Saharan Africa, and particularly in rural areas within those regions. Even when economists take into account differences in purchasing power, the average American enjoys an income 20 times greater than the average sub-Saharan African.[10] As prosperity has increased, so too has inequality, not only around the globe but also within countries. The gap between rich and poor is growing in China, for instance. In Bolivia, fewer than 100 families own five times more property than the land that 2 million families cultivate. Poverty afflicts women and children and certain minorities disproportionately; the Bolivian poor include 88 percent of the indigenous population.[11] In many countries, poverty has disappeared only from view, concentrated in disadvantaged regions or neighborhoods or households. Troubled by the growing disparity between "haves" and "have-nots," the United Nations made halving extreme poverty and hunger between 1990 and 2015 the first of its eight Millennium Development Goals (MDGs).

DEFINITIONS OF POVERTY

Participants at the 1995 UN World Summit on Social Development in Copenhagen, Denmark, defined *absolute poverty* as "a condition characterized by severe deprivation of basic human needs, including food, safe drinking water, sanitation facilities, health, shelter, education and information."[12] While people living in absolute poverty struggle first and foremost to stay alive, problems compound one another: Hunger, homelessness, illiteracy, discrimination, low self-esteem, ill health, and early death overlap and interlock.

It is easier to define poverty than to characterize the poor, although stereotypes abound—"helpless victims," for instance, or "lazy bums." The poor have in common an insecure situation, and their vulnerability and invisibility combine to undermine their social standing and political power. "Lack of work worries me," admits an Egyptian father, one of the 60,000 poor men and women whose voices the World Bank collected at the turn of the 21st century. "My children were hungry and I told them the rice is cooking, until they fell asleep."[13] Although anyone can experience short-term or intensified hardship after natural disasters, such as hurricanes or earthquakes, poverty is usually a chronic condition, a complex trap. "If you were born to a poor father, he cannot educate you and cannot give you any land, or very little land of poor quality; every generation gets poorer," observes a Ugandan.[14] Because of prejudice or corruption, the poor often encounter barriers that prevent them from taking advantage of public services, from roads to schools. In India, "If you don't know anyone, you will be thrown to the corner of a hospital!"[15]

Social systems—legal, economic, political, traditional—often exclude the poor from rights, resources, and relationships.[16] "Poverty is humiliation, the sense of being dependent on them [the better off], and of being forced to accept rudeness, insults, and indifference when we seek help," says one Latvian.[17] In Bulgaria, Roma (Gypsy) men and women complain that officials always turn down a Roma's application: "They drop their voices and tell him to come some other time. . . . If you decide to lodge a complaint they tell you, 'Who do you think you are, what are you fighting for?' You might be slapped in the face so hard that they'll send you flying through the door."[18] As the poor recognize, people's experiences shape who they are or imagine they could be. Poverty shackles dreams. As a Georgian citizen concludes, "Poverty is lack of freedom, enslaved by crushing daily burden, by depression and fear of what the future will bring."[19]

Experts often distinguish between *absolute poverty*—the scramble for survival—and *relative poverty*—lack compared to other people, or households, within a given region. Absolute poverty is rare in industrialized countries such as Japan and the United States, where the poor seldom die of hunger, for instance. Being poor may mean choosing between medicine and groceries or owning a car that doubles as a bedroom because housing is too expensive. Still, in the United States as abroad, poverty deprives people not only of their physical needs but often of their hope, self-respect, and human rights. "My name is not 'Those People,'" wrote Julia Dinsmore in 1998, when she was living on $621 a month in cash welfare benefits supplemented by $169 in food stamps. "My name is not 'Ignorant, Dumb or Uneducated.'"[20] Although the richest country in the world, the United States has one of the highest poverty rates among industrialized nations. Poverty persists in pockets and bands concentrated in the Southeast, Southwest, Appalachia, and Native American reservations. According to the U.S. Census Bureau, 36.5 million Americans were living in poverty in 2006, and many scholars consider that official figure conservative.

Contemporary definitions of both absolute and relative poverty acknowledge that people have more than physical needs. Nobel Prize–winning economist Amartya Sen, for instance, has described four dimensions of poverty that interfere with functioning in society: lack of opportunity, capability, security, and empowerment. All sorts of barriers, from unreliable transportation to political cronyism, may block access to good jobs, and women often carry extra burdens of childcare and household responsibilities. Shoddy education and health care erode human potential. Just getting by, the poor rarely have financial cushions to carry them through a flood or a layoff, and little protects them from domestic or civil violence. To call the poor "downtrodden" is to acknowledge that power holders in the home, the town, and the nation ignore or silence their voices.[21]

MEASURES OF POVERTY

Governments and donors depend on poverty assessments to allocate aid, evaluate programs, and track change over time. "If you can't measure it, you can't manage it," according to PARIS 21, a worldwide consortium of number crunchers affiliated with the United Nations.[22] Sizing up poverty is an inexact and controversial science, however. Researchers commonly use three tools: poverty lines, participatory appraisals, and poverty indexes.[23] Poverty mapping, a relatively new technique, color codes data gathered from other instruments and paints it onto maps to highlight regional inequality.

Poverty Lines

The study of poverty draws heavily from economics, a mathematically inclined social science. Poverty lines quantify deprivation. Experts set a baseline of income or expenditures, survey households, and count who falls below the cutoff. As long as researchers design the model carefully and gather accurate information from a representative sample, this method provides precise, objective, and standard results, with figures that can be easily compared from year to year or group to group. Drawbacks, however, include the high cost of large-scale surveying and the need to avoid new variables. Critics also question the long-standing practice of gathering information from households and then extrapolating figures for individuals, which overlooks inequalities within the household, such as between men and women, or among adults, children, and the elderly.

At the beginning of the 20th century, as understanding of nutrition deepened, social scientists began measuring poverty by food consumption. Hunger resonates with the public. It represents the most absolute poverty and stirs the conscience; no one wants to deny a starving person a bowl of soup. Since most people require about 2,000 calories a day to maintain their weight, researchers figured out the cheapest shopping list for a balanced diet. Next, they decided what proportion of income families should spend on food (in the United States, the rule of thumb is about a third). Then they drew a line: If a family did not earn enough to fill the hypothetical grocery cart, the family qualified as poor. To this day, the U.S. Census Bureau defines a "poverty threshold" using a formula adjusted for family size and inflation that was developed from 1960s U.S. Department of Agriculture (USDA) emergency food budgets.

Although many countries still use calorie-based poverty lines, critics point out their many limitations. First of all, the 2,000-calorie model does not fit all. Farmers and other manual laborers burn more energy than sedentary urbanites and office workers. Furthermore, men usually need to eat more than women and children. Nor do cheap calories always equal the variety that people crave and good nutrition requires. In addition, food costs and eating patterns differ geographically and culturally. When estimating poverty, experts have incorporated more and more of these variables. Instead of measuring hunger, a physical sensation, the USDA now surveys Americans' *food insecurity* through a variety of indicators it considers more precise: In households with very low food security, a high percentage of adults not only worry that food will run out but skip meals, lose weight, and often do not eat for a whole day.[24]

But tinkering with how information is gathered or how levels are calculated compromises a poverty line's major advantage: the ability to compare results year to year. Although no one considers the Census Bureau's poverty threshold an accurate gauge of food consumption or needs, keeping the same formula allows researchers to chart trends.

Societies cannot measure poverty by bread alone, however. As people begin to pull out of destitution, they devote a smaller percentage of their budget to food, a behavior pattern dubbed Engel's law, after the German statistician Ernst Engel who first noticed it in 1857.[25] Yet the poor still face difficult choices about how to spend limited resources. Most poverty lines have expanded their shopping list to include a bundle of "basic" goods and services.

What is a necessity, though? Clothes, obviously, and a place to sleep. But what about conveniences that improve quality of life, such as electricity or telephone service? Or a goat or a sewing machine, which might enable someone to earn more income? What about a TV for entertainment and information? In deciding the parameters of poverty thresholds, experts look for objective—and quantifiable—answers to value-laden questions.

Lines also imply a false divide between poverty and prosperity. In 2006 the U.S. Census Bureau set a poverty threshold for a U.S. family of two adults and two children at $20,444.[26] But that does not mean that all families below the threshold endured the same hardship or that a family earning $21,000 was living on Easy Street. To gauge the depth and extent of poverty, experts have developed other tools. A head count index, for example, reports the percentage of the population that lives below the poverty threshold. Experts also quantify the poverty gap by taking into account how far people fall below the threshold. Multiplying the head count by a poverty-gap index that gives more weight to the poorest households paints a more accurate picture of the severity of poverty: the higher the number, the more destitute the country overall.[27]

Many economists now prefer poverty lines based on spending rather than income. On a practical level, the self-employed may not keep good records or may underreport income to avoid taxes, and many people feel more comfortable discussing what they buy rather than what they earn. Secondly, the poor's wages often vary seasonally, so an income survey's timing may skew the picture; migrant farmworkers, for instance, often take home regular pay in summer but next to nothing in winter. Yet essential expenses—food, housing, and the like—usually remain constant. Thirdly, charting what the poor consume helps researchers more accurately capture a standard of living.[28] Two American families earning $20,000 a year may experience very different levels of hardship if one lives rent-free in an inherited house or taps a savings account or benefits from government-provided health insurance or free groceries from a local food pantry.

While statistics give insight into poverty, the larger the field surveyed, the more problematic the comparisons. It makes sense to match up income levels in two neighboring Mississippi counties, but income, expenses, and to some extent needs vary widely among cities, states, and regions. To determine who qualifies for certain benefits, the U.S. Department of Health and Human Services uses guidelines adapted from the census threshold but added for a family of four in 2008 an extra $3,180 for Hawaii and $5,300 for Alaska.[29]

On an international scale, is it even possible to make meaningful comparisons between farmers in the southeastern United States and northeastern Syria, or inner-city youth in New York and New Delhi, India? In many ways, no. Some economists consider poverty in developing countries a different phenomenon than poverty in the United States, which ensnares a small subset of the population rather than a broad swath of society. When the World Bank set its $1 and $2 a day benchmarks in 1990, it drew upon the poorest countries' strikingly similar poverty lines but excluded developed nations, leaving them to define poverty by their own domestic standards. An American whom the Census Bureau officially designates as "poor" earns about $28 a day. Designers of poverty thresholds are always weighing the advantages of standardization against more accurate complexity.

Participatory Appraisals

In close-knit communities, most folks can point to who is poor and who is well off without a bar graph. Vietnamese, for instance, assess their neighbors by looking at their house, yard, modes of transportation, possessions, and level of education. A motorbike, a well, a TV, a garden, savings, and children in school indicate wealth; by contrast, the Vietnamese poor live in unstable mud huts, pull their children out of class to work, lack easy access to water, and fall short of food several months before the harvest.[30] Participatory appraisals draw on this deep well of local knowledge, usually assessing poverty through group and individual interviews.

Although outsiders may frame and facilitate discussions, this method honors community members' expertise, redressing one of the consequences of poverty—disempowerment—in the very process of gathering information. Whereas lines describe disadvantage with broad strokes, appraisals fill in details. They often reveal problems particular to a certain area, such as domestic violence or contamination from a leaking chemical tank.

But bottom-up data are often expensive to gather, difficult to verify, and almost impossible to compare. Unlike quantitative tools, which send survey takers into the field with uniform questionnaires, qualitative assessments require interviewers with more social skills who can engage people and groups in substantial conversations. Sometimes misunderstanding or outside motives distort informants' reporting. Unlike a misplaced decimal point or underreported wage, evaluators may find it hard to recognize a statement colored by family rivalry or by angling for aid. Studies have also found that ground-level poverty appraisals follow a sliding scale: the richer people are, the higher they set life's minimum requirements. Subjective, unlike objective, poverty ratings push human complexity and regional differences to the foreground.

Despite their limitations, participatory appraisals yield insightful results. Researchers use them as both a shortcut to understanding an area's deprivation and a long-term bridge between measuring and alleviating poverty. Within an afternoon, a community forum can air a host of grievances. Over weeks, months, and years, discussion groups can engage the poor in defining and solving their own predicaments. However well intentioned, poverty measures and solutions imposed by outsiders may rob the poor of agency, perpetuating a victim mentality. Participatory appraisals, on the other hand, affirm competence. When local involvement shapes not just problem identification but also intervention, antipoverty programs are more likely to succeed.

Poverty Indexes

Indexes try to combine the benefits of other measures. Like poverty lines, they aim for quantifiable results that allow comparisons and objective distribution of benefits. Like participatory appraisals, they recognize lack of money as only one dimension of poverty and often incorporate community input to generate assessments. Some agencies use a single index as a yardstick; in South Asia, many microfinance agencies quickly and inexpensively gauge clients' poverty by inspecting homes and then plugging numbers about roof quality, etc., into a housing index formula. For a comprehensive representation of poverty, however, experts recommend not just a single stem but a bouquet of indexes, some weighted more heavily than others and "drawn from at least four areas: human resources, housing, food security and household assets."[31]

The United Nations relies on a variety of indexes to capture relative and universal aspects of world poverty. While the world body uses separate human poverty indexes (HPIs) for industrialized and underdeveloped countries, the criteria are similar—life expectancy, literacy, standard of living. HPI-2, for industrialized nations, also tries to gauge perpetuation of poverty: a high proportion of extremely low income and long-term unemployment points to the poor's social exclusion.[32] Expanding upon the poverty indexes, the UN Human Development Index (HDI) addresses additional aspects of well-being, from technology access and safety from crime to political participation by both men and women. Dividing nations into high, medium, and low development, the HDI ranks them in order. In 2007/2008, Iceland topped the list, with the United States ranked twelfth. Medium development countries included Ukraine (76), Syria (108), Guatemala (118), and India (128). African countries predominated in the bottom tier, with the Democratic Republic of the Congo at 168 and Sierra Leone in last place (177).[33]

Most poverty measures, as well as maps, present only a snapshot of poverty. Although repeated snapshots capture overall trends, harder to pin down is the movement of people in and out of poverty. For instance, even if a given poverty rate remains steady from one year to the next, that does not mean that exactly the same people qualify as poor. As incomes rise in a growing economy, a family may do a bit better but remain vulnerable to shocks; with a sudden surge in fuel prices or a diagnosis of cancer, it may tumble back into severe hardship. Research suggests that individuals do not march out of destitution in a straight upward line but may zigzag for years, or a lifetime, above and below the poverty threshold, what one expert calls "bottom-end churning."[34] Only a survey that follows individuals over time will reveal long-term gains or setbacks.

CAUSES OF POVERTY

As economists and development specialists debate the accuracy and usefulness of various poverty calculations, even bigger battles center on causes and cures. For much of human history, destitution was a fact of life, the bad luck of birth, the fate of the masses at the bottom of the social pyramid. In ancient civilizations—from Sumerian to Mayan, Egyptian to Chinese—a ruling class of kings and nobles exploited and enslaved the less fortunate. In the feudal societies of medieval Europe, serfs toiled in fields, supporting the vassals who served the lords. Inequality was a given, not so much created as inherited.

Being so commonplace, destitution did not carry the burden of shame it often does today. Most people accepted widespread poverty as God's will, part of humankind's trial before the respite of heaven. "The poor you always have with you," explains the Christian New Testament (Matthew 26: 11). Honoring, sometimes even romanticizing, the poor, religions all over the world exhort charity, a spiritual duty and ticket to salvation. Rooted in ancient India, Jainism holds that "charity—to be moved at the sight of the thirsty, the hungry, and the miserable and to offer relief to them out of pity—is the spring of virtue," as written in the *Pancastikaya* by Kundakunda. "One should give even from a scanty store to him who asks," advises a Buddhist verse (224) in the Dhammapada. The Jewish Talmud echoes that theme: "Even a poor man who himself subsists on charity should give charity" (Gittin 7b). Why? "Blessed is he who considers the poor; the Lord delivers him in the day of trouble," proclaims the Bible in Psalm 41 (1). According to the Qur'an (Sura 9: 60), charity, known as *zakat*, is an obligation for Muslims, one of the five pillars of faith. A hadith narrated by al-Bukhari attributes the following to Muhammad: "The one who looks after and works for a widow and for a poor person is like a warrior fighting for God's cause."[35] Although some people still characterize poverty as an act of God or an accident of circumstances, few accept it as inevitable. Instead of merely alleviating misery, the concerned now aspire to eliminate it—and that requires understanding cause.

One difficulty lies in disentangling poverty's roots from its results—a chicken-and-egg conundrum. A study of 34,000 psychiatric patients in Massachusetts, for instance, linked low socioeconomic status to mental illness.[36] But does that mean that mental illness leads to poverty, or instead that unemployment and low income stress the disadvantaged to the point of breakdown? Poverty's correlates—malnutrition, vulnerability, etc.—double back to exacerbate hardship. Many poor settlements suffer from environmental degradation not only because residents may be chopping down trees for firewood but because powerful companies may be dumping waste on purpose in a community that lacks the clout to protest. Across the Caribbean and sub-Saharan Africa, girls struggling to pay school fees and widows struggling to feed children often resort to "survival sex," which puts them at risk for HIV infection. Once ill, they cannot afford state-of-the-art treatment, so HIV develops into full-blown AIDS, which often stigmatizes families, draining them emotionally and financially while a beloved wastes away.[37] Poverty snowballs. Cause and effect suggest a simple line with a one-way arrow, but as a multidimensional problem, poverty sits at the center of a web, with lines radiating in and out from all directions.

Resource Distribution and Climate

One school of thought holds that geography is destiny. The world is not a level playing field: Some countries benefit from fertile soil, vast forests, and valuable mineral and fossil-fuel deposits, while others lack such natural bounty. Climate affects agriculture and disease rates, often determining who prospers and who struggles. Even as global poverty retreated in the 20th century, it remained concentrated in certain regions, most of them in the tropics. Sometimes dubbed the Third World (a term that originally did not designate an economic ranking but instead referred to countries that had not picked sides in the cold war between the United States and the Soviet Union), least developed nations now often fall under another umbrella term that acknowledges their geographic similarity: the Global South.

Oil dramatically illustrates the wealth-generating power of natural resources. In the 20th century, world demand for heating, driving, and manufacturing fuel catapulted countries with vast reserves of this "black gold" into major exporters. From Venezuela to Nigeria to Iraq, oil revenue both spurred and complicated development. In Saudi Arabia, harsh desert had long isolated and segmented the nomadic population, which clustered around oases. Discovery of oil in 1938 bolstered the nascent kingdom united and ruled by the Al Saud family. As oil prices skyrocketed—between 1973 and 1980, Saudi revenues leaped from $4.3 billion to $101.8 billion—the government transformed the tribal economy, settling the Bedouin, building roads and cities, establishing electric and phone lines, and providing services such as public schooling. With free, unlimited health care for all citizens, life expectancy has increased from 40-some years in 1960 to more than 75 years today.[38]

Yet resource wealth does not automatically translate into general well-being. Despite its relatively high per-capita income (45th in the world), Saudi Arabia ranked 61 on the 2007/2008 UN HDI, lagging particularly in women's equality and empowerment.[39] In oil-rich nations, export income has disproportionately benefited a ruling class that fiercely guards its political and economic privileges. According to one political-science theory, authoritarian regimes of resource-rich nations have succeeded in fending off democracy movements because the government does not depend on taxpayers for funding. These rentier (landlord) states can afford the security apparatus to suppress dissent and can buy accommodation with promises of stability and subsidies for all.

Oil wealth also distorts the economy. Even though everyone knows that fossil fuels will run out one day, there is not much incentive to develop other industries. Local manufacturers and other companies often receive government subventions (subsidies) so they avoid hard lessons about efficiency and marketing and competition. After Holland discovered a natural-gas bonanza under its feet in the 1960s, the export boom inflated the currency. With foreign goods cheaper than local ones, many businesses closed, a phenomenon that economists dubbed the "Dutch disease." Yet fuel prices fluctuate, and when they drop, the boom goes bust. Not only does the oil industry scale back, but money does not flow as freely across the entire economy. Unemployment soars, and the poor, least able to weather shocks, suffer the most.[40]

Climate similarly gives and takes away. Abrupt changes in weather upend farmers all over the world, but in the Global South, where millions of families barely scrape by, one bad harvest can spell disaster. Droughts ravage broad swaths of Africa and Asia. In Ethiopia, farmers depend on two rainy seasons, a short one in February and a long one in summer. When cooler-than-usual ocean temperatures lower rainfall across the Horn of Africa, crops shrivel, livestock collapse, and people die of hunger and disease—nearly 1 million during the 1984–85 famine.[41] Several years of poor rains again plunged Ethiopia into crisis in 2000. Chronic water shortages handicap desert nations such as Niger, Mali, Turkmenistan, and Yemen. At the other extreme, floods periodically devastate China and Bangladesh, which is swamped annually by monsoon rains and melting Himalayan snows that swell four major rivers. Global warming will only intensify extreme weather. Calling climate change "the defining human development issue of our generation," the United Nations warns that it lashes the poor in particular and threatens to "erode human freedom" and "undermine international efforts to combat poverty."[42]

Water brings another set of problems in hot climes as it harbors parasites and their carriers. Mosquitoes transmit malaria, characterized by debilitating fever, chills, muscle aches, and malaise. The most severe malarial parasite, *Plasmodium falciparum*, thrives in sub-Saharan Africa. Hardest hit are people with reduced immunity, such as children and pregnant women. In Uganda alone, 100,000 people die of the disease annually. "It's like a jumbo jet crashing every day," observes Dr. Andrew Collins, deputy director of the Malaria Consortium, an international nonprofit group.[43] In Africa, malaria kills 2,000 children a day, and it is the fourth leading cause of death in children under five worldwide according to the World Health Organization.[44]

Number three is diarrhea, caused by a variety of parasites, viruses, and bacteria that infect people as a result of contaminated drinking water or poor hygiene. In India, more than 500,000 children die from diarrhea every year.[45] Like other tropical diseases, when diarrhea does not kill, it weakens, leaving people more susceptible to other infections, such as tuberculosis and HIV.

While geography spawns tropical diseases, global inequality has allowed them to persist. In parts of Asia, Africa, South America, and the Middle East *Schistosoma* worms live in freshwater snails and release their larvae into lakes, streams, and canals. Schistosomiasis-linked cancer is the number-one killer of Egyptian men between the ages of 20 and 40, mostly farmers and family breadwinners.[46] If schistosomiasis afflicted the Global North, chances are that industrial nations would have long ago funded an all-out war on it, with epidemiologists devising strategies for its treatment and eradication. But schistosomiasis ranks among the "neglected" tropical diseases, along with hookworm, trachoma, ascariasis, trichuriasis, lymphatic filariasis, and onchocericiasis.[47]

Moral Geography

A subset of those who hold earth and sky responsible for poverty have linked climate to character and character to prosperity. While some conceded that hot climes might require a different lifestyle, such as an afternoon siesta in the energy-sapping heat, most cast difference as inferiority and poverty as proof of "backwardness." Even temperature assumed values: *cool* equals rational, thoughtful, scientific, and disciplined; *hot* implies emotional, physical, superstitious, and out of control.[48] In the 14th century, the North African scholar Ibn Khaldun remarked in his famous *Muqaddimah,* a world history treatise, that temperate zones produce more "civilized" people with more refined buildings, horticulture, crafts, science, religion, and political leadership. Ironically, as Western social scientists later embraced moral geography, they dismissed as inferior the Arab Muslim civilization that had produced Ibn Khaldun.[49]

Centuries later, Max Weber, another pioneer sociologist, amplified the argument that certain cultural traits lend themselves to prosperity. In *The Protestant Ethic and The Spirit of Capitalism* (1905), Weber theorized that religious values underlay the West's increasing prosperity. In Protestant sects, the pious dedicated themselves to their occupation and shunned lavish spending. Although getting rich was not the goal, Protestant communities accumulated wealth because of their high productivity and thriftiness, Weber noted, and they could invest this capital in new industries. Even as religious fervor and distinctions faded, the "Protestant work ethic" survived as a capitalist value, with financial success vaguely associated with moral goodness and God's favor.[50] Especially in the late 19th and early 20th centuries, with global inequality intensifying, prominent Westerners attributed their good fortune to what they saw as their own virtues—ingenuity and industriousness.

At the end of the 19th century, moral geography joined forces with scientific racism. According to Charles Darwin's theory of evolution, in nature only the fittest survive, and Social Darwinists explained global and local inequality through genetics. Anthropologists traveled the world measuring skulls to "prove" the superiority of white-skinned Caucasians. Darwin's cousin, Francis Galton, a doctor, geographer, and explorer, pioneered intelligence testing, ranking Africans two grades below Anglo-Saxons.[51] While some scientists argued that the "colored" peoples who populated the poorer south would eventually evolve with "tutelage," others held out less hope for the "mentally and morally deficient" classes within their own societies whose biology doomed them to pauperism.

Individual Character

The ongoing effort to root out bias in science and a growing appreciation for human commonality have largely discredited notions of an inborn hierarchy of civilizations, races, and classes. Many Americans, however, hold individuals responsible for their hardship. Almost half of respondents in a 2001 poll blamed poverty on "people not doing enough" rather than on circumstances. While only 34 percent of respondents considered a shortage of jobs as a "major cause" of poverty, drug abuse (70 percent) and lack of motivation (52 percent) ranked higher. More than 20 percent surveyed, across all income categories, attributed lower moral values to the poor.[52] In another poll that year, half of respondents blamed poverty on a combination of biological and cultural factors.[53] Call behavior a lifestyle choice, a failing, or a physical inclination, popular opinion links destitution to laziness, drug abuse, and sexual promiscuity.

Because racial and cultural dimensions to poverty exist, bigoted undertones persist in character explanations of poverty. Non-Western nations and certain minority communities within almost all nations experience more destitution. In the United States, blacks fall below the poverty line at roughly triple the rates of non-Hispanic whites: 24.3 versus 8.2 percent, respectively, in 2006, according to U.S. Census Bureau statistics.[54] Among children, those with immigrant parents are twice as likely as native-born whites to be poor.[55] Poverty is by no means exclusively a minority phenomenon. Yet, studies reveal that American schoolbooks and the media create and reinforce stereotypes about who is poor. Through use of images, for instance, introductory college economic texts disproportionately cast poverty as a black phenomenon.[56]

Culture of Poverty

Poverty creates a vicious cycle, with side effects of stressful circumstances—such as crime, domestic violence, HIV/AIDS—in turn contributing to cause. Although education may offer a way out, poor children often have trouble taking advantage of public schooling because of ill health, hunger, family need for their labor, and lack of support—from a steady supply of pencils to a quiet spot to do homework. Parents who have experienced workplace discrimination may question the value of investing time, effort, and scarce resources into studying or job training. And because people with similar income levels tend to marry each other, income gaps widen.[57]

After studying villagers and slum dwellers in Mexico, Puerto Rico, and the United States, American anthropologist Oscar Lewis in the 1960s introduced the theory of a "culture of poverty" among the poorest of the poor that transcends regional and even national borders. Poverty persists, Lewis argued, because the desperately poor develop a "design for living that is passed down from generation to generation."[58] Oriented to the here and now rather than the future, this culture emphasizes short-term pleasures (a pack of cigarettes, for instance) over long-term benefits (savings and good health). Growing up in households with little privacy and much violence, where adults borrow money at exorbitant rates between paychecks and run to the convenience store for overpriced snacks because no one had the means or foresight to stock the cupboards with supermarket bargains, very poor kids are socialized into a community in many ways cut off from mainstream society. Although Lewis mentioned many positive qualities he observed among the poor, from hope to gaiety to courage, he concluded that the culture of poverty produced "badly damaged human beings."[59] They feel helpless, dependent, inferior, unworthy—"aliens in their own country."[60]

Although a theory in progress, at points vague and inconsistent, the "culture of poverty" generated much interest and controversy. It offered an explanation for the tenaciousness of poverty, and later scholars reformulated it in discussions of a permanent "underclass." But critics have faulted this idea for circular reasoning (poverty causes poverty), polarization (the poor—"them"—differ from the rest of society—"us"), nihilism (how can interventions counteract something so encompassing as culture?), and implicit racial and cultural prejudices. While Lewis maintained that only the deeply destitute developed a culture of poverty, he exempted certain groups, such as eastern European Jews, whose religion and scholarly traditions gave them a sense of history and belonging to a worldwide faith community.[61]

In the United States, the public usually associates "underclass" with poor, urban African Americans, so the notion of a "culture of poverty" has become entangled in contentions about race. While some researchers have argued that 20th-century housing "hypersegregation" by whites spawned this inner-city underclass by intensifying black communities' isolation,[62] others have argued that the chronically poor share blame for their dysfunctional lifestyle. Black entertainer Bill Cosby, for instance, set off a firestorm in 2004 when he remarked in a prominent speech that "the lower economic people are not holding up their end in this deal. . . . These people are not parenting. They are buying things for kids—$500 sneakers for what?"[63] In a less judgmental tone, recent research has focused on the power of "social interactions." For good and for ill, communities influence individual decisions by offering role models, a vision of what is normal and appropriate, a sense of belonging. For a child growing up in a poor neighborhood, street talk often speaks louder than more positive, distant messages about staying in school and just saying no to drugs. Peers may sanction poor economic choices (sneakers instead of books) and poverty-associated behaviors ranging from smoking to out-of-wedlock births to crime.[64] Inequality grows. Acknowledging that long-term poverty sometimes gives rise to self-defeating conduct still leaves unanswered the question of what causes stark economic stratification.

Overpopulation

No issue better illustrates the complex overlap of culture, correlation, and cause than population growth. While fertility rates are dropping worldwide, they remain high in the poorest countries and particularly in rural areas. According to the World Bank, the citizenry in low- and middle-income countries will more than double between 1980 and 2030 and will outnumber that of high-income countries seven to one (billion). Because developing nations have a younger population (a third under age 15), they experience "population momentum" as large numbers of people reach child-bearing age.[65] On a simplistic level, more people usually means smaller slices of pie; the more heads, the higher the divisor in per-capita income. (On the other hand, a big and highly productive population can generate more wealth to go around.) Rapid population growth may also stretch local resources beyond their "human carrying capacity."

In 1798, English clergyman Thomas Malthus published *An Essay on the Principle of Population* postulating that human reproduction grows at a faster rate than food production and would outpace it if not for two restraints. Death is one, caused by "all unwholesome occupations, severe labour and exposure to the seasons, extreme poverty, bad nursing of children, great towns, excesses of all kinds, the whole train of common diseases and epidemics, wars, plague, and famine."[66] The second is reduced fertility, brought about through abstinence and later marriage—in other words, birth control. Malthus's grim but influential vision spurred research to improve both agriculture and contraception.

Malthusian alarm that population would outstrip the food supply resurfaced in the mid-20th century as vaccines, antibiotics, and technology contributed to increasing life expectancy.[67] In *The Population Bomb* (1968), biologist Paul Ehrlich predicted massive starvation within a decade. But improved agriculture and contraception again averted catastrophe. In 1967, the United Nations declared family planning a basic human right, and the development of birth-control pills in the 1960s and IUDs (intrauterine devices) in the 1970s offered more contraceptive options. Between 1960 and 1980, fertility declined by a third around the globe, with women having an average of four children instead of six.[68] At the same time, the Green Revolution—a movement promoting irrigation, fertilizers, pesticides, machinery, double-cropping, and improved varieties of wheat, rice, corn, and millet—boosted crop yields from Mexico to Pakistan.

In the 21st century, Malthusian fear of "overpopulation" has given way to a broader concern about population pressures on the environment in both rich and poor countries. Although most industrial nations are now experiencing minimal (less than 1 percent in the United States) or negative population growth, they guzzle energy. In 1998, the United States, with roughly 5 percent of the world's population, consumed 23 percent of global coal and natural gas production and 40 percent of its oil.[69] As a result, it ranks number one in carbon dioxide emissions from burning fossil fuels.[70] As population expands in the developing world, so, too, do energy demands and water demands and intensity of agriculture. Without careful management, meeting these demands leads to air pollution, water contamination, deforestation, and desertification.

Although birth-control proponents emphasize a causal link between population growth and poverty, the poor do not always see large families as a burden. Sex is a cheap pleasure. Children can bring joy to a hard life as well as extra hands to help in the house or the fields or to earn outside income. Offspring provide insurance the needy cannot find or cannot afford: Sick or elderly parents depend on sons and daughters. Since many poor children die of malnutrition, disease, and accidents, parents need more than two (the replacement rate) to guarantee a family's survival. Does fertility lead to impoverishment then, or does destitution encourage people to bear more children?

Social Structures

Many experts argue that while geography and demography entwine to contribute to poverty, the fundamental cause of inequality lies in economic and political systems so closely linked that many scholars prefer the term *political economy.* Were geography the sole determinant of wealth, then wealth should remain as constant as continents. Yet fortunes have changed places, and the economic divide between the world's richest and poorest countries has stretched from a three to one ratio in 1820, to 11:1 in 1913, 35:1 in 1950, 44:1 in 1973, and 72:1 in 1992.[71] Were individual differences in talent and motivation the only factors in economic success, then poverty would follow a pattern related to those variables, not cluster around easily discriminated subsets of the population: women, children, the disabled, indigenous people, immigrants, disfavored minorities, or oppressed majorities. Social institutions, not some "natural order," direct the polarized distribution of wealth.

CAPITALISM

Poverty took on many of its contemporary characteristics after feudalism gave way to capitalism in Europe in the 16th century. The roots of capitalism lay in mercantilism, trade to turn a profit. Commerce motivated people all over the medieval world to move from farms to cities—Hangzhou in China, Delhi in India, Baghdad in the Middle East—and especially port cities, such as Tripoli in the eastern Mediterranean or Kilwa Kisiwani, an island off East Africa. In urban hotbeds of commercial activity, scholarship bloomed, fed by cross-cultural contact and spurred in part by commercial needs—math for transactions, linguistics for communication, astronomy for navigation. Although Europeans participated in this international market, its heart beat in the Global South.

A merchant class began to distinguish itself from the traditional nobles, who were religious leaders or the landed gentry (feudal lords). In Europe, philosophers began to apply observations about nature to human behavior. This intellectual revolution, the Enlightenment, championed human potential and individual freedom; in elevating reason above faith, it challenged the traditional authority of church and state. Out of the Enlightenment grew European democracy as well as capitalism. In an ideal "free market," individuals pursued their own self-interest, accumulating land, material, and tools (capital) in order to produce or deliver goods and services.[72]

Within European society, wealthy merchants gained an edge on landlords. Profits turned into capital, a pool of money available for investing in new technology, such as light and fast cargo ships, and for buying people's labor.[73] Government furthered mercantile interests, keeping taxes low, giving military support to overseas ventures, and outlawing workers' petitions for higher wages or shorter days. During the Industrial Revolution of the late 18th and 19th centuries, capitalists were able to invest in machinery, opening factories along rivers (for water power) or near cities (for access to consumers), mechanizing agriculture, and amassing tremendous fortunes. Economic growth created a substantial middle class.

Industrial capitalism lowered as well as lifted social and financial status, however. As workers abandoned the countryside to fill manufacturing jobs, they left behind communities that knew them personally, the network of friends and family who offered emotional and financial support during crises and the parish church that had coordinated aid to the needy. While employers needed cheap labor at hand, desperately poor strangers alarmed urban residents, who supported laws regulating vagabonds, beggars, and unemployed laborers, deporting them or consigning them to public or private workhouses.

Because economic and political power tended to dovetail, poverty disenfranchised the poor, who fought back by organizing labor unions or populist political parties. Skillful politicians took advantage of the poor's strength in numbers, an infamous 19th-century example being William "Boss" Tweed of New York City's Tammany Hall, who bought Irish immigrant votes with money and food. Particularly in England and the United States, business interests prevailed at the highest level of government, which adopted laissez-faire policies that gave capitalists a free hand. In pursuit of profits, companies often exploited workers and sometimes defrauded consumers.

Citing the alienation of the masses who toiled in miserable working conditions, alternative economic systems challenged private enterprise. In the early 20th century, socialists and communists argued against excessive individualism, advocating instead for economic systems in which the government owns and operates the means of production, in theory for the good of all citizens. Yet, centrally managed economies frequently suffered from inefficiency and abuse of power, degenerating into authoritarian states that tried to control thought as well as factory output.

In the 1950s, economist Simon Kunetz charted data in a curve that suggested that while inequality may rise initially after industrialization because of all the dislocation, in the long term countries do better to move from traditional to industrial economies. During the cold war, the United States, representing capitalism and the market economy, and the Soviet Union, representing communism and the command economy, vied to influence the shape of emerging industrial economies. Although all systems, particularly those in the Global South, mix private and public elements, the collapse of the Soviet Union in the 1990s marked a triumph for free-market capitalism.

At the end of the 20th century, more and more nations sought integration into the world market, a process known as globalization. In developing nations, the transition has uprooted many of the poor from homes and livelihoods, but many economists believe short-term pain will segue into long-term gain. Already experts attribute dramatic rising per-capita incomes in countries such as China, India, Vietnam, and Uganda to participation in international trade and direct foreign investment (DFI). Critics of globalization and the huge multinational corporations at its vanguard contend that it destroys traditional culture and delivers uneven economic benefits that widen inequality, a long-term problem as pernicious as poverty.[74] Look to history, they say: Western capitalists grew rich by ill-using other people.

LEGACY OF COLONIALISM—A HISTORICAL PERSPECTIVE

At the turn of the first millennium, no one would have predicted that Europe and North America would top the human development charts at the second. Under the Song dynasty (960–1279), China led the world in innovations—including gunpowder, movable type, the compass, and paper money—thanks in large part to its political stability. As population grew, so did urban centers, and the agricultural economy diversified to include cash crops such as tea and cottage industries such as silk. Trade and travel brought cosmopolitan development to the Arab world from the eighth to the 15th century. As Muslim merchants sailed and caravanned across Asia, North Africa, and the entire Mediterranean basin, students followed in their tracks, creating extended scholarly networks. Building upon ancient Greek and Indian traditions, Muslim scholars pioneered the sciences, from astronomy to botany to medicine. In wealth, technology, and other measures of "civilization," Europe lagged behind, reeling in the 14th century from the triple whammy of the Great Famine (1315–22), the Hundred Years' War (1337–1453), and the Black Death (1347–52), or bubonic plague.

Europe's fortunes began changing, however, with Christopher Columbus's "discovery" of the Americas in 1492. From timber to silver to land, the vast resources of this "new" world enriched the "old"—at the expense of indigenous peoples—and spurred capitalism and industrialization, which reinforced European power. To the New World, Europe often delivered not just an economic but a physical blow: Diseases new to the Americas, such as measles and smallpox, decimated indigenous populations.

At its most basic, colonialism involves removing raw materials, often with the help of cheap, local labor; processing them in the mother country; and selling manufactured goods back to a captive market. Colonialism has taken many forms, however, colored by local conditions. In the settler colonies of North America, Australia, South Africa, and Algeria, for instance, Westerners homesteaded individual farms on land they called "vacant"—even when indigenous people, with different concepts of property rights, were using it. In exploitation colonies, a profit-oriented outpost, such as a Haitian sugar plantation or a South African gold mine, extracted resources and shipped them home.

After Columbus, competing nation-states from Norway to Italy combed the globe for places to establish a foothold. While trade required exchange and negotiation, colonialism implied conquest and domination, although colonizers often insisted they were "protecting weaker states" or "civilizing backward natives." Backed by blunderbusses, warships, and loans with stiff default penalties, colonizers coerced "agreements" from locals; force overcame resistance. Culminating with a multinational "scramble for Africa" at the end of the 19th century, Europeans carved up the world into empires, among them the Spanish who claimed Latin America, the British who ruled India, the French who controlled North Africa, and the Dutch who dictated the East Indies.

"Until lions have their historians, tales of the hunt shall always glorify the hunters," warns an African proverb, and Western history has long portrayed colonialism as colonizers liked to see it—as inevitable, necessary, and often beneficial to the colonized. Colonialism's defenders point to European "gifts" to the Global South: railroads and hospitals, civil service ladders and legal codes, literacy in languages that opened access to Western technology, markets, and ideas about democracy and women's rights.

Yet colonial administrations disrupted and denigrated local institutions, possible hotbeds of dissent. They prohibited instruction in indigenous languages, cutting off parents from children and graduates from their cultural heritage. The infrastructure and institutions imposed upon local cultures served European commercial and political interests first.

During the cold war, Soviet propaganda cast American and European businessmen as reverse Robin Hoods, robbing the poor to feed the rich. But colonial relationships were much more complicated than that simplistic portrayal; they blended some good intentions and many bad practices, and they changed both the colonizer and the colonized. Nor was colonialism exclusively capitalist foreign policy. Command economies, too, trampled indigenous culture "for its own good." In the Soviet Union's satellite republics, state factories and collective farms supplanted local enterprise. Eager to suppress dissent and instill loyalty, the Russia-centric Politburo outlawed religious expression and imposed Russian-language instruction across Eastern Europe and Central Asia.

The violence and double standards of the colonial experience left lasting scars on people and institutions. Especially in the wave of decolonization that followed World War II, optimists hoped that newly independent nations would vault to prosperity once resident foreigners were no longer siphoning off the best of everything, and democracy, or at least democratic socialism, would bloom. Instead, colonial rule left a legacy of elite domination of a less advantaged majority. Authoritarian rule and corruption dog the Global South. In addition to Iraq, long a site of international intervention, former British colonies Sudan and Myanmar (Burma), former French colonies Chad and Haiti, former Belgian colony the Democratic Republic of the Congo, former Italian colony Somalia, and former Soviet satellite Uzbekistan ranked among the worst in misuse of public office for private gain in 2007; most also fell in the lower tiers of the UN HDI.[75]

Scholars now also speak of internal colonization, one group's oppression of another within the same society. In India and Nepal, for instance, the Hindu caste system relegated the dirtiest work to Dalits, the so-called Untouchables, about a quarter of the population; this tradition persists today even though the newly independent Indian government outlawed discrimination against Dalits and established affirmative action for "scheduled castes" and others in 1955. Discrimination has long existed within many societies, but Western colonial administrators often fanned local ethnic, religious, and class tensions through both ignorance and a deliberate strategy of "divide and conquer." They drew arbitrary borders, ignored complex local balances of power, and imposed their own racial prejudices. The Belgian colonial authority in Rwanda, for instance, issued identity cards that cemented distinctions between the majority Hutus and minority Tutsis, whom the Belgians favored. After independence, Hutus assumed power and attributed many of the country's problems to the former Tutsi elite. Fanned by food and land shortages, discord escalated into a savage Hutu spree of violence that killed roughly 800,000 Tutsis and Hutu moderates in April 1994.[76] Long poor, Rwanda now struggles to rebuild its coffee and tea industry, regain investors' confidence, and care for millions maimed, widowed, and orphaned by the genocide.

SLAVERY AND ITS AFTERMATH

Slavery stands as the most extreme form of economic exploitation. For eons, cultures all over the world have practiced slavery, commandeering the labor of the less powerful—war captives, for instance. In some situations, slaves could earn manumission for themselves or their children, a famous example being Roxelana, a Russian concubine who eventually married the Ottoman sultan and whose son, Selim, acceded to the throne in 1566.[77] More often, however, children inherited their parents' servile status.

In chattel slavery, the type prevalent in the Americas, masters bought and sold human beings as pieces of property, without regard for family and other ties. While apologists for slavery once argued that masters shielded slaves from extreme poverty because they had an economic interest in feeding and housing them, bondage stripped slaves of their human rights and protection from verbal, sexual, and other physical abuse. Slaves underpinned the preindustrial economy: Many British and American merchants made fortunes in the trans-Atlantic slave trade, which provided manpower for rice, sugar, cotton, and tobacco cultivation.

In the 19th century, Britain abolished slavery throughout its empire, as did France, the United States, and many other countries. But slavery has not disappeared. Particularly in Southeast Asia, the impoverished and their children continue to work as prostitutes or menial laborers under coercion—despite a worldwide ban on slavery encoded in the 1948 UN "Universal Declaration of Human Rights."[78]

Ending slavery does not immediately stop its negative impact, especially when race makes visible former slave status. Slaves and their descendants must overcome personal and institutional bias, discrimination that permeates society and contributes to poverty in all its dimensions, from reduced income to lower self-esteem. In the United States, the founders wrote discrimination into the Constitution, defining a slave as three-fifths of a person for purposes of taxing the owner. The descendants of the more than 8 million Africans enslaved between 1619 and 1865 have been fighting a long legal battle to overturn laws that denied them equal rights and opportunity.

BAD GOVERNANCE

"In a country well governed, poverty is something to be ashamed of," observed Chinese philosopher Confucius (551–479 B.C.E.). "In a country badly governed, wealth is something to be ashamed of." As Confucius points out, political leadership affects the distribution of wealth. Societies prosper when their institutions 1) protect property rights, 2) prevent the powerful from bullying, and 3) create equal opportunity for a broad cross-section of people.[79] Leaders fail their constituents when they mismanage the economy, embroil a society in conflict, and put personal gain before the public good. Through action or inaction, government plays a major role in delivery of services, from trash pickup to sewage treatment. Whether command or market economies, some countries are more successful than others in administering education, sanitation, and basic health care.

Money obviously makes a difference: Developing countries may lack cash to pay more teachers or lay water pipelines. Epidemic AIDS has overwhelmed underfunded health systems, especially in sub-Saharan Africa, where between 1995 and 2005 life expectancy plunged from 62 to 38 years.[80] Nonetheless, some poor states achieve substantial "bang for the buck" because of efficient management and careful prioritizing. In Iran, for example, where 87 percent of mothers have a skilled birth attendant, one in 370 expectant mothers dies; in neighboring Afghanistan, where skilled birth attendants assist at only 8 percent of deliveries, the mortality is one in six. (In the United States, the figure is one in 2,500, and in Sweden, one in 29,000.)[81] While for-profit companies often offer services lacking in destitute neighborhoods, they may contribute to inequality. For example, in the Tanzanian city Dar es Salaam, the poor pay up to five times more for water than other users because the government does not regulate the pricing and service of private vendors.[82]

Governments compound problems from poor administration when they incite or tolerate civil or international conflict. Poverty and armed conflict have a strong association: Fighting is ongoing in 80 percent of the world's 20 poorest countries. Researchers are still trying to tease out if poverty causes conflict: Do rebels take up arms to right inequality (grievance) or simply to help themselves to a share of resources (greed)? It seems clearer, however, that chronic conflict contributes to chronic instability, which in turn causes poverty.[83] On both the individual and national level, investing in weaponry highjacks funds and energy that could have been spent improving quality of life. Eritrea, for example, which ranks near the bottom on the UN HDI (157 out of 177), spends more than 19 percent of its gross domestic product (GDP) on the military versus 4.1 percent on education and 3.1 percent on health.[84] Once fighting breaks out, it robs families of breadwinners, leaves orphans, disrupts agriculture, destroys infrastructure such as roads and bridges, and often uproots populations.

Experts distinguish among the world's 175 million migrants, who move to seek work or to escape an insecure situation; 10.6 million refugees, who cross borders because of the risk of human-rights abuses (including death) at home; and 25.8 million internally displaced persons (IDPs), who stay within their country but flee to another region because of violence or disaster.[85] Although migrants may leave home voluntarily, conflict compels most refugees and IDPs. Poverty, however, dogs all three categories of people, often poor to begin with, who forsake the support networks of home. In the regional war that followed the UN partition of Palestine in 1947, for example, about two-thirds of the indigenous Arab population—726,000 according to a UN survey—fled or were driven from their homes. More than 50 years later, this refugee population has grown to more than 4 million (UN figures) or 5 million (Palestinian Authority figures) through further dislocation as well as reproduction.[86] One-third registered with the United Nations Relief and Works Agency (UNRWA) live in squalid UNRWA refugee camps in the Arab countries surrounding Israel. Their poverty and statelessness has strained local resources and inflamed political tensions in a region where international cooperation on issues ranging from water to trade is much needed to alleviate hardship.

Corruption is the third hallmark of bad governance. A web of indirect associations links official malfeasance to poverty. On the economic side, graft, favoritism, and embezzling hinder a country's economic growth (which correlates directly to poverty). They discourage foreign investment and domestic entrepreneurship, lower tax revenues and divert public spending, and intensify inequality. Studies reveal that the poor in developing countries pay a higher proportion of their income on taxes and bribes than do the rich. In Romania, for instance, bribes cost the poorest third of citizens more than 10 percent of their income, while the richest third pay two percent.[87]

On the government side, corruption weakens institutions and public trust in them. When politicians allocate money to capital projects with more potential for lining powerful pockets than improving quality of life (palace and office construction versus education and health care), the poor again suffer disproportionately. Corrupt countries have higher school drop-out rates and infant mortality. When citizens perceive unfairness in the system, public trust plummets, as does public participation. What motivates self-starters to graduate from school, excel on a job, start a business, or pursue leadership positions when their experience shows only that the wealthy and well connected get ahead?[88] Although corruption afflicts both command and market economies, it is less likely to persist in democracies, where a free press can expose wrongdoing and the electorate can vote corrupt officials out of office. Shame and blame can motivate governments to tackle poverty.

REMEDIES FOR POVERTY

With so much disagreement about the scope and roots of poverty, no easy consensus has emerged about how to attack the problem, only that it must be done. At the UN Millennium Summit in New York in September 2000, the General Assembly declared: "We will spare no effort to free our fellow men, women and children from the abject and dehumanizing conditions of extreme poverty, to which more than a billion of them are currently subjected. We are committed to making the right to development a reality for everyone and to freeing the entire human race from want."[89] The imperative is both moral and practical. As South African civil rights leader Nelson Mandela once said, "Overcoming poverty is not a gesture of charity. It is an act of justice."[90] Poverty qualifies as a security as well as a humanitarian concern. Although researchers have discredited the assumption that poverty automatically breeds terrorism,[91] it does endanger world peace. The ills associated with destitution—such as crime, disease, civil conflict—spill over borders and disturb everyone's prosperity.

Talk dollars, and poverty is a pocketbook issue. Better-off nations spend sizable sums (but not enough, many say) to send peacekeeping forces to trouble spots, to arrest drug and sex traders, to ship grain during famines. Within nations, too, poverty exacts social as well as human costs. When the poor lack affordable primary care, for instance, they often forgo treatment at initial stages of illness. With infectious diseases, this delay contributes to epidemics, including AIDS, tuberculosis, and flu. Illness debilitates workers; it keeps them home from jobs, hurting business productivity. Once the very sick seek treatment, it is more expensive and often less effective.

In the United States, since hospitals cannot turn patients onto the street, they have to charge other consumers more to cover those who cannot afford to pay. Disability and even the premature death of a parent may put a whole family at risk for poverty. The U.S. Institute of Medicine estimated that in 2003 lack of health insurance for 41 million Americans cost the country between $65 and $130 billion a year, and the number of uninsured has continued to rise.[92] Although attacking poverty requires long-term commitment and investment, advocates call it effort and money well spent. The principle holds true globally. Oxfam International estimates that for every dollar put into improving access to clean drinking water and sanitation, a developing nation saves $3–$4.[93]

Weighing Different Approaches

Tackling a problem as diffuse as poverty seems daunting. Where to start? Despite the nearly universal wish to eliminate hardship, difficult questions complicate the undertaking.

- Should antipoverty measures address a broad spectrum of problems or focus on one or two key areas? Which ones? Out of the UN Millennium Summit emerged the commitment of 189 nations to reaching eight Millennium Development Goals (MDGs). The first, to "eradicate extreme poverty and hunger," sets specific targets between 1990 and 2015 of halving the proportion of people who live on less than $1 a day and halving the proportion of people who suffer from hunger. The other seven MDGs aim to redress miseries that attend and aggravate poverty: achieve universal primary education; promote gender equality and empower women; reduce child mortality; improve maternal health; combat HIV/AIDS, malaria, and other diseases; ensure environmental stability; and create a global partnership for development. Within these broad categories, a gamut of agencies focus on small or large slices of the total pie, from establishing "Integrity Awards" for corruption fighters to producing low-cost ceramic water filters.[94]

- Should interventions target individuals, groups, communities, or whole nations? Many aim for the poorest of the poor. Others focus on women because of their disproportionate share of hardship and because of their central role in the family and in reproduction not just of people but of culture. Study after study links economic improvement to advances in women's health and education. Early development projects often failed, in fact, because they ignored women's essential but sometimes invisible economic roles. Although in many countries women raise crops and livestock essential for survival (accounting for 53 percent of agricultural labor in Egypt, for instance), they receive a scant 5 percent of extension services, traditionally oriented toward men, particularly toward farmers who own land and can get credit to buy new technology.[95]
- Should antipoverty strategies redress specific historic wrongs? Projects that attempt to reduce inequality do this implicitly, but strong emotions and political disagreements complicate assistance to certain disadvantaged groups, such as African Americans or Palestinian refugees. Many countries practice affirmative action, favoring previously excluded groups. India reserves a quota of state jobs, seats in parliament, and educational admissions for scheduled tribes, scheduled castes (such as Dalits), and "other backward classes," such as women.[96] In Malaysia, where a Chinese minority has long dominated financially, *bumiputera* (sons of the soil) laws require that native Malays own a set stake in businesses.[97] Noting that in 2002 women constituted less than 7 percent of board members in public companies, Norway called for representation of at least 40 percent for each gender—guaranteeing more females in management.[98] Yet what some call "positive discrimination," a step toward equal opportunity, others decry as "reverse discrimination," an insult to fairness and meritocracy (success based on talent) that actually perpetuates stereotypes of certain groups' inferiority. Protest and legal challenges have quashed affirmative-action measures in Britain, France, and the United States.
- Who should be in charge of designing, paying for, and assessing the effectiveness of antipoverty strategies? Should leadership come from the top down or the bottom up? Pointing out that imposed strategies often

meet resistance, advocates for local control champion planning and evaluation at village or regional levels. Others argue for national campaigns. Still others urge tapping a global knowledge base and requesting help or supervision from expert, objective outsiders.

- What roles should the United Nations and the rest of the international community—donors, governments, and NGOs—play? Although developing nations need money and technical expertise, assistance often comes with strings attached. Out of goodwill but also in hope of conversions, missionaries have long traveled the world opening schools and hospitals for the poor. From Britain to Japan to Saudi Arabia to the United States, many wealthy countries promote domestic agendas through their foreign-aid budgets, opening markets, protecting energy sources, and spreading religious or political values. While sensitive to hardship, diplomats also give and withhold aid to reward cooperation and punish disagreement. Some aid contracts require recipients to buy goods and services from donor nationals, along the model of the Marshall Plan. (Proposed by U.S. secretary of state George Marshall in 1947 to reverse Europe's industrial derailment after World War II, the Marshall Plan entailed massive U.S. grants to European nations, who were required to buy American products, shipped on American vessels.) But "tied aid" can drive up costs and undermine local "ownership."[99] As a result, aid does not always reach those who need it most.

With the MDGs, the United Nations is monitoring progress toward each goal based on specific indicators. For trends in extreme poverty, for instance, the United Nations monitors 1) the proportion of population subsisting on less than $1 per day (this figure must fall from 29 percent to 14.5 percent of all people in low- and middle-income countries), 2) the poverty-gap ratio (how much poverty multiplied by how deep), and 3) the poorest fifth's share of national consumption. Hunger is measured by 1) the prevalence of underweight children under five and 2) the proportion of the population consuming less than a minimum level of calories.[100] The United Nations does not assign tasks, however, instead welcoming all development activities—those that nibble, those that gnaw, and those that take a huge bite out of poverty. In order to combat the multifaceted problem of poverty, it has urged the public and private sectors to partner on a multipronged attack. While a "big tent" approach that puts everyone on the same team seems to make sense with a problem so sprawling, vehement disagreement at times leaves players working at cross-purposes.

Although many people credit the MDGs for reenergizing the fight against global poverty, critics cite lack of accountability as one of their major shortcomings. With no one ultimately responsible for meeting goals, failure carries no penalty. Columbia University professor Thomas Pogge, for one, has argued that the first MDG was unambitious, allowing affluent nations to applaud their good intentions without requiring major changes to practices that preserve their wealth and perpetuate poverty. Some cynics go so far as to call the recent compassion boom "social money laundering."[101] True "sharing" would require the rich as well the poor to adjust lifestyles. The United States consumes more corn, coffee, copper, lead, zinc, tin, aluminum, rubber, oil seeds, oil and natural gas than any other nation.[102] If the rich did not grab the lion's share, say advocates of wealth redistribution, the poor would have more resources at their disposal.

Poverty alleviation strategies generally take three forms. **Welfare** approaches redistribute wealth, usually taking money from the rich in the form of taxes and giving it to the poor as cash or subsidies for food, housing, etc. **Capital** approaches build up individuals' and communities' assets, which in turn improve capacity for economic growth. Almost all antipoverty projects aim to develop human capital—through improved nutrition, health care, and especially education and training. After the 1995 World Summit in Copenhagen, many nations signed onto the 20/20 Initiative, an agreement between donors and developing nations that those receiving foreign aid would devote at least 20 percent of it, as well as 20 percent of their national budget, to basic social services.[103] Whereas capital strategies try to improve people's potential to earn, **economic** approaches cut straight to income. How will the poor move into the ranks of the better off? By earning more money.[104] Just as the causes of poverty overlap, so do antipoverty measures, which often combine strategies.

Welfare Strategies

Although most people associate welfare with government programs, such as free school lunches, it encompasses private giving as well, from donating canned beans to food banks to dropping quarters in a beggar's cup. Welfare provides immediate relief and often addresses inequality. Donations do not always flow from highest- to lowest-income areas, however. Natural disasters, for instance, prompt outpourings of charity: After Hurricane Katrina barreled into the U.S. Gulf Coast in 2005, Tunisia sent detergent, Thailand sent rice, and Israel sent baby food to tide over residents flooded out of their homes.[105]

Many people consider welfare a stopgap measure at best, most effective in emergencies. Because it treats symptoms and not underlying causes of persistent poverty, it requires an ongoing commitment, expensive over the long haul. It distorts the natural development of the economy. When broadly administered, as in subsidized pensions for the elderly, welfare wins popular support, but when targeted to the indigent, it often faces opposition and may stigmatize recipients. Critics blame welfare for creating a culture of dependency among the able-bodied poor, who in theory lose incentive to work when promised giveaways.

Proponents, on the other hand, point out its essential role in insulating vulnerable groups from such sudden shocks as the loss of a father or the loss of a job. When sufficient, welfare frees the poor from the grind of meeting daily needs and helps them "get back on their feet" and stay there.

SOCIAL SECURITY

Most countries subsidize various "safety nets" to prevent absolute poverty. With the United Nations, the Niger government has set up an early warning system to identify those most at risk of starvation during food crises, such as widows, single mothers, the elderly, and the disabled. Even before crops fail and stockpiles run out, Niger distributes sorghum, millet, and beans to the vulnerable and food supplements to children who live far from health centers.[106] At the other end of the HDI, affluent, egalitarian Sweden has served as the poster child for the welfare state. There the government levies high income and inheritance taxes in order to provide or subsidize benefits, some of them universal (health care, child care, parental leave and allowances, pensions for the elderly) and some based on economic need (housing, sick pay, disability support, unemployment pay). Poverty is rare and income relatively evenly distributed although non-Europeans (mostly refugees from the developing world) experience higher unemployment and immigrants lag behind other citizens.[107]

CONDITIONAL AID

Because Sweden bases benefits to a large extent on work, some have called it "workfare" rather than welfare.[108] Canada and the United States practice strict workfare, requiring the able-bodied to work, the goal being to wean them off public aid. Other countries also set conditions on welfare benefits. Instead of withholding benefits as punishment, some Latin American countries are experimenting with offering them as an incentive to build human capital. For example, under its Bolsa Familia program, Brazil is paying about 11 million low-income families cash if they send their children to school and take them for health checkups.[109]

Capital Strategies

Capital may come in the form of technology, such as farm machinery or computers, or infrastructure, such as paved roads and electric lines. Many projects focus on building human capital. In these projects, people are the asset, made more valuable and more productive through education and health care.

While capital approaches may involve substantial upfront investments and sometimes require a generation to produce results, they often transform the lives of participants. "Give a man a fish, and you feed him for a day. Teach a man to fish, and you feed him for a lifetime," observes a Chinese proverb, a cliché that nonetheless captures the hope of capital approaches.

However, development projects come with their own set of problems. Although they aim to reduce inequality, they may reinforce it by producing a new group of haves (with tractors or college degrees) who pull away from have-nots. Big-budget projects almost inevitably generate graft as contractors from donor nations and power brokers from recipient nations try to tap into the pipeline. Development has tended to impose a Western blueprint for progress that often underestimates the integrity of local culture. Even the Green Revolution, for all of its success in making nations self-sufficient in food, had a downside: Chemical fertilizers caused pollution, and new irrigation systems encouraged water use beyond some landscapes' ability to sustain it. Because development projects operate on sensitive turf, sometimes challenging long-standing cultural mores and ecological balances, they require careful design. One size does not fit all.

SURMOUNTING GEOGRAPHICAL DISADVANTAGES

Activists generally find it easier to muster political and financial support to fight problems blamed on geography rather than human failings. A case in point is the international campaign against malaria that has been rejuvenated by the foundation launched by Microsoft billionaire Bill Gates and his wife, Melinda. Not only has the Gates Foundation funded tried-and-true prevention, such as mosquito nets and bug spray, but in 2005 it announced $258.3 million in grants for research on new drugs, new insecticides, and a vaccine.[110] Led by economist Jeffrey Sachs, the Earth Institute at Columbia University in New York City is pushing treatment of neglected tropical diseases through a "rapid-impact" package of donated and generic drugs.[111]

Other development specialists are calling for a second Green Revolution. India led the first, increasing land under cultivation, double-cropping, and planting improved cereal strains. By the end of the 1970s, India gained self-sufficiency in food production—even producing a surplus to export. Damming rivers for irrigation, engineers also generated water-powered electricity. This not only improved village life, but it also fueled manufacturing, spurred by the need for fertilizers, pesticides, and farming equipment. Between cereal exports and industrial growth, India was able to pay back loans for the Green Revolution and gain solid credit status.[112]

Although genetic engineering allows scientists to tailor-make plants resistant to certain pests and tolerant of drought, agriculture advocates stress that the key to a second Green Revolution lies in sustainable low-tech practices. They favor integrated crop management, an environmentally sensitive balancing act of crop rotation, fertilizers, and so on, over high-tech seeds and pesticides.[113] After Kenya's extension service directed an information campaign toward women, corn production rose 28 percent and bean and potato production more than 80 percent. According to the World Bank, simply increasing the number of girls studying in primary school would boost farm output by almost a quarter. In general, education, particularly of women, has far-reaching positive effects.[114]

MANAGING POPULATION

Similarly, efforts to curb population growth now focus less on technological breakthroughs than on birth planning as a way of life. Planned Parenthood and allies around the world have promoted development of better contraceptives and easier access to them. With reason, however, the poor often suspect experts' eagerness to curb their fertility, and they resist imposed solutions, especially from cultural outsiders.

While Western feminists cast birth control as reproductive freedom of choice, ethnic and class prejudice have long tainted reform, especially at the turn of the 20th century, the heyday of "scientific racism." Specious theories of genetic difference inspired the Western eugenics movement, which proposed improving the human race through selective breeding. Launched in 1910, the American Eugenics Records Office lobbied hard for forced sterilization of the intellectually and morally "unfit," a category that included people with epilepsy, alcoholism, mental illness, physical disabilities, a criminal record, and an inherited "shiftlessness or laziness."[115] While acknowledging the environmental component of "pauperism," such as how a father's illness could impoverish a family, one expert argued that "poverty means relative inefficiency and this in turn means mental inferiority."[116] By 1940, more than 30 states had sterilization laws on the books.

Many U.S. eugenicists also attributed unsavory characteristics to the southern Europeans arriving in massive numbers and settling in teeming urban slums. Breeding grounds for diseases, overcrowded and unsanitary tenements became a symbol of contamination of health and also of bloodlines. Settled generations of white Americans spoke of safeguarding the human race. For all of her empathy for immigrant mothers, nurse Margaret Sanger embraced eugenics rhetoric in her birth-control campaign that spurred the founding of Planned Parenthood. In a 1932 article, she endorsed immigration quotas and recommended controlling "the intake and output of morons, mental defectives, epileptics." She went on to suggest that authorities should put "illiterates, paupers, unemployables, criminals, prostitutes, [and] dope-fiends" under government medical protection and "segregate them on farms and open spaces as long as necessary for the strengthening and development of moral conduct."[117] Historical ties to eugenics and moral geography still cloud family-planning initiatives worldwide.

As developing nations embraced Western science, they helped strip out its bias. Scientists used precise mathematical models rather than vague theories of racial refinement to argue for birth control. In the 1970s, demographers in India and China convinced officials that through strict limits on family size they could stem the environmental toll and economic burdens of a large population. Elites, less likely to depend on their children for income and insurance, often saw the benefits of smaller families. The poor, who bore the brunt of government intervention, often resented policies that infringed on their reproductive freedom and cultural traditions. Rewards and punishments buttress China's one-child policy, launched in 1979–80 with massive propaganda about propelling the nation to modernity. Despite its name, the policy limits only urban couples and government employees to one child, allowing a second to most rural residents after a five-year interval, along with other exceptions. One-child families enjoy privileges in housing, among other things, while violators face fines, job loss, and coerced sterilization or abortion. Critics of the authoritarian approach point to research indicating that China's voluntary "late, long, few" policy of the 1970s (delaying, spacing, and limiting births) produced more dramatic results than the mandatory one-child plan that tramples on the human rights of dissenters.[118]

Today, most organizations involved in population issues steer away from the word *control*. They speak of human rights, not the human race. They advocate for women's health and women's schooling, voluntary human-capital improvements. Educating women about health not only reduces maternal ailments and child mortality but also increases the effectiveness of any method of birth control.

Treading carefully, the United Nations Population Fund (UNFPA) emphasizes that it "supports countries in using population data for policies and programmes to reduce poverty and to ensure that every pregnancy is wanted, every birth is safe, every young person is free of HIV/AIDS, and every girl and woman is treated with dignity and respect."[119] Assured that most children will survive, families will not have to produce so many "spares." Once parents are truly planning their families, economists point out, they are likely to consider "opportunity costs," what they give up in order to bear, nurse, and nurture each child. When a society improves a woman's job prospects and/or schooling, it increases the "productive value" of her time. Since motherhood pulls her away from wage-earning, children become more "expensive," and people tend toward smaller families.[120]

Economic Strategies

Experts differ on which economic levers to pull to eliminate poverty. Economists point out the obvious correlation between prosperity and widespread employment but disagree on how to achieve that. Should government simply stabilize the money supply and let businesses compete, or should it create jobs, particularly for low-skill workers, as Sweden has done? Many economists believe economies should grow, on the proverbial theory that a rising tide raises all boats, even though inequality widens if the rich get richer faster than the rest.

THE WASHINGTON CONSENSUS

Why did the West pull ahead of the rest in the 19th century? Many Westerners believe the answer is three-pronged: capitalism, democracy, and the Industrial Revolution. Powering the engine of this trinity into the 21st century is free trade.

After World War II, the United States emerged as a major trade promoter. Even before the fighting had ended, representatives from 45 countries met at Bretton Woods, New Hampshire, in July 1944 to discuss how to rebuild after the war and how to avoid another worldwide depression. Although delegates represented countries with diverse political and economic systems, from China to Czechoslovakia and Liberia to Luxembourg, they shared a common goal: fiscal stability. To achieve it, they established two new institutions—the International Monetary Fund (IMF) and the International Bank for Reconstruction and Development (today one part of the World Bank)—and paved the way for a third, the World Trade Organization (WTO).[121]

The 29 nations who first joined the IMF agreed to a predictable currency-exchange system measured against the U.S. dollar to facilitate international trade. Over the years, the IMF has added more than 150 other members, who share information about their economic policies and currency. To help members weather economic crises, the IMF offers advice and short-term loans. The World Bank was established to lend money at favorable rates for reconstruction projects. Since that mission covered mostly battle zones,

Latin American delegates far from World War II fronts pushed for an equal (and later primary) emphasis on development in other parts of the world.[122]

Loans alone could not reverse Europe's economic depression or stem widespread hunger and homelessness. Under the Marshall Plan, Britain, France, Germany, and other countries collaborated on an economic recovery strategy that worked, thanks to a $13 billion infusion from across the Atlantic. The Marshall Plan lay the groundwork for the European Union (EU) and inspired donor-funded global development efforts.[123]

These macroeconomic interventions succeeded in Europe and set a pattern for rejuvenating ailing national economies. Although the IMF and World Bank complement each other, they operate differently. Only developing nations may borrow from the World Bank, which sets interest rates based on a country's gross national product (GNP), the value of its goods and services, divided by population. Countries with a very low GNP per capita receive interest-free loans. At its start, the World Bank concentrated on large urban transportation and electrical power projects, but over the years, learning hard lessons about where aid is most effective, it has shifted emphasis to smaller enterprises and rural development. With a staff of about 10,000 and branches around the world, the bank also provides technical assistance with its loans.

Serving both poor and rich countries, the IMF has strengthened its supervisory role over the years. Financial crises occur when countries spend more than they take in. Although the IMF will lend money to tide them over, it looks at countries' borrowing records and balance of payments (how much they import versus how much they export) and then conditions loans on borrowers' willingness to make far-reaching policy changes (structural adjustments) to balance the budget. Many other lenders and donors withhold funds until a country implements a structural adjustment program (SAP).[124]

In the 1980s, a recession caused by the international oil crisis precipitated a debt crisis. Cash-strapped Mexico nearly defaulted on its loan payments, which drew attention to the staggering debt poor countries were carrying. In 1980, Mexico was paying more than 30 percent of its annual GNP as external debt, but it was in the middle range of countries that included Poland (16 percent), Syria (27 percent), Algeria (47 percent), Peru (51 percent), and Nicaragua (112 percent).[125] To prevent a banking collapse, lenders agreed to reduce and forgive some loans while the IMF and World Bank guaranteed the rest. Those two Washington-based institutions, as well as the U.S. Treasury and Federal Reserve, advised Latin American governments to privatize public companies, eliminate trade barriers (such as tariffs and quotas), invite foreign investment, secure property rights, restructure taxes, raise interest rates, and redirect spending to basic services and infrastructure, among other reforms—a formula for fiscal discipline that economist John Williamson dubbed in the 1990s "the Washington Consensus."[126]

Although many hail the Washington Consensus for improving the macroeconomic balance sheet in many countries, opinion is deeply divided over its effect on the poor. Structural adjustments, which may include eliminating food subsidies and levying user fees for schools and clinics, often disproportionately burden the poor. Servicing debt preempts spending on services. Privatized industries may cut wages to compete. In an economy oriented toward exports rather than self-sufficiency, production for local needs often takes second place; farmers emphasize growing coffee, for instance, instead of a variety of food crops.[127] SAPs at times provoke popular revolt, especially when development projects enrich Western contractors and corrupt elites or when the glitter of Western culture lures the young away from local traditions. Can structural adjustment be called voluntary when countries have borrowed money out of desperation and reform is a requirement for debt relief? To some critics, the Washington Consensus has become a synonym for "free trade" or "globalization" or "neoliberal policies" in which governments forsake regulation and hand the keys of the house to profit-making businesses, particularly multinational corporations.

Proponents of structural adjustment argue that plans tailored for each country that put in place safety nets as well as promote economic growth turn some short-term pain into long-term gain that trickles down. In a study of the two dozen developing countries that have significantly opened to foreign trade around the turn of the millennium, the World Bank points to accelerated economic growth in two-thirds, accompanied by poverty reduction. The percentage of people living on less than $1 a day fell from 43 to 36 percent in Bangladesh, for instance, and from 13 to 10 percent in Costa Rica.[128] Because the "post-1980s globalizers" include highly populated countries such as India and China (as well as much smaller countries such as Nepal and the Dominican Republic), their gains have put a dent in global poverty. Other progrowth policies promoted by the Washington Consensus help the poor, according to the World Bank. In Vietnam, for instance, rice farmers benefited from land privatization, and real income and consumption increased for the poorest 5 percent of the population.[129]

MICROCREDIT

Whereas macroeconomic strategies aim to spread prosperity from the top down, microcredit campaigns aim to build it from the bottom up. Most business activity or housing improvement starts with a loan, which borrowers pay back over time. To get the loan, they have to show collateral. Too often, antipoverty activists say, financial institutions exclude the poor, whom they deem unworthy of credit because they have no assets or no history of making payments reliably. Although the poor can sometimes access cash through pawn shops, informal moneylenders, or credit cards, these often charge "high-risk" borrowers usurious interest, trapping them in a cycle of debt rather than giving them the opportunity to improve their livelihood and living standard. Microcredit projects unleash entrepreneurship among the poor by providing access to small pools of capital and teaching the poor to save and invest.

Muhammad Yunus launched the microcredit movement in the mid-1970s. An economics professor at the University of Chittagong in Bangladesh, he supervised a research project on offering banking services to the rural poor, especially women. Out of it grew the Grameen Bank (*grameen* means "village"), which aims to build social capital as it encourages self-employment. Instead of collateral, it relies on trust and peer pressure. Borrowers own the bank and help set policy. They must join a group and agree to the "16 decisions" that grew out of member discussions; for example, they promise to boil water, build pit latrines, keep families small, grow and eat vegetables, and "always be ready to help each other."[130] In return, the bank advances seed money, usually less than $200, which borrowers pay back, with interest, in tiny weekly installments.

With almost 1,200 village branches and 4.5 million borrowers, the Grameen Bank boasts a repayment rate around 98–99 percent—far better than the 30 percent rate for agricultural loans and 10 percent rate for industrial loans at Bangladeshi commercial banks.[131] At first donor funded, Grameen Bank has been self-sustaining since 1995. Its clients buy chickens, goats, and inventory for roadside stands (and even begging); in one of the bank's most successful projects, women lease cell phones, which they share for a fee, bringing telecommunication services to isolated areas. Once borrowers have a track record, the bank will advance larger sums, including home and education loans. Because women plow their benefits back into their families, Grameen loans have a tremendous ripple effect, and studies have shown borrowers are more likely to vote, to bear fewer children, and to have a say in household decisions. Like all antipoverty initiatives, the "barefoot bank" has drawn its share of criticism for rescheduling so many loans (especially in the wake of a flood) and for enmeshing the very poor in yet another cycle of debt. But its success has spawned a global microcredit movement that broadly interprets capitalism to wed market forces and social good.[132]

CONCLUSION

With its host of causes, effects, and potential remedies, human hardship is so vast and varied a problem that a plural noun might better capture its sprawl: We should think not of "poverty" but of "poverties." Although they share many characteristics, poverties also differ, rural from urban, female from male, disaster-related from conflict-entwined. So dissimilar is the widespread poverty in the Global South from the selective poverty in developed nations that some economists consider them two separate phenomena. People in absolute poverty toil first to feed, cloth, and maintain their bodies. In the long run, many experts believe, globalization will raise incomes around the world, relieving much basic misery. As Americans well know, however, poverty can persist even in the richest economy. With relative poverty, especially in prosperous nations, physical burdens may diminish but often psychological burdens grow as citizens experience inequality. As concern shifts from surviving to thriving, countries must make a commitment to equal opportunity in education, employment, and political representation.

---

[1] World Bank. "Poverty Drops Below 1 Billion, says World Bank." Press release # 2007/159/DEC accompanying release of "World Development Indicators 2007" (April 15, 2007). Available online. URL: http://go.worldbank.org/TQDI2FZ4F0. Downloaded May 10, 2007. The United States Census Bureau estimates the 2007 world population at 6.605 billion. U.S. Census Bureau. "Table 094. Midyear Population by Age and Sex." Available online. URL: http://www.census.gov/cgi-bin/ipc/idbagg. Downloaded May 10, 2007.

[2] U.S. Department of Labor, Bureau of International Labor Affairs. "The Department of Labor's Findings on the Worst Forms of Child Labor, 2005," p. 7. Available online. URL: http://www.dol.gov/ilab/media/reports/iclp/tda2005/tda2005.pdf. Downloaded May 10, 2007.

[3] UN Office for the Coordination of Humanitarian Affairs. "Pakistan: Focus on Kidney Sales by Bonded Labourers" (April 7, 2005). Available online. URL: http://www.irinnews.org/report.asp?ReportID=46508&SelectRegion=Asia&SelectCountry=PAKISTAN. Downloaded November 14, 2007.

[4] BBC News. "Niger's President in Famine Zone" (July 21, 2005). Available online. URL: http://news.bbc.co.uk/1/hi/world/africa/4698943.stm. Downloaded Nov 14, 2007.

[5] CNN.com, "Inside and Beyond Niger" (August 15, 2005). Available online. URL: http://www.cnn.com/2005/WORLD/africa/08/15/niger.perspective. Downloaded Nov 14, 2007.

[6] Abhijit Vinayak Banerjee. "Introduction." In Banerjee et al. *Understanding Poverty.* Oxford and New York: Oxford University Press, 2006, pp. xvii–xix.

[7] Robert F. Clark. *Victory Deferred: The War on Global Poverty (1943–2003).* Lanham, Md.: University Press of America, 2005, p. 7.

[8] World Bank. "Fighting Poverty: Findings and Lessons from China's Success." Available online. URL: http://go.worldbank.org/QXOQI9MP30. Downloaded May 10, 2007.

[9] Banerjee. "Introduction." In *Understanding Poverty,* p. xviii.

[10] Daron Acemoglu, Simon Johnson, and James Robinson. "Understanding Prosperity and Poverty: Geography, Institutions, and the Reversal of Fortune." In Banerjee et al. *Understanding Poverty,* pp. 19–20. Economist Stephen C. Smith, in *Ending Global Poverty* (New York: Palgrave Macmillan, 2005, p. 1), says Americans are 50 times richer than sub-Saharan Africans.

[11] United Nations Development Programme. "Human Development Report 2005: International cooperation at a crossroads: Aid, trade and security in an unequal world," p. 166. Available online. URL: http://hdr.undp.org/reports/global/2005/pdf/HDR05_chapter_5.pdf. Downloaded May 10, 2007.

[12] United Nations. "Programme of Action of the World Summit for Social Development," Chapter 2, No. 19. Available online. URL: http://www.un.org/esa/socdev/wssd/agreements/poach2.htm. Posted August 21, 2000.

[13] Deepa Narayan et al. *Voices of the Poor: Crying Out for Change.* New York: Oxford University Press for the World Bank, 2000, p. 34. Available online. URL: http://www1.worldbank.org/prem/poverty/voices/reports/crying/cry.pdf. Downloaded May 11, 2007.

[14] Deepa Narayan et al. *Voices of the Poor: Can Anyone Hear Us?* New York: Oxford University Press for the World Bank, 2000, p. 35. Available online. URL: http://www1.worldbank.org/prem/poverty/voices/reports/canany/vol1.pdf. Downloaded May 11, 2007.

[15] Narayan et al. *Voices of the Poor: Crying Out for Change,* p. 139.

[16] Simon Maxwell. "The Meaning and Measurement of Poverty." ODI Poverty Briefing 3 (February 1999). Available online. URL: http://www.odi.org.uk/publications/briefing/pov3.html. Downloaded May 11, 2007.

[17] Narayan et al. *Voices of the Poor: Can Anyone Hear Us?,* p. 217.

[18] Narayan et al. *Voices of the Poor: Crying Out for Change,* pp 134–135.

[19] Narayan et al. *Voices of the Poor: Can Anyone Hear Us?,* p. 31.

[20] Julia Dinsmore. "My Name Is Not 'Those People.'" In D. Stanley Eitzen and Kelly Eitzen Smith. *Experiencing Poverty: Voices from the Bottom.* Belmont, Calif.: Thomson Wadsworth, 2003, p. 64. The essay originally appeared in the September-October 1998 issue of *People United for Families (PUFF) Poverty to Prosperity Newsletter.*

[21] Heba El-Laithy and Khalid Abu-Ismail. "Poverty in Syria: 1996–2004: Diagnosis and Pro-Poor Policy Considerations." United Nations Development Programme (June 2005), p.86. Available online. URL: http://www.undp.org.sy/publications/national/Poverty/Poverty_In_Syria_en.pdf. Downloaded September 12, 2006.

[22] Quoted in "Using Research and Data to Advance Development Goals." United Nations Population Fund Web site. Available online. URL: http://www.unfpa.org/pds/research.htm. Updated December 15, 2005. For more information about Paris21, see "Paris21—Background & Presentation." Available online. URL: http://www.paris21.org/pages/about-paris21/paris21-background-presentation/presentation/. Downloaded May 11, 2007.

[23] United Nations Population Fund. "Characterizing Poverty." Available online. URL: http://www.unfpa.org/swp/2002/english/ch2/page4.htm. Downloaded May 11, 2007.

[24] USDA Economic Research Center. "Food Security in the United States: Hunger and Food Security." ERS Web site. Available online. URL: http://www.ers.usda.gov/Briefing/FoodSecurity/labels.htm. Updated November 15, 2006.

[25] Angus Deaton. "Measuring Poverty." In *Understanding Poverty*, pp. 4–7.

[26] U.S. Census Bureau. "Poverty Thresholds 2006." Available online. URL: http://www.census.gov/hhes/www/poverty/threshld/thresh06.html. Downloaded January 23, 2008.

[27] El-Laithy and Abu-Ismail. "Poverty in Syria: 1996–2004," Annex 1, p. 2.

[28] El-Laithy and Abu-Ismail. "Poverty in Syria: 1996–2004," Annex 1, p. 2.

[29] United States Department of Health and Human Services. "The 2008 HHS Poverty Guidelines." Available online. URL: http://aspe.hhs.gov/poverty/08poverty.shtml. Downloaded January 23, 2008.

[30] Hanoi, Vietnam, Research and Training Center for Community Development, 1999. Quoted in Narayan et al. *Voices of the Poor: Can Anyone Hear Us?*, p. 28.

[31] United Nations Population Fund. "Characterizing Poverty."

[32] United Nations Development Programme. "Overview." *Human Development Report 2006*. Available online. URL: http://hdr.undp.org/hdr2006/statistics/indices/. Downloaded May 11, 2007.

[33] United Nations Development Programme. "Human development index." Human Development Report 2007/2008. Available online. URL: http://hdrstats.undp.org/indicators/1.html. Downloaded January 23, 2008.

[34] Stephen Jenkins. Quoted in Maxwell. "The Meaning and Measurement of Poverty."

[35] See Andrew Wilson, ed. "World Scripture: Charity and Hospitality." International Religious Foundation. Available online. URL: http://www.unification.net/ws/theme141.htm. Downloaded May 13, 2007. Also see, "Good Manners and Form (*al-Adab*)." USC-MSA Compendium of Muslim Texts. Available online. URL: http://www.usc.edu/dept/MSA/fundamentals/hadithsunnah/bukhari/073.sbt.html. Downloaded May 13, 2007.

[36] American Psychological Association. "Low Socioeconomic Status Is a Risk Factor for Mental Illness, According to a Statewide Examination of Psychiatric Hospitalizations." APA online press release (March 6, 2005). Available online. URL: http://www.apa.org/releases/lowses.html. Downloaded May 13, 2007.

[37] Marc Airhart. "AIDS Linked to Poverty, Violence, Discrimination." Interview with Maria Jose Alcala (Fall 2005). Earth and Sky Web site. Available online. URL: http://www.earthsky.org/humanworld/interviews.php?id=49422. Downloaded May 14, 2007.

[38] Library of Congress, Federal Research Division. "Country Profile: Saudi Arabia" (September 2006). Available online. URL: http://lcweb2.loc.gov/frd/cs/profiles/Saudi_Arabia.pdf. Downloaded May 14, 2007. Onn Winkler. "Rapid Population Growth and the Fertility Policies of the Arab Countries of the Middle East and North Africa." *Yale F&ES Bulletin* 103, p. 449. Available online. URL: http://environment.yale.edu/documents/downloads/0-9/103winckler.pdf.

[39] United Nations Development Programme. "Saudi Arabia." Human Development Indicators Country Fact Sheets. Available online. URL: http://hdrstats.undp.org/countries/country_fact_sheets/cty_fs_SAU.html. Downloaded January 23, 2008.

[40] Daphne Eviatar. "Petrol Peril: Why Iraq's oil wealth may do more harm than good." Boston.com News. (April 13, 2003). Available online. URL: http://www.boston.com/news/packages/iraq/globe_stories/041303_ideas2.htm. Downloaded May 14, 2007.

[41] Tsegay Wolde-Georgis. "The Impact of Cold Events on Ethiopia." Review of the Causes and Consequences of Cold Events: A La Niña Summit (1998). Available online. URL: http://www.ccb.ucar.edu/lanina/report/wolde.html. Downloaded May 14, 2007.

[42] United Nations Development Programme. Human Development Report 2007/2008: *Fighting Climate Change: Human Solidarity in a Divided World*, p. 1. Available online. URL: http://hdr.undp.org/en/media/hdr_20072008_en_complete.pdf. Downloaded January 23, 2008.

[43] Celia W. Dugger. "Push for New Tactics as the War on Malaria Falters." *New York Times Online* (June 28, 2006). Available online. URL: http://www.nytimes.com/2006/06/28/world/africa/28malaria.html?pagewanted=1&ei=5070&en=e732b6df8ba53117&ex=1157601600. Downloaded November 14, 2007.

[44] Centers for Disease Control and Prevention. "The Impact of Malaria, a Leading Cause of Death Worldwide." Available online. URL: http://www.cdc.gov/malaria/impact/index.htm. Updated September 13, 2004.

[45] U.S. Agency for International Development. "India's Largest Ever Race Against Diarrheal Deaths on July 29." USAID press release (July 27, 2006). Available online. URL: http://www.usaid.gov/in/newsroom/press_releases/july27_6.htm. Updated July 31, 2006.

[46] Information from the World Health Organization quoted on a microbiology class Web page. "Schistosomiasis." Tulane University. Available online. URL: http://www.tulane.edu/~dmsander/WWW/224/Schisto.html. Updated February 16, 1999.

[47] Jeffrey D. Sachs and Peter J. Hotez. "Fighting Tropical Diseases." *Science* 311 (March 17, 2006), p. 1,521. Available online. URL: http://www.sciencemag.org/cgi/content/summary/311/5767/1521. Downloaded May 14, 2007.

[48] J. M. Blaut. *The Colonizer's Model of the World: Geographical Diffisionism and Eurocentric History*. New York and London: Guilford Press, 1993, pp. 13–18.

[49] Ibn Khaldun. *The Muqaddimal*. Trans. Franz Rosenthal. Princeton, N.J.: Princeton University Press, 1967, p. 61.

[50] "Max Weber." History of Economic Thought Web site. Available online. URL: http://cepa.newschool.edu/net/profiles/weber.htm. Downloaded August 6, 2007.

[51] Jonathan Plucker. "Francis Galton." Indiana University. Available online. URL: http://www.indiana.edu/~intell/galton.shtml. Downloaded November 14, 2007.

[52] Daniel T. Lichter and Martha L. Crowley. "American Attitudes about Poverty and the Poor." Population Reference Bureau. Available online. URL: http://prb.org/Template.cfm?Section=PRB&template=/ContentManagement/. Downloaded November 14, 2007.

[53] D. Stanley Eitzen and Kelly Eitzen Smith. *Experiencing Poverty: Voices from the Bottom*. Belmont, Calif.: Thomson Wadsworth, 2003, p. 6.

[54] U.S. Census Bureau. "Household Income Rises, Poverty Rate Declines, Number of Uninsured Up." Press release (August 28, 2007). Available online. URL: http://www.census.gov/Press-Release/www/releases/archives/income_wealth/010583.html. Downloaded January 23, 2008.

[55] Michael Zimmermann, Wendy Zimmermann, and Jeffrey S. Passel. *The Integration of Immigrant Families in the United States*. Washington, D.C.: Urban Institute, 2001.

[56] Rosalee Clawson. "Poor People, Black Faces: The Portrayal of Poverty in Economics Textbooks." *Journal of Black Studies* 32, no. 3 (January 2002): 352–361.

[57] Nancy Birdsall. "Life Is Unfair: Inequality in the World." *Foreign Policy* 111 (Summer 1998): 76 ff.

[58] Oscar Lewis. *The Children of Sanchez: The Autobiography of a Mexican Family.* New York: Random House, 1961, p. xxiv.

[59] Quoted in Susan Rigdon. *The Culture Façade: Art, Science, and Politics in the Work of Oscar Lewis.* Urbana and Chicago: University of Illinois Press, 1988, p. 65.

[60] Oscar Lewis. "The Culture of Poverty." *Society* 35, no. 2 (January–February 1998): p. xxiv.

[61] Lewis. "The Culture of Poverty."

[62] Douglas Massey and Nancy Denton. *American Apartheid Segregation and the Making of the Underclass.* (Harvard, Mass.: Harvard University Press, 1998). Description available online. URL: http://www.hup.harvard.edu/catalog/MASAMA.html. Downloaded July 16, 2007.

[63] Quoted in Benin Daker. "Cosby and Black Underclass." *Christian Science Monitor,* July 20, 2004, p. 9. Available online. URL: http://www.csmonitor.com/2004/0720/p09s01-coop.html. Downloaded July 16, 2007.

[64] Blume, Lawrence E., and Steven Durlauf. "Identifying Social Interactions: A Review," working paper from Wisconsin Madison—Social Systems, July 22, 2005, EconPapers Web site. Available online. URL: http:///www.ssc.wisc.edu/econ/archive/wp2005-12.pdf. Downloaded August 7, 2007.

[65] "Population Growth Rate." World Bank DEP Web. Available online. URL: http://www.worldbank.org/depweb/english/modules/social/pgr/. Downloaded July 16, 2007.

[66] Thomas Robert Malthus. "An Essay on the Principle of Population: A View of Its Past and Present Effects on Human Happiness; with an Inquiry into Our Prospects Respecting the Future Removal or Mitigation of the Evils Which It Occasions." 6th ed. Book I, Chapter 2. London: John Murray, 1826. Available online. URL: http://www.econlib.org/library/Malthus/malPlong1.html#bottom. Downloaded July 16, 2007.

[67] Colin D. Butler. "Human Carrying Capacity and Human Health." *PLoS Med* 1, no. 3 (December 28, 2004): e55. Available online. URL: http://medicine.plosjournals.org/perlserv/?request=get-document&doi=10.1371%2Fjournal.pmed.0010055. Downloaded July 16, 2007.

[68] Centers for Disease Control and Prevention. "Achievements in Public Health, 1900–1999: Family Planning." *MMR* 48, no. 47 (December 3, 1999):1,073–80.

[69] Solar Energy International. "Energy Facts." Available online. URL: http://www.solarenergy.org/resources/energyfacts.html. Downloaded July 16, 2007. U.S. Geologic Survey. " United States Energy and World Energy Production and Consumption Statistics." Available online. URL: http://energy.cr.usgs.gov/energy/stats_ctry/Stat1.html. Downloaded July 16, 2007.

[70] U.S. Central Intelligence Agency. "United States." *CIA Factbook.* Available online. URL: https://www.cia.gov/cia/publications/factbook/geos/us.html. Downloaded July 16, 2007.

[71] United Nations Development Programme. Human Development Report 2000. Available online. URL: http://hdr.undp.org/en/media/hdr_2000_en.pdf. Downloaded February 6, 2008.

[72] Richard Hooker. "The European Enlightenment: Glossary." Available online. URL: http://www.wsu.edu/~dee/GLOSSARY/CAPITAL.HTM. Downloaded July 16, 2007.

[73] Richard Robbins. *Global Problems and the Culture of Capitalism.* Boston and London: Allyn & Bacon, 1999, pp. 84, 86–88.

[74] World Bank. "Assessing Globalization." Available online. URL: http://www1.worldbank.org/economicpolicy/globalization/issuesbriefs.html. Downloaded July 17, 2007.

[75] Transparency International. "Corruption Perceptions Index 2007." Available online. URL: http://www.transparency.org/policy_research/surveys_indices/cpi/2007. Downloaded February 6, 2008.

[76] BBC News. "Rwanda: How the Genocide Happened." April 1, 2004. Available online. URL: http://news.bbc.co.uk/1/hi/world/africa/1288230.stm. Downloaded July 17, 2007. Human Rights Watch. "History." Available online. URL: http://www.hrw.org/reports/1999/rwanda/Geno1-3-09.htm. Downloaded July 17, 2007. Human Rights Watch. "Numbers." Available online. URL: http://www.hrw.org/reports/1999/rwanda/Geno1-3-04.htm. Downloaded July 17, 2007.

[77] Applied History Research Group. "The Ottoman World to 1600: Roxelana." University of Calgary. 1998. Available online. URL: http://www.ucalgary.ca/applied_history/tutor/islam/empires/ottoman/roxelana.html. Downloaded July 17, 2007.

[78] American Anti-Slavery Group. "Types of Slavery." Available online. URL: http://www.iabolish.com/slavery_today/primer/types.html. Downloaded July 17, 2007.

[79] Acemoglu, Johnson, and Robinson. "Understanding Prosperity and Poverty." In Banerjee et al. *Understanding Poverty,* pp. 19–20.

[80] United Nations Population Fund. "Population Issues: Meeting Development Goals," p. 2. Available online. URL: http://www.unfpa.org/pds/facts.htm. Downloaded July 17, 2007.

[81] Nikola Krastev. "World: Maternal Mortality Numbers Still Climbing." July 4, 2004. Radio Free Europe/Radio Liberty Web site. Available online. URL: http://www.rferl.org/featuresarticle/2006/07/10d24de4-cc8d-459c-9eed-629ee1bccc4c.html. Downloaded May 16, 2007. United Nations Population Fund. "Regional Workshop on Skilled Birth Attendants in South and West Asia." Report from workshop in Islamabad, Pakistan, held April 19–21, 2004, p. 21. Available online. URL: http://www.rferl.org/featuresarticle/2006/07/10d24de4-cc8d-459c-9eed-629ee1bccc4c.html. Downloaded May 17, 2007.

[82] Bethan Emmett. "In the Public Interest: Health, Education, and Water and Sanitation for All." Oxford: Oxfam International, 2006, p. 49. Available online. URL: http://www.reliefweb.int/rw/lib.nsf/db900SID/AMMF-6T8GMT/$FILE/OXFAM-Aug2006.pdf?OpenElement. Downloaded May 17, 2007.

[83] Bryan Michael. "Poverty and Conflict." January 16, 2004. Development Gateway. Available online. URL: http://topics.developmentgateway.org/poverty/sdm/previewDocument.do~activeDocumentId=860864?activeDocumentId=860864. Downloaded July 16, 2007. Jonathan Goodhand, "Violent Conflict, Poverty, and Chronic Poverty." CPRC Working Paper 6 (May 2001). Available online. URL: http://www.chronicpoverty.org/pdfs/06Goodhand.pdf. Downloaded August 14, 2007.

[84] Emmett, "In the Public Interest," p. 52. United Nations Development Programme. "Eritrea." Available online. URL: http://hdr.undp.org/hdr2006/statistics/countries/country_fact_sheets/cty_fs_ERI.html. Downloaded August 14, 2007.

[85] Amnesty International. "Refugees Have Rights—Questions and Answers." Available online. URL: http://web.amnesty.org/pages/refugees-background-eng. Downloaded August 14, 2007.

[86] Benny Morris. *The Birth of the Palestinian Refugee Problem Revisited.* Cambridge: Cambridge University Press, 2004, pp. 1, 602. Donna E. Arzt. *Refugees into Citizens: Palestinians and the End of the Arab-Israeli Conflict.* New York: Council on Foreign Relations, 1997, p. 14. David P. Forsythe. "The Palestine Question: Dealing with a Long-Term Refugee Situation." *Annals of the American Academy of Political and Social Science* 467 (May 1983): 90.

[87] Oxfam International. "Our Generation's Choice." Oxfam Briefing Paper 94 (November 2006), p. 14. Available online. URL: http://www.oxfam.org.au/media/files/ourgenerations choice.pdf. Downloaded August 14, 2007.

[88] Eric Chetwynd, Frances Chetwynd, and Bertram Spector. "Corruption and Poverty: A Review of Recent Literature." Management Systems International Executive Summary (January 2003), pp. 3–5. Available online. URL: http://pdf.dec.org/pdf_docs/PNACW645.pdf. Downloaded August 14, 2007.

[89] Resolution adopted by the United Nations General Assembly [without reference to a Main Committee (A/55/L.2)] 55/2. United Nations Millennium Declaration, September 8, 2000. Available online. URL: http://www.un.org/millennium/declaration/ares552e.htm. Downloaded February 6, 2008.

[90] Quoted in Emmett. "In the Public Interest," p. 99.

[91] Alan B. Krueger and Jitka Maleckova. "Education, Poverty, and Terrorism: Is There a Causal Connection?" *Journal of Economic Perspectives* 17, no. 4 (Fall 2003): 119–144. Alvin Powell. "Freedom Squelches Terrorist Violence." *Harvard University Gazette* 4 (November 2004). Available online. URL: http://www.hno.harvard.edu/gazette/2004/11.04/05-terror.html. Downloaded August 14, 2007.

[92] Institute of Medicine of the National Academies. "Hidden Costs, Value Lost: Uninsurance in America." Prospectus available online. URL: http://www.iom.edu/CMS/3809/4660/12313.aspx. Downloaded February 8, 2008. Charles Marwick. "Lack of insurance costs up to $130 b in illness and premature death." *BMJ* 326, no. 7,404 (June 28, 2003): 1,418.

[93] Emmett. "In the Public Interest," pp. 91–99.

[94] Transparency International. "Corruption Perception Index 2006." Available online. URL: http://www.transparency.org/publications/newsletter/2006/november_2006/spotlight. Downloaded August 14, 2007. Potters for Peace. Web site. Available online. URL: http://www.pottersforpeace.org/. Accessed August 14, 2007.

[95] Food and Agriculture Organization. "Education, Extension, and Communication." Available online. URL: http://www.fao.org/Gender/en/educ-e.htm. Downloaded August 14, 2007.

[96] Andre Betaille. "Caste, Inequality and Affirmative Action." Geneva: International Institute for Labour Studies, 2002, p. 4. Available online. URL: http://www.ilo.org/public/english/bureau/inst/download/andre.pdf. Downloaded August 14, 2007.

[97] Chang Teck Peng. "The Long-waited Freedom of Expression and Poverty Eradication: Malaysians Challenge." United Nations Educational, Scientific and Cultural Organization. Available online. URL: portal.unesco.org/ci/en/ev/php=URL_ID/21947&URL_DO/DO_TOPIC&URL_SECTION-201.html. Downloaded August 14, 2007.

[98] United Nations. "Norway Called 'Haven for Gender Equality.'" Press release WOM/1377 (January 20, 2003). Available online. URL: http://www.un.org/News/Press/docs/2003/wom1377.doc.htm. Downloaded August 14, 2007.

[99] United Nations Development Programme. "UN Human Development Report 2005," p. 8. Available online. URL: http://hdr.undp.org/reports/global/2005/pdf/HDR05_overview.pdf. Downloaded August 14, 2007.

[100] United Nations. "Millennium Development Goals Indicators." Available online. URL: http://millenniumindicators.un.org/unsd/mdg/Host.aspx?Content=Indicators/Official List.htm. Downloaded August 14, 2007.

[101] Branko Milanovic. "Why we all do care about inequality (but are loath to admit it)." October 8, 2003. Available online. URL: http://www.worldbank.org/research/inequality/pdf/freldstein.pdf. Downloaded August 14, 2007. Paul Krugman. "Wages, Wealth, and Politics." August 18, 2006. Available online. URL: http://economistsview.typepad.com/economistsview/2006/08/paul_krugman_wa.html. Downloaded August 14, 2007.

[102] American Academy for the Advancement of Science "Introduction to Population and Resources." *AAAS Atlas of Population and Environment*. Available online. URL: http://atlas.aaas.org/index.php?part=2. Downloaded August 14, 2007.

[103] United Nations Children's Fund. "Implementing the 20/20 Initiative." Available online. URL: http://www.unicef.org/publications/pub_implement2020_en.pdf. Downloaded August 14, 2007.

[104] El-Laithy and Abu-Ismail. "Poverty in Syria," p. 85.

[105] Associated Press. "Baby Food from Israel, Blankets from India." September 19, 2005. Available online. URL: http://www.msnbc.msn.com/id/9363899/. Downloaded August 14, 2007.

[106] United Nations Office for the Coordination of Humanitarian Affairs. "Niger: When development is an emergency," August 29, 2006. IRINnews.org. Available online. URL: http://www.irinnews.org/S_report.asp?ReportID=55313&SelectRegion=West_Africa. Downloaded August 14, 2007.

[107] Helen Lachs Ginsburg and Majorie Rosenthal. "The Ups and Downs of the Swedish Welfare State: General Trends, Benefits, and Caregiving." *New Politics* 11, no. 1. Available online. URL: http://www.wpunj.edu/newpol/issue41/Ginsburg41.htm. Downloaded August 14, 2007. Joachim Palme. "Income Distribution in Sweden," *Japanese Journal of Social Security Policy* 5, no. 1 (June 2006). Available online. URL: http://www.ipss.go.jp/webj-ad/WebJournal.files/SocialSecurity/2006/jun/palme.pdf. Downloaded August 14, 2007. Katja Vuori. "Protecting (im)migrants and ethnic minorities from discrimination in employment: Finnish and Swedish experiences," chapter 3. International Labour Organization. June 16, 1998. Available online. URL: http://www.ilo.org/public/english/protection/migrant/papers/sw-fipro/ch3.htm. Downloaded August 14, ?007.

[108] Anders Bjorklund and Richard B. Freeman. "Generating Equality and Eliminating Poverty, the Swedish Way." NBER Working Paper 4945 (December 1994). Available online. URL: http://papers.ssrn.com/sol3/papers.cfm?abstract_id=226545. Downloaded August 14, 2007.

[109] Monte Reel. "Cash Aid Program Bolsters Lula's Reelection Prospects." *Washington Post*, October 29, 2006, A14.

[110] Gates Foundation. "Gates Foundation commits $258.3 Million for Malaria Research and Development." Available online. URL: http://www.gatesfoundation.org/GlobalHealth/Pri_Diseases/Malaria/Announcements/Announce-051030.htm. Downloaded August 14, 2007.

[111] Sachs and Hotez. "Fighting Tropical Diseases," 1,521.

[112] Saby Ganguly. "From the Bengal Famine to the Green Revolution." Available online. URL: http://www.indiaonestop.com/Greenrevolution.htm. Downloaded August 14, 2007.

[113] United Nations Food and Agriculture Organization. "FAO Director-General appeals for a second Green Revolution." September 13, 2006. Available online. URL: http://www.fao.org/newsroom/en/news/2006/1000392/index.html. Downloaded August 14, 2007.

[114] UN Food and Agriculture Organization. "FAO Director-General appeals."

[115] Allan Chase. *The Legacy of Malthus: The Social Costs of the New Scientific Racism*. Urbana, Chicago, and London: University of Illinois Press, 1975/1980, pp. 119, 129.

[116] Charles Davenport, in *Heredity in Relation to Eugenics* (1911, p. 80), quoted in Chase. *The Legacy of Malthus*, p. 157.

[117] Margaret Sanger. "A Plan for Peace." *Birth Control Review* (April 1932), 106. Available online. URL: http://www.lrainc.com/swtaboo/taboos/ms_apwp.html. Downloaded May 17, 2007.

[118] Therese Hesketh, Li Lu, and Zhu Wei Xing. "The Effect of China's One-Child Family Policy after 25 Years." *New England Journal of Medicine* 353 (September 15, 2005), pp. 1,171–76. Available online. URL: http://content.nejm.org/cgi/content/full/353/11/1171. Downloaded August 14, 2007.

[119] United Nations Population Fund. "Our Mission." Available online. URL: http://www.unfpa.org/about/. Downloaded August 14, 2007.

[120] T. Paul Schultz. "Fertility and Income." In Banerjee et al. *Understanding Poverty*, pp. 133, 136.

[121] World Bank. "Bretton Woods Conference." Available online. URL: http://web.worldbank.org/WBSITE/EXTERNAL/EXTABOUTUS/EXTARCHIVES/0,,contentMDK:64054691~menuPK:64319211~pagePK:36726~piPK:36092~theSitePK:29506,00.html. Downloaded August 14, 2007. Government of Canada. "1944—Bretton Woods Agreement." Available online. URL: http://www.canadianeconomy.gc.ca/English/economy/1944Bretton_woods.html. Downloaded August 14, 2007.

[122] "IMF History and Structural Adjustment Conditions." Available online. URL: http://ucatlas.ucsc.edu/sap/history.php. Downloaded August 14, 2007. Allison Berg. "History of the IMF." Available online. URL: http://filebox.vt.edu/users/aberg/Imf.content.html. Downloaded August 14, 2007.

[123] U.S. State Department. "The Marshall Plan (1947)." Available online. URL: http://usinfo.state.gov/usa/infousa/facts/democrac/57.htm. Downloaded August 14, 2007.

[124] David D. Driscoll. "The IMF and World Bank: How Do They Differ?" International Monetary Fund Web site. Available online. URL: http://www.imf.org/external/pubs/ft/exrp/differ/differ.htm. Downloaded August 14, 2007. World Bank. "About Us." Available online. URL: http://go.worldbank.org/B6U4HPNDS0. Downloaded February 6, 2008.

[125] Vincent Ferraro and Melissa Rosser. "Global Debt and Third World Development." In Michael Klare and Daniel Thomas, eds. *World Security: Challenges for a New Century*.

New York: St. Martin's Press, 1994, pp. 332–355. Available online. URL: http://www.mtholyoke.edu/acad/intrel/globdebt.htm. Downloaded May 17, 2007.

[126] Harvard University Center for International Development. "Washington Consensus." Global Trade Negotiations home page. Available online. URL: http://www.cid.harvard.edu/cidtrade/issues/washington.html. Updated April 2003.

[127] Walden Bello. "Structural Adjustment Programs: Success for Whom?" In Edward Goldsmith and Jerry Mander, eds. *The Case Against the Global Economy and for a Turn Towards the Local.* San Francisco: Sierra Club Books, 1996. Available online. URL: http://www.converge.org.nz/pirm/structur.htm. Downloaded May 17, 2007.

[128] David Dollar and Aart Kray. "Trade, Growth, and Poverty." *Finance & Development* 38, no. 3 (September 2001). International Monetary Fund Web site. Available online. URL: http://www.imf.org/external/pubs/ft/fandd/2001/09/dollar.htm. Downloaded May 17, 2007.

[129] David Dollar and Aart Kray. "Growth Enhancing Policies Are Good for Poor People." World Bank Institute Web site, Development Outreach. Summer 2000. Available online. URL: http://www1.worldbank.org/devoutreach/summer00/article.asp?id=55. Downloaded May 17, 2007.

[130] Grameen Bank. "A Short History of Grameen Bank." Available online. URL: http://www.grameen-info.org/bank/hist.html. Updated September 18, 2002. Grameen Bank. "The 16 Decisions of Grameen Bank." Available online. URL: http://www.grameen-info.org/bank/the16.html. Downloaded May 17, 2007. Muhammad Yunus. "What Is Microcredit?" Grameen Bank Web site. January 2003. Available online. URL: http://www.grameen-info.org/mcredit/. Downloaded May 17, 2007.

[131] S. Kamaluddin. "Lender with a Mission—Bangladesh's Grameen Bank Targets Poorest of Poor." Global Development Resource Center Web site. Available online. URL: http://www.gdrc.org/icm/grameen-article4.html. Downloaded May 17, 2007.

[132] Evaristus Mainsah, Schuyler Heuer, Aprijita Kaira, and Qiulin Zhang. "Grameen Bank: Taking Capitalism to the Poor." Columbia Business School Web site. *Chazen Web Journal of International Business* (Spring 2004). Available online. URL: http://www1.gsb.columbia.edu/mygsb/faculty/research/pubfiles/848/Grameen_Bank_v04.pdf. Uploaded May 17, 2004. Muhammad Yunus. "Social Business Entrepreneurs Are the Solution." Grameen Bank Web site. Available online. URL: http://www.grameen-info.org/bank/socialbusinessentrepreneurs.htm. Downloaded May 17, 2007.

2

Focus on the United States

Unfortunately, many Americans live on the outskirts of hope, some because of their poverty, and some because of their color, and all too many because of both.
—Lyndon Baines Johnson (1908–73)

The American embrace of capitalism has made the United States an economic powerhouse. Although government at various levels regulates business practices and provides some safety nets, the market rules the economy: Individuals and private firms decide when to expand, whom to employ, and what goods and services to produce. Since 1945, the high-tech focus of American industry has riven the labor pool into two tiers, boosting workers with skills or education and depressing the rest, according to the U.S. Central Intelligence Agency. "Since 1975, practically all the gains in household income have gone to the top 20% of households."[1]

Released just before Labor Day, the U.S. Census Bureau's annual report on income and poverty usually prompts a flurry of op-ed pieces. Some highlight good news. Between 2005 and 2006, for instance, real median household income rose to $48,200—the second consecutive gain since 1999—and the poverty rate, which had been rising after the turn of the millennium, declined slightly to 12.3 percent of the population. Other editorials underscore troubling figures. In that same time, more Americans—47 million, or 15.8 percent of the population—lacked health insurance.[2]

Apportioning blame or credit, editorialists try to make sense of trends. In the first half of the 20th century, the gap between the rich and the rest narrowed, yet inequality has resurged since the 1970s.[3] As economist Robert Samuelson noted in the *Washington Post*, "the rich are getting an ever-bigger piece of the economic pie": In 1981, the richest 5 percent of American households enjoyed 16.5 percent of total income; by 2005, that share had swollen to 22.2 percent. Yet he admitted that no one really knows why middle- and working-class Americans are losing ground although fingers point to "globalization, weaker unions, increasingly skilled jobs, the frozen minimum wage and the 'winner-take-all society' (CEOs, sports stars and movie celebrities getting big payouts)" as well as expensive health insurance.[4] Despite antipoverty policies and programs, hardship refuses to disappear. In 2006, 36.5 million Americans (12.6 percent) lived below the poverty threshold—about a quarter of Native Americans and African Americans, a fifth of Hispanics, and a sixth of all children and of all foreign-born immigrants.[5]

Regardless of their political orientation or their critique of official measuring tools, writers decry the prevalence and persistence of poverty. After all, America is supposed to be a land of plenty.

HISTORY

Popular history paints a picture far rosier than actual research supports. According to American myth, the natural bounty of the New World, especially the abundance of "empty" land, offered all newcomers prosperity unattainable in other countries. Immigrants needed only the gumption to make the crossing and a willingness to work hard. Pioneers "civilized the wilderness" by carving it into small homesteads, and yeoman farmers, so idolized by Thomas Jefferson and the other founding fathers, formed the backbone of the new republic. Until the 1960s, school textbooks focused on U.S. riches and triumphs, almost never mentioning its poor.[6]

Colonial Poverty

Poverty has long been part of the American landscape. Historians estimate that 90 percent of ship passengers arrived destitute in the 17th and 18th centuries. Three out every four people who crossed the Atlantic during that time period were enslaved Africans. Of white immigrants, two-thirds toiled as indentured servants, many of whom died before they earned their freedom. A small fraction established livelihoods as farmers and artisans, but more scraped by as vagrants and day laborers.[7]

Although access to land, game, wood, and other natural resources did foster social mobility and improve nutrition in the colonies, Indian wars, economic ups and downs, and epidemics of smallpox and yellow fever contributed to poverty for a third of the population.[8] New England settlers followed English poor law, with towns caring for their own but rebuffing outsiders. Struggling families might receive a tax break or a pair of shoes, permission to cut firewood or graze sheep on common land, or even a loaner cow for a season so that they could drink milk and churn butter. Often town fathers arranged apprenticeships for orphans or poor children.[9] Believing that salvation lay in work and self-sufficiency, donors favored temporary aid and job opportunities over long-term support and outright gifts.

While the transition to commercialized agriculture (growing crops for sale as well as survival) and early industrialization in the 18th century improved the fortunes of merchants, manufacturers, master craftsmen, financiers, and landlords, it also pushed have-nots to the bottom. The high cost of food and other goods prompted 30 riots between 1776 and 1779. More citizens spent a lifetime without owning land.[10] Private charity and public relief funded by "poor taxes" increased, but so, too, did the strings attached. Whereas Puritans and other early colonists had accepted poverty as part of God's plan, citizens of the new democratic republic shifted more responsibility onto the individual.[11] They distinguished between the "deserving" poor, usually widows and abandoned wives they considered victims of circumstance, and the "undeserving" poor, usually able-bodied men whom they blamed for laziness, drinking, and other moral failings. Led by Quaker merchants, the Philadelphia business community opened Bettering House around 1768, a cost-efficient tough-love institution to confine, supervise, and "uplift" the poor. Although mothers sometimes convinced authorities to allow them to remain at home, by the 1820s most cities were institutionalizing destitute men, women, and children either in almshouses or workhouses that had onsite employment, such as looms to weave textiles. Angry about separation of families and loss of control over their personal lives and labor, resisters either defied almshouse rules or fled town.[12]

The New Republic

As in England, the Industrial Revolution in the United States transformed the economy, prompting an internal migration from country to city and drawing immigrants from around the world. In the first half of the 19th century, inventions and developments in transportation spurred larger-scale agriculture and manufacturing. In 1831, farmer Cyrus McCormick developed a mechanical reaper for harvesting grain and then built a company that sold it widely through easy credit and advertising. Blacksmith John Deere in 1837 improved the plow with a steel blade that helped farmers cut through the Great Plains' thick grass and heavy soil, earning them the nickname of "sod busters." This and many other new tools saved time and labor but favored farmers who had the wherewithal to buy them. Some went on to enlarge their spreads. Those without means to invest in horse-drawn plows, seeders, harrows, binders, threshers, and wagons—and later gas-powered tractors and chemical fertilizers—began to be left behind.

While working as a tutor on a Georgia plantation, Eli Whitney patented the cotton gin in 1793, a hand-cranked or horse-powered device that extracted sticky seeds from cotton bolls. Thanks to the gin, cotton soon supplanted tobacco, sugar, and rice as the South's major crop and the United States's major export. Cotton fed the Northern textile industry, which improved upon British spinning and weaving machines and benefited from time-saving shipping breakthroughs such as steamboats and railroads. Although Congress outlawed slave importation in 1808, cotton production depended on cheap labor, so trade in human beings continued both internally and covertly. By 1860, enslaved African Americans constituted a third of the Southern population.[13] At the same time, thriving cloth mills and other manufacturing plants lured women off hardscrabble New England farms and immigrants from French Canada and northern Europe.

Civil War Aftermath

In 1860, 11 slaveholding Southern states seceded from the Union and formed the Confederate States of America. At the height of the subsequent Civil War (1861–65), President Abraham Lincoln issued the Emancipation Proclamation, which freed slaves in the Confederate states. The war devastated the South. By contrast, the North rebounded quickly and continued its industrial development. Oil refineries, steel mills, meat-packing plants, railroads, and factories making everything from knives to shirts created fortunes for their owners and jobs for millions. Immigrants flocked to the United States, often settling in East Coast cities. A reflection of a growing economy, per-capita income rose more than 5 percent a year around 1870. Optimism characterized the national mood and made its way into Horatio Alger's popular stories of shoeshine boys and other urchins who pulled themselves up by their bootstraps through a combination of "luck and pluck." States and municipalities invested in public education to open opportunities.[14]

As an economic strategy, the federal government encouraged expansion, arranging generous loans for big businesses and granting land to railroads and the like. Since the 1840s, journalists had been talking about America's "Manifest Destiny" to settle the continent from coast to coast, and the 1862 Homestead Act fueled westward migration by awarding 160-acre parcels to pioneers who lived on and "improved" their claims over five years. Since Native Americans stood in the way of this land grab, however, the U.S. Army fought a series of Indian wars from 1865 to 1890 that displaced tribes and confined survivors to reservations.

Prosperity did not rain down evenly. State and local poor relief grew tenfold between 1860 and 1870. The national government stepped in with a pension plan for Civil War widows and disabled veterans.[15] From roughly 1865 to 1868, the federal Freedmen's Bureau supplied food, clothes, and fuel; ran hospitals; started schools; and advocated for former slaves.[16] Congress defeated a provision to redistribute plantation land to African Americans, however, and President Andrew Johnson rescinded General William T. Sherman's land grants in South Carolina, Georgia, and Florida—popularly known as "40 acres and a mule"—under which every ex-slave family was to receive 40 acres of farmland. Despite ambitious plans to rebuild the South, Northern corruption and white Southern resistance scuttled Reconstruction. The 19th century's changing demographics established poverty patterns that persist to this day. In 2006, the Northeast had the highest median household income, and the South, the lowest, with blacks and Native Americans enduring disproportionate hardship.

The national mood darkened in the mid-1870s. Because of improved production, crop supply outstripped demand, and falling prices for wheat, cotton, and corn hit farmers hard, especially in the South and West, and especially those who had borrowed money to buy tools or land. Banks failed; small businesses went bankrupt. As the government's laissez-faire philosophy left big business unfettered but also unregulated, corporations often exploited workers and merged into giant trusts that stifled competition. As the U.S. economy metamorphosed from a rural, agricultural plow horse to an urban, industrial engine, intellectuals worried about Americans' physical and moral decline.

The Gilded Age

Mark Twain nicknamed the period between the Civil War and the turn of the century "the Gilded Age" because of its materialism. Dinner parties were the rage in the late 19th century: Mrs. Stuyvesant Fish even threw one for her dog, dressed for the occasion in a $15,000 collar (the equivalent of more than $300,000 in 2005); another at Delmonico's restaurant in New York City in the 1880s featured a $10,000 indoor "lake" complete with real swans. The frivolous spending of the newly or the obscenely rich, imitated on a lesser scale by the growing middle class, contrasted with the penury of most Americans, more than 90 percent of whom lived on less than $1,200 a year (about $26,500 today). Of this latter group, the average annual income was $380 ($8,400 in 2005 dollars).[17] By 1900, 30 million Americans (30 percent of the population) lived in cities, and one in three of them was nearly starving.[18]

Stark was the contrast between Caroline Astor's Fifth Avenue mansion with its ballroom–art gallery that could hold 1,200 guests and the tenements on Manhattan's Lower East Side, where immigrant families lived and often worked in small, dark, grimy apartments.[19] In a typical New York slum block in 1900 stood 39 tenements with 605 apartments, 2,781 residents (a sixth of them children under five), shared toilets, and no baths. Only 40 apartments had hot water, and more than 440 rooms had no windows, hence no direct light or air.[20] In such close quarters, sweltering in summer and frigid in winter, diseases like tuberculosis and typhoid fever spread quickly, hitting children and the malnourished particularly hard.

Although many Americans admired enterprising "captains of industry," others reviled the richest of the rich as unscrupulous "robber barons." Free-market capitalists countered that inequality was as natural as evolution: In business, as in nature, the fittest survived, and the poor had only their own failings to blame for their misfortune. For all their Social Darwinism, however, many tycoons donated generously to charity—out of a sense of religious obligation, upper-class noblesse oblige, or fairness. A weaver's son who immigrated from Scotland to the United States at age 13, steel magnate Andrew Carnegie preached what he called "the gospel of wealth," giving away more than $350 million to fund community projects—most famously libraries and universities—that enabled individuals to succeed on their own merits.[21] Even as great wealth passed from generation to generation in select families, Carnegie wanted to keep alive the possibility of Horatio Alger's rags-to-riches stories, much like Carnegie's own.

Still, poverty outstripped philanthropy. The widening divide between rich and poor ran counter to core American values about the equality of man. As farmers united in a political movement known as populism and workers joined unions, their sometimes violent protests and strikes raised awareness about abusive work sites and the unevenness of prosperity. Journalists, too, exposed the underside of a society growing more and more diverse as waves of immigrants arrived from eastern and southern Europe. While some readers accused these "muckrakers" of exaggerating tales of human misery in order to sell papers, these same writers found a receptive audience among moralistic middle- and upper-class Americans. Surely something was wrong with a society in which hard workers, the "deserving" poor, suffered so many hard knocks. Vivid reports such as Jacob Riis's *How the Other Half Lives* (1890), a photo-and-text documentary of squalid New York tenement life, and Upton Sinclair's *The Jungle* (1906), a novel about Chicago's corrupt meatpacking industry, revealed that poverty not only degraded the poor, but it also "contaminated" the better off—from the lady who caught the flu from her maid, to the gentleman who surrendered his wallet to a jobless mugger, to the child who developed diarrhea after buying an ice-cream sandwich from an unsanitary peddler. Underlining "the close relations between bad housing, bad health, bad morals, and bad citizenship," many a writer linked the condition of the poor to the well-being of the nation as a whole.[22]

The Progressive Era

Outrage spurred action in the Progressive Era, roughly 1890–1929. Reformers espoused change: new regulations on business and a more systematic approach to preventing poverty than "the patchwork of local poor laws and private charities" that provided relief without challenging the status quo.[23] Founding Hull-House in Chicago in 1889, Jane Addams inspired a national movement of settlement houses, neighborhood centers that aimed to "Americanize" immigrants and improve their living conditions. Besides offering classes in everything from sewing to English to art, Hull-House operated a library, a day care, a public bath, and health and legal clinics, and it encouraged political and social connections by opening its space to lecturers, mutual-aid societies, and discussion groups.[24] In a science-enamored age, progressives believed in studying as well as addressing problems such as poverty, and Hull-House pioneered the academic fields of social work and sociology.

Led by W. E. B. DuBois, a sociologist with a Harvard Ph.D., a small group of prominent African Americans in 1905 formed the Niagara movement to demand civil rights and economic opportunity for the black community. After the Civil War, Southern states had enacted a series of black codes to keep freed slaves from voting, serving on juries, marrying whites, etc. With the Fourteenth and Fifteenth Amendments, ratified in 1868 and 1870, respectively, the Constitution guaranteed all citizens equal protection under the law and men of any color the right to vote. But in the post-Reconstruction South, segregation and disenfranchisement continued both de jure (by law) and de facto (by practice), under a system that became known as Jim Crow. It received official sanction in the Supreme Court ruling in *Plessy v. Ferguson* (1896): "Laws permitting, and even requiring, their [black and white] separation in places where they are liable to be brought into contact do not necessarily imply the inferiority of either race to the other," the Court stated; separate could be equal. In fact, schools, railroad cars, and other services set aside for blacks suffered from underfunding and neglect, and beaches, parks, theaters, and even hospitals turned away African Americans.

Underorganized and underfunded, the Niagara movement floundered for three years until an antiblack riot in the Illinois capital of Springfield, Lincoln's hometown, drew shocked national press coverage. Since 1890, southern blacks had been moving north to escape Jim Crow, part of the "Great Migration" that lasted until 1970. But newcomers faced discrimination and de facto segregation. In Springfield, as elsewhere, discrimination had shunted blacks to low-pay, low-prestige positions as waiters, servants, wagon drivers, and the like. Out of more than 1,000 black workers in Springfield, only four held skilled factory jobs.[25] Seeking out folks from home—and facing hostility if they tried to settle next door to whites—most African Americans lived in all-black neighborhoods, many of them economically diverse.

In the Springfield riot, a white mob destroyed a small black business district and burned 40 homes in a nearby poor neighborhood, beating many blacks and lynching two, a barber and a wealthy elderly man who lived in a mostly white neighborhood. Alas, white-on-black violence was nothing new, and more race riots followed during World War I as black migrants continued to head north to fill wartime factory jobs. But in the wake of the Springfield rampage, white activists joined Niagara leaders in forming the National Association for the Advancement of Colored People (NAACP), which later played a crucial role in the civil rights movement of the 1950s.[26]

Progressives had a mixed record of success. They did clean up city governments, tighten building codes, rein in big business, and promote (as well as bureaucratize) public education so that by 1920 more than 86 percent of children were attending school.[27] In 1906, the Food and Drugs Act mandated accurate labeling to protect consumers; patent medicines had to list all ingredients, including alcohol and heroin, and processors could no longer mask inferior flour or tainted milk with concealed additives like chalk. That same year, the Meat Inspection Act, a direct consequence of *The Jungle*, led to safer food for consumers and, indirectly, cleaner working conditions for slaughterhouse employees. Ratification of the Sixteenth Amendment to the Constitution in 1913 solidified Congress's authority to levy an income tax—first instituted in 1861 to fund the Civil War—as a way of modestly redistributing wealth to benefit the public.

Although reformers lobbied hard, they lost focus and backers at times because of their diffuse agenda, which spanned women's rights to temperance to environmental conservation. While many states passed laws limiting children's work to 10 hours per day, for instance, enforcement was spotty. Sounding the alarm about tenements as breeding grounds for disease and vice aroused antipathy more often toward poor immigrants than toward the profiteering slumlords and sweatshop owners who abused them.

In the 1920s—just four decades after France had presented the United States with the Statue of Liberty, a symbol of welcome—Congress enacted a series of strict quotas limiting immigration by national origin. For later immigrants who entered the United States without proper papers or overstayed their visas, illegal status often compounded economic difficulties.

A sense of well-being also undercut the progressive agenda. Although Word War I ravaged Europe, it stimulated U.S. industry. Workers benefited from a labor shortage, and companies honed both management and technology to improve efficiency. At his Detroit, Michigan, auto plant, Henry Ford led the revolution in mass production, standardizing parts and tasks in order to turn out cars at a fast clip and low price. While critics noted that assembly lines robbed skilled craftsmen of their autonomy and authority, they also created slots for many unskilled laborers. Ford needed to keep his machine-like operation humming; to prevent factory hands from quitting numbing jobs—or joining unions in protest—he dramatically increased pay to $5 per day. Higher wages not only lowered turnover but enabled Ford to turn his workforce into car buyers, expanding the market for his Model T's.

Ford and other major industrialists also bought loyalty and improved productivity through benefits, a philosophy dubbed "welfare capitalism." Companies trimmed the workday to eight hours and offered health insurance, paid vacation, retirement pensions, and in-plant infirmaries, cafeterias, and sports teams. While welfare capitalism did not cover the millions working for small businesses or not working at all, a factory job could lift a family out of poverty and into the middle class. Adequately paid workers fueled a boom in profusely advertised consumer goods, from sofas to washing machines to toothpaste.

Depression and the New Deal

Many government interventions proposed in the Progressive Era did not materialize until the Great Depression of the 1930s, when hardship rather than merchandise became the great equalizer. Although the economy had always experienced dips and swells, when the stock market crashed in October 1929, an ordinary downturn rippled out of control. Average investors lost everything, and speculators who had bought on margin found they owed money. Confidence shattered, Americans pulled the reins on spending, so manufacturers cut production, laid off workers, and sometimes folded. The optimism of the roaring 1920s had fueled widespread borrowing by both individuals and businesses, and with so many suddenly unable to pay debts and mortgages, banks ran short of funds. More than a third failed in the early '30s as jittery depositors clamored to make withdrawals.

Panic fueled recession, as did poor government decisions. By passing the Smoot-Hawley Act in 1930, for instance, Congress slapped a huge tariff on imports, provoking retaliatory moves by foreign countries that undermined world trade and internationalized the depression. In the midst of fiscal crisis, the United States also experienced the worst drought in its history, which exacerbated erosion from "sod-busting" and other environmentally unsound farming practices on the Great Plains. Hot, dry winds soon whipped up choking "black blizzards" in what became known as the dust bowl.[28]

As John Steinbeck dramatized in his 1939 novel *Grapes of Wrath*, dust and debt drove farmers off their land and propelled impoverished "Okies" to migrate from the Midwest to sunnier central California. In cities, poverty moved beyond the slums into the house next door. By 1933, almost 13 million (some sources say 15 million) Americans—a quarter of the labor force—were out of work. Hungry and humbled, the unemployed lined up to eat in soup kitchens run by churches and other private charities, and those evicted from apartments or foreclosed homes slept in shantytowns dubbed "Hoovervilles," a sarcastic swipe at President Herbert Hoover (1874–1964) and his assurances that prosperity awaited "just around the corner." When 20,000 out-of-work World War I veterans marched on Washington to claim their service bonus, Hoover angered the public by ordering troops to break up the protest.[29] This depression's length and depth, along with government's inability to deal with it, rattled American faith in progress.

Elected in 1932, Franklin D. Roosevelt pledged candor and bold federal action to stem the flood of misfortune. In his first inaugural address, he critiqued the get-rich-quick mentality of jazz-age financial speculators and applauded old-fashioned values: "The joy and moral stimulation of work no longer must be forgotten in the mad chase of evanescent profits." But in a break with the past, Roosevelt and the Democratic-controlled Congress asserted a much stronger federal role in managing and democratizing the economy. Under Roosevelt's New Deal administration, an alphabet soup of agencies created jobs, dispensed aid, and tightened regulations.

This economic experiment was not always successful or popular. Laissez-faire capitalists, accustomed to a free hand, generally resented government interference. To some, Roosevelt's central planning smacked of socialism. Yet most Americans supported New Deal legislation to protect consumers and workers. A new Securities and Exchange Commission supervised the stock market, and the Federal Deposit Insurance Corporation (FDIC) guaranteed bank accounts up to $5,000. In 1938, Congress passed the Fair Labor Standards Act, which set a minimum wage of 25¢ an hour, required extra pay for overtime, and limited the hours and types of jobs that children could work. That same year, after a drug with an ingredient related to antifreeze killed 100 people, the Food, Drug, and Cosmetic Act gave broad new powers to the Food and Drug Administration (FDA). The laws benefited everyone but especially the most exploited, those who had no choice but to work 12-hour shifts or to buy cheap brands of medicine and tinned meat.[30]

Concern for public welfare spurred the Federal Emergency Relief Administration (FERA), headed by onetime social worker Harry Hopkins (1890–1946). Between 1933 and 1935, FERA dispensed $3 billion, mostly in grants to states.[31] Besides direct aid, such as shelters for transients along travel routes or utility bill payments for cash-strapped families, FERA funded programs that put the unemployed to work—including large numbers of white-collar workers who had never imagined that they would land on the dole. States created adult education and literacy classes for teachers, theater projects for actors and stagehands, and digs for archaeologists; they tapped engineers and architects as well as construction workers to build playgrounds, schools, roads, and dams. In Washington, scientists tested the amount of vitamin C in the state's apples. In bankrupt Key West, Florida, artists from around the country painted murals and designed postcards and brochures to lure tourists. FERA also underwrote part-time jobs for college students who otherwise would have had to drop out.[32]

Public service dominated New Deal initiatives. Planting trees, fighting fires, and making maps, youths in the Civilian Conservation Corps (CCC) earned room, board in wilderness barracks, and $30 a month, of which the government docked $25 for their families.[33] The Tennessee Valley Authority (TVA) put on line a hydroelectric plant that controlled flooding and delivered cheap rural electricity. In 1935, the Works Progress (later Work Projects) Administration (WPA) succeeded FERA and until its disbanding in 1943 employed more than 8.5 million Americans.[34] Because the agency tried to match skills to task, its projects ranged from airports to surveys to guidebooks, the last thanks to the Federal Writers' Project. In addition to setting up migrant camps and lending more than $1 billion to farmers, the Farm Security Administration (FSA) assigned photographers—future greats such as Gordon Parks (1912–2006), Walker Evans (1903–75), Ben Shahn (1898–1969), and Dorothea Lange (1895–1965)—to document the plight of sharecroppers and dust bowl refugees. Although many Americans belittled make-work, few could deny the utility of highway bridges or the virtuosity of symphony orchestras. With their focus on American workers and American themes, WPA projects intensified patriotism, arts appreciation, and respect for the struggles of ordinary citizens. In the 1930s, poverty moved out of the shadows and into the light.

With one in five Americans benefiting from federal assistance, negative attitudes about relief softened during the depression. At the same time, people's expectations of government grew, along with a sense of entitlement, that aid to the needy was not a gift but a due. As Roosevelt assured Congress in 1935, he was not seeking to destroy individual ambition or the profit motive in business; he did not aim to divide the American pie into equal slices. But, he said, government had a duty to provide "security against the major hazards of life." Recognizing the limits of welfare capitalism, Congress passed the landmark Social Security Act of 1935. Under its plan for "old-age insurance," about 60 percent of workers and their employers paid a tax, based on wages, to fund benefits available after age 65. By 1939, the government extended coverage to families when a worker died. Children of divorced, widowed, or unwed mothers qualified for Aid to Dependent Children (ADC), which states administered. While ADC aimed to alleviate poverty among a targeted population, Social Security strove to prevent it among the nation at large.

As wartime production lifted the United States out of its slump, the government canceled its first food-stamp program, which from 1939 to 1943 had distributed coupons to the poor so that they could buy "unmarketable" surplus, such as ripening produce.[35] Still, Roosevelt continued to stress the importance of a social safety net. In his 1944 State of the Union address, he outlined "a second bill of rights": besides religious and press freedom, all Americans had a right to "a useful and remunerative job . . . adequate food, clothing, and recreation . . . a decent home . . . adequate protection from the economic fears of old age, sickness, accident, and unemployment . . . [and] a good education."[36] To what extent should the government intervene to secure these rights? While Democrats, like Roosevelt, believed in a strong state role, Republicans favored fewer taxes and fewer regulations, unshackling business so that it could go about creating jobs. Attitudes about how to address poverty divided Democrats and Republicans and contributed to contentious partisanship as the century progressed.

Since 1945

Popular as the New Deal was, many Americans considered the Great Depression an exceptional crisis. Objections to relief lingered amid notions that the poor failed because of their own shortcomings and needed a can-do attitude more than public assistance. Raised to cherish individualism, independence, and free enterprise, Americans resisted the welfare-state model developing in Western Europe. There, to varying degrees over the next decades, governments taxed citizens heavily in order to provide comprehensive social services—including child care, medical treatment, and education—and income support, such as paid maternity and sick leaves and unemployment compensation.

Although Social Security marked a major shift in U.S. policy and expanded in the 1950s to raise the payout during retirement and add disability insurance, Americans did not charge the federal government with cradle-to-grave management of their well-being. Into the 21st century, the U.S. government guaranteed no universal health care, for instance; health insurance was a benefit larger employers offered as a perk and many Americans did without. Free public education, which differed significantly in quality depending on locality, ended at 12th grade. Nor did Americans embrace redistribution of wealth or rationing of services. Many felt Europe's *industrial socialism*—a loaded term during the cold war years that pitted the United States and capitalism against the Soviet Union and communism—sapped initiative and independence. Some called European nations "nanny states." What motivates hard work if the go-getter and the slacker end up with the same portion?

POSTWAR BOOM—FOR SOME

Still haunted by the bread lines of the Great Depression, Americans nonetheless believed that government should intervene to stabilize the economy, a philosophy well articulated by British economist John Maynard Keynes (1883–1946), one of the architects of the Bretton Woods institutions. Keynesian policy did not assure everyone a subsistence income but encouraged steady employment and prevented boom and bust cycles through taxes and state spending.

Bracing for the economic shock of millions of World War II veterans returning to civilian life, Congress had already enacted the Serviceman's Readjustment Act of 1944, also known as the G.I. Bill of Rights. Its most controversial benefit turned out to be its least used: unemployment pay of $20 a week for a year if needed. But 7.8 million veterans took advantage of Veterans Administration (VA) support for training or education: up to $500 a year for tuition, books, and fees, as well as a living stipend. In 1947, almost half of entering college students had served in the military. That same year, the government also backed more than 640,000 G.I. loans, mostly for homes but also for farms and businesses, which stimulated construction and other industries.[37] Because of the G.I. Bill, millions of Americans of modest means were able to buy a house and earn a certificate or diploma, entering the labor force over the next few years with better prospects.

Magazines brimmed with stories of Americans "getting back to normal," marrying, starting families, and buying new cars, which helped them commute to white-collar service and sales jobs from their new houses in the suburbs. Spurred by wartime exigencies, the United States began its technological breakaway in computers, medicine, weaponry, and space engineering. More and more workers were reporting to the lab or the office rather than the field or factory floor (the percentage of the labor force who farmed dropped from 38 in 1900 to 3 in 1970).[38] Birth rates soared, creating a "baby boom" from 1946 to 1966. Jets whisked travelers from coast to coast and across the Atlantic. In the 1950s as in the 1920s, advertising whetted appetites for consumer products from cake mix and cigarettes to Tupperware and televisions. Abundance, proposed historian David Potter in *People of Plenty* (1954), had hard-wired optimism into the American character.

But other academics warned that superficial bounty hid a national deficit. Harvard economist John Galbraith argued in his best-seller *The Affluent Society* (1958), for instance, that the United States should be investing in the public rather than the private sector, in capital more than economic strategies of eliminating poverty. Instead of producing and marketing lipstick and the like, the country should be building infrastructure and improving schools. While materialism generated a buzz of prosperity, it masked the "forgotten fifth," the more than 22 percent of Americans still in poverty.[39]

THE CIVIL RIGHTS MOVEMENT

Among those being left behind were African Americans. Published in 1944, Swedish economist Gunnar Myrdal's influential *An American Dilemma: The Negro Problem and American Democracy* laid black poverty at the feet of discrimination. Daily humiliations reminded African Americans of their status as second-class citizens. Racism in the United States was not just personal but institutional, with law, government, and other entities giving advantages to whites. Social Security and unemployment insurance, for instance, originally excluded agricultural and domestic workers, the majority of whom were blacks or immigrants. Aid to the needy and nonworking remained a patchwork of private and public assistance, the latter administered largely by states, each with its own eligibility criteria. Some screened out "unsuitable" families, which married white officials often defined as those headed by never-wed African-American women, even though only the children, never the mothers, received ADC aid.[40]

Institutional racism also reinforced housing segregation. Another New Deal agency, the Federal Housing Administration (FHA) had fostered home ownership by changing laws so that banks could offer long-term mortgages to people making small down payments. But the FHA discouraged lending on easy terms to African Americans by painting entire neighborhoods as a credit risk. Nor could blacks move out of these districts. On the theory that racial or ethnic mixing drove down property values, the FHA encouraged, and state courts sanctioned, restrictive covenants that forbade white property owners from selling to anyone but Caucasians. As a result, neighborhoods remained segregated, and blacks had more difficulty building wealth the way most middle-class Americans did, through buying a home that rose in value as they enjoyed the use of it.

In 1948, the Supreme Court ruled against enforcing racially restrictive covenants in *Shelley v. Kraemer,* but redlining took its place. The FHA and banks color coded neighborhoods, denying loans to anyone in red zones, regardless of qualifications—usually blacks or other minorities, such as Hispanics—who could not then join the exodus to new housing developments in the suburbs.[41]

Having fought and died for the United States during World War II, black veterans expected a grateful nation to live up to long-standing promises of equal opportunity. In 1948, President Harry Truman (1884–1972) did order the U.S. military to desegregate, but Jim Crow kept rearing its ugly head, especially in the South, where whites who beat and killed blacks went unpunished, as the murder of 14-year-old Emmett Till in Mississippi underscored in 1955. African Americans could not collect their full due under the G.I. Bill: Not only did educational institutions deny them entrance, but so, too, did suburbia, since the VA followed the FHA's lead in redlining.

Frustration fueled the civil rights movement of the 1950s, which ranged from sit-ins at lunch counters to legal challenges in the courts. In *Brown v. Board of Education* (1954), the NAACP won a major victory as the Supreme Court reversed *Plessy v. Ferguson* and ruled that "in the field of public education, the doctrine of 'separate but equal' has no place. Separate educational facilities are inherently unequal." Writing the unanimous decision, Chief Justice Earl Warren pointed out that racial separation generates among young blacks "a sense of inferiority as to their status in the community that may affect their hearts and minds in a way unlikely ever to be undone."

The Court then ordered local jurisdictions to desegregate public schools "with all deliberate speed," provoking a backlash in the South. Nineteen U.S. senators and 81 congressmen penned a "Southern Manifesto" urging resistance. Georgia passed a law converting public schools to private schools to avoid the order, and the Arkansas National Guard tried to turn away nine African-American students enrolling at Little Rock Central High School. When James Meredith enrolled at the University of Mississippi in 1963, President John Kennedy had to send in 16,000 troops to quell a rioting white mob that killed two and injured 160, shooting 28 federal marshals.[42] In the end, all schools desegregated, yet patterns of race-tinged inequality remained because of schools' link to unofficially segregated neighborhoods.

WAR ON POVERTY

Momentum was building to remove institutional barriers to political and economic equality. In the 1960s and 1970s, Congress passed a series of acts that secured the civil rights of all Americans. Strong-armed through Congress by President Lyndon Johnson, the Civil Rights Act of 1964 not only outlawed discrimination in schools, hotels, and workplaces, but it created the Equal Employment Opportunity Commission to root out bias based on race, religion, gender, or national origin. The Fair Housing Act of 1968 outlawed redlining and was reinforced by the Equal Credit Opportunity Act of 1974. Between 1940 and 1990, the percentage of blacks graduating from high school rose from 7.7 to 63.1 percent, with the greatest gains in the 1970s.[43]

The cumulative federal effort to improve equal opportunity in schools and workplaces yielded significant economic progress for African Americans, particularly from 1965 to 1975.[44] From 1940 to 1960, blacks improved their earnings mostly by moving out of the South. After 1975, the advance slowed because the economy stagnated and unskilled workers' wages in particular lagged. But in the golden years in between, when the civil rights movement had won over or beaten down most of its opponents and government measures tackled discrimination head-on, poverty and inequality retreated. Thanks to strong enforcement of fair laws and policies, black Americans began to catch up to their white peers.

Rippling out from the civil rights movement was attention to economic injustice in many forms. On Thanksgiving in 1960, CBS television aired *Harvest of Shame*, a documentary exposing how large agribusiness exploited Hispanic farmworkers in Florida. Two years later, socialist writer Michael Harrington (1928–89) described in his best-selling *The Other America* a poverty both invisible and new, "more isolated and politically powerless than ever before."[45] Setting out to give statistics a human face, he interviewed "the rejects of the affluent society," folks beyond the reach of welfare capitalism and union-secured benefits: small farmers tied to their land unable to compete with huge corporate spreads, hotel maids earning 55¢ an hour, laid-off miners in company towns with a skill that does not travel, skid-row alcoholics. At least in the Progressive Era, politicians courted the vote of tenement residents, who dreamed the American dream of a better life. At least in the Great Depression, the government could not ignore the needs of a majority of Americans. At least in poverty-stricken developing nations, "aspiration becomes a national purpose that penetrates to every village and motivates a historic transformation," Harrington wrote.[46] But the American poor no longer enjoyed the same strength in numbers. Into the 1960s, as the U.S. economy was picking up steam, poverty receded (dipping to 12.9 percent in 1969).[47] At the same time, it became entrenched.

Contributing to a culture of poverty, Harrington and others argued, was 1950s urban renewal. As whites fled to the suburbs, so went much of the tax base that had supported city services and schools. Buildings deteriorated, and vacancies increased. At rush hour, traffic choked the streets. In response, municipalities decided to "clean up" the core, with the federal government contributing funds for razing slums and building superhighways that allowed commuters a quick in and out. But urban-renewal projects often tore the fabric of the inner city. Pedestrians could not walk as easily from one section of town to another. Small shops closed without foot traffic. The down-at-the-heels appearance of ethnic neighborhoods often belied their vitality and economic diversity, but African Americans and immigrants lacked the political clout to challenge decisions about what constituted a slum.

Those who could afford to move out of the city usually did. While the federal government subsidized housing for the poor left behind, Harrington foresaw many of the problems that developed with "projects" such as Chicago's Robert Taylor Homes, a two-mile line of 28 identical high-rises. Need outpaced availability, and concentrating poverty in a small space intensified problems associated with it, especially drugs and crime.[48]

Harrington concluded, nonetheless, that only the federal government could abolish poverty. In his 1961 inaugural address, President Kennedy had proclaimed that "man holds in his mortal hands the power to abolish all forms of human poverty" and pledged American aid to "peoples in the huts and villages across the globe struggling to break the bonds of mass misery." Spurred in part by Harrington's book, Kennedy's administration began to take aim at domestic as well as international inequality. The program of issuing coupons to the poor to buy food revived, tentatively at first, then formally after the Food Stamp Act of 1964. That year, Kennedy's successor, Johnson, declared an all-out "War on Poverty." Attention begot attention: Academic studies and investigative commissions spawned media coverage and legislative initiatives.

In a time of perceived plenty, as the United States was asserting itself abroad as "leader of the free world," pictures and stories of home-grown destitution shocked Americans. In 1967, for instance, the Senate Subcommittee on Employment, Manpower, and Poverty held hearings in Mississippi, where testimony about hunger so stunned senators that several left the hotel ballroom and headed into the field, trailed by reporters. They visited a mother in a fetid shack who fed nothing but rice and biscuits to her six children, listless from hunger, their bellies swollen from malnutrition. "I didn't know this kind of thing existed," said an appalled senator, Robert Kennedy. Later that year, a team of pediatricians sent to the Mississippi Delta by the nonprofit Field Foundation testified about boys and girls weak and in pain. "They are suffering from hunger and disease and directly or indirectly they are dying from them, which is exactly what starvation means."[49] Although skeptics questioned broad and dramatic claims, stories and pictures of misery from

Southwest American Indian reservations to housing projects in the Bronx (New York) spurred a growing antihunger lobby. By 1974, all 50 states were issuing food stamps.[50]

The War on Poverty took place on many fronts. As with the New Deal, many of its human-capital interventions became fixtures of U.S. policy. With $1 billion in funding behind it, Title 1 of the 1965 Elementary and Secondary Education Act launched long-lasting programs aimed at disadvantaged children, such as Head Start preschools and support for extra reading teachers. Enacted that same year, Medicare and Medicaid subsidized health care for elderly and low-income Americans. In 1972, Congress authorized the Special Supplemental Nutrition Program for Women, Infants, and Children (WIC), which provides referrals, nutrition advice, and subsidized milk, eggs, cheese, carrots, cereal, and baby formula for low-income pregnant women, new mothers, and children under five. Also in the '70s, Social Security added Supplemental Security Income (SSI) for the disabled, which enabled more families to care for handicapped children at home and permitted some mentally impaired adults at hospitals and institutions to live on their own or in group homes.[51]

Complementing government initiatives and traditional faith-based charities were a host of new think tanks and nonprofit agencies, of all political colors, concerned with both poverty alleviation and prevention in the United States and abroad. The long-lived among them include Reading Is Fundamental, which distributes books and promotes literacy; the Southern Poverty Law Center, which takes on discrimination cases and promotes diversity; and the Children's Defense Fund, which conducts research and promotes child-sensitive public policies.

In the 1960s and 1970s, inspired in part by the civil rights and women's liberation movements, more poor people began to advocate on their own behalf. A founder of the United Farmworkers Union, Cesar Chavez (1927–93), for example, brought to national attention not just the plight but the dignity of migrant and immigrant laborers. Throughout the 1970s and 1980s, antipoverty activists formed nonprofit organizations such as ACORN (Association of Community Organizations for Reform Now) and the National Mental Health Consumers' Self-Help Clearinghouse. These put affected communities in charge of describing and rectifying their circumstances.

WELFARE REFORM

In 1973, the U.S. poverty rate hit a low of 11.1 percent before creeping back up. By then, the Vietnam War had upstaged the War on Poverty, and war in the Middle East sparked an Arab oil embargo that drove up energy prices.

"Stagflation," high interest and high unemployment, pinned the U.S. economy in a recession.

Voting for change, Americans elected as president Republican Ronald Reagan, who promised to reverse Keynesian policy by cutting taxes, rolling back regulations, pruning government spending, and stabilizing the money supply. In this era, Milton Friedman (1912–2006) emerged as the prevailing economic guru. Author of *Capitalism and Freedom* (1962), Friedman championed the free market. Whenever possible, government should get out of the way; when not possible, it should maximize individual choices: For example, he proposed that instead of pumping money into failing public schools, districts should issue parents tuition vouchers that they could apply to any private or public school, allowing competition to improve the educational system.[52] While many antipoverty activists howled that "Reaganomics" served the rich and harmed the poor, conservative Republicans accused liberal Democrats of patronizing the disadvantaged by underestimating and overproviding for them. What the poor needed, argued conservatives, were fewer handouts and higher expectations.

As the United States ended the 20th century with a political toss-up between Democrats and Republicans, policy makers continued to debate the merits of Keynesian versus other economic philosophies in spreading prosperity. While many business executives have hailed globalization as a boon for the U.S. economy overall, labor leaders have countered that it has been a bust for American and foreign workers as companies outsourced jobs overseas in order to skimp on wages and benefits. Economists likened the changing economic landscape at the millennium to the transition following the Industrial Revolution. To some, the end of the 19th century was the worst of times; the rich romped as they pleased while poverty calcified. To others, it was the inevitable grinding of shifting gears. Eventually, economic growth trickled down, as free trade proponents argue will eventually occur today.

One issue, however, united pundits and politicians of both parties: dissatisfaction with welfare, most often understood as a monthly check for needy families with children even though cash made up a small fraction of government benefits.[53] Since the 1930s, ADC had undergone a number of revisions, including name changes, and its rolls had grown, nearly tripling between 1965 and 1992. It was big, and it was expensive. By 1993, Aid to Families with Dependent Children (AFDC) supported about 10 percent of American mothers, including 25 percent of African-American mothers—most single and living in cities, almost half never married, almost half without high school diplomas.[54] Most collected benefits for a short spell, but about 10 percent stayed on welfare for a decade or more.[55] A lightning rod, AFDC drew censure from all directions. Liberal critics said the program offered too few benefits, forcing women to raise children in rat- and crime-infested neighborhoods and contributing to a culture of poverty. Conservatives said it offered too many benefits, taking away incentives to get married and find work.

Passed in 1996, the Personal Responsibility and Work Opportunity Reconciliation Act (PRWORA) overhauled welfare with a conservative orientation that also addressed liberal concerns. It capped spending; more needy people or rising cost of living would not lead to more funding. It changed welfare from an entitlement (a legal right for any who qualify as long as needed) to a temporary bridge. PRWORA ordered most adults off the rolls and into jobs within two years and set a lifetime five-year limit on assistance. To help discourage out-of-wedlock births, it required teen mothers to live with an adult in order to receive a check. Anyone who did not cooperate or committed a felony drug crime could lose benefits, including food stamps. Declaring "self-sufficiency" a principle of U.S. immigration policy, the act restricted aid to legal immigrants. At the same time, however, PRWORA addressed problems that had torpedoed previous reform attempts, such as mothers making the transition to entry-level work who needed affordable child care, continued health insurance, and job training. By funding Temporary Assistance for Needy Families (TANF) as block grants to states, PRWORA hoped to encourage innovation and flexibility in administering welfare.[56]

Because of this leeway, programs differ considerably from state to state, making it difficult to evaluate the overall impact of the new welfare-to-work strategy.[57] A decade after PRWORA, states supported significantly fewer clients; welfare caseloads had shrunk about 6 percent in Indiana, 48.5 percent in California, and more than 93 percent in Wyoming. Lawmakers reauthorized TANF as part of the Deficit Reduction Act of 2005. But are welfare "graduates" better off?[58] Many more single mothers are working, earning more, and child poverty rates have dropped, particularly among blacks and Hispanics. At the same time, however, many Americans who left welfare have turned into the working poor. Since 2000, the number of families receiving TANF has continued to shrink even though child poverty has crept back up. Deep poverty among children (when family income falls below half the poverty line) has increased. Eligibility for assistance does not equal funding, however: More than half of poor families who qualify for TANF never receive benefits. Researchers speculate that PRWORA's get-to-work tough love lies behind this trend, prompting states to throw out an unwelcome mat that discourages the needy from seeking TANF.[59] As the media spotlight revealed after Hurricane Katrina in August 2005, in a sink-

or-swim economy, many Americans are struggling to keep their heads above water.

CONTEMPORARY PROBLEMS AND INTERVENTIONS

Hunger and Nutrition

Thanks to its "amber waves of grain," the United States produces enough food and animal feed to sustain its population—and more. The world's largest agricultural exporter, it sold $64 billion worth of farm products abroad in 2005.[60] But the country also imports almost as much as it exports: off-season or exotic fruits, vegetables, and nuts as well as cheaper processed foods, such as wine, beer, cheese, pasta, coffee, candy, and canned goods. Overall, Americans are eating more than ever, with per-capita food consumption rising between 1983 and 2002 from 1,800 to 2,000 pounds per year.[61]

Yet this bounty masks problems in food production, distribution, and consumption. The United States wastes up to half of its harvests between field and table, according a University of Arizona study. While farmers cannot prevent bad weather or a bit of rot, some gamble on the commodity markets and plough under crops that will not pay off. On the consumer end, the average family of four overshops and tosses out almost $600 worth of groceries a year.[62] Americans overeat, too: About 30 percent of adults are obese, and among children and teens, 16 percent are overweight—triple the percentage in 1980.[63] Yet more than a tenth of American households experienced food insecurity at some point in 2006, although exact figures vary significantly from state to state—from more than 18 percent of the population in Mississippi to less than 7 percent in North Dakota.[64]

The USDA now distinguishes four categories of food security: high, marginal, low, and very low. In the 4 percent of households at the very bottom of the scale, people were more likely to skip meals and lose weight. But the majority of food-insecure families reported that sometimes they could not afford balanced meals and often ran out of groceries (and almost always worried about running out).[65] What is missing on the plate often shows up on the report card: Studies show that children growing up under these conditions have more behavioral problems and worse academic records than their food-secure classmates.[66] Ironically, food insecurity and obesity often overlap: The highest rates of obesity (and one of its correlates, type-2 diabetes) coincide with high-poverty, low-education populations.[67]

Often heavily advertised, processed foods—high in fat, added fat, and added sugar—are cheap and filling and appealing to people who may not have the transportation or the time after school and work to shop for chicken breasts and broccoli. When consumers fled to the suburbs at the end of the 20th century, grocers followed, leaving behind pricier take-outs and convenience stores, which stock fewer fresh fruits and vegetables. Studies have shown that high-income neighborhoods average about 30 percent more supermarkets than low-income areas; in Philadelphia, the difference is 156 percent.[68] Higher prices and fewer choices usually equal poor nutrition. "We think of obesity as being predicted by genetics; believe me, it is also predicted by incomes and zip codes," says Dr. Adam Drewnowski, director of the Nutritional Sciences Program for the University of Washington School of Public Health and Community Medicine.[69] Antihunger initiatives, therefore, usually address both the quantity and the quality of food available to the poor.

FOOD STAMPS, WIC, AND SCHOOL LUNCH

Administered by both federal and state government, food stamps remain the nation's biggest antihunger—and entitlement—program. To qualify, applicants must present documentation of income and living expenses. Almost 26 million low-income Americans—half of them children—collect food stamps, which no longer come as paper coupons but as an electronic debit card to buy groceries. Benefits depend on need and state of residence; the average payout is $209 a month. Because of PRWORA, the percentage of food stamp households on cash welfare dropped from 42 to 15 percent between 1990 and 2005, and many (29 percent) reported earnings from work. Nonetheless, measured by lines and gaps, these households are very poor: less than 12 percent topped the poverty threshold, and 40 percent survived on half or less.[70]

In addition to food stamps, low-income mothers and young children may be eligible for WIC, a short-term program that serves almost 8 million Americans a month. It issues vouchers, opens warehouses, or makes deliveries of food rich in protein, calcium, iron, and vitamins A and C. To qualify, applicants must not only fill out paperwork but visit a health professional who certifies their "nutritional risk."[71]

Most American children also eat better because of the National School Lunch Program. Since 1946, its yearly cost and outreach has grown from $70 million and 7.1 million children to $7.9 billion and more than 26.9 million children. Any public or nonprofit private school or day care may participate. In return for serving meals that meet federal nutrition guidelines (less than 30 percent fat and a third of the recommended daily amount of protein, calcium, vitamins, and calories), schools receive money and donated staples from the USDA, as well as bonuses (such as fruit) now and then from agricultural surplus. By design, low-income families benefit most. Kids whose families top the poverty line by no more than 30 percent get free lunches (and sometimes breakfasts and snacks), while those slightly better off may buy them at a reduced price. Although the USDA subsidizes costs for needier students, it also pays participating schools cents for every other meal served, and all pupils profit from the balanced menu and nutrition education.[72]

Experts credit federal food aid with eliminating the gross malnutrition that shocked Americans in the 1960s. Pregnant women who receive WIC during pregnancy are more likely to give birth to full birthweight, and therefore healthier, babies. According to one study, girls from food-insecure households who participate in the school lunch program face a 71 percent lesser risk of being overweight. Food programs also have positive financial ripple effects. Sometimes criticized for inaccuracy and inefficiency, the food stamp program has reduced its over- and underpayments. During economic downturns, increased circulation of food stamps helps the food industry. And prevention saves money: For every $1 spent on WIC, the government saves $3.89 in health expenses as the child grows up.[73]

Unfortunately, many needy Americans miss out on federal food aid. Food stamps reach only about 60 percent of those eligible.[74] Among the reasons are offputting bureaucracy, language and culture differences, stigma, and lack of information.[75] Aware of these barriers, the USDA publishes materials widely in Spanish and English. Many people also credit the debit card with helping to make food stamps less visible at the grocery store and therefore less embarrassing to beneficiaries.

FOOD BANKS AND CORNER STORES

Hosts of agencies tackle hunger locally. Often with grants from the USDA, outreach projects offer food stamp counseling and application assistance. In Texas, where more than half of eligible residents do not receive food stamps, Lone Star Legal Aid (LSLA) sends bilingual paralegal-attorney teams to community events with laptop computers hooked to scanners and projectors. Besides giving PowerPoint presentations and advice, they often gather required documentation on the spot, shepherding food stamp applications through the system.[76]

Other nonprofit groups fill gaps in the federal food programs. America's Second Harvest Network moves almost 2 billion pounds of donated and purchased edibles to food banks. These in turn distribute food either directly to hungry clients through open pantries or to homeless and domestic-violence shelters, churches that run soup kitchens, and neighborhood groups that operate lunch programs in the summer or "kids cafés" in the evening.[77] Founded in 1954, Meals on Wheels delivers a hot, balanced dinner and a moment of social contact to shut-ins and senior citizens whose limited mobility as well as resources may interfere with shopping and cooking. Need here will only grow, predicts Meals on Wheels, as the U.S. population continues to age.[78]

Still other organizations address broad problems in the American food chain. Worrying that nutrition suffers because of the disconnect between producers and consumers, the Center for Food and Justice sponsors projects that link schools and hospitals with local farms.[79] A number of groups are working with businesses to bridge the "grocery gap." Many supermarkets resist locating to impoverished neighborhoods because of higher security costs, employee turnover, and disappearance of carts, which carless shoppers may wheel far from the store. One solution is to provide free shuttle service to existing stores: Customers gain access, while stores gain customers. Another solution is to help markets open and profit in underserved urban and rural communities. The Pennsylvania Fresh Food Financing Initiative, for instance, offers grants, loans, tax credits, and human-resource support to retailers settling and hiring in needy areas.[80]

Homelessness and Housing

On any given night in the United States, a population the size of a major city has no place to call home. Sometimes 440,000 (roughly the population of Kansas City), sometimes 842,000 (more than that of San Francisco), the number of homeless Americans is hard to pin down. Point-in-time counts may miss the many people temporarily or intermittently without housing, instead catching more of the "chronically" homeless, particularly "street people" with mental illness or drug addiction. For that reason, researchers often prefer surveys that cover a period of time (period prevalence counts). Both measures fall short, however, for the homeless are often on the move or out of sight, doubling up with friends for a few days or sleeping in cars, at stations, or under overpasses. At some point in a year, the National Law Center on Homelessness and Poverty estimates that 3.5 million people, including 1.35 million children, experience homelessness. Families with children now constitute about a third of the homeless population in cities and probably a higher fraction in rural areas.[81]

Homelessness is just the outer edge of a national housing crisis. Many more Americans put up with problems (overcrowding, cranky plumbing, few electrical outlets, unsafe neighborhoods) or pay more rent or mortgage than they can afford just to keep a roof over their heads. By the government rule of thumb, households should spend no more than 30 percent of their income on housing. But with housing prices rising faster than earnings, low- and middle-income Americans are increasingly spending a bigger share: 12 to 14 million families devote half their budget to shelter.[82] More than 5 million households have what the U.S. Department of Housing and Urban Development (HUD) defines as "worst-case needs": Their income falls below half the local median, and lacking assistance, they live in substandard housing or spend more than half their income on rent.[83]

PUBLIC HOUSING AND VOUCHERS

Since the 1930s, the federal government has encouraged home ownership, first by guaranteeing mortgages and later by adding income-tax breaks for interest payments. During the Great Depression, it began building affordable rental housing in city slums to be run by local public housing authorities. By the Johnson era, the federal government was also subsidizing private developers to construct more multi-unit buildings for low-income renters screened by local housing authorities.[84] As many of these "projects" deteriorated, tenants and neighbors complained: Often managed by profit-minded landlords, these isolated "warehouses" for the poor seemed to breed social problems. Under President Richard Nixon, the Housing and Community Development Act of 1974 marked a shift from public (or public-private) housing toward the private market. Under Section 8, eligible families or individuals found a place to rent and paid a share of their income; government funding made up the difference, up to a "fair market" ceiling.[85]

These three strategies—making mortgages fair and affordable and subsidizing either public-housing units or rent vouchers—continue to underpin poverty relief at HUD. Also under Nixon, the federal government shifted more decision making to state and local authorities through community development block grants. Into the 21st century, many municipalities were demolishing "distressed" projects and supporting through tax and other incentives private development of affordable housing sprinkled throughout town. Over the years, HUD has also experimented with "rent to own" schemes for tenants, from selling them public-housing units to setting aside a portion of rent to accumulate a down payment to buy a house.[86] But because subsidized apartments and rental vouchers are not an entitlement, need outstrips supply. Most local housing authorities have enormous lines. In Minnesota alone in 2006, 48,000 individuals and families were on the eligible list, and some wait years for assistance.[87]

AFFORDABLE HOUSING AND A LIVING WAGE

Many housing activists aim to increase the stock of affordable housing. From a Georgia farm devoted to Christian service grew Habitat for Humanity, a nonprofit organization promoting "partnership housing" worldwide. Those in need of housing build it—with the help of Habitat volunteers and a capital fund that buys land and supplies. Instead of a down payment, Habitat homeowners contribute "sweat equity" at the construction site, and they then make monthly payments on a no-interest mortgage that, along with donations, replenishes Habitat's operating fund. Habitat affiliates operate in every state, and although affordable lots are often hard to find, the organization estimates that it has built more than 200,000 houses around the world since the mid-1970s. Other groups support first-time homeowners through counseling and other services.

Although owning a home may be the "American dream," some advocates focus on improving the rental market. While many Americans accumulate wealth by buying houses incrementally and then selling them for a profit, low-income families often own homes in "temporary spells," paying closing costs repeatedly and missing out on long-term benefits. Also, owning is risky. First, housing prices fluctuate; during a market downturn, owners may find their property worth less than what they paid for it. Second, lenders around the turn of the millennium courted low-income and credit-poor buyers with "subprime loans," many of which offered a low introductory interest rate. Home ownership expanded. But in 2007, as interest rates on many loans began resetting to a higher level, nearly 16 percent of all subprime borrowers fell behind in their payments. Experts feared that they and many more cash-strapped Americans would lose their homes over the next few years—a crisis for the U.S. economy (and therefore the world's). In Detroit alone, lenders foreclosed on one out of every 21 houses in 2006.[88] Many nonprofit groups have joined forces with local government, private developers, foundations, banks, and local businesses to improve the rental housing stock.

The Arlington Partnership for Affordable Housing, for instance, buys and renovates apartment buildings in a Virginia suburb of Washington, D.C., where the average rent ($1,375 per month) exceeds the budget of a starting teacher and where high housing prices drive 91 percent of firefighters and 75 percent of police officers to live outside the county.[89] Long commutes contribute to snarled traffic and poor air quality. For the working poor who earn even less than public servants, housing availability can make or break a job. Companies that depend on low-wage service workers in Arlington and other parts of the country are finding they have a stake in maintaining close-in affordable rental units.

If municipalities cannot lower housing prices, then businesses need to raise wages, many advocates say. Some speak of a "housing wage" based on what people must earn in order to spend no more than 30 percent of their income on an average two-bedroom apartment. Nationwide, experts placed it at $16.31 per hour in 2006, but it varied locally, from $22.86 in California to $11.82 in South Carolina. By comparison, the federal minimum wage was $5.15 per hour, not enough to lift a working mother with two kids above the poverty threshold. In 2007, Congress passed the first minimum wage hike in a decade, phasing in a new hourly rate of $7.25 by the summer of 2009. Economists predicted that approximately 13 million workers would benefit from the raise (either directly or from "spillover effects" for those earning a bit more than minimum wage)—but would still struggle to find decent housing.[90] Even employees earning the national median wage of $14.57 per hour must pay an oversize share of income on their rent or mortgage.[91] Yet many businesses opposed even a modest hike in the federal minimum wage, arguing that higher labor costs will make their product or service too expensive and therefore less competitive.

Broad coalitions of antipoverty activists, from college students to church ministers, are campaigning locally for "living wage" ordinances. These require that private contractors who receive public money pay employees a salary substantial enough to cover basic needs. More than 140 such laws have passed. The Sandia Pueblo in New Mexico pays all its employees a minimum of $8.10 an hour, for instance, while Hartford, Connecticut, ensures that workers involved in large projects earn $10.58 with $4.81 per hour in health benefits.[92]

Illness and Access to Health Care

On average, the United States spends more per person on health care than any other country, but it trails other Western nations in life expectancy, infant mortality, doctor visits, and patient satisfaction. High-tech procedures successfully treat many serious illnesses, but costs of the U.S. free-market, fee-for-service system put even basic care—from monitoring high blood pressure to filling cavities—beyond the reach of many citizens. In theory, welfare capitalism is providing workers and their families with health insurance, which spreads costs among a large pool, reducing any one person's catastrophic bill. But rising health-care costs are driving up the price of insurance, and many employers are either passing along more of that expense to employees, reducing benefits, or opting out altogether, especially for their low-wage workers.[93]

The 47 million Americans without health insurance still seek treatment—but they often postpone it until illness reaches crisis proportions. By federal and state law, hospitals must provide emergency care to any patient, but many write up a bill even steeper than what they have negotiated to charge insurance companies and then send it to collection agencies when patients cannot pay. Medical debt contributes to stress, financial hardship, and roughly half of all personal bankruptcies (a middle-income phenomenon since the very poor are less likely to seek court protection and more likely to have Medicaid insurance).[94]

Delayed and in some cases lesser-quality care exacerbates illness among the poor. Less apt to get flu shots or primary care, low-income Americans are more likely to develop pneumonia; once hospitalized, they more often receive second-rate treatment. Although it is difficult to weigh precisely each cause (genetics, environment, diet, lifestyle, health-care access and quality), people who live in high-poverty areas have higher hospitalization rates for diabetes and lower survival rates for cancer, particularly lung and prostate cancer. Of Americans with HIV, the poor and certain minorities are more likely to die of AIDS-related diseases.[95] Even more than low income, inequality seems to have a negative correlation with mortality. Perhaps more crowded public housing in highly stratified communities leads to more disease. Perhaps, as studies have shown, the bigger the gap between rich and poor, the less a community spends on public services, from clinics to hospitals to education.[96]

MEDICARE, MEDICAID, AND SCHIP

The federal government has put into place several health safety nets for 80 million of its most vulnerable citizens. Launched as part of the 1965 Social Security Act and later expanded, Medicare offers insurance to all seniors, younger people with long-term disabilities, and Americans with serious kidney disease. Medicaid targets the poor and people with extremely high medical bills. Since 1997, the State Children's Health Insurance Program (SCHIP) grants to states matching funds to help cover the youngest uninsured.

A federal program funded by a tax on workers, Medicare pays for hospitalization (Part A) and subsidizes various options at various premiums for health expenses (Part B). A recent add-on improves coverage for prescription drugs. Under Medicare, beneficiaries may enroll in managed-care plans or carry their insurance to individual providers that may accept what Medicare reimburses or charge patients more. Because Medicare serves more than 42 million Americans, critics have faulted its bureaucracy for waste and susceptibility to fraud by unscrupulous providers. At the same time, however, size has helped Medicare negotiate favorable rates for service and contain health-care costs. Most experts credit Social Security with reducing elder poverty dramatically since the Great Depression: between 1960 and 1995, with the addition of Medicare, the poverty rate declined from 35 to 10 percent. Once the poorest of the poor, senior citizens are now no worse off than the rest of the adult population.[97]

Some low-income seniors also qualify for Medicaid, which covers more services. Although the federal government pays a little more than half the cost, states administer Medicaid, so, as with TANF, rules vary somewhat by locale. After welfare reform in the mid-1990s, Medicaid shifted from being a program for those receiving cash assistance to one for the working poor. Some states also include better-off residents whose chronic health conditions make it difficult for them to find or pay for private insurance. Between 1999 and 2004, the Medicaid rolls expanded from 34 million to 47 million Americans, as did costs, to $295 billion nationwide.[98] Like many states, Tennessee devotes a substantial chunk of its budget—more than a quarter—to its version of Medicaid and began in 2005 to institute some unpopular cutbacks to save money.[99] Many needy children also qualify for Medicaid, and for 6 million more SCHIP fills in gaps, such as when a working parent is not offered or cannot afford family coverage. The Bush administration's vow to hold the line on spending for SCHIP and Medicare/Medicaid in 2008 drew heated opposition.

UNIVERSAL HEALTH INSURANCE AND TARGETED CAMPAIGNS

A number of nonprofits work to complement government programs. The powerful AARP, formerly the American Association of Retired Persons, educates seniors about their health insurance options under Medicare and Medicaid and lobbies to close gaps in coverage for long-term care and the like.[100] To inform the 20 million or so Americans who are eligible for Medicaid but have not signed up, groups such as the Center for Healthy Communities, operating out of an Ohio medical school, sponsor outreach activities.[101]

Still other health activists aim for no less than an overhaul of the entire health-care system to benefit all Americans. Between Medicare, Medicaid, and plans for the military and federal employees, the government already insures about a third of Americans.[102] Six times in the 20th century reformers tried—but failed—to introduce some sort of universal health insurance.[103] Many argue that it is not only insurance but health-care delivery that needs fixing. Freedom to sue in the United States compels doctors to practice "defensive medicine" that drives up costs, some complain. Others fault medical schools for emphasizing high-tech specialty care instead of selecting and training physicians who will deliver primary care in underserved rural and inner-city communities.

Some antipoverty activists focus on specific health problems that compound the disadvantages of the poor—mental illness, for instance, or HIV infection. Many initiatives address substance abuse in Native American communities, where alcohol plays a role in at least 17 percent of deaths, versus under 5 percent for the general population.[104] Besides contributing to suicide, domestic violence, and accidents, heavy drinking and alcoholism account for the relatively high incidence in certain tribes of fetal alcohol disorders. When pregnant women drink, alcohol passes into the womb, leading at times to altered brain development and to permanent impairments such as low IQ, poor impulse control, and other behavior problems that interfere with school and job performance—which in turn perpetuate poverty. Collaborations among the U.S. Indian Health Service, local governments, foundations, and tribal leaders include the Cherokee's Healthy Nations project and the Fetal Alcohol Syndrome Epidemiology Research project sponsored by the Cheyenne River Sioux tribe and the University of New Mexico, which screens pregnant women, runs clinics for children, and sponsors preventive education about alcohol abuse.[105]

Illiteracy and Education

Education, most Americans believe, can most effectively break the cycle of poverty. It certainly improves the pocketbook. In 2006, high school dropouts earned an average annual income of $19,915; high school graduates, $29,448; and college graduates, $54,689. Furthermore, people without high school diplomas had a much higher unemployment rate than those holding bachelor's degrees.[106] Through 12th grade, the nation's more than 95,000 public schools deliver most of the country's instruction, and experts estimate that improving that system over 20 years would raise the GDP by more than $400 billion.[107] As newsman Tom Brokaw has remarked, public education "is the underpinning of our cultural and political system . . . the engine that moves us as a society toward a common destiny."[108]

As a result of strong local roots, public education remains far more decentralized than other major antipoverty programs. Of the $536 billion that the United States spends on elementary and secondary education, less than 9 percent comes from the federal government, with state and district governments sharing most of the rest of the burden (roughly 45 percent and 37 percent, respectively).[109] Per-pupil spending varies widely, with New York averaging $12,093 in 2004 and Mississippi $6,237.[110] Because property taxes finance the local contribution, wealthy neighborhoods tend to have well-funded schools, and schools serving disadvantaged students in lower-income neighborhoods usually have the fewest resources. Although more spending often leads to higher quality, many critics of American public education complain that it delivers too little "bang for the buck." Among faulted school districts, Washington, D.C., stands out; it spends $12,801 per pupil but ranks among the worst in the nation for student achievement.[111]

NO CHILD LEFT BEHIND

To help overcome disparities in public education, Congress passed the No Child Left Behind Act at the end of 2001. It boosted federal education spending but tied it to "accountability," measured through test scores and teacher certification, for example. Building on the 1965 Elementary and Secondary School Act, it increased Title 1 funding for programs targeting poor students (those eligible for free and reduced-price lunches) and schools serving high-poverty neighborhoods. No Child Left Behind also expanded English instruction for immigrant children and reinforced special education for students with disabilities.[112]

Among its more contentious provisions, No Child Left Behind allowed parents to transfer students out of schools failing to make "adequate yearly progress" either into better performing schools or into charter schools. Publicly funded, charters have leeway to experiment with different curricula, emphasizing the arts or Chinese culture, for instance, or offering boys- or girls-only classes. In theory, competition and choice challenge all schools to improve. Critics charge, however, that progress measured by test scores has undermined education in its broadest sense and caged teachers' creativity. While charter advocates point to local success stories, charter and other public schools differ little in test scores, according to national studies. Opponents blame charter schools for siphoning off students backed by concerned parents, teachers filled with energy and ideas, and money needed to rehabilitate decrepit buildings.[113]

CHOICE, EQUALITY, AND OPPORTUNITY

A number of foundations and citizen groups have launched public-private ventures to improve American education. Charter schools belong to a broader, controversial movement for more school choice. California, for instance, allows parents to request bilingual education, which can take various forms but involves significant instruction time in a non-English language, almost always Spanish. For Latino students from low-income families, learning to read in their native language as well as in English encourages family involvement and respect for their heritage.[114] Vouchers offer another choice, allowing all families to carry their share of per-pupil spending to any school they choose, including private and parochial schools.

Experimental programs aimed at disadvantaged learners abound. They range from "power lunches," during which community volunteers read with struggling second graders, to "early college" high schools, where students may earn an associate's degree by graduation.[115] In Baltimore, where three-fourths of African-American boys drop out before the end of high school, the Abell Foundation partnered with the public school system to send a score of at-risk seventh- and eighth-grade boys to a boarding school in Kenya, East Africa. Far from the violent turf of home, many boys at Baraka School bloomed under close attention, strict discipline, and spartan living conditions, including no television and electricity only six hours a day.[116]

Other groups seek redress for educational inequalities through the courts. In the spirit of *Brown v. Board of Education,* they have sued almost every state as well as local school districts to even out teacher salaries, building funds, or access to Advanced Placement classes.[117] In 2005, California settled a class-action lawsuit brought by the American Civil Liberties Union on behalf of families in low-performing schools and promised $800 million in emergency repairs and $139 million in new textbooks and materials.[118] Recognizing that businesses have a stake in an educated workforce, groups such as the Council for Corporate and School Partnerships open the way for companies to donate money, time, and management advice to public schools.[119]

Still other organizations work to make higher education affordable. In contrast to state-subsidized systems abroad, where academic achievers are usually guaranteed a free university education on a straight and narrow track, higher education in the United States operates as more of a free market, blending admission by merit and completion by ability to pay. On one hand, the system welcomes more nontraditional learners and late bloomers, but the price tag often puts a diploma out of reach. To downsize costs, the federal government subsidizes loans for all, makes outright grants to some low-income students, and offers tax credits for tuition paid. Many groups sponsor scholarships to supplement federal aid, among them the United Negro College Fund (often for undergraduates at historically black institutions), the Mexican American Legal Defense and Educational Fund (for law students), and Google (for Hispanic students majoring in computer science or engineering).[120]

LITERACY IS FUNDAMENTAL

Although law mandates school attendance only until age 16, education is a lifelong process. On paper, at least according to the Central Intelligence Agency, the United States boasts a fabulous literacy rate: 97 percent for both men and women.[121] That statistic, however, masks a darker truth: In 2003, 93 million American adults (43 percent of the population) had only basic or below basic prose skills, struggling with such everyday tasks as writing a check, reading a prescription label, filling out a job application, or deciphering a pay stub. Among the lowest literacy group, more than a third live in poverty.[122]

Many nonprofit organizations aim to boost reading skills. Organizations such as New Jersey Reads or affiliates of Literacy Volunteers of America run adult-education programs, pairing functionally illiterate adults with tutors, for instance, or offering English as a Second Language (ESL) classes. Others prepare high school dropouts to take the test to earn a high school general equivalency diploma (GED). Whether directly acknowledged, literacy is a building block of almost all human-capital antipoverty strategies. As former Louisiana governor Kathleen Blanco observed, "Every educated person is not rich, but almost every educated person has a job and a way out of poverty."[123]

By all accounts, the United States has a robust economy. Between 1959 and 2004, the real GDP more than doubled. The percentage of women working has soared, and women now make up nearly half of the work force. After the turn of the millennium, education levels reached record levels: In 2006, 86 percent of adults over age 25 reported that they had completed at least high school, and 28 percent boasted bachelor's degrees.[124] Yet, after falling to a low of 11.1 percent in 1973, the U.S. poverty rate has weaved up and down without dipping below 11 percent.[125] Why, even with more two-earner families, has growth not lifted more Americans out of poverty?

Economic trends, lingering racial bias in education and employment, and family structure have contributed to poverty's stubbornness. Since 1970, declining wages for low-skilled workers have fueled increasing income inequality. At the same time, while more women are working, more are also raising children alone. Today roughly a quarter of American children (and more than half of African-American children) grow up in single-parent families, which are twice as likely to live in poverty as two-parent families—and nearly three times as likely if the single parent is a woman. Single mothers, who made up 84 percent of custodial parents in 2003, often have difficulty collecting full child support from fathers.[126] As a result of the pay and parenting double punch, the United States entered the 21st century with the highest level of inequality among rich nations.

Can policy bridge that gap between haves and have-nots so that more Americans have enough? Many poverty watchers point to Britain's successful inroads against child poverty through a combination of tax credits (including one similar to the U.S. Earned Income Tax Credit for low-income workers). Suggestions abound for reducing poverty, from national health insurance to subsidized child care, from higher tax credits for the poor to fewer tax breaks for the rich, from universal prekindergarten to more help for the unemployed and ex-prisoners. As Steve Durlauf points out in the foreward to this book, some economists are making an argument for major investments to improve the environment of very young children during the critical years of brain development. The bigger question is, Do Americans have the political will to take bold action on behalf of the poor?[127]

[1] Central Intelligence Agency. "United States." CIA World Factbook Web site. Available online. URL: https://www.cia.gov/library/publications/the-world-factbook/geos/us.html. Updated May 10, 2007.

[2] U.S. Census Bureau. "Household Income Rises, Poverty Rate Declines, Number of Uninsured Up." Press release (August 28, 2007). Available online. URL: http://www.census.gov/Press-Release/www/releases/archives/income_wealth/010583.html. Downloaded January 24, 2008.

[3] Thomas Piketty. "The Kuznets Curve: Yesterday and Tomorrow." In Abhijit Vinayak Banerjee et al. *Understanding Poverty*. Oxford and New York: Oxford University Press, 2006, p. 63.

[4] Robert J. Samuelson. "Trickle-Up Economics: Our Growing Inequality Problems." *Washington Post*, September 27, 2006, A27.

[5] U.S. Census Bureau. "Household Income Rises, Poverty Rate Declines, Number of Uninsured Up."

[6] Gary B. Nash. "Poverty and Politics in Early America." In Billy G. Smith, ed. *Down and Out in Early America* University Park: Pennsylvania State University Press, 2004, p. 1.

[7] Nash. "Poverty and Politics," pp. 6–7.

[8] Nash. "Poverty and Politics," pp. 9–11.

[9] Ruth Wallis Herndon. "'Who Died an Expence to This Town': Poor Relief in Eighteenth-Century Rhode Island." In Smith, ed. *Down and Out in Early America*, pp. 136–142.

[10] Nash. "Poverty and Politics," pp. 3–5, 13–14, 24.

[11] J. Richard Olivas. "'God Helps Those Who Help Themselves': Religious Explanations of Poverty in Colonial Massachusetts, 1630–1776." In Smith, ed. *Down and Out in Early America*, pp. 262–265.

[12] Nash. "Poverty and Politics," pp. 16–19. Karin Wulf. "Gender and the Political Economy of Poor Relief in Colonial Philadelphia." In Smith, ed. *Down and Out in Early America*, pp. 165–169.

[13] Joan Brodsky Schur. "Teaching with Documents: Eli Whitney's Patent for the Cotton Gin." National Archives Web site. Available online. URL: http://www.archives.gov/education/lessons/cotton-gin-patent/. Downloaded May 16, 2007.

[14] Benjamin M. Friedman. *The Moral Consequences of Economic Growth*. New York: Alfred A. Knopf, 2005, pp. 114–115.

[15] Friedman. *The Moral Consequences*, p. 115.

[16] Elaine C. Everly. "Freedmen's Bureau Records: An Overview." Available online. URL: http://www.archives.gov/publications/prologue/1997/summer/freedmens-bureau-records.html. Downloaded July 19, 2007.

[17] *American Experience*. "Gilded Age." Public Broadcasting System Web site. Available online. URL: http://www.pbs.org/wgbh/amex/carnegie/gildedage.html. Downloaded May 14, 2007. Sylvia Whitman. *What's Cooking? The History of American Food*. Minneapolis, Minn.: Lerner Publications, 2001, pp. 38–39. To provide equivalents in 2005 dollars, the author used the consumer price index (CPI) and the calculator at MeasuringWorth.com. Available online. URL: http://measuringworth.com/calculators/uscompare/#. Accessed May 14, 2007.

[18] Library of Congress. "The Progressive Era to the New Era, 1900–1929: Cities in the Progressive Era." Available online. URL: http://lcweb2.loc.gov/ammem/ndlpedu/features/timeline/progress/cities/cities.html. Downloaded July 19, 2007.

[19] *American Experience*. "Gallery: Millionaire's Row." Public Broadcasting System Web site. Available online. URL: http://www.pbs.org/wgbh/amex/carnegie/gallery/astorman.html. Downloaded July 19, 2007.

[20] E. R. L. Gould. "The Housing Problem in Great Cities." *Quarterly Review of Economics* 14 (1899–1900): 378–393. Available online. URL: http://www.tenant.net/Community/LES/gould.html. Downloaded July 19, 2007.

[21] Carnegie Corporation of New York. "Andrew Carnegie's Philanthropic Vision." Available online. URL: http://www.carnegie.org/sub/philanthropy/carn_phil_vis.html. Downloaded July 19, 2007.

[22] Gould. "The Housing Problem in Great Cities."

[23] Alice O'Connor. *Poverty Knowledge: Social Science, Social Policy, and the Poor in Twentieth-Century U.S. History*. Princeton, N.J., and Oxford: Princeton University Press, 2001, p. 26.

[24] Margaret Luft. "About Hull House." Available online. URL: http://www.hullhouse.org/about.asp. Downloaded July 19, 2007.

[25] Roberta Senechal. "The Springfield Race Riot of 1908." Illinois Publications Online, Northern Illinois University Libraries. Available online. URL: http://www.lib.niu.edu/ipo/1996/iht329622.html. Downloaded July 19, 2007.

[26] ———. "The Springfield Race Riot of 1908."

[27] Feldmeth, Greg. "The Progressive Era." U.S. History Resources Web site. Available online. URL: http://www.polytechnic.org/faculty/gfeldmeth/lec.prog.html. Downloaded August 13, 2007.

[28] Friedman. *The Moral Consequences*, pp. 160–165. Sylvia Whitman. *This Land Is Your Land: The American Conservation Movement*. Minneapolis, Minn.: Lerner Publications, 1994, pp. 50–54.

[29] Friedman. *The Moral Consequences*, pp. 164–166.

[30] Friedman. *The Moral Consequences*, pp. 168–172. U.S. Food and Drug Administration. "History of the FDA: The 1938 Food, Drug, and Cosmetic Act." Available online. URL: http://www.fda.gov/oc/history/historyoffda/section2.html. Downloaded July 19, 2007.

[31] "Harry Hopkins to Ferguson, January 3, 1935." Texas State Library and Archives Web site. Available online. URL: http://www.tsl.state.tx.us/governors/personality/mferguson-hopkins.html. Updated November 2, 2005.

[32] Utah History Research Center. "Emergency Relief Administration: Agency History 343." Available online. URL: http://www.historyresearch.utah.gov/agencyhistories/343.html. Downloaded July 19, 2007. University of Washington Libraries. "Federal Emergency Relief Administration (FERA)." Available online. URL: http://content.lib.washington.edu/feraweb/essay.html. Downloaded July 19, 2007. Colorado State Archives. "Illustrated History of FERA in Colorado." Available online. URL: http://www.colorado.gov/dpa/doit/archives/fera/home.htm. Downloaded July 19, 2007. "History of the Key West Art Project."

Available online. URL: http://www.keysarts.com/WPA-Spotlight.htm. Downloaded July 19, 2007.

[33] Whitman. *This Land Is Your Land*, pp. 54–57.

[34] Library of Congress. "American Memory, Works Progress Administration." Available online. URL: http://memory.loc.gov/ammem/today/apr08.html. Downloaded July 19, 2007.

[35] USDA Food and Nutrition Service. "A Short History of the Food Stamp Program." Available online. URL: http://www.fns.usda.gov/fsp/rules/Legislation/history.htm. Downloaded July 19, 2007.

[36] Friedman. *The Moral Consequences*, pp. 170–172. Franklin D. Roosevelt. "The Economic Bill of Rights." Available online. URL: http://www.worldpolicy.org/globalrights/econrights/fdr-econbill.html. Downloaded July 19, 2007. Excerpt from the January 11, 1944, address to Congress.

[37] U.S. Department of Veterans Affairs. "History of the G.I. Bill." Available online. URL: http://www.75anniversary.va.gov/history/gi_bill.htm. Downloaded July 19, 2007.

[38] Friedman, *The Moral Consequences*, p. 184.

[39] National Poverty Center, University of Michigan. "Poverty Facts: How Has Poverty Changed over Time?" Available online. URL: http://www.npc.umich.edu/poverty. Downloaded July 19, 2007.

[40] Susan W. Blank and Barbara B. Blum. "An Early History of ADC." In *A Brief History of Work Expectations for Welfare Mothers in The Future of Children: A Publication of The Woodrow Wilson School of Public and International Affairs at Princeton University and The Brookings Institution*, p. 3. Available online. URL: http://www.futureofchildren.org/information2827/information_show.htm?doc_id=72243. Downloaded July 19, 2007.

[41] Adam Gordon. "The Creation of Homeownership: How New Deal Changes in Banking Regulation Simultaneously Made Homeownership Accessible to Whites and out of Reach for Blacks." *Yale Law Journal* 115 (October 2005): 186–224.

[42] Atlanta Regional Council for Higher Education. "1950–1959 Retrenchment and Redirection." Available online. URL: http://www.atlantahighered.org/civilrights/essay_detail.asp?phase=2. Downloaded July 19, 2007. National Park Service. "Desegregation of Central High School." *The Encyclopedia of Arkansas History and Culture*. Available online. URL: http://encyclopediaofarkansas.net/encyclopedia/entry-detail.aspx?entryID=718. Downloaded July 19, 2007. U.S. Department of Justice. "Education." Kids Page. Available online. URL: http://www.usdoj.gov/kidspage/crt/edu.htm. Downloaded July 19, 2007.

[43] "Taking Measure of the Black-White Higher Education Gap." *The Journal of Blacks in Higher Education* (summer 1994): 6.

[44] Donohue, John J. III, and James Heckman. "Continuous Versus Episodic Change: The Impact of Civil Rights Policy on the Economic Status of Blacks," *Journal of Economic Literature* 29, no. 4., December 1991, pp. 1,603–1,605.

[45] Michael Harrington. *The Other America: Poverty in the United States*. New York: Penguin Books, 1962/1971, p. 15.

[46] Harrington. *The Other America*, p. 167.

[47] National Poverty Center. "Poverty Facts."

[48] Harrington. *The Other America*. D. Bradford Hunt. "What went wrong with public housing in Chicago? A history of the Robert Taylor homes." *Journal of the Illinois State Historical Society* (Spring 2001). Abstract. Available online. URL: http://findarticles.com/p/articles/mi_qa3945/is_200104/ai_n8939181. Downloaded July 19, 2007.

[49] Peter K. Eisinger. *Toward an End to Hunger in the United States*. Washington, D.C.: Brookings Institution Press, 1998, pp. 75–78. Nicolaus Mills. "Hurricane Katrina and Robert Kennedy." *Dissent* (Spring 2006). Available online. URL: http://www.dissentmagazine.org/article/?article=405. Downloaded July 19, 2007. Nancy Amidei. "Rethinking Hunger in America: Adapting the Sullivan Principles." *Christian Century* (January 21, 1987): 51. Available online. URL: http://www.religion-online.org/showarticle.asp?title=979. Downloaded July 19, 2007.

[50] Harrell R. Rodgers, Jr. *American Poverty in a New Era of Reform*. 2d ed. Armonk, N.Y., and London: M.E. Sharpe, 2006.

[51] Rodgers. *American Poverty in a New Era*, p. 82.

[52] Robert Samuelson. "A Man of Ideas in the Arena." *Newsweek* (November 27, 2006), 44.

[53] Rodgers. *American Poverty in a New Era*.

[54] U.S. Census Bureau. "Mothers Who Receive AFDC Payments." Available online. URL: http://www.census.gov/population/socdemo/statbriefs/sb2-95.html. Updated September 13, 2000.

[55] R. Moffitt. "Incentive effects of the U.S. welfare system: A review." *Journal of Economic Literature* 30 (1992): 1–61. Available online. URL: http://www.poverty.smartlibrary.org/NewInterface/segment.cfm?segment=1913. Downloaded July 19, 2007.

[56] Rodgers. *American Poverty in a New Era*, pp. 97–104. Stanley D. Eitzen and Kelly Eitzen Smith. Experiencing Poverty: Voices from the Bottom. Belmont, Calif.: Thomson Wadsworth, 2003, pp. 116–117.

[57] "Welfare Reform and Children." Available online. URL: http://www.urban.org/publications/308014.html. Downloaded July 19, 2007.

[58] Richard Wolf. "How Welfare Reform Changed America." *USA Today*, July 18, 2006. Available online. URL: http://www.usatoday.com/news/nation/2006-07-17-welfare-reform-cover_x.htm. Downloaded July 19, 2007.

[59] Parrott, Sharon, and Arloc Sherman. "TANF AT 10: Program Results Are More Mixed Than Often Understood." Center on Budget and Policy Priorities Web site. Available online. URL: http://www.cbpp.org/8-17-06tanf.htm. Updated on August 17, 2006.

[60] USDA. "Foreign Agricultural Trade of the United States: Monthly Summary." Available online. URL: http://www.ers.usda.gov/data/FATUS/MonthlySummary.htm. Updated July 13, 2007.

[61] Alberto Jerardo. "U.S. Ag Trade Balance, More Than Just a Number." USDA *Amber Waves* (February 2004). Available online. URL: http://www.ers.usda.gov/amberwaves/February04/Features/USTradeBalance.htm. Downloaded July 19, 2007.

[62] Food productiondaily.com. "Half of U.S. Food Goes to Waste." November 24, 2004. Available online. URL: http://www.foodproductiondaily.com/news/ng.asp?id=56340&n=dh330&c=tzlvsrxywshqwyj. Downloaded July 19, 2007.

[63] CDC. "Overweight and obesity: Introduction." Available online. URL: http://www.cdc.gov/nccdphp/dnpa/obesity. Updated May 2[illegible], 2007.

[64] Nord, Mark, Margaret Andrews, and Steven Carlson. "Household Food Security in the United States, 2006." USDA Economic Research Report No. (ERR-49), November 2007, pp. iv, 20. Available online. URL: http://www.ers.usda.gov/Publications/ERR49/ERR49.pdf. Downloaded January 25, 2008.

[65] ———. "Household Food Security in the United States, 2006," p. 4.

[66] Janet Raloff. "Academic Cost of Food Insecurity." *Science News* 168, no. 4, (December 10, 2005). Available online. URL: http://www.sciencenews.org/articles/20051210/food.asp. Downloaded July 13, 2007.

[67] Lynn Parker. "Obesity, Food Insecurity and the Federal Child Nutrition Programs: Understanding the Linkages." Food Research and Action Center (FRAC), October 2005. Available online. URL: http://www.frac.org/pdf/obesity05_paper.pdf. Downloaded May 15, 2007.

[68] UC Davis Health Service."Free Shuttles Can Close the Grocery Gap." Available online. URL: http://www.ucdmc.ucdavis.edu/news/grocery_gap.html. The Food Trust. "Food for Every Child: The Need for More Supermarkets in Philadelphia." 2001. Available online. URL: http://www.thefoodtrust.org/php/about/index.php. Downloaded July 13, 2007.

[69] Craig Degginger, "USDA study to address obesity and poverty," University of Washington Office of News and Information, June 22, 2004. Available online. URL: http://uwnews.washington.edu/ni/article.asp?articleID=4798. Downloaded August 14, 2007.

[70] USDA Food and Nutrition Service, "Characteristics of Food Stamp Households: Fiscal Year 2005—Summary," September 2006. Available online. URL: http://www.fns.usda.gov/oane/menu/Published/FSP/FILES/Participation/2005CharacteristicsSummary.pdf. Downloaded August 14, 2007.

[71] USDA, "WIC." Available online. URL: http://www.fns.usda.gov/wic/WIC-Fact-Sheet.pdf. Updated March 2006; USDA Food and Nutrition Service, "About WIC," Available online. URL: http://www.fns.usda.gov/wic/aboutwic/. Updated October 28, 2005.

[72] USDA Food and Nutrition Service, "National School Lunch Program," July 2007. Available online. URL: http://www.fns.usda.gov/cnd/Lunch/AboutLunch/NSLPFactSheet.pdf. Downloaded August 14, 2007.

[73] Dorothy Rosenbaum and Zoe Neuberger. "Food and Nutrition Programs: Reducing Hunger, Bolstering Nutrition." Center on Budget and Policy Priorities. July 19, 2005. Available online. URL: http://www.cbpp.org/7-19-05fa.htm#_edn17. Downloaded August 14, 2007.

[74] Christine Vestal. "States Expand Food Stamp Programs." December 6, 2006. Statline.org. Available online. URL: http://www.stateline.org/live/details/story?contentId=162244. Downloaded August 14, 2007.

[75] "Food Stamp Participation Overall Steady in May 2006," Food Research and Action Center Web site. Available online. URL: http://www.frac.org/html/news/fsp/2006.5_FSP.html. Downloaded August 14, 2007.

[76] "Food Stamp Outreach Initiative Lone Star Legal Aid," Legal Services Corporation Research Library Web site, July 2006. Available online. URL: http://www.Iri.Isc.gov/abstracts/abstract.asp?level1=SPA&level2=Public%20Benefits&AbstractID=060023. Downloaded August 14, 2007.

[77] "Who We Are," America's Second Harvest Web site. Available online. URL: http//www.secondharvest.org/. Accessed August 14, 2007.

[78] Meals on Wheels Association of America Web site. Available online. URL: http://www.mowaa.org/index.asp?mid=37. Accessed August 14, 2007.

[79] Center for Food and Justice. "CFJ Projects." Urban and Environmental Policy Institute Web site. Available online. URL: http://departments.oxy.edu/uepi/cfj/projects.htm. Downloaded August 14, 2007.

[80] The Reinvestment Fund. "Commercial Real Estate Pennsylvania Fresh Food Financing Initiative." TRF Web site. Available online. URL: http://www.trfund.com/financing/real estate/supermarkets.html. Downloaded August 14, 2007.

[81] National Coalition for the Homeless. "How Many People Experience Homelessness?" June 2006. Available online. URL: http://www.nationalhomeless.org/publications/facts/How_Many.pdf. Downloaded August 14, 2007; "Top 100 Biggest Cities." City-Data.com Web site. Available online. URL: http://www.city-data.com/top1.html. Downloaded August 14, 2007; National Coalition for the Homeless. "Who Is Homeless?" June 2006. Available online. URL: http://www.nationalhomeless.org/publications/facts/Whois.pdf. Downloaded August 14, 2007.

[82] National Coalition for the Homeless. "Who Is Homeless?" U.S. Department of Housing and Urban Development. "Affordable Housing." Available online. URL: http://www.hud.gov/offices/cpd/affordablehousing/. Downloaded August 14, 2007.

[83] HUD User. "Affordable Housing Needs: A Report to Congress on the Significant Need for Housing." Report Abstract. December 2005. Available online. URL: http://www.huduser.org/publications/affhsg/affhsgneed.html. Updated October 16, 2006; Habitat for Humanity. "Affordable Housing Statistics." Available online. URL: http://www.habitat.org/how/stats.aspx. Downloaded August 14, 2007.

[84] National Coalition for the Homeless. "Who Is Homeless?" U.S. Department of Housing and Urban Development. Available online. URL: http://www.hud.gov/. Downloaded August 14, 2007.

[85] Minneapolis Public Housing Authority. "The History of the Tenant-Based Housing Programs." Available online. URL: http://www.mphaonline.org/section8.cfm. Downloaded August 14, 2007.

[86] "Government's Role in Low Income Housing." Rental Housing Online Web site. Available online. URL: http://rhol.org/rental/housing.htm. Downloaded August 14, 2007.

[87] Carissa Wyant. "Report Reveals 48,000 on Public Housing Waiting List in Minnesota." *Minneapolis/St. Paul Business Journal,* December 6, 2006. Available online. URL: http://twincities.bizjournals.com/twincities/stories/2006/12/04/daily27.html. Downloaded August 14, 2007.

[88] Noelle Knox. "'Subprime' borrowers help set foreclosure record." *USA Today,* June 14, 2007. Available online. URL: http://www.usatoday.com/money/economy/housing/2007-06-14-subprime-foreclosures_N.htm. Downloaded January 25, 2008. Peter Henderson, Tim McLaughlin, Andy Sullivan, and Al Yoon. "Frenzy of Risky Mortgages Leaves Path of Destruction." *Boston Globe,* May 8, 2007, p. 2. Available online. URL: http://www.boston.com/news/nation/articles/2007/05/08/frenzy_of_risky_mortgages_leaves_path_of_destruction/?page=2. Downloaded May 15, 2007. National Low-Income Housing Coalition. "The Crisis in America's Housing: Confronting Myths and Promoting a Balanced Housing Policy," pp. 13–16. January 11, 2005. Available online. URL: http://www.nlihc.org/doc/housingmyths.pdf. Downloaded May 7, 2007.

[89] "Housing Facts." Arlington Partnership for Affordable Housing Web site. Available online. URL: http://www.apah.org/facts/. Downloaded August 14, 2007.

[90] Economics Policy Institute. "Minimum Wage: Facts at a Glance." EPI Web site. Available online. URL: http://www.epinet.org/content.cfm/issueguides_minwage_minwagefacts. Updated April 2007.

[91] Keisha Lamothe. "Rent Increases Trump Workers' Income Growth." CNNMoney.com. December 12, 2006. Available online. URL: http://money.cnn.com/2006/12/12/news/. Downloaded August 14, 2007. Heather Boushey and John Schmitt. Center for Economic and Policy Research. Available online. URL: http://www.cepr.net/documents/publications/labor_market_2005_12.pdf. Downloaded August 14, 2007.

[92] ACORN. "City and County Campaigns." Living Wage Resource Center. Available online. URL: http://www.livingwagecampaign.org/index.php?id=1958. Downloaded August 14, 2007.

[93] Elise Gould. "Health insurance eroding for working families. Employer-provided coverage declines for fifth consecutive year." EPI Briefing Paper #175, Economic Policy Institute. September 28, 2006. Available online. URL: http://www.epi.org/content.cfm/bp175. Downloaded August 14, 2007. Malcolm Gladwell. "The Moral-Hazard Myth. The Bad Idea Behind Our Failed Health-Care System." *The New Yorker* (August 29, 2005). Available online. URL: http://www.newyorker.com/fact/content/articles/050829fa_fact. Downloaded August 14, 2007.

[94] David U. Himmelstein, Elizabeth Warren, Deborah Thorne, and Steffie Woolhandler. "MarketWatch: Illness and Injury as Contributors to Bankruptcy." *Health Affairs* (February 2, 2005). Available online. URL: http://content.healthaffairs.org/cgi/content/full/hlthaff.w5.63/DC1. Downloaded August 14, 2007.

[95] National Cancer Institute. "Area Socioeconomic Variations in U.S. Cancer Incidence, Mortality, Stage, Treatment, and Survival, 1975–1999." Abstract. Available online. URL: http://seer.cancer.gov/publications/ses/abstract.html. Downloaded August 14, 2007. U.S. Department of Health and Human Services Agency for Healthcare Research and Quality. "The National Health-Care Disparities Report." February 2004. Available online. URL: http://www.ahrq.gov/qual/nhdr03/nhdrsum03.htm. Downloaded August 14, 2007.

[96] J. W. Lynch, G. A. Kaplan, E. R. Pamuk, R. D. Cohen, K. E. Heck, J. L. Balfour, and I. H. Yen. "Income Inequality and Mortality in the Metropolitan Areas of the United States." *American Journal of Public Health* 88, no. 7 (July 1998): 1,074–1,080. Available online. URL: http://www.pubmedcentral.nih.gov/articlerender.fcgi?artid=1508263. Downloaded August 14, 2007.

[97] "Insurance." AARP Web site. Available online. URL: http://www.aarp.org/health/insurance/. Downloaded August 14, 2007.

[98] "Medicaid Outreach Consortium." Center for Healthy Communities Web site. Available online. URL: http://www.med.wright.edu/CHC/programs/medoutreach.htm. Downloaded August 14, 2007.

[99] Kari Lydersen. "Tennessee Medicaid Cuts Stir Fear Among State's Poor." *The New Standard*, January 27, 2005. Available online. URL: http://newstandardnews.net/content/index.cfm/items/1415. Downloaded August 14, 2007.

[100] AARP. Available online. URL: http://www.aarp.org/health/insurance/. Downloaded August 14, 2007.

[101] Medicaid Outreach Consortium. Available online. URL: http://www.med.wright.edu/CHC/programs/medoutreach.htm. Downloaded August 14, 2007.

[102] Dennis Cauchon. "Medicaid Insures Historic Number," August 1, 2005. Available online. URL: http://www.usatoday.com/news/washington/2005-08-01-medicaid_x.htm. Downloaded February 6, 2008.

[103] Gladwell. "The Moral-Hazard Myth."

[104] Indian Health Service cited in Eric Newhouse. "Bane of the Blackfeet." *Great Falls Tribune* August 22, 1999. Available online. URL: http://www.gannett.com/go/difference/greatfalls/pages/part8/blackfeet.html. Downloaded August 14, 2007.

[105] Susan G. Parker. "Cherokee Nation Project Promotes Fitness to Fight Substance Abuse." Robert Wood Johnson Foundation Web site. Available online. URL: http://www.rwjf.org/reports/grr/028250.htm. Updated October 2003. "Tribal Health Department." Cheyenne River Sioux Tribe Web site. Available online. URL: http://www.sioux.org/health_dept.html. Downloaded August 14, 2007.

[106] U.S. Census Bureau. "Earnings Gap Highlighted by Census Bureau Data on Educational Attainment." March 15, 2007. Available online. URL: http://www.census.gov/Press-Release/www/releases/archives/education/009749.html. Downloaded May 16, 2007.

[107] U.S. Dept of Education, A Guide to Education and No Child Left Behind. October 2004. Available online. URL: http://www.ed.gov/nclb/overview/intro/guide/guide_pg12.html#history. Downloaded August 14, 2007.

[108] "Education Quotes." National Education Association Web site. Available online. URL: http://www.nea.org/aew/quotes.html. Downloaded August 14, 2007.

[109] U.S. Department of Education. "Overview: 10 Facts about K-12 Education Funding." Available online. URL: http://www.ed.gov/about/overview/fed/10facts/index.html. Updated November 2, 2005.

[110] U.S. Census Bureau. "National Spending Per Student Rises to $8,287." April 3, 2006. Available online. URL: http://www.census.gov/Press-Release/www/releases/archives/economic_surveys/006685.html. Downloaded November 30, 2007.

[111] Lori Montgomery and Jay Mathews. "The Future of D.C. Public Schools: Traditional or Charter Education?" *Washington Post,* August 22, 2006, A1.

[112] U.S. Department of Education, "The Elementary and Secondary Education Act (The No Child Left Behind Act of 2001)." Available online. URL: http://www.ed.gov/policy/elsec/leg/esea02/index.html. Downloaded November 30, 2007.

[113] Lori Montgomery and Jay Mathews. "The Future of D.C. Public Schools: Traditional or Charter Education?" *Washington Post,* August 22, 2006, A1.

[114] San Diego County Office of Education. "Successful Bilingual Schools: Six Effective Programs in California." October 2006. Available online. URL: http://www.sdcoe.k12.ca.us/lret2/els/pdf/SBS_Report_FINAL.pdf. Downloaded August 14, 2007.

[115] Jennifer Jacobson. "Kirst Comments on Early College High School Experiments." *Chronicle of Higher Education,* March 11, 2005. Available online. URL: http://ed.stanford.edu/suse/faculty/displayFacultyNews.php?tablename–otify1&id=306. Downloaded August 14, 2007.

[116] Afefe Tyehimba, "The Baraka School Gets Back on Its Feet." Available online. URL: http://www.citypaper.com/news/story.asp?id=4754. Downloaded August 14, 2007. Public Broadcasting System. "'The Boys of Baraka' Lesson Plan: The Influence of Environment on Education." Available online. URL: http://www.pbs.org/pov/pov2006/boysofbaraka/for.html. Downloaded August 14, 2007.

[117] "Persistent Funding Disparities," Clearinghouse on Educational Policy and Management Web site. University of Oregon. Available online: URL: http://eric.uoregon.edu/trends_issues/finance/02.html. Downloaded August 14, 2007.

[118] American Civil Liberties Union. "California Judge Finalizes Historic Education Settlement in ACLU Lawsuit," press release, March 23, 2005. Available online: URL: http://www.aclu.org/rightsofthepoor/edu/13461prs20050323.html. Downloaded August 14, 2007.

[119] Council for School and Corporate Partnerships, "Guiding Principles." Available online. URL: http://www.corpschoolpartners.org/guiding_principles.shtml. Downloaded August 14, 2007.

[120] "Scholarship Programs," Mexican American Legal Defense and Educational Fund Web site. Available online: URL: http://www.maldef.org/education/scholarships.htm. Downloaded August 14, 2007; "Low Income College Scholarships," College Scholarships.org Web site. URL: http://www.scholarships-ar-us.org/scholarships/low-income.htm. Downloaded August 14, 2007.

[121] Central Intelligence Agency, "United States," World Factbook Web site. Available online. URL: https://cia.gov/cia//publications/factbook/geos/us.html. Downloaded December 3, 2007.

[122] U.S. Department of Education National Center for Education Statistics, "National Assessment of Adult Literacy." Available online. URL: http://nces.ed.gov/NAAL/index.asp?file=KeyFindings/Demographics/Overall.asp&PageID=16; http://www.newjerseyreads.org/utility/showArticle/?objectID=47. Downloaded August 14, 2007.

[123] "We Can End Poverty." Better World Project. Available online. URL: http://www.betterworld.net. Downloaded December 3, 2007.

[124] U.S. Census Bureau. "Earnings Gap Highlighted by Census Bureau Data on Educational Attainment." Press release (March 15, 2007). Available online. URL: http://www.census.gov/Press-Release/www/releases/archives/education/009749.html. Downloaded May 16, 2007.

[125] U.S. Census Bureau. "Table 2. Poverty Status of People by Family Relationship, Race, and Hispanic Origin: 1959 to 2005." Available online. URL: http://www.census.gov/hhes/www/poverty/histpov/hstpov2.html. Downloaded May 16, 2007.

[126] Laura Lippman. Indicators of Child, Family, and Community Connections, U.S. Department of Health and Human Services Web site. Available online. URL: http://aspe.dhhs.gov/hsp/connections-charts04/ch1.htm. Updated October 24, 2005. Timothy Grall. Custodial Mothers and Fathers and Their Child Support: 2003. U.S. Census Bureau Web site, pp. 2–7, July 2006. Available online. URL: http://www.census.gov/prod/2006pubs/p60-230.pdf. Downloaded August 8, 2007; Christine Todd. Poverty Reduction and Welfare Provision for Single Parents in Aotearoa/ New Zealand and the United States—A Comparative Analysis, paper for U.S. Basic Income Group Network conference p. 3, February 2007. Available online. URL: http://www.usbig.net/papers/164-Todd-NewZealand.doc. Downloaded August 8, 2007.

[127] Hilary W. Hoyes, Marianne E. Page, and Ann Huff Stevens. "Poverty in America: Trends and Explanations." *Journal of Economic Perspectives* 20 (Winter 2006): 47–48, 66. Timothy M. Smeeding. "Public Policy, Economic Inequality, and Poverty: The United States in Comparative Perspective." *Social Science Quarterly* 86 (2005): 959–961, 979–981. David R. Francis. "The War on Poverty Is Winnable." *Christian Science Monitor,* April 2, 2007, 17. Available online. URL: http://www.csmonitor.com/2007/0402/p17s01-cogn.htm. Downloaded May 15, 2007.

3

Global Perspectives

One day our grandchildren will go to museums to see what poverty was like.
—Muhammad Yunus, founder of Grameen Bank

Since 1990, the annual UN Human Development Report has tracked global wrestling with poverty. Each year, teams of scholars and development specialists highlight a theme: the "lack of political commitment rather than financial resources" in fighting poverty (1991), "the wide and persistent gap between women's expanding capabilities and limited opportunities" (1995), technology's contribution to development (2001), democracy as power sharing (2002), the need for "multicultural policies . . . so that all people can choose to speak their language, practice their religion, and participate in shaping their culture" (2004), the water crisis as a result of competition and imbalance rather than scarcity (2006), and climate change (2007/2008).[1] For all of the local complexity they sometimes note in sidebars, the reports underscore the commonalities in poverty that transcend cultural differences.

Although they congratulate and inspire, the reports also goad. In 2005, for instance, the authors note that the "overall report card on progress makes for depressing reading" because most countries were lagging behind in the MDGs. Despite profound gains—a two-year increase in life expectancy in developing countries, for instance, and the lifting of 130 million people out of extreme poverty—18 countries slipped down the ladder on the HDI. Calling the HIV/AIDS pandemic "the single greatest reversal in human development," the report nonetheless labeled extreme inequality the worse and underlying culprit.[2]

To the 2005 experts, the primary corrective is international aid effectively delivered. It needs to be 1) massive enough to kick-start development, 2) predictable and not laden with transaction costs and conditions, and 3) "owned" by the recipient. In the 1990s, many rich countries slashed aid, and while the report praises the reversal of that trend in the 21st century, it points out that rich nations contribute just 0.25 percent of their income. Promises often fail to materialize. Although the world's largest donor by share (0.22 percent), the United States ranks with Japan and Italy near the bottom on the Assistance Committee of the Organisation for Economic Co-operation and Development (OECD). Since the September 11, 2001, terrorist attacks, the United States has increased international aid as a security strategy, and development advocates applaud its greater commitment, particularly to Africa.[3] But in the troubled wake of its invasion of Iraq, the United States spent a third of its 2005 official aid budget there on reconstruction and debt relief.[4] Moreover, "for every dollar that rich countries spend on aid," the *Human Development Report 2005* notes, "they allocate another $10 to military budgets."[5]

The report identified 2005 as a turning point. Will world citizens make the necessary sacrifices and commitments to achieve the MDGs? Or, will the global war on poverty turn out to be merely a skirmish? The following case studies, in descending HDI order, survey some of the battlefronts in this war.

Some countries, such as India, have made tremendous economic gains thanks largely to globalization, which has helped boost millions of the once-poor into the middle class even as millions more remain destitute. Other countries have lost ground. Once secure Ukrainians experienced a wrenching transition from a centrally planned to a market economy in the 1990s; the drop in living standards was dramatic, but perhaps short term. In the Democratic Republic of the Congo, by contrast, hardship went from bad to worse. Although poverties differ from region to region and country to country, the poor do not. They have in common a longing for a better life.

UKRAINE

I worked my whole life. For 42 years I was officially employed.
My husband and I never had to deny ourselves anything.
We had really exceptional savings. I was at peace. I thought,
even if I don't have children, in my old age, I'll be well provided for
and that even if I get sick or something happens, I'll have the money
to hire a caregiver or a nurse to look after me.
I'll have money for good food, medical care, for my funeral,
and for other things. And now I'm a beggar. . . .
This feeling of my own powerlessness,
of being unnecessary, of being unprotected
is for me the worst of all.
—Ukrainian senior citizen, 1996[6]

Part of the Soviet Union since the 1920s, Ukraine achieved independence in 1991. The second largest nation in Europe and a crossroads between Europe and Asia, Ukraine enjoys a mostly temperate climate, access to the Black Sea, and generous natural resources: iron ore, coal, natural gas, minerals, timber, and extremely fertile black soil (*chernozem*). Yet, on the UN 2007/2008 HDI, Ukraine ranked only 76, well below northern and western European nations such as Norway (2), Ireland (5), and France (10) and behind neighboring Hungary (36), Poland (37), Slovakia (42), Romania (60), Belarus (64), and Russia (67).[7] Ukraine fell 17 steps on the index between 1990 and 2000.[8] The struggles of this "breadbasket of Europe" illustrate the difficulties of many eastern European nations after the disintegration of the USSR.

History

Roots of Ukrainian nationalism lie in the early medieval kingdom of Rus (860–1240), centered in Kiev, Ukraine's capital on the Dnieper River. A powerful trading empire, Christian Rus dominated eastern Europe for centuries until infighting among nobles weakened the state and Kiev fell to Mongol invaders. When Poland annexed much of Ukrainian territory in the 14th century, some peasants resisted. Renowned for their independence and military skill, these Cossack rebels held off encroaching neighbors until the Russian Empire gobbled up most of Ukraine in the late 18th century. During the upheaval of World War I and the 1917 Bolshevik Revolution that overthrew the Russian czar, Ukraine wrested back its independence—but only for a few years. By 1922, the Bolsheviks had firmly established Communist rule in Ukraine, renaming it the Ukrainian Soviet Socialist Republic, part of the new Russia-centric Union of Soviet Socialist Republics.

In colonial style, Moscow tapped the resources and orchestrated the politics of its satellite nations, often to their detriment. With almost 70 percent of its land arable, Ukraine fed the Soviet Union, producing meat, milk, grain, and vegetables, and its factories turned out metal pipes and drills and other essential equipment.[9] But when drought led to poor harvests in 1932–33, Soviet policies turned hard times into a humanitarian disaster. The Soviets championed collective rather than individual farming not only because communism stressed group ownership and state direction but also because collectivization stifled Ukrainian nationalism and resistance. Convinced that socialist greatness lay in industrial production, Soviet premier Joseph Stalin sold Ukrainian agricultural produce to buy machinery and expand the military and channeled food to Russian factory workers rather than distributing it to the native population. At the height of the famine in

1933, 25,000 people a day were dying in Ukraine, even in the countryside, their unburied bodies ravaged by wild dogs. An eyewitness described the hungry eating "dogs, horses, rotten potatoes, the bark of trees, grass—anything they could find," including babies and small children. "The people were like wild beasts, ready to devour one another. And no matter what they did, they went on dying, dying, dying. They died singly and in families. They died everywhere—in yards, on streetcars and on trains."[10] Moreover, Stalin never acknowledged the suffering, so the rest of the world did not rush in with aid. Ukrainians call the 1930s famine Holodomor, "murder by hunger."[11]

Some Ukrainians welcomed the Germans who invaded the Soviet Union in 1941. In retreat, the Stalinist government carted off everything from cattle to tractors and blew up much of what they could not carry—fuel, grain, forests—lest it fall into enemy hands. The civilians left behind found no succor from the occupying army, however, because Adolf Hitler intended for Germans to colonize Ukraine's fertile farmlands and enslave much of the local population. Hundreds of thousands of Ukrainian Jews died during the Nazi occupation. The worst massacre took place in September 1941, when the Nazis rounded up Kiev's Jewish residents, stripped them of their valuables, and shot more than 30,000 over a day and a half. While nationalists battled both Germans and Soviets, many Ukrainians collaborated with one side or the other to survive and perished in the crossfire. During World War II, roughly 2.5 million soldiers and 5.5 million civilians died, accounting for 19 percent of Ukraine's population.[12]

Since 1945

Ukrainians continued to suffer after World War II from another famine, massive homelessness, and Stalinist repression. Nonetheless, the country's economy slowly recovered in the following decades. In addition to producing wheat, barley, corn, sugar, and other foodstuffs, Ukraine developed a broad industrial base, manufacturing everything from fertilizers to airplanes. It became a hub of Soviet rocket science, and among the cosmonauts blasting into the space race in the early 1960s was Ukrainian Pavel R. Popovich.

In contrast to freewheeling market economies in capitalist countries, the command economies of Soviet republics like Ukraine regulated business—and personal life—to a high degree through central planning. Aiming for maximum employment and at least a basic minimum of social services, the state set goals of what goods and services to produce and how to distribute them. Layered with bureaucracy, centralized economies could not respond nimbly to shifts in supply and demand, so sometimes stores flooded with unwanted goods even as they lacked basics. Ukrainians grew accustomed to waiting in lines for rationed treasures, from bread to shoes to apartments. To get what they wanted or needed, citizens resorted to bribes, workplace theft, and the black market. On one hand, communism guaranteed citizens jobs, education, housing, and health care. But it demanded ideological loyalty, a commitment to the system. In theory, the party distributed national wealth equally, but in practice, top officials enjoyed privileges and luxuries denied to the masses. Ukrainians who resisted Soviet control, questioned procedures, or exposed corruption faced punishment. In state-run industries, workers had few incentives to work hard, avoid waste, or catch mistakes.[13]

In April 1986, an electrical experiment gone awry caused a chemical explosion at the Ukrainian nuclear power plant at Chernobyl that shot flames, chunks of nuclear fuel, and a burst of radioactive dust and gas into the night sky. Estimates vary on the amount of radiation released, but a Swiss agency affiliated with the United Nations puts the magnitude at 100 times more than the atomic bombs the United States dropped on Hiroshima and Nagasaki in World War II. Carried by the wind, 70 percent of the fallout settled on Belarus and spread into Scandinavia, the Baltic states, and other parts of northern Europe. Radioactive strontium and cesium-137 also fouled a large swath of northern Ukraine and spread south as rain drove contaminants into lakes and rivers.[14]

In typical Soviet style, the communist leadership took charge of disaster management but restricted information. Although the government conducted health screenings among nearby residents and soldiers sent to clean up the reactor site ("liquidators"), it forbade individuals from wearing radiation dosimeters. It trucked in food, dammed rivers, dug up and dumped contaminated soils, but resettled only hundreds of the millions in the fallout zone. Years passed before both the local and international communities learned the causes of the accident—engineers who ignored safety guidelines, miscalculations, a faultily built reactor—and the magnitude of the catastrophe.[15]

Anxiety and anger with the Soviet response to Chernobyl fueled the Ukrainian independence movement. All across the Soviet Union, satellite republics were chafing against Russian central rule and blaming heavy military spending for a decline in social services. In the late 1980s, Soviet leader Mikhail Gorbachev instituted reforms intended to strengthen the Communist empire through economic restructuring and more democratic openness. But a groundswell was building to dissclve the Soviet Union. In Kiev, students dramatized their call for political reform through hunger strikes, boycotts, and street protests, resulting in the prime minister's resignation, nationalization of Soviet property, and multiparty elections.[16] Full independence followed in 1991.

Survey of Contemporary Problems and Interventions

ECONOMIC TRANSITION AND DECLINE

As their first president Ukrainians elected a former Communist Party bigwig, Leonid Kravchuk, a political economist they hoped would lead them swiftly into the prosperous company of the democratic nations of the European Union (EU). Ukraine joined the IMF and World Bank in 1992. Because of the country's rich natural resources, developed industries, and educated population (99 percent of men and women are literate),[17] observers expected the country to thrive. But the transition from a centrally planned to a free-market economy, difficult all across Eastern Europe, proved especially painful in Ukraine.

Under communism, the state used surpluses in profitable sectors across the empire to cover costs elsewhere; subsidies compensated for inefficiency and controlled prices. After independence, Ukrainian factories suddenly had to buy the imported oil and gas they had used extravagantly, and farmers had to pay full price for fertilizers, insecticides, and animal feed. As prices rose, demand fell, both at home and abroad. Other former communist-bloc nations no longer had to buy Ukrainian goods; they could develop their own industries or shop from the West.[18] Ailing Ukrainian enterprises stopped paying workers. Not only did demand fall further, but many households faced extreme poverty.

To prop up employers, the government loaned money, printing it as needed. As a result, the currency lost value. By 1993, inflation was running at 10,255 percent, meaning that consumers were paying as much as 100 times last year's price for steaks, televisions, cars, and the like.[19] Savings evaporated. Next, the government borrowed from abroad. To pay interest on this debt, the state had to cut spending in other areas, such as salaries, health care, and education.[20] Declining wages and layoffs delivered a second whammy.

Disagreement slowed economic and political reform. While some Ukrainians, especially in the west of the country, leaned toward capitalism, easterners favored a more socialist model, and the government remained a "massive centralized bureaucracy" with "a cumbersome regulatory system."[21] Taking advantage of the fray were greedy "rent-seekers" who stole state assets, avoided taxes, and abused subsidies and privileges meant to stimulate the economy and protect citizens. With corrupt managers and politicians in cahoots, bankers, traders, and entrepreneurs made fortunes on natural-gas deals and the like.

Although the party elite had usually cornered luxuries and privileges, communism on the whole had been a great equalizer. It guaranteed almost everyone a job. The transition of the early 1990s, however, abruptly and starkly divided Ukrainians. Market-savvy businessmen, honest and dishonest, grew rich while the standard of living for most Ukrainians plummeted. Experts estimate the poor at 2 percent of the Ukrainian population in 1987–88, the peak of a prosperous decade, and at 63 percent in 1993–95.[22] By 2001, when Ukraine established an official poverty line of $4.30 measured by consumption, the percentage had shrunk to 27.2, but many more felt disadvantaged as the newly rich flaunted their wealth, conspicuous consumption that the "classless" communist system had discouraged.[23]

As usual, hardship increased vulnerability. As Ukrainians migrated to other countries to find work, families suffered, and women in particular fell prey to traffickers who lured them abroad with promises of good jobs and then trapped them in prostitution rings.[24] Even as the birth rate fell, orphanages swelled with children mothers could not care for.[25] Primary and secondary school enrollment shrank because parents could not afford informal fees or needed more hands to work.[26] During the 1990s, Ukrainians cut their consumption of meat, eggs, milk, fish, and fruit in half and ate more bread and potatoes. Yet the iron-poor, carbohydrate-high diet, especially common in large families, contributed to more tuberculosis and anemia in pregnant women and portended nutrition-related health problems to come for children.[27]

RIGHTING THE ECONOMY, MENDING THE SAFETY NET, AND FIGHTING CORRUPTION

At independence, Ukraine set its sights on joining the international business community through membership in the World Trade Organization and the EU. But government corruption and lack of transparency have slowed Ukraine's acceptance into the EU and deterred foreign investment and aid. Only at the end of a dismal decade did the country undertake reforms to bring its policy more in line with Western economies and begin to establish credibility as an equal trading partner.

Under Prime Minister Viktor Yushchenko, the government standardized budgeting and decision-making procedures, eliminated hundreds of unfair special privileges, and privatized state enterprises, including distributing land from collective farms to private owners. Although observers disagree on how much credit Yushchenko deserves, the Ukrainian economy grew, creating jobs that helped lift the "new poor" out of poverty. But a combination of Communists and oligarchs drove him from office. In 2004, when he ran for president as an opposition candidate, opponents not only harassed him but likely poisoned him with dioxin, which scarred his face. After he lost a narrow election marked by massive fraud, millions of Ukrainians dressed in orange protested for weeks until a fair vote count established Yushchenko's victory.[28] While powerful interests and old habits still work to enrich a criminal elite in Ukraine, the "orange revolution" offered hope that ordinary citizens working together could help equalize opportunity and stabilize the country. With technical assistance from the United Nations, the World Bank, the IMF, the EU, USAID, and assorted NGOs, Ukraine has started to clean up its financial practices.

As one plank of this new economic platform, the government is trying to target aid to its neediest citizens and nurture a middle class. A first basic step, related to transparency, is assembling accurate information that had not always been systematically gathered and published before, such as socioeconomic data about per-capita income, labor conditions, health care, school enrollment, calorie consumption, and social privileges. Official statistics often overlooked the underground economy that had developed in the Soviet era as Ukrainians bartered for goods and services. Furthermore, regardless of income, groups such as police officers, judges, and politicians had benefited from perks such as free phone service or free medicine; war veterans received half off housing costs.[29] Yet, because of narrow criteria, in 1999 only 4.5 percent of Ukrainian families qualified for low-income cash assistance.[30] Surveys are helping officials determine who is poor and in what way.[31]

Research has revealed that poverty has become an increasingly rural problem, for instance. Although the head of most poor households either worked or received a pension, the less educated experienced more hardship.[32] With data, state officials have outlined a series of problems, including "extremely low per capita income and living standards among most of the population, . . . depopulation as the result of a mortality rate that is higher than the birth rate, . . . mass emigration of the most talented and qualified professionals, . . . mass hidden and disguised unemployment, . . . deteriorating general health and reduced life expectancy, . . . declining quality in both education and human potential, . . . [and] unsatisfactory environmental conditions."[33]

International agencies such as the UN Development Programme have encouraged Ukrainian leaders to consider the poor when making all kinds of policy decisions and to support human capital development through measures such as education reform. As the government pursued more jobs and better pay through free-market reforms, observers worried that top-heavy growth would leave out the underprivileged. Breaking up collective farms, for instance, may fail to decrease rural poverty if land ends up concentrated in a few hands rather than titled to family farmers. Similarly, small and medium enterprises (SMEs) could generate many jobs, but they need tax breaks and access to loans, through credit unions, for instance.[34] One project that USAID has funded advised vegetable growers on making contracts with supermarket chains, which guarantee steadier and higher sales than open-air stalls. Another contributed to the Energy Alliance, which helps manufacturers install mini power stations that produce energy more cheaply than the state system and recycle thermal waste.[35] Technical assistance encompassed legal reform in business: Regulations not only allow smaller companies to compete but may also improve public health when they address pollution and workplace safety.

Ukraine has also been trying to turn a hodgepodge of social benefits into a more fair and consistent safety net. In the 1990s, the state expanded the size and number of household agricultural plots, a Soviet innovation that helped many families garden their way beyond hunger. Less successful has been the pension system, which promised more than it could deliver. With the deficit growing, Ukraine cut monthly payouts from a minimum of about $60 in 1990 to about $20 in 1999. Since the turn of the millennium, Ukraine has been working on pension reform, but pressures pull the government two ways. On the one hand, people have been clamoring for relief, and Ukraine borrowed money to substantially increase pensions. On the other, the World Bank, while applauding Ukraine for improved recordkeeping and other changes, warned that the system could not sustain itself without reducing expenses and increasing revenues—by raising the retirement age, for instance, which in 2005 stood at 55 for women and 60 for men.[36] Poverty reduction may require other unpopular decisions, such as redistributing housing subsidies so that only those most in need receive benefits.

ENVIRONMENTAL DEGRADATION

Complicating economic and health problems for Ukrainians is pollution. The government estimates that by 2015, coping with the Chernobyl disaster will have cost the country $201 billion. After independence, Ukraine levied a Chernobyl disaster tax on all businesses—18 percent at first—to help pay for cleanup, resettlement, and health benefits. But state spending, even when supplemented by international aid, could not keep pace with problems. Soil and forests in the sizable northern fallout zone, making up more than 7 percent of Ukraine's territory, remain contaminated, and unmapped debris dumps threaten groundwater. To reduce radioactivity in milk and meat, the Ukrainian government continues to distribute uncontaminated hay and free feed additives and monitors state-farm produce headed for shops. But many rural Ukrainians survive on contaminated food from contaminated land: They hunt and fish, garden a small plot, graze a few animals on wild grass, and gather radioactive mushrooms and berries. Of the 3 million Ukrainians exposed to radiation in the Chernobyl disaster, 84 percent—including 1 million children—were still on government sick rolls in March 2002.[37]

Although Chernobyl represents an extreme, all of eastern Europe struggles with industrial pollution and occupational dangers largely ignored in the Soviet era. Ukraine burned much coal for energy, especially for its inefficient factories, and carbon emissions fouled the air while manufacturing runoff tainted the Dnieper River. Although industrial setbacks temporarily reduced that source of pollution, after independence Ukrainians rushed to buy cars, most often without expensive catalytic converters to filter carbon-monoxide exhaust.[38] While life expectancy has been increasing in most nations of the world, in Ukraine mortality is increasing. In the working-age bracket of 20–49, men die at almost four times the rate of women—likely because they work dangerous (but better compensated) jobs denied to women.[39]

CREATING CITIZEN WATCHDOGS

Although the world community pledged massive Chernobyl aid, the United Nations was able to raise, in 1998, only $1.5 million of the $90 million that affected countries said they needed for long-term cleanup and assistance for survivors. Contaminated areas languished because industries could not lure workers from other parts of the country, and locals with skills or means often moved away. Government plans to resettle much of the remaining population proved expensive and unpopular since many communities did not welcome radiation refugees who might compete for jobs. With funds limited, the United Nations asked Ukraine, Belarus, and Russia to prioritize projects. Antipoverty strategies shifted from welfare to human capital, empowering locals with information and education to overcome a "victim" mentality. Working with the Ukrainian government and particularly NGOs, UN agencies are supporting the medical needs of women, children, and liquidators, as well as regional economic and mental/physical-health projects to empower residents.[40]

On paper, the Ukrainian government has promised an open society committed to protecting its citizens. The constitution, adopted in 1996, guarantees in article 50 the right to a safe and healthful environment—and the right to information and to compensation should that right be violated. It also established separate legislative, executive, and judicial branches that act as a check on one another's power. But democracy and the rule of law are new to a society that so long had to defer to a cloaked, authoritarian government. Many Ukrainians are unaware of environmental problems—and unaware of their rights and how to exercise them.[41]

A variety of Ukrainian NGOs are trying to raise the country's environmental consciousness among officials as well as citizens. MAMA-86, for one, has partnered with British organizations on an "environmental democracy" project. After Ukrainian experts surveyed natural resource management, they shared the results through regional roundtable workshops for all "stakeholders." They then publicized the process by publishing their findings and holding press conferences.[42] The Vermont-based Institute for Sustainable Communities (ISC) supports Ukrainian environmental initiatives, such as teacher training and school curricula development. Through its Ukraine Citizens Action Network, ISC strengthens local organizations with advice about ethics, outreach, financial viability, and strategies for advocacy and legal change.[43]

The Ukrainian NGO Ecopravo-Lviv has met success and failure in class-action suits on behalf of citizens. It backed a group of mothers suing a coal-mining company for polluting the water supply of the small town of Sosnivka with fluoride, which in large amounts has sickened about 2,500 children. The mothers wanted the company build a water-treatment plant, but a court ruled that just to file suit, the claimants must pay a state fee of 5 percent of what they were demanding—a price beyond their reach. Ecopravo-Lviv won a major victory, however, in stopping the construction of a chemical fertilizer terminal in Mykolaiv. The sponsors, an Irish-Russian-Ukrainian group, had "donated" trams and buses to the city and won quick approval by authorities of the project. But a local environmental nonprofit concerned about endangered fish in a nearby estuary and a shipbuilding company worried about workers' health objected. On their behalf, Ecopravo-Lviv sued on the grounds that the builders had not followed proper procedures: They had not published an environmental impact statement or submitted the project for evaluation by local EcoSafety officials. Eventually 100,000 local citizens signed petitions opposing the terminal. In his ruling against the terminal builders and the ministry that sided with them, the judge noted that they had failed to consider public opinion.[44]

Conclusion

After strong performance early in the decade, Ukraine's economy then settled into "solid" but not "spectacular" growth by 2007. Observers remained confident the country and the economy could weather a political crisis between the president and his prime minister.[45] Yet, even as the national balance sheet improved, assessments of the trickle-down effect varied widely. The World Bank, on the one hand, reported deep inroads against poverty, down to 19 percent of the population in 2003.[46] On the other hand, while the government conceded that extreme hardship diminished, the overall poverty rate, around 27 percent of the population, did not budge between 2001 and 2003.[47] In fact, poverty persisted among more than a quarter of the population into 2005—despite economic growth and despite pension and other safety-net improvements.[48]

Unemployment has become less of an issue than low income is: Half the working population in Ukraine does not make a living wage. On top of that hardship, inflation is resurging. Ukraine must untangle a knot of low demand, monopolies, and corruption. People cannot afford goods and services, but without a market, factories and businesses cannot boost production and pay. Because the privileged few control industry, they can conspire to keep wages low. Many monopolists rely on corruption to drive small entrepreneurs out of business, avoid taxes, and subvert government spending. Instead of division at the highest levels of government, Ukraine needs a consensus to tackle widespread poverty and widening inequality by expanding workers' opportunities.[49]

SYRIA

I left school five years ago. My parents didn't give me
any money for books, so I started working. . . .
My boss always shouts at me, and sometimes
he hits me. Sometimes, I cry when I see my friends
go [to] school—I want to wear clean clothes
and go to school with them.
—Syrian carpenter, age 14[50]

When colonial powers drew the borders of modern Syria after World War I, they extracted the nation-state from a broad territory known as Bilad al-Sham, which also included parts of modern Jordan, Lebanon, Israel, and the Palestinian territories. Slightly bigger than North Dakota, the Syrian Arab Republic borders the Mediterranean Sea to the west. Its narrow, humid coast bumps into mountains; on the other side, a huge, mostly treeless steppe covers most of the territory, giving way to desert south and east. Although Syria boasts arable land, a literate workforce, a diverse economy, and natural resources that include oil, gas, and phosphates, volatile politics have contributed to privation in this mostly Arab, Muslim nation.[51]

Like other Middle East and North Africa (MENA) nations, Syria is "richer than it is developed."[52] On the 2007/2008 UN HDI, it ranked 108, in the medium range. About 2 million people, 11.4 percent of the population, could not meet their basic needs; by a measure of expenditure, the poverty rate rises to 30 percent, according to a 2005 joint Syrian and UN report. In general, rural poverty is greater than urban, but the overall poorest region lies in the northeast, home to a large Kurdish minority. Illiteracy runs high among the most destitute, with a "disturbingly low rate" of poor girls enrolled in school. Since poverty is shallow, however, small improvements in income and schooling can make a significant difference in lifting people out of hardship.[53] Repressive leadership, disputes with neighboring Israel over water and borders, and interference in neighboring Lebanon's affairs have earned Syria black marks from the world community, and the country's isolation has complicated efforts at economic reform.

History

Archaeologists digging through Syria's past have found layer upon layer of settlement, which Syrian tourism officials mine today. Excavations at Ebla, in the west, have placed ancient Syria within a far-reaching Semitic trading empire that peaked after 2500 B.C.E. Around that time, people also settled at Damascus, making Syria's present capital one of the oldest continuously occupied cities in the world. Artisans wove silk brocade, crafted wood and mother-of-pearl mosaics, and blew glass so fine that Italians later imported their techniques to Venice. On the coast, Phoenicians honed shipbuilding: From their city-states, they sailed the Mediterranean peddling rare dye made from mollusk shells so expensive that its deep purple became the hallmark color of royal robes.

Like tides, empires have long rolled in and out of Greater Syria, a nexus for Europe, Asia, and Africa. Assyrians, Babylonians, Persians, and the Macedonian Alexander the Great conquered the region. An influx of Greek immigrants energized trade and cities where philosophers flourished. Next, the Romans marched in, building roads, digging wells, and irrigating fields with aqueducts; they taxed farmlands based on its harvest potential, a system that survived until 1945.[54]

Religious diversity also figures into the conglomeration. Jews and Aramaeans had settled in Syria in the 13th century B.C.E. On the road to Damascus, Paul converted to Christianity and established the first organized Christian church at Antioch. Soon after the death of Muhammad, founding prophet of Islam, Muslim invaders swept north from the Arabian Peninsula, and Damascus surrendered in 635 C.E. About 90 percent of Syrians today identify themselves as Muslims and about 10 percent as Christians.[55]

Muhammad's successor, Uthmān established the Umayyad dynasty, which ruled from Damascus until the Abbasids seized the caliphate and established their capital in Baghdad. From the 11th to 13th century, Europe mounted the Crusades, a series of wars across Greater Syria. Although Western history has traditionally cast the Crusades as a "clash of civilizations" between West and East, with noble Christians fighting to reclaim the Holy Land from Muslim infidels, recent scholarship has offered alternate readings, pointing to the modest place of holy war in Arab histories of the era, the plunder motive of many impoverished Christian warriors, and the sometimes shifting allegiances of combatants on both sides.[56] The European intrusion spurred Kurdish commander Saladin to unite Greater Syria and Egypt and to expel crusaders from the prized Palestinian city of Jerusalem.[57]

In the early 16th century, Greater Syria came under control of the Turkic Ottoman Empire, which ruled indirectly through pashas, administrative and military leaders. Although poverty was widespread, trade thrived. So did charity. Family members looked after one another, and religious communities tended to their poor, in part to stem conversions to other faiths. While Ottoman law discriminated against religious minorities, it also protected *dhimmi,* Christians and Jews, allowing them to practice their faith, teach classes, and distribute aid. Based on the Qur'an, Islamic law is very specific in urging benevolence, requiring believers with free and clear assets to donate about 2.5 percent to the poor every year (*zakat*), to give additional alms to beggars or needy neighbors *(sadaqa)*, and to care for orphans. To bolster their standing among their majority Muslim subjects, the sultan and lesser Ottoman rulers made sure that the public was aware of their private philanthropy. At the end of Ramadan, for instance, they distributed food to the hungry. From bureaucrats to merchants to widows, wealthy individuals endowed religious trusts (*waqfs* or *awqaf* [Arabic pl.]), which supported hospitals, schools, and mosques, many of them with shelters and soup kitchens. In Ottoman Syria, as elsewhere throughout the Muslim world, alleviating poverty solidified community ties.[58]

Struggling against European encroachment, the Ottomans entered World War I on the side of Germany in 1914 and soon began drafting Arab men into the military, at least those who could not afford to buy an exemption. Anticipating misery, richer residents fled before the Triple Entente—France, Britain, and Russia—blockaded Ottoman ports, cutting off fuel and food supplies. At the same time, locusts swarmed over fields in Lebanon, and several years of poor harvests touched off a devastating famine in Bilad al-Sham. While black marketers profited from soaring prices, in Damascus women and children begged for a bite to eat and the starving "ate orange peels from the street." Convinced that hardship would foment Arab revolt against the Ottomans, the British refused pleas to allow aid through the blockade. Roughly one-sixth of the Syrian and Lebanese population died during World War I of hunger, disease, or battle wounds—more than double and perhaps triple the losses of either France or Germany. The misery and later memory of war and famine intensified Arab nationalism, a sense of ethnic and cultural solidarity.[59]

For a few months in 1920, Syria did become an Arab kingdom, but with the Treaty of Sèvres, the World War I victors carved up Ottoman land, drawing boundaries that sometimes contradicted historical, ethnic, and economic ties. With a "mandate" from the League of Nations, France occupied Syria and Lebanon, in theory to prepare locals for independence. In practice, the French put their own interests first. To suppress Pan-Arab unity, they divided the territory, accentuating religious differences and splitting Lebanon from Syria. French companies benefited from special concessions, including control of utilities and railroads, and French administrators imposed French in schools, the franc in currency, and strict limits on freedom of the press. Although the French coopted some local elites, a broad spectrum of Syrians banded together, using mandate rhetoric to demand their political and economic rights.[60]

Since 1945

Weakened by World War II, France could not hold Syria, which achieved its official independence in 1946. As was soon to happen elsewhere in the Middle East and North Africa, the unity inspired by anticolonialism crumbled in Syria. While nationalists promised democracy, rivalries derailed political transformation, and leaders often pursued private gain at the expense of public benefit. What survived in the new nation-state of Syria was not the French ideals of *liberté* and *égalité* but "the paternalism and authoritarianism that were the legacies of the colonial civic order."[61]

Arab nationalist feelings ran strong in Syria. When Britain withdrew from Palestine and Israel declared a Jewish state in 1948, Syria and other Arab neighbors invaded, accusing the West of breaking promises and favoring Jews over Arabs. Although Israel prevailed in its war of independence, Palestinians recall that moment as *al-nakba*, "the catastrophe." Ongoing hostility has frequently erupted into outright war. In 1967, Israel seized Syria's Golan Heights, a plateau that Syria reclaimed in battle—but only temporarily—in 1973.

In the meantime, military coups in Syria periodically overturned civilian rule. In 1958, Syria merged with Egypt, led by charismatic Arab nationalist Gamal Abdel Nasser (1918–70), but the United Arab Republic dissolved three years later when Syria seceded after another coup. The Arab Socialist Resurrection Party (Baath) began dominating politics in the 1960s, and in 1970, Syrian defense minister and Baathist Hafiz al-Assad (1930–2000) took charge after a bloodless military coup. Assad belonged to a minority Muslim sect, the Alawis. Poverty and discrimination at the hands of the Sunni Muslim majority had driven many Alawis to join the military and the Baath Party, and under Assad—in a twist on the usual pattern—they came to dominate the ruling elite. Since the 1960s, a "state of emergency" law has allowed military elites to seize property, censor publications, and ban groups from meeting.[62]

With the Baath Party's rise to power a strong secular, socialist bent emerged in Syria, which drew military and economic support from the Soviet Union.[63] From the 1960s through the 1980s, the government nationalized many enterprises and private assets such as land. The discovery of oil enabled the state to meet the country's energy needs and subsidize many social services, muting complaints. In 1976, Syria sent troops into neighboring Lebanon, destabilized by civil war, and the occupying force remained into the 21st century, with Syria meddling in Lebanese politics and profiting from the more laissez-faire nation's ports, casinos, black market, and banking and telecommunications industries.[64]

The Assad government ruthlessly silenced dissent. Syria's independent syndicates for professionals—doctors, pharmacists, lawyers, engineers, and so on—often challenged the military, and in 1980, they organized a nationwide strike to end torture, free political prisoners, and restore rule of law. Jailing (and later executing some) leaders, the government dissolved all these organizations, reforming them with new, approved directors and mandatory membership.[65] Among religious opponents of the dictatorship was the Muslim Brotherhood. At first a democratic opposition group, a voice for the poor and disenfranchised, the Brotherhood was driven underground and coordinated sometimes violent protest and assassination campaigns against an increasingly corrupt regime. In 1982, state security forces led by Assad's brother bombed, shelled, and gassed the Brotherhood stronghold of Hama, leveling Syria's fourth-largest city and killing, by conservative estimates, from 10,000 to 25,000 people, mostly civilians.[66]

Although wary of groups that might challenge the regime, Syria has supported armed Arab factions committed to reclaiming Palestine. Politics has put Syria at odds with the United States, Israel's chief ally. Even though Syria no longer backs attacks on Westerners or strikes from its own territory and has indirectly accepted Israel's right to exist, the U.S. State Department continues to list the country as a state sponsor of terrorism, accusing it of supporting the Lebanese militia Hezbollah and letting militants who support the Iraqi insurgency slip through its border with Iraq.[67]

Since the 1980s, many Syrians with means have fled the country. Of students earning Ph.D.s abroad, for instance, only 20 percent return home—a "brain drain" that has contributed to Syria's impoverishment.[68]

After Assad's death in 2000, his son Bashar al-Assad ran unopposed for the presidency. Pledging reform, the younger Assad's government has released some political prisoners, legalized private banking, promoted computer technology and Internet access, and spoken out against cronyism. Necessity is pushing Syria to diversify its economy and to shift away from central planning to allow SMEs flexibility to compete in a global marketplace. Although no match for the output of Persian Gulf states, Syria's oil production peaked in the mid-1990s, and experts predict the rentier state will be importing oil before 2020. Losing that income (oil accounted for about 65 percent of exports in 1996), Syria will find it harder to continue subsidizing basic commodities, such as diesel, cement, flour, rice, sugar, vegetable oil, and tea.[69] But to attract investors and stimulate trade, the government must loosen censorship and state control. Observers wonder how much mild-mannered Bashar—who was training in London to be an eye doctor when his family summoned him home after the death of his more politically minded brother Basil in a car crash in 1994—can reorient an oppressive military regime and an economy "plagued by corruption, aging state industries, a volatile and underperforming agricultural sector, rapidly depleting oil resources, an anachronistic educational system, capital flight, and lack of foreign investment."[70]

Survey of Contemporary Problems and Interventions

BORDER CLASHES

Conflict is expensive, but none more so than the Israeli-Palestinian standoff. One scholar estimates that it has cost the United States about $3 trillion in aid and investment losses,[71] and no estimate can quantify the toll in death, destruction, and lost opportunities for the countries directly involved. It stands in the way of regional solutions to common problems, such as water distribution. It diverts funds and attention from economic growth and poverty alleviation. Syria spends 80 percent of its tax revenue on its sizable military—some 400,000 troops.[72]

Palestinian refugees began pouring into Syria after the first Arab-Israeli war in 1948. As of 2003, more than 407,000 Palestinian refugees officially registered with UNRWA were living in Syria, more than a quarter of them in crude UNRWA camps and some others in locally run camps. More welcoming than some other Arab states, Syria has granted refugees all but political rights, so Palestinians may own a house (but not farmland), fill government jobs, and attend state universities, where many train for teaching and nursing. The less educated tend to work in agriculture or construction. Although many Palestinians have integrated into Syrian society, almost half of refugee families live on or below the poverty line. While UNRWA runs schools and clinics and Syria supplies basic utilities, camps were never meant to be permanent, so generations of Palestinian children have grown up in crude mud and cement-block structures with faulty water and sewage systems.

In addition to the UNRWA-tracked refugees, Syria has absorbed 125,000–170,000 people displaced in 1967, mostly former residents of the Golan Heights.[73] About 1.5 million Iraqis have also fled into Syria because of the violence and insecurity that followed the U.S. invasion and occupation of their country in 2003.[74]

The political and social costs of challenging Israel and interfering in Lebanon have also hampered Syria's ability to provide for its poor. Since designating Syria a state sponsor of terrorism in 1979, the United States has denied it economic aid and opposed loans by the World Bank and other financial institutions.[75] In 2004, U.S. president George W. Bush imposed additional sanctions on Syria, cutting off direct flights between the two countries and prohibiting U.S. investment, among other punishments. Although more symbolic than substantial since many American businesses already steer clear of Syria, sanctions nonetheless carry the potential to warn off trading partners.[76]

While many Syrians appreciate that peace lays the foundation for regional prosperity, it remains elusive. Conflicting visions of history and justice abound in the Middle East. Because Syria represses homegrown political organizations, it has no outspoken peace lobby. And the United States's special relationship with Israel has tainted the U.S. role as peacemaker. Nor do experts agree on how to bring Syria to the negotiating table. While the United States has often isolated Syria through sanctions and the like, another school of diplomacy believes that the world community should engage with Syria through talks, trade, and aid.

TARGETING POOR POPULATIONS

UNRWA and other international relief organizations serve the Palestinian refugee community within Syria. The UN Development Programme is also working with the Syrian government to analyze poverty and direct resources to the nation's neediest citizens. The greatest "incidence, depth, and severity" of poverty falls in the northeast, home to a large Kurdish minority. At a macro level, the United Nations is advising Syria on "pro-poor" growth strategies combined with reinforcement of safety nets such as pensions, insurance, and welfare.[77] On a micro level, cooperative programs include health services for the handicapped and microfinance institutions (*sanduq*) in impoverished rural regions such as Jabal al-Hoss. Each *sanduq* must include female members, and some cater only to women. Besides loans, *sanduqs* offer instruction in everything from mushroom cultivation to beekeeping, hairdressing to refrigerator maintenance, literacy to nursing.[78]

Some private charities, international as well as local, supplement government efforts. The Britain-based SOS Children runs two orphanages, near Damascus and the northeastern city of Aleppo.[79] Operating around Damascus, Hefez al-Na'amah (Protection of Prosperity) repackages hotel and restaurant leftovers and clothes and unused furniture from the wealthy.[80]

But NGOs that cross over the line from economic support to political challenge, linking poverty to government corruption or repression, risk calling down the security apparatus. The Human Rights Association in Syria lobbies on behalf of people for whom human-rights abuses often lead to poverty, including women, children, political prisoners and their families, and Kurds.[81] After World War I and the breakup of the Ottoman Empire, Kurds who had hoped for the reestablishment of a homeland found themselves divided among Turkey, Iraq, and Syria, where they face ongoing discrimination. In Syria, the government stripped a subset of Kurds of their citizenship in 1962, and they and their descendants may not work for the government or practice medicine or law.[82] By calling for economic and social rights, however, the Human Rights Association in Syria has invoked harassment, and authorities have several times detained its president, Haytham al-Maleh, and other lawyer activists and prevented them from leaving the country.

REDUCING UNEMPLOYMENT

Although the Syrian government stated an unemployment rate under 12 percent in 2002, independent experts put the figure closer to 20 percent. About a quarter of the population works for the government and public sector at low pay.[83] With a young and growing population, about 40 percent under the age of 15, Syria is struggling to expand its economy to provide this rising generation with work. Every year, about 350,000 young people enter the labor market.[84]

As Syria's main trading partner and donor, the EU has funded programs such as the Syrian-European Business Centre (SEBC) to encourage private-sector businesses. It has helped train managers; one Syrian participating in an SEBC international trade fair returned home with orders for Syrian companies worth 25 million euros.[85] To improve job prospects for rural youths, the United Nations has helped fund a "smart community project" in Qusaybeh, an impoverished five-village cattle-farming area with steady electricity. Local residents donated land for an Agro-Food Processing Unit that works on marketing local produce; the processing unit is linked to agricultural research institutions and a global marketplace through the Multipurpose Technology Community Centre (MTCC). Based around a computer lab, the MTCC offers free Internet access as well as training in computer literacy, Arabic and English, accounting, secretarial skills, and eventually e-commerce.[86] *Sanduqs* also foster entrepreneurship. In Umjern village, for instance, women borrow money to buy beads, thread, and wood for looms and hope to sell their embroidery in Aleppo, or even Lebanon.[87]

Employment is also on the agenda of NGOs such as the Society for Developing the Role of Women in Syria, which has launched a program to shelter and train divorced women. Pawns in nasty divorces, children often lose their childhood along with their home; according to a 2003 UNICEF study, more than 85 percent of Syria's child laborers have divorced parents.[88] Improving women's economic self-sufficiency also helps their children.

NARROWING EDUCATION GAPS

Although Syria offers free primary education and requires attendance until age 12, achievement varies by region and gender.[89] Women lag behind men in school enrollment and literacy (64 versus 90 percent) since poor families especially need their daughters' labor and then often marry them off in their early teens.[90] Schooling even more than type of job or other variables correlates closely with poverty: More than 81 percent of the poor have less than a ninth-grade education.

The Syrian government has partnered with UN agencies to improve its public schools. Contributing to dropout rates are large classes and overwhelmed teachers who may deliver instruction with a lecture and a snap of a ruler. The Child-Friendly Schools project in northeast Syria limits class sizes to 30 (down from more than 50), invites student and parent feedback, and introduces newer teaching methods such as round tables for working groups instead of rows of desks.[91] Also in the north, a pilot "second-chance" learning project welcomes female dropouts back to school.[92] In 2003, Syria signed onto the international Convention on the Elimination of All Forms of Discrimination Against Women (CEDAW), and based on CEDAW recommendations, it has rewritten school textbooks to portray women in a wider variety of roles.[93]

The officially sanctioned Syrian Women's Union also reaches out to women. On the education front, it runs numerous training programs for illiterate girls.[94] Its members visit house to house convincing mothers to obey the law and keep their daughters in school.[95]

Conclusion

In a joint document outlining the UN Development Assistance Framework (UNDAF) for 2007–2011 for Syria, the government set a target of full integration into the world economy by 2020. After a brainstorming session that included NGOs, the Syrian government and UN agencies identified five priority areas for the country's short- and longer-term development: 1) "faster economic growth, with social protection and sustainable livelihoods," 2) "improved efficiency and accountability of government structures," 3) "reduced disparities in basic social services (with emphasis on disadvantaged areas, mainly in the north and east)," 4) "sustainable environmental management," and 5) "disaster management." With the United Nations stressing a "rights-based and results-based approach," Syria acknowledged the need for comprehensive reform involving citizens across society. Hailed as a "landmark" first in Syrian-UN cooperation, this UNDAF envisions a decentralized Syria where by 2020 "freedom of expression, democracy, pluralism and the rule of law prevail."[96]

Even as Syria signed on to this lofty goal, the government continued to arrest and jail dissidents. On May 13, 2007, for instance, a Syrian court sentenced journalist Michel Kilo to a three-year prison term for "weakening national sentiment" by criticizing Syria's meddling in Lebanon.[97] In an authoritian state rife with official corruption and stagnant bureaucracy, "better governance" may be the most needed but least likely antipoverty measure.

While decrying the country's human rights record, American politicians began in spring 2007 to reach out to Syria. First House Speaker Nancy Pelosi led a delegation to the country, then Secretary of State Condoleeza Rice met with Syrian foreign minister Walid al-Moualem at an international conference about Iraq in May. As the U.S. occupation of violence-wracked Iraq ground on, Syria struggled to absorb about a million and a half refugees; what concerned Rice, however, was border crossings in the other direction, and she urged Syria to stop fresh fighters from entering Iraq to join the insurgency. Many observers saw that brief talk as a modest diplomatic breakthrough that nourished hope for more cooperation between Syria, the United States, and other nations in resolving many of the region's security and development problems.

GUATEMALA

If a poor man gets sick, who will support the household?
—Guatemalan man, 1994[98]

Orchids, parrots, and woven textiles splash bright colors across the Republic of Guatemala. Between fertile coastal plains bordering the Gulf of Honduras to the east and the Pacific Ocean to the west rise mountains and volcanoes. Agriculture employs half the population and accounts for about three-quarters of exports, which include coffee, bananas, and sugar, as well as other fruits and flowers. Like other Latin American countries, Guatemala gets a boost on the UN HDI (it ranks 118) from its per-capita income, but its ranking masks appalling inequality in its distribution. More than half the population—and perhaps as much as 80 percent, according to the U.S. State Department—lives in poverty, which is deep, severe, and chronic. About the size of Tennessee, Guatemala is the largest, most populated (12.3 million), and probably poorest country in Latin America, with one of the world's worst child malnutrition rates. As is true elsewhere in Latin America, poverty predominates in rural areas, particularly among the indigenous 60 percent or so of the population, descendants of the ancient Maya.[99]

History

A group of affiliated states strung across tropical Mesoamerica, Maya civilization flourished from about 250 to 900 C.E. The Maya cultivated maize, developed an accurate calendar based on astronomy, built elaborate stone temples and pyramids, crafted detailed pottery and metal ornaments, discovered the mathematical concept of zero, and recorded history in writing. After competition between rival city-states likely escalated into warfare, the civilization declined,[100] and conquistadores led by Pedro de Alvarado defeated the Maya in 1523–24, claiming the land for Spain. Maya diversity survives to this day in Guatemala, where indigenous people belong to about 21 ethnolinguistic groups, such as the Quiché, Cakchiquel, Mam, and Kekchi.[101]

Immediately after the conquest, colonists and church orders appropriated communal land and enslaved the indigenous people to raise cocoa and indigo. Even after the Spanish king abolished slavery, racism bolstered exploitation. Indians had to pay a tax, for instance—a powerful incentive to disown their Maya heritage.[102] Under Spanish law, anyone born to at least one Spanish parent qualified for citizenship, and locally born and often mixed-blood "Ladinos" came to form a powerful class. In 1821, they led a break from Spain. For the next century, through coups, revolts, and the rare election, government changed hands often, with liberal elites favoring capitalism and republicanism and conservative elites siding with church and landowners. With most schooling reserved for Ladino males, widespread illiteracy served as a pretext for excluding women and indigenous people from political participation.[103]

In the late 1800s, a series of liberal dictators spurred development, building roads and setting up a national school system, but modernization often came at the expense of the poor. The state passed a law obliging all male citizens to work on the roads or a pay a fee, but in practice only the indigenous labored without wages under the hot sun. As the world's thirst for coffee grew, so did the need for cheap labor on plantations (*fincas*). Many of the poor ended up in debt servitude as *patrones* advanced them money and then deducted the bill at harvest, in effect binding workers from season to season. So acute was the need for hands that an 1877 *mandamiento* (order) required villages to muster up to 60 men to work on nearby *fincas* for a fortnight or a month—and set a precedent for legalized forced labor through *mandamientos*. Continued privatization of communal land, with coffee and fruit growers grabbing prime spreads, often left indigenous farmers with plots so tiny or so marginal that they had little choice but to work for wages.[104]

Nor was the exploitation all internal. In 1901, General Manuel Estrada Cabrera (1857–1924) invited the United Fruit Company to complete a railroad and later telegraph lines between the capital and Puerto Barrios, the country's main Atlantic port. In return, Estrada Cabrera granted the American company a concession to run these systems and to grow bananas on land it could buy for a nominal price along the tracks. Over time, United Fruit came to control most of Guatemala's communications and transportation, levying a tariff on freight arriving and leaving the country.

Elsewhere in Central America, too, United Fruit became so deeply enmeshed in commerce and politics that locals referred to the company as "El Pulpo" (the Octopus). In their defense, multinational companies such as United Fruit made the colonialist argument that they paid their workers better-than-average wages; built schools, houses, hospitals, and infrastructure; and tackled some of the region's problems, such as dengue fever and agricultural diseases. But multinationals also supported dictatorial regimes as long as they were good for business. Derisively, Americans referred to countries such as Guatemala as "banana republics," corrupt and dysfunctional.[105]

Seizing power in 1931, General Jorge Ubico (1878–1946) enamored Americans with his anticommunism. Supporting large landowners, his government oversaw a 1934 vagrancy law that commanded landless peasants to work 150 days a year on *fincas*, with compliance monitored in personal workbooks laborers had to carry and produce on demand. An emerging middle class of teachers, shopkeepers, and mid-level officials began to regard rule by feudal landowners as a detriment to their progress. They supported Ubico's overthrow in 1944 and in the free elections that followed elected a socialist reformer and educator, Juan José Arévalo (1904–90).[106]

Since 1945

A new constitution "ended censorship, forbade presidential re-election for more than two periods, classified racial discrimination as a crime, freed higher education from governmental control, banned private monopolies, established a 40-hour work week, forbade payment to the workers in tokens changeable for goods at the landowner's store (a common practice by landowners who did not pay wages in cash) and legalized labor unions."[107] Women voted for the first time in 1946. With education reform, literacy rose to a still paltry 29 percent in 1950.[108]

Under popular president Jacobo Arbenz (1913–71), Guatemala passed an agricultural reform act intended to rectify a gross imbalance: 2 percent of the population held 72 percent of the nation's arable acres. Expropriating unused land from large estates, the state would pay owners its declared tax value over 25 years, with interest, and in the meantime redistribute it to poor and landless peasants. Investing in agriculture, the state hoped not only to empower the indigenous community but also to reorient the Guatemalan economy away from heavy dependence on a few export crops and toward modest industrialization.[109]

As the Arbenz government claimed hundreds of thousands of fallow United Fruit acres, the company protested the compensation as insufficient. Losing in the Guatemalan courts, United Fruit enlisted the U.S. government to press its claim, but when Guatemala refused to back down, tensions escalated. American business and political leaders mounted a public relations campaign to color the Arbenz regime as a Communist threat within the Western Hemisphere. In 1954, the U.S. Central Intelligence Agency coordinated a coup to overthrow Arbenz—a victory for large landowners and multinationals and a pattern mirrored in other Latin American nations.[110]

Overtly and covertly, the United States backed brutal right-wing military regimes across Latin America in the 1960s and 1970s. The United States also supported modernization, but in the 1970s, development specialists worldwide were confronting failure: Infrastructure building and economic growth—the focus of World Bank lending in the 1950s and 1960s—were not transforming the lives of the poor. Led by Robert McNamara, former U.S. business "whiz kid" and secretary of defense, the World Bank expanded and reoriented its lending toward human-capital projects such as education, family planning, and even land reform. McNamara also called upon leaders of developing countries such as Guatemala to meet the basic needs of their poorest citizens.[111] Under pressure, Guatemala borrowed heavily in the 1980s, so its foreign debt tripled to more than $3 billion by the mid-1990s, approaching a crushing fifth of its GDP.[112]

Popular unrest simmered. The 1973 Arab oil embargo hit Guatemala and other oil-importing Latin American countries hard; farmers could no longer afford petroleum-based fertilizers, and the rising cost of basic goods outpaced urban salaries. Teachers and other workers went on strike and won wage increases. After a 1976 earthquake killed almost 30,000 Guatemalans and left almost a million homeless, neighborhood groups stepped in where a corrupt government was failing to distribute food, prevent looting, or pull corpses from the rubble.[113] Agitating labor unions, opposition political parties, and groups such as the National Slum-Dwellers Movement began reaching out from the city to the indigenous living in rural areas and remote mountain villages.[114]

But the government struck back, assassinating and "disappearing" opponents. What began as a failed revolt within the army in 1960 degenerated into a civil war that lasted more than three decades. Rebels fled to the countryside and enlisted disaffected indigenous people. As part of a "scorched-earth" campaign in the '80s to break the insurgency, the army destroyed hundreds of villages. Perhaps a million peasants fled, forced into resettlement camps or escaping into Mexico. Government-authorized paramilitary "civilian self-defense patrols" terrorized those left behind in the countryside, torturing, raping, and killing. In the war's orgy of violence, 11 percent of the victims were Ladino and the rest Maya or other ethnicities, such as the African-Caribbean Garífunas. About 200,000 people died or vanished.

The cost in dollars and development was steep as well. According to a UN estimate, just sponsoring the paramilitary patrols cost 39 percent of Guatemala's GNP in 1990. Antipoverty efforts by and large halted—just before a slump in coffee prices on the world market hurt its poorest cultivators.[115]

Misery finally forced negotiation. Peace accords signed in 1996 not only bound both sides to lay down arms but addressed exclusion and inequality within Guatemalan society. In the decade after, the country made some progress in implementing the peace agenda. It reduced the size of the military, for instance, increased tax collection and spending on rural development, and extended education and utility services.[116] But government corruption and violence in many forms, including youth gangs, street crime, political assassinations, and domestic violence, contribute to widespread insecurity, especially for antipoverty activists.[117]

Survey of Contemporary Problems and Interventions

DISCRIMINATION

Racism lies at the root of indigenous oppression. The conquistadores imposed their language and their religion on the "superstitious savages." Although the church converted many Maya to Catholicism, the indigenous population nonetheless held fast to much of their heritage. To this day about 84 percent speak an indigenous language, often in addition to Spanish, Guatemala's official tongue.[118] At the turn of the 20th century, a Ladino writer described the Maya as "closer to beast than man," fit only for "the lash."[119] According to indigenous activist Rigoberta Menchú (1959–), who won the Nobel Peace Prize in 1992, Ladinos once treated the Maya as if they "didn't exist," but the push to assert native identity as part of the country's cultural fabric has provoked more "verbal aggression" and overt racism. Menchú has tried to sue politicians who called her a "tomato seller" and "market Indian." Restaurants, hotels, theaters, and parks often turn away Maya women in traditional dress, saying they cater only to "respectable people," not Indians.[120] As a UN investigator noted, Guatemalans of indigenous and African descent live in areas of "economic impoverishment and social marginalization . . . a glaring example of the systemic and structural nature of racial discrimination."[121]

The Accord on the Identity and Rights of Indigenous Peoples, part of the 1996 peace accords, proclaimed Guatemala a multiethnic nation and outlined reforms, such as multilingual and multicultural education, to redress discrimination and bias. It also proposed antipoverty measures such as recognition of communal landownership and redistribution of farm plots. But inertia and resistance have slowed these initiatives, and the indigenous lack the political and social clout to force change. Past land grabs drove them into remote highlands, particularly in the north, now one of Guatemala's poorest regions. Although allowed to vote, the poor and often illiterate must overcome many structural barriers to political participation, including transportation difficulties, registration formalities, and timing of elections during harvest season.[122]

Intimidation is judicial as well as political. In a majority Maya country, the indigenous make up only 14 percent of the police. The accused face trial in Spanish, a language many do not speak. Corruption is rife within the courts. Although authorized by the peace accords, human rights activists trying to prosecute military and government officials for the civil war's genocidal violence have been kidnapped and killed.

EMPOWERING INDIGENOUS PEOPLES

The government has attempted some structural change. Recent laws outlaw broadcasting racial remarks in the media and discriminating in civil service hiring. Judges found guilty of bias face a 20-day unpaid suspension. Set up in 2002, the presidential Commission on Discrimination and Racism against Indigenous Peoples (CODISRA) has enlisted Maya, Xinca, and Garífuna representatives to track discrimination claims and advise the state on eliminating prejudice and favoritism in policy making. CODISRA lacks funds, however, as well as enforcement power.[123]

Often at personal risk, Guatemalan activists are working to raise awareness of the peace accords and indigenous rights. Some groups campaign for indigenous access to Maya religious sites—as well as a share of the tourist dollars generated there. Other groups promote the survival of native languages; the Academia de Lenguas Mayas de Guatemala (Guatemalan Academy of Mayan Languages), for instance, offers language training in 15 provinces. The Centro de Actividades Múltiples e Investigación (Center for Multiple Activities and Research), which focuses on documentation and support of culture and popular education in Guatemala, invites Maya to study folkloric music and dance and to learn how to investigate environmental problems. Other NGOs, such as the Centro de Investigación y Educación Popular (Center for Investigations and Popular Education), founded by exiles in Mexico City, organize around labor and human rights issues. The Rigoberta Menchú Tum Foundation has focused on voter turnout in indigenous communities. Sometimes allying poor Maya and Ladinos, peasant groups protest, strike, and even occupy fallow fields to push for land reform, raises in the minimum wage, and an end to the military presence in the countryside.[124]

Many Guatemalans and development specialists see education as the best weapon against inequality. Education reform instigated by the peace accords has improved elementary school enrollment. Particularly successful has been the government's National Program for Community Management of Educational Development (PRONADE), which funds teacher salaries, learning materials, and snacks for communities that want to open their first school and that show much local involvement. As intended, PRONADE reaches the very poor, and its schools report higher attendance and fewer dropouts than other public elementary schools.[125]

Religious groups are also active in education. Recognized in the Guatemalan constitution, the Catholic Church does not have to register as other religions and NGOs do. In the past few decades, however, evangelical Protestant missions have wooed away converts, and presently about 50–60 percent of Guatemalans are thought to be Catholic and 40 percent Protestant, with many indigenous people simultaneously practicing Maya rituals.[126] Churches often draw on their worldwide affiliations and resources to fund projects in Guatemala. Working through the local diocese, for instance, U.S.-based

Catholic Relief Services funds scholarships for 380 destitute girls, offers literacy classes for adults, and sponsors libraries—and vegetable gardens—in schools in the western highlands town of San Marcos.[127] After Hurricane Mitch triggered floods, landslides, and widespread erosion in 1998, a Tennessee Protestant church sent missionaries to Sayaxché in the north, where they helped build a small educational and theological center. Members of the U.S. congregation now sponsor each of the 15 Kekchi students there.[128]

Many other NGOs have also forged international links. Partnering with local teachers and leaders, three former U.S. Peace Corps volunteers launched Sa Q'achool Nimla Kalebal (SANK), Harmony for Our Community. In a Maya Kekchi area, SANK has awarded scholarships to scores of child laborers.[129] In Guatemala, as elsewhere, families may recognize school as a long-term investment but cannot afford the short-term costs of fees, books, and lost income.

SAFEGUARDING MATERNAL AND CHILD HEALTH

Poor, indigenous, and rural Guatemalans—groups that often overlap—suffer poor health. Guatemala has the lowest life expectancy and highest infant mortality rates in Central America. Malnutrition stunts the growth of 44 percent of children under five.[130] Driven into the mountains by Ladino land grabs, the rural poor often lack access to health care and well-stocked facilities. For women, who generally give birth young and average five children, health illiteracy and geographic isolation compound pregnancy risks. In 2000, for every 100,000 births, about 240 women died in Guatemala. In the United States, 17 did, and in Canada, six.[131] The Catholic Church's ban on abortion and artificial contraception complicates family planning in Guatemala. Less controversial are initiatives to improve birth outcomes for mothers and children. Although modernizers initially leaned toward Westernized health-care development, the centralized high-tech and hospital-oriented model did not serve poor Guatemalans well. First of all, many indigenous people live scattered in isolated communities, far from health centers. Secondly, state-of-the-art treatment is expensive—and often overkill in communities where iron supplements to treat anemia and vaccinations to prevent diphtheria could avert much serious illness. Thirdly, many Indians find institutional medicine "cold" and insulting—with public hospitals staffed by Ladino professionals hostile to the herbalists, midwives, and priests patients like to consult alongside doctors.[132]

Since the 1970s, the development community has been discovering that "small is beautiful."[133] With funding from abroad, the Guatemalan Ministry of Health has contracted with NGOs to build simple village clinics and birthing centers right where people need them.[134] More programs are now tapping traditional healers to help deliver health care. Since the vast majority of the poorest women give birth at home, USAID and other donors are underwriting training programs for midwives. They learn to handle minor complications and to recognize problems that require referrals. Most important, they educate patients in their own language and own setting. Since maternal well-being translates into healthier infants, improved prenatal care also strikes a blow at malnutrition. So does support for breastfeeding and hygiene advice to prevent diarrhea. Many international organizations "train the trainers." Save the Children, for example, enlists teen educators to share knowledge about reproduction and mothers to teach about childhood diseases.[135]

Nutrition and health aid intersect. Supporting the Guatemalan government's food security programs, USAID donates pinto beans, black beans, soy-fortified bulgur, rice, and oil for school lunches; NGOs receiving the food sometimes distribute it to families or sell it to pay for other projects. Some assessments have criticized Guatemala's focus on school lunches and emergency feeding because the most serious consequences of malnutrition occur on an ongoing basis in children under two.[136] In Guatemala City, the women's cooperative Better to Live enriches bread and more than 160 meals a day with soy milk byproducts to boost the diet of women and children living in a neighborhood jerry-rigged over a garbage dump.[137] Although beans and bread fill stomachs, what Guatemala children need, according to World Bank researchers, are not piecemeal programs but "an aggressive, integrated approach to malnutrition" that ranges from drinking water to deworming medicine.[138] And many peasants and their advocates argue that land reform would allow the poor to grow their way out of poverty.

Conclusion

Stopping in Guatemala as part of a weeklong Latin American tour in March 2007, U.S. president George W. Bush applauded Guatemalan president Oscar Berger for building "a government that is accountable to all its citizens." While emphasizing U.S. aid for education and health care, including clinics held by U.S. military medical teams, Bush praised the Central American Free Trade Agreement (CAFTA) for helping lift vegetable farmers and other Guatemalans out of hardship.[139] Yet Bush's tour also drew attention to the country's high rate of deep poverty, what the World Bank calls its "remarkably unequal distributions of income, resources and opportunities."[140]

Journalists noted that Guatemala's destitution has fueled emigration of 10 percent of the population to the United States. The February 2007 assassination of visiting Salvadoran politicians by Guatemalan police officers exposed corruption within government and security forces.[141] The country is lagging in several MDGs, especially in reducing maternal mortality and illiteracy.[142] Despite significant aid and higher national income than neighboring Honduras, Guatemala has made far less progress toward safe motherhood, in large part because it is a low political priority.[143] According to Amnesty International, "threats, attacks and intimidation against human rights defenders, in particular those focusing on economic, social and cultural rights, intensified" in Guatemala in 2006.[144] For peace to hold and the country to prosper, government will have to be accountable to the least powerful majority as well as the privileged elite.

INDIA

In our village the women cannot do much.
They do agricultural labor, bring fuel wood
from the jungle, and look after children.
—Indian villager, 1997[145]

Besides such natural resources as coal, gas, diamonds, and farmland, people are the Republic of India's greatest asset—and liability. With a third of its 1.1 billion citizens under age 15 and approaching reproductive age, India will likely overtake China as the world's most populous nation by 2050. Even now Indians make up more than 15 percent of the world's population but occupy a South Asian subcontinent that is only a generous third the size of the United States, just 2.4 percent of the world's land.[146] Although about 70 percent of Indians still live in villages, many rural residents have migrated to urban areas so that Mumbai (Bombay), Delhi, and Kolkata (Calcutta) rank within the top 10 largest cities and urban areas in the world, with Chennai (Madras), Bangalore, Hyderabad, and Ahmadabad also falling within the top 50.[147] A cultural mosaic of 28 states and seven territories, with at least 16 official languages (headed by Hindi and English), India hums with activity and diversity. It has produced some of the world's most innovative thinkers, including Nobel Prize winners Rabindranath Tagore (1861–1941, literature), Subramaniam Chandrasekar (1888–1970, physics), and Amartya Sen (1933– , economics), as well as pioneers in postcolonial scholarship.

As is true elsewhere in South Asia, population multiplies the effect of social and economic developments. Even small changes represent large gains or setbacks because of the number of people involved. In 2001, more than 34 percent of Indians (perhaps 350 to 400 million) were surviving on less than $1 a day, according to one set of UN statistics. But since breaking free of British colonial administration in 1947, India has cultivated a new middle class of roughly equal proportions. Thanks to a large, growing, varied economy, poverty shrank by about a tenth in just the decade around the turn of the millennium.[148] Once synonymous with destitution, India now sits at 128 on the UN HDI, at the low end of the middle tier.

History

Cities on the subcontinent date back to Harappa and Mohenjo-Daro, built by Indus Valley civilizations before 2500 B.C.E. The warlike Indo-European Aryans next moved in, settling in tribal kingdoms, *jana-padas*, that eventually evolved into modern India's ethnolinguistic territories. In a charged debate, historians disagree over the relative input of "outsiders" versus "insiders" in ancient India, but no one disputes that Aryans mixed with local cultures and that eventually their military values took a more spiritual turn.[149] Orally composed and then written in Sanskrit, the Aryans' hymns, the Rig-Veda, formed the basis of Hinduism, India's majority religion. Vedic culture also established a hierarchy symbolically corresponding to the god Brahma's body: priests and teachers made up the Brahmans (mouth); warriors and rulers, Kshatriyas (arms); traders and craftsmen, Vaishyas (thighs); and farmers, laborers, and servants, Shudras (feet). Within these four main categories, occupational groups sorted themselves into a complex ladder of castes. One group, the Dalits, fell beyond the pale and were considered ritually "polluting" and therefore "untouchable."[150]

Many of the lower castes resented Brahman privilege. One Kshatriya, Siddhartha Gautama (c. 560 B.C.E.), broke with his role as a tribal chief's son and preached a new philosophy, a "middle way" of meditation and right conduct, that came to be known as Buddhism. When the Mauryan king Aśoka (died c. 235 B.C.E.) converted to Buddhism at the end of the third century, he sent missionary monks across Asia, but he also set a precedent for tolerating religious pluralism at home. Although Buddhism later diminished in India, it shaded Hindu practice.[151]

Empire succeeded empire in northern India, while many independent kingdoms thrived elsewhere on the subcontinent. Over the centuries, Indian traders cross-pollinated the ancient world. In India, the Maurya gave way to the Gupta, who patronized art, literature, and learning and presided over a prosperous golden age. Building on a long tradition of scholarship in medicine, law, and astronomy, Indian scientists calculated the value of pi, refined the decimal system, and theorized that the world is round.[152]

Arab traders introduced Islam, and Muslim conquerors staked out fiefdoms and even a sultanate in the medieval period. The Turkic invader Babur defeated and conglomerated them into the Mughal Empire, which dominated

Hindu India in the 16th and 17th centuries. As Islam became an important part of India's cultural mosaic, Europeans vied with one another for a share of the subcontinent's profitable trade. In the late 1620s, the British East India Company won permission from the Mughal emperor to build a fortified factory near present-day Mumbai. Growing fabulously rich from triangular trade among India, China, and England, the company undercut Asian and Mediterranean merchants and exploited divisions within the disintegrating empire. Allying itself with the emperor *and* with states both independent of and in revolt with the Mughals, the company demanded concessions and tribute for military defense.[153]

Historians have few kind words for the greedy and double-crossing East India Company. Collecting taxes on behalf of the Mughal emperor, the company plundered Bengal and ignored a catastrophic famine in 1769–70 that killed perhaps a third of the population. With corruption slowly bankrupting the company, it appealed for more support from the British Crown, its quasi-official sponsor. With the help of an army that by the mid-19th century employed about 200,000 sepoys (Indian soldiers), it also annexed more and more territory to stay afloat.[154]

East India Company misrule bred unrest. Across the subcontinent, speculation drove up land prices; squeezed for taxes, peasants borrowed money with their plots as collateral and then lost them when they could not pay back their loans. In 1857, sepoys mutinied and triggered a widespread, bloody rebellion that cinched Britain's decision to replace the East India Company with outright colonial rule.

British colonial rule in India, dubbed the "British Raj," exacerbated poverty. Building railways, roads, and a postal system, Britain asserted it was bringing efficiency and technology ("civilization") to "superstitious" and "backward" people. Yet the British "de-industrialized" the economy. Although India had long produced trade goods and, in fact, influenced the British textile industry with its advanced dyeing techniques, policies suppressed Indian handicrafts, turning artisans into peasants and India into a captive market for British manufacturers.[155] What peasants grew or mined or made depended largely on what British industry demanded. When the Civil War disrupted cotton supplies from the United States, for instance, colonial administrators steered farmers away from food to cotton, a shift that contributed to famine in the 1870s and beyond.[156]

For all of their business-facilitating investment in infrastructure, the British spent relatively little developing human capital. Advances in health care did not reach the masses on the subcontinent: In 1921, the average Indian lived 25 years—in contrast to 55 years for someone in England. More than 3 million people died during the Bengal Famine of 1943–44, when Britain was preoccupied with World War II. Amartya Sen, who as a nine-year-old boy passed cigarette tins of rice to starving beggars, concluded decades later from his economics research that Bengal Province had been producing sufficient food, but prices had risen beyond the means of landless rural laborers. Others have noted that the British prioritized food for soldiers, urban industrial workers, and more strategic parts of the empire. Descending on Kolkata and other provisioned cities, hungry Bengalis culled through garbage, and women sold their bodies and sometimes their children. Even as Britain turned down offers of aid, colonial authorities deported tens of thousands back to the countryside, where they perished out of sight.[157]

The benefits of schooling reached just a fraction of young Indians. Missionaries, administrators, and reformers had varied motives for promoting English-language education, from eliminating Hindu practices such as sati (a widow's suicide by burning on her husband's funeral pyre) to producing a cadre of bureaucrats and spreading Western scientific knowledge. But between 1911 and 1947, the literacy rate grew only from 6 to 11 percent.[158]

In higher education, the British goal of making "them" more like "us" backfired. Forming the backbone of the late 19th- and early 20th-century nationalist movements were Indian lawyers and intellectuals educated abroad, from Muhammad Iqbal (1875–1938) of the Muslim League to Jawaharlal Nehru (1889–1964) of the India Congress Party. At first, many of the elite lobbied only for greater involvement in colonial affairs, but soon leaders were calling for home rule.

Leading the call for the colonizers to leave, Mohandas Gandhi (1869–1948) recognized that the independence movement needed to tap into and empower the country's poorest citizens. In one of his most successful acts of civil disobedience, he led a march to the sea, where he publicly broke colonial law by making salt. This protest against the British monopoly on a substance needed by every Indian—none more so than sweating laborers—spurred thousands to boycott salt, as well as British cloth.[159] Gandhi campaigned for both economic and social reforms within Indian society, from a revival of rural handicrafts (emblemized by spinning thread) to an end to caste prejudice. He called Dalits "Harijans" (children of God). Other leaders also championed the disenfranchised, among them Bhimji Ramji Ambedkar (1891–1956), a lawyer born a Dalit, who campaigned for women's and Dalits' rights.[160]

Since 1945

Although Indians largely united behind the push for national sovereignty, deep divisions within society also surfaced, divisions long fomented by the

British. Despite Congress Party promises of fair treatment for all, lingering Hindu resentment over Mughal rule gave grounds for Muslim fears about losing identity and power as a minority within a Hindu state. In the past, the Hindu elite had benefited from closer relationships with the British; during World War II, however, the Congress Party urged continued noncooperation in the war, while mostly Muslim soldiers served with distinction beside British forces. Urged on by the Muslim League, Britain partitioned the subcontinent, cleaving off a two-pronged Muslim state on the shoulders of India—East and West Pakistan, which later became the separate nations of Pakistan and Bangladesh.[161]

A humanitarian disaster ensued. In the tense year leading up to partition, Hindu-Muslim rioting killed thousands. When Britain announced the exact borders two days after independence, bisecting the northern states of Bengal and Punjab, extremists on both sides of the line began attacking—expurgating—the minority. Caught in the middle of the looting and fighting were Sikhs and other religious groups, and particularly targeted were women, symbol of home and honor. Kidnapped, raped, branded, their breasts cut off, women then faced stigma within their own community. Each assault provoked revenge or flight, with families abandoning everything they could not carry on their backs or in an oxcart. Assailants struck the streams of fragile refugees; one nine-car train heading north to Pakistan arrived with only eight survivors. By the time the violence subsided, more than a million had died and 10 million relocated. Nor did the bloodbath bring an end to communal conflict, for India and Pakistan continued to fight over disputed territory, such as the former princely state of Kashmir, and Hindu and Muslim minorities remained embedded in both nations, with tensions sometimes exploding into violence.[162]

Despite the unleashing of sectarianism, India enshrined in its 1950 constitution an idealistic vision of an inclusive, secular, socialist democracy. Guaranteeing freedom of speech and religion, it outlawed discrimination. Mindful of the poor, the document abolished "untouchability," prohibited bonded labor and human trafficking, outlawed child labor under age 14, and pledged "equal pay for equal work for both men and women." In a socialist vein, the state promised to intervene—"within the limits of its economic capacity and development"—to secure the "right to work, to education, and to public assistance" for the unemployed, the elderly, the sick, the disabled, and others in a state of "undeserved want."[163] Amended many times, the constitution set goals that the republic is still struggling to achieve.

India's first prime minister, Nehru, dominated the political scene between 1947 and his death in 1964. A leader of the nonaligned movement across the developing world, he refused to choose sides during the cold war.

Economically and somewhat politically, India inclined toward the Soviet Union. The central government took a leading role in transportation, telecommunication, and heavy industry such as steel; it also regulated and sometimes financed private-sector initiatives. At the same time, India's constitution, legal structure, and pluralism aligned the country with Western democracies.[164] Much more than the communist bloc, India recognized the limitations of the state. With encouragement and funding, political leaders enlisted voluntary agencies in the monumental task of development. By the end of the 1990s, an estimated million NGOs were operating in India, many of them self-help groups.[165]

Through a series of five-year plans, the central government tackled poverty. It focused first on agriculture, which employed almost three-quarters of all Indians, and then on industry, aiming for self-sufficiency and then production for export. In rural communities, the government ended the zamindari system of tax collecting from large estates, which had encouraged absentee landlordism at the expense of tenant farmers. It also organized *panchayats*, village councils, that involved rural residents in regional agricultural planning, but these benefited wealthier and higher-caste peasants rather than the desperate landless poor.

Inspired by Gandhi, many postindependence reformers formed organizations committed to social justice through a gift (*dan*) of service, labor, or money. Lawyer T. Prakasam (1872–1957) helped create rural reconstruction institutions that promoted adult education, village industries, and water-supply initiatives. Journalist Vinoba Bhave (1895–1982), a deeply spiritual Brahman, walked from village to village preaching nonviolence and wealth sharing. He inspired "haves" to donate land to "have-nots," and although much of it was unfit for farming, his Boodan movement distributed more than a 1.2 million acres.[166]

Food topped priorities. At partition, India had lost most of its jute and cotton-growing areas to West Pakistan, so it had to devote some cereal-growing land to these industrial crops. Food shortages continued into the 1960s; during a mid-decade drought, India had to import 11 percent of its grains.[167] In the late '60s and early '70s the Green Revolution—better seeds, more irrigation, and fertilizers and pesticides—finally boosted India into the black for food, although harvests varied from region to region. With the population ever expanding, however, many of the rural poor migrated to cities searching for opportunity. They survived as best they could, but many ended up squatting on sidewalks and scavenging garbage dumps.

Promising to eliminate poverty in the early 1970s, Prime Minister Indira Gandhi (1917–84), Nehru's only child, nationalized banks, capped personal incomes, and instituted land reform. But her imperial style cost her local support, and increased centralization in decision making enabled corruption among her associates. India's economy also was not growing as robustly as hoped. War—with China (1962) and Pakistan (1965 and 1971, the latter bringing another surge of refugees)—drought, and the international oil crisis contributed to inflation (especially in food prices), government spending cuts, and factory closings. Although the IMF gave India a loan, it demanded more cutbacks and economic liberalization. In response to strikes, protests, and charges of government corruption, Gandhi declared a "state of emergency" in 1975, jailing and censoring her opposition. In those years, her thuggish son Sanjay undertook "urban beautification," razing shacks and slums and sparking riots by the poor.[168]

In the 1980s, politicians began to move away from the secular, socialist vision of India. Elected out and then back into office, Gandhi was assassinated in 1984, as was her son Rajiv while on the campaign trail seven years later. Religious friction and populism were on the rise. Although the government since independence had reserved jobs, scholarships, and political posts for tribes, "scheduled" lower castes, and "other backward classes," many of the disadvantaged wanted an expansion of affirmative action. Dalits staged mass conversions to Islam to protest continued discrimination and began flexing muscle through new political parties. Hindu nationalists, in turn, were organizing to defend "majority rights"; they represented Indians who felt that Muslims and Christians were undermining the Hindu way of life and that government set-asides unfairly penalized upper castes.[169]

In the early '80s, the economy fared better. Some credit early investment in infrastructure, others the Green Revolution, and still others a boom in consumer goods, such as televisions, cassette tape players, and computers. But India still relied heavily on foreign aid, mostly in the form of loans.

Although many have hailed India's capitalist reorientation, for others, a 1984 gas leak at an idle pesticide plant in Bhopal—the largest industrial accident in history—has served as a cautionary tale about globalization. That December a fog of methyl isocyanate rolled over the shantytowns around the factory and into the city, immediately suffocating at least 3,800 people and perhaps as many as 8,000. The gas seared the eyes and lungs of many more and triggered so many cancers and birth defects that India now estimates the death toll at more than 22,000. Much about the disaster remains disputed. The U.S.-based multinational Union Carbide Corporation, the majority stockholder in the plant, responded with millions in aid and in 1989 paid a $470 million legal settlement to the Indian government to cover costs of the disaster and compensation (in the range of $500) to each survivor. But activists charge that Indian officials let the company off too easily because they did not want to frighten away foreign investors. Pointing to contested evidence about lax safety standards at the plant, they have pressed murder charges against the company and its chief executive, but neither has stood trial. Nor have advocates for the ailing Bhopal poor had success in getting Union Carbide's new parent company, Dow Chemical, to take responsibility for long-term medical treatment or groundwater cleanup. Because the victims are Indian slumdwellers and not American suburbanites, advocates charge, the corporation has evaded legal and moral obligations.[170]

In 1990–91, when the Persian Gulf War suddenly interrupted oil supplies it also eliminated the jobs of many Indians who had been working in Gulf States and sending home remittances. India needed to borrow more, but corruption and religious violence rattled foreign confidence in the country. To maintain its credit line, India had to agree to more structural adjustment, solidifying a turn toward a free-market economy.[171] At the beginning of the 21st century, economists were marveling at India's "economic miracle" over the past decade—steady growth, stable prices, and an expanding service sector that now accounts for more than half of the country's GDP. But for all the press about India's high-tech prowess and latte-drinking entrepreneurs—the "Bangalore boom"—prosperity is relative. The Indian middle class is growing, modestly, but it is a minority. About 40 percent of the population cannot read and write, and more than three-quarters still subsist on less than $2 per day.[172]

Survey of Contemporary Problems and Interventions

POPULATION GROWTH AND RURAL POVERTY

Since independence, India's population has soared even though the government has promoted modern contraception. The fertility rate (number of children per woman) has declined by more than 40 percent since the mid-1960s, although that percentage varies tremendously from state to state. But, the death rate has declined, too, thanks to vaccinations and improved medicines. Consequently, more people survived, and for a longer period of time, to reproduce.

Less than half of Indian women use contraception. With couples averaging more than two children, population has grown exponentially—more than 20 percent each decade. The birth rate is highest in rural areas, home to the majority of Indians and the majority of disadvantaged Indians, so population pressures tangle with the conglomeration of other problems contributing to rural poverty.[173]

India's initial population-control programs educated the public about contraception and set specific numeric targets. At government behest, health professionals promoted sterilization as the most fail-safe method, with the result that by the early 1990s, of those married women who used contraception more than two-thirds had been sterilized. Bureaucrats offered incentives ranging from priority for housing to cash, as well as sometimes disincentives for resisting government goals. Critics charged coercion.

During the 1970s "emergency," Indira Gandhi's government rounded up men in poor neighborhoods for forced sterilization. Although short lived, the tactic cast a long shadow of resistance and distrust, with villagers 30 years later rejecting polio vaccines out of fear health workers might be sterilizing children. Also unpopular have been recent disincentives that place poor parents in a bind. Pressured by her mother-in-law and others into a third pregnancy, Vijaykumari Markande lost her affirmative-action seat on an Indian village council in 2004 because of a law barring elected council members from having more than two children.[174] To many, race, caste, or religious prejudice seems to factor into whom the government punishes for not cooperating with population policies.

WOMEN'S EMPOWERMENT

Like many other countries that participated in the UN-sponsored 1994 Cairo Conference on Population and Development, India has shifted its focus from numbers and devices to a more holistic approach to family planning and reproductive health. Many women in India want to space or limit their children but lack the means. They may face pressure from their husbands or extended families to produce sons; they may not have access to providers who offer reversible contraception such as IUDs or birth-control pills; illiterate, they may never have learned about their bodies. Although India has a dedicated Maternal and Child Health service, its reach and quality suffer from lack of funding and staff. Maternal and infant mortality are much higher in villages than in cities, in part because most rural women marry young and have their first baby before they turn 18, and more than half have no trained midwife or doctor attending their deliveries.[175]

Preventing deaths encourages families to have fewer children, giving them confidence that their offspring will survive to adulthood. With funding from UNICEF and the World Bank, India in 1992 launched the Child Survival and Safe Motherhood (CSSM) program in some of its poorest, most populated states: Bihar, Uttar Pradesh, Rajasthan, and Madhya Pradesh. Success has been mixed at best. More children are getting immunized, but although CSSM aimed to bring expectant mothers into the fold of pre- and postnatal primary care, studies revealed that clinics had neither the equipment nor the knowledge to deal with common pregnancy complications.[176]

Benefiting from flexibility, community ties, and fluency in local languages, NGOs have complemented government efforts to train traditional birth attendants in basic hygiene. They also have helped poor women—and girls—understand and advocate for their health needs. Although legislators have long tried to alter Hindu and Muslim custom of marrying off young daughters (building upon the 1929 British Child Marriage Restraint Law, India established 18 as the minimum marriage age for girls), the practice continues, especially in the poor and populous north. Wed to older men at eight or 10 or 12, girls give birth soon after reaching puberty, before their bodies have matured. Many NGOs are working not only to educate adolescents about reproduction but also to raise the "value" of an unwed daughter. The Azad India Foundation, for instance, has been educating adolescent girls in 15 Bihar villages about sexual health. In a district with an 18 percent literacy rate for women, it also runs informal education centers that teach reading and train girls in money-making skills such as candle and detergent making.[177]

MICROCREDIT

Women secure in their knowledge, rights, and worth speak up and are heard in making family-planning decisions. Broad efforts to empower rural women not only contribute to curbing population but also to reducing poverty. Local and international agencies work in India on all seven of the gender-equality priorities set by a UN Millennium Development task force: educational opportunities for women; access to sexual and reproductive health and rights, reducing time burdens, guaranteeing property and inheritance rights, improving income-generating opportunities, improving political participation, and reducing violence against girls and women.[178]

Microcredit ventures have proliferated in India. Some, such as the Activists for Social Alternatives (ASA), closely follow the Grameen Bank model. In an area of the southernmost Indian state of Tamil Nadu where low-caste illiterate laborers toil for large landholders, ASA lends small sums to women. With the money, they buy dairy cows and goats, sewing machines, farm stands, and even land. Meeting weekly with a group, they pay back loans and begin saving. With earnings from their entrepreneurial ventures, they have been able to free their children to go to school. Some borrowers and their husbands have even challenged landlords in court, and almost three dozen women have won election to village councils.[179]

But microcredit operations take many forms. Businesses have partnered with state and international NGO lenders to penetrate the rural market. Hindustan Lever, a subsidiary of the multinational Unilever corporation (maker of Lipton tea and Dove soap, among many other household products), employs village women in door-to-door sales, their loan being the seed money to buy their first round of supplies.[180] Some microfinanciers are introducing high technology to rural banking: To reduce paperwork costs, Swayam Krishi Sangham (SKS) Microfinance is experimenting with issuing borrowers "Smart Cards" with embedded microchips. According to SKS chief executive officer (CEO) Vikram Akula, borrowers increase their income by about 10 percent annually, moving out of poverty within about six years. At the same time, however, he cautions that "microfinance is not a silver bullet."[181] Microfinance skeptics and even fans caution that lenders must tailor programs to communities' unique needs and must incorporate empowerment measures such as literacy classes or health insurance to address poverty on many fronts.[182]

CHILD LABOR

India's 1950 constitution defended the right of children under 14 to study rather than work. It outlawed child labor in factories, mines, and other "hazardous employment" and pledged "free and compulsory" public education within a decade. Yet, good intentions have failed to materialize on a large scale. Quoting the 1991 census, the Indian embassy in Washington, D.C., put the number of working children at 11.28 million. Most are rural, and nine out of 10 worked in a family setting farming, fishing, and learning crafts alongside their parents. Human Rights Watch, on the other hand, estimated in 2003 that 60 to 115 million Indian children worked, mostly raising crops, but also "picking rags, making bricks, polishing gemstones, rolling beedi cigarettes, packaging firecrackers, working as domestics, and weaving silk saris and carpets." Many were bonded laborers (although the constitution prohibits that, too), "virtual slaves" leased out by parents in return for a loan and trapped because they earned so little that they could not pay off the debt. "Poverty is one of the causes of child labor but also one of the consequences," notes a rapporteur for India's National Human Rights Commission (NHRC), "because it is so cheap, it causes adult unemployment and wage suppression."[183]

In its defense, the Indian government notes that India has more children under 14 than the United States has people. India signed the UN Declaration of the Rights of the Child (1959) and the World Declaration on the Survival, Protection and Development of Children (1990) and has set up the National Authority for the Elimination of Child Labor. The capstone of a series of laws, the 1986 Child Labor (Prohibition & Regulation) Act bars employers from hiring children to tan leather, bag cement, dye cloth, or engage in a host of other dangerous jobs, such as peddling snacks near moving trains. It also sets health and safety rules for legal occupations, requiring that children get at least one day off per week and allowing states to set rules for everything from spittoons to explosive or flammable dust. Under 1996 directives from the Supreme Court, officials must remove children from hazardous worksites and use penalties charged to violators to fund special schools. Lawful employers must work children no more than six hours a day and pay for education for at least an additional hour.[184]

Yet, as child advocates point out, many employers openly violate the law while others have found ways to skirt it, sending work home, for instance, or employing very distant relatives in order to qualify as an exempt family business. Inspectors often overlook girls, designated as "helpers" rather than workers or employed as maids in private houses where abuse may range from verbal to sexual. In 2003, Human Rights Watch charged that because of "apathy, caste bias, and corruption," officials often do not enforce labor laws, especially for bonded children, who are usually Dalits.[185]

ENDING ABUSE AND UNIVERSALIZING PRIMARY EDUCATION

Although activists oppose bonding, most do not want to end all forms of child labor—at least not yet. So essential is child labor to the survival of poor families that a blanket ban would only hurt the people it means to help. Some NGOs insist that working children be involved in making decisions about how to address the problem. Most groups campaign for child workers along two tacks: improving grievous conditions and promoting education.[186]

Some expose abuse. International activists often go after multinational corporations, hoping to shame them into hiring adults, paying better wages, and/or improving working conditions. Dutch activists, for instance, have pointed out that British-Dutch Unilever and American multinational Monsanto employ tens of thousands of children in harvesting and processing cotton seed, an ingredient in cooking oil, detergents, and cosmetics. Paid less than half a man's wage and about a third of a woman's wage, children aged six to 14 work 12-hour days, exposed to pesticides, and sleep in migrant camps.[187] Many Indian NGOs pressure officials to enforce laws on the books.

Other groups feel they serve children better with less antagonistic tactics. Both bonded labor and sari weaving are illegal, for instance, but sometimes activists simply use scarce funds to help families pay off debts and free children from crippling years at the loom. In cities, activists for Pratham have had to win the trust of employers in order to get to know the needs and dreams of working children.[188]

For long-term as well as short-term benefits to the poor, education holds the most promise. As the Indian government boasts, all states have lifted school fees through the upper primary grades. But children often work during school hours, and once they have missed the early grades, they cannot step easily into a classroom. Working families—garbage sorters, rock quarriers, peddlers, beggars—often move. With grant funding from the government, many organizations "rehabilitate" children pulled out of dangerous worksites and run welfare projects for those employed legally. They offer meals, health care, job training, and summer and after-hours classes. Meeting kids at or near their work, sometimes on sidewalks, sometimes at train stations, Pratham staffers first befriend children through "hobby" classes, such as play or crafts, and then draw them into small study sessions that eventually lead to their mainstreaming into public schools.[189] Reformers ranging from foreign missionaries to native-born philanthropists have also opened private schools. At Shanti Bavan, a boarding school outside Bangalore, Dalit children often encounter pencils and toilets for the first time. "[At first] we don't make them sleep on beds because it is a culture shock," says principal Lalita Law. "Our goal is to give them a world-class education so they can aspire to careers and professions that would have been totally beyond their reach."[190]

Conclusion

India has become the poster child for globalization's benefits. Since the early 1990s, the economy has grown robustly—more than 8 percent a year from 2002 to 2006. Since the government loosened its hold on business, competition from multinational corporations has not shut down local industries but rather spurred manufacturing for both the national and international market. Although the top 20 percent of the population has benefited the most from the boom, prosperity and self-confidence have trickled down.[191] Not only do officials have more money to invest in physical capital such as roads and rural electrification, but development specialists and social investors are fanning entrepreneurship among the poor.[192] By the Indian government's calorie-only measure, poverty shrank from 26.1 percent of the population in 1999–2000 to an estimated 21.8 percent in 2004–05.[193]

Still, one in five Indians cannot afford enough to eat. Ill-being assessed by everything from corruption to HIV infection rates to lack of schooling remains high, particularly in rural areas and particularly in left-behind states such as Bihar and Uttar Pradesh. Until reduction in human misery outpaces growth, many observers feel it is too soon for trade liberalizers to crow about India's economic "miracle."[194]

DEMOCRATIC REPUBLIC OF THE CONGO

I voluntarily entered the army because I came to
the conclusion that my family was suffering too much.
There was no more food or clothes.
They lost everything. . . . I was fifteen. . . .

Global Perspectives

I was a combatant and going to the battlefield.
We had many children but only four girls in our small group.
One night, two of the commander's men
came to get me and bring me to him.
Since he was the commander, I had to obey.
I went and lived together with him.
I felt that I was raped.
—demobilized Congolese soldier, 2005[195]

The fabulous mineral wealth of the Democratic Republic of the Congo (DRC), known from 1971 to 1997 as Zaire, contrasts with devastating poverty. The third largest country in Africa and the size of western Europe, the DRC straddles the equator, a riverine basin bordered by highlands. Trees cover more than three-quarters of the country, dense rain forests of mahogany, ebony, teak, and other tropical hardwoods to the north and northeast that merge into savannas to the south and southeast. In addition to timber and the potential for hydroelectric power from the massive Congo River, the DRC's natural resources extend into deep deposits of copper, cobalt, zinc, cadmium, tin, uranium, diamonds, gold, silver, and oil. Yet, these riches have not brought well-being to the Congolese, a fusion of more than 200 ethnic groups, 80 percent of whom live on less than 20¢ per day.[196] In addition, the DRC owes $12 billion to foreign lenders, although under the IMF and World Bank's 1996 Heavily Indebted Poor Countries (HIPC) Initiative, they have promised to forgive 80 percent of the debt if the country reforms its economy.[197]

From the colonial period through independence, rapacious rulers enriched the few at the expense of the many. In the decade since 1997, civil conflicts have killed up to 4 million Congolese, most of whom died from hunger and disease. Fighting has displaced another 2–4 million. Although estimates of per-capita income vary widely, in most rankings the DRC falls below its many impoverished neighbors, including Zambia and Angola to the south, Tanzania and Rwanda to the east, Sudan and the Central African Republic to the north, and the smaller Republic of the Congo to the west. Because of the near collapse of the state, statistics are approximations at best but reveal declining quality of life. As in much of sub-Saharan Africa, infant and maternal mortality and food insecurity run high. AIDS has piggybacked on malaria and tuberculosis, contributing to a downturn in life expectancy, which hovers around 50 years. More than 40 percent of the population has no schooling, while less than 1 percent has reached university level. On the 2007/2008 UN HDI, the DRC ranked an abysmal 168.[198]

History

More than 10,000 years ago, Stone Age hunter-gatherers crisscrossed the Congo River basin. Around 1000 B.C.E., Bantu speakers began migrating into the region, cultivating yams and oil palms and eventually developing iron tools. From the northeast came speakers of Sudanese languages who introduced cattle herding and new grains. Other migrants brought bananas and other tropical fruits.[199] To this day, the majority of Congolese farm for their living without tractors or fertilizers, raise goats, sheep, and pigs, and use traditional techniques of slashing and burning and leaving fields fallow. As groups intermingled, the small-statured first peoples—later known to the West as pygmies and locally as Bitwa or Twa—were driven into the northern jungle, where they continue to live communally by hunting, fishing, and gathering honey, roots, and nuts.[200]

In the north, in and along the dense rain forests, clans organized into villages, sometimes merging into chiefdoms, but they remained segmented and loosely organized. To the south, centralized states emerged, usually ruled by a king claiming divine authority. They absorbed neighboring communities and oversaw trade developing with Arabs, whose networks extended across the Mediterranean and into Asia. Crossing deserts, camel caravans brought Indian silk, Chinese ceramics, European beads, and Saharan salt to central Africa to exchange for ivory, slaves, ebony, gold, carvings, cloth, copper, steel, gum, and spices. Europeans wanted a piece of this lucrative action, and in 1482, Portuguese explorer Diogo Cão (c. 1450–86) sailed from the Atlantic coast up the Congo River and planted a stone cross in the name of Portugal and Christianity.[201]

The Portuguese encountered the Kongo, a well-organized Bantu kingdom. A high priest who bridged the worlds of the living and the dead, the king ruled with his nobles from a central palace in Mbanza Kongo, later São Salvador in Angola. Able to muster an army of 80,000, the king collected taxes and tribute through provincial governors, also responsible for services such as road maintenance and courts of appeal.[202]

Within a decade, the Portuguese sent a missionary expedition that included priests, soldiers, peasants, craftsmen, and women. They soon converted the aristocracy to Catholicism, driving a wedge between court and commoners. After they helped Afonso I (reigned 1506–43) assume power, he established diplomatic relations with Portugal, declared Catholicism the state religion, and welcomed Portuguese missionaries and merchants. But the Portuguese tried to isolate the Kongo from contact with other Europeans and upset the balance of the local economy. Although the kingdom had long traded slaves, usually war captives, many had remained locally as servants and advisers. With fortunes to be made shipping slaves across the Atlantic to New World plantations (especially the Portuguese colony of Brazil), the Portuguese paid Africans to capture and sell their neighbors. Also divisive were competing missionaries, some of whom bound followers to the fields, growing fruit, tobacco, sugarcane, and other cash crops. Rival European and Arab traders armed their allies and their slavers, sparking civil wars. By the 17th century, slavers were exporting up to 15,000 people a year, depopulating the region.[203]

Even as the Kongo disintegrated, vast inland kingdoms flourished. In the southeast grasslands, the Songye Luba empire spawned the Lunda, a more militaristic state also known for producing fine metalwork and incorporating foreign chiefs into its political hierarchy. The Kuba kingdom prospered from iron production and adaptations of New World crops such as beans, corn, tobacco, and cassava (manioc), which became the Congolese staple. But the competitive international slave and ivory trade undermined Luba and Lunda stability. With the Industrial Revolution, demand shifted in the early 19th century from slaves to raw materials, including peanuts, wood, palm oil, ivory, and rubber. Since growing and collecting these cash crops was labor intensive, subsistence farming suffered. So, too, did local industries as traders sold European-made cloth, weapons, and other manufactured goods.[204]

Belgian king Leopold II (r. 1865–1909), whose ambitions far outsized his tiny kingdom, enlisted Congo explorer Henry Stanley (1841–1904) to quietly cobble together a "confederation of free negro republics." He did so by conning mostly illiterate chiefs into signing away land rights. Then, at a 1884 conference in Berlin that included not a single African's participation, contending European nations divided up the "dark continent." Cunning Leopold claimed for himself a colony of more than a million square miles, which he named the Congo Free State—a darkly ironic choice given the terror he catalyzed over the next two decades.[205]

While the Berlin Act bound Leopold to allow free access to European merchants and missionaries, he set about expropriating "vacant" land. His private monopoly extracted resources—first mostly ivory for piano keys, billiard balls, and the like (until hunters had killed most of the elephants) and then rubber, which quadrupled in price on the world market between the 1880s and 1910s to satisfy Western demand for bicycle and car tires. Leopold forbade Congolese from selling to any traders (Arab, African, or European) other than the state and its concessionary companies. Then he "taxed" villages for laborers, who had to penetrate deeper and deeper into the rain forest to gather rubber sap from vines while their fields lay unattended. As food supplies dwindled, hunger and disease spread. When men balked at rubber duty, field supervisors backed by the Force Publique—foreign African troops armed and commanded by Europeans—seized chiefs, wives, and children as hostages, usually gang-raping the women. Crew leaders and soldiers, many of them children "recruited" by raids, had license to burn villages and shoot resisters or workers who failed to meet "quota." To prove they were not wasting bullets, they cut off hands from the dead—and the living—sometimes smoking them to preserve them for counting.[206]

A few horrified witnesses, mostly Protestant missionaries, began to leak word of atrocities to the West, where calls mounted to replace Leopold. In 1908, the Belgian government took over the Congo, but trauma long survived the Congo Free State. From 5 to 8 million Congolese died under Leopold's rule, which established patterns of violence that afflict the Congo region to this day: forced labor, rape, capricious shooting by child soldiers, death and maiming by hacking, and genocide.[207]

In a more benevolent guise, from 1908 Belgian colonials continued to milk Congo for its riches, shifting from rubber to copper, diamonds, and other minerals. Coercing Africans to mine and plant for large companies and build roads and railways for the state, colonial employers offered some welfare benefits in return, such as housing and health care. As they encouraged villagers to bring along their families, work camps evolved into multiethnic towns and cities, sites of fusion and confusion, assimilation and resistance. Like other Europeans in Africa, Belgians proclaimed their civilizing mission, with an emphasis on order. They replaced local chiefs with cooperative appointees and disciplined their Congolese "children" with curfews and bans on palm wine. Although Catholic and Protestant missionaries opened schools, the Belgians strictly limited higher education, political expression, and contact beyond the colony.[208]

Since 1945

World War II helped end Congo's isolation. To the Allied cause, the country contributed essential raw materials (such as uranium for the first atom bomb) and troops, who returned home stirred by European vulnerability, contact with nationalists from other African colonies, and the battle against Hitler's racism. Under pressure both in the colony and from abroad, Belgians loosened their grip, allowing Africans to own land, use European courts, and buy alcohol. Although political parties remained outlawed, French-speaking Congolese, the *évolué*, harnessed discontent with the colonial regime through ethnic cultural associations.

As colonies across Asia and Africa expelled their war-depleted European masters, the Belgians began speaking of gradual withdrawal. Congolese insistence coupled with 1959 riots in Leopoldville accelerated the timetable, and in 1960, the Democratic Republic of the Congo declared its independence, electing Joseph Kasavubu (c. 1913–69) as president and accountant Patrice Lumumba as prime minister (1925–61).[209]

Although the Belgians had intended to stay on "supervising," an army mutiny and other violence prompted white flight, including financial and human capital, such as government administrators. The Belgians had done almost nothing to prepare the Congo for self-rule. At independence, less than three dozen Congolese had graduated from universities at home or abroad, and they included not a single lawyer, doctor, judge, or engineer. Civil war erupted, with the wealthy copper-producing province of Katanga seceding, and Western powers intervened to protect their mining interests, distrusting Lumumba's ardent nationalism and accusing him of communist leanings. After Lumumba's assassination in 1961, onetime journalist Joseph-Désiré Mobutu (1930–97) seized power in a CIA-backed coup and ruled until 1997.[210]

On the surface, Mobutu championed African identity. Calling for "authenticity," he argued that the DRC should return to its precolonial roots and denounced Christianity. He rechristened the country *Zaire* (big river); the capital Leopoldville, Kinshasa; and himself, Mobutu Sese Seko Kuku Ngbendu wa za Banga, "the all-powerful warrior who, because of his endurance and inflexible will to win, will go from conquest to conquest leaving fire in his wake." But his Africanization ignored two realities: Paternal chiefs of yore had ruled and dispensed justice with the consent of the village, and Congolese society had fused many different belief systems—including Catholicism (about 50 percent of the population), Protestantism (20 percent), and Islam (10 percent)—with traditional beliefs. When he nationalized colonial companies, from mines and plantations to small shops, he distributed them not to needy Congolese but to his small cohort, most members of which lacked business skills.

In his "kleptocracy," literally "rule by thieves," corruption ran rampant. Living lavishly, Mobutu siphoned off about $5 billion of the country's wealth; he licensed regional warlords and gagged opposition with soldiers and police so brutal that observers likened him to a second Leopold. Yet, fearing a coup, he underpaid and undermined the regular army, thugs who also preyed on the citizenry. In the 1970s, falling world copper prices dealt Zaire's economy a blow from which it never recovered. The country fell behind on debt payments and, nearly bankrupt, resisted IMF pressure for structural adjustment in the 1980s.

As elsewhere across Africa, the United States had led other Western powers in backing the abusive strongman in the name of stability and anti-communism. But once it had gained the upper hand in the cold war, the

West tempered its support for Mobutu. In 1990, the U.S. Congress cut off military and economic aid.[211]

The 1990s brought painful transition. So frustrated were unpaid soldiers and impoverished civilians that they rampaged through the capital and elsewhere in 1991 and 1993, burning buses and factories, looting stores and mines, and breaking into elite homes—a destructive pillage that further set back the country. Dissidents finally forced Mobutu to allow elections in the 1990s, but confusion reigned as the entrenched regime resisted democracy. In eastern Zaire, Hutu refugees poured over the border in the wake of the 1994 Rwandan genocide, adding to ethnic tensions. Backed by Rwanda, Uganda, and Angola, rebels led by Laurent-Désiré Kabila (c. 1939–2001) fought their way to Kinshasa and drove Mobutu into exile.[212]

Kabila renamed Zaire the Democratic Republic of the Congo. Initial hopes for change soon dissolved as Kabila took up where Mobutu left off, installing cronies, silencing opposition, and pilfering national resources. He also alienated his foreign backers. Civil war broke out, compounded by meddling from neighboring countries. While Zimbabwe, Angola, and Namibia supported Kabila, Rwanda, Uganda, and Burundi joined rebels against the government. Caught in the middle again were the Congolese poor.

After Kabila's assassination in 2001, his son Joseph Kabila (1971–) assumed the presidency. In contrast to his father, the young Kabila seriously pursued peace talks, and in 2002, parties to the conflict met in Pretoria, South Africa, and agreed to form a representative government in the DRC. Multiparty democratic elections in 2006—the first in more than four decades—inspired hope that better governance might begin to lead the Congo out of desolation.[213]

Survey of Contemporary Problems and Interventions

CIVIL CONFLICT

Some scholars have blamed the 1998 Congo war—sometimes called "Africa's World War I"—on greedy rebels and a collapsing state. Others point out that civil conflicts both predated Kabila's reign and have continued beyond the Pretoria Accords, continuing to cause around 30,000 deaths a month. This deep-rooted and complex ethnic strife snakes from the colonial through the postcolonial era. Whether European or African, a small, profiteering elite bought loyalty by awarding land and privileges to select leaders and their cultural communities. This sowed discord that prevented united opposition.

Even the favored rarely felt secure, for autocrats guarded their power by changing allegiances when it suited their ambitions. In a complex twister of political winds, for instance, Mobutu stripped the Banyamulenge of citizenship in 1981. These relatively prosperous—and therefore resented- -ranchers and businesspeople, traced their ancestry to Tutsi cattle herders who became "Congolese" more than a century ago when colonial powers divvied up Africa on the map. Yet, the Mobutu regime cast them as outsiders and scapegoats. When the Rwandan Hutu-Tutsi feud spilled over the eastern border in the 1990s, it drew in the Banyamulenge.[214]

"When the elephants fight, the grass dies," observes a popular African proverb. The death rate in the DRC during the war ran 40 percent higher than in the rest of sub-Saharan Africa, already the world leader in mortality. About half of the almost 4 million deaths resulted not from violence but from poverty-related causes, such as malnutrition and diarrhea, with 65 percent of the casualties being children. War further demolished the DRC's dysfunctional economy. Military spending diverted funds from schools and health clinics, which stopped operating altogether in rebel-controlled areas. Fighting disrupted transportation, especially along the essential Congo River, cutting off trade and isolating businesses from both suppliers and markets. Fearing rape, murder, assault, and looting, many villagers did not dare travel to their fields, so the DRC ran short of food. Many farmers switched from raising goats to guinea pigs, which they could carry with them when they had to escape. Of course mining and logging—the big moneymakers—continued, drawing more workers off the land, but the race to extract as much as possible before the land fell into the hands of the next militia aggravated environmental destruction.[215]

AID TO CIVILIAN SURVIVORS

Groups from around the world have rushed emergency humanitarian aid to the millions of Congolese hiding in forests or gathering in formal and informal IDP (internally displaced person) camps. UNICEF, the UN World Food Program, the Red Cross, and many NGOs have distributed salt, water, high-protein biscuits, measles vaccines, mats, soap, buckets, plastic sheeting, hoes, kitchen utensils, and so on, but dirt roads, when there are roads at all, complicate delivery. Cholera outbreaks raise fears of epidemics within crowded camps. Security remains dicey for civilians and aid workers alike, despite the presence of 17,000 UN peacekeeping troops.[216]

Development specialists also note that despite its horrific death toll, the Congo civil war has attracted less media attention than other disasters, such as the tsunami that washed over Indonesia, Thailand, and other parts of South Asia in December 2004. As in the past, most of the world knows little of Congolese suffering. "Aid goes where the TV cameras are," notes Richard Brennan, health director of the International Rescue Committee, as evidenced in the $136 per person for tsunami relief versus $3.60 to the DRC.[217]

Some on the scene worry that urgent crises draw this limited aid toward welfare, such as providing food and materials to recently displaced groups, rather than human capital, such as improving health care and education.[218] For the long term, the DRC must rebuild. While the IMF works with the government on stabilizing the macroeconomy, the World Bank is funding scores of reconstruction projects—from fishing to law, energy to education. As refugees and demobilized soldiers return to razed or abandoned villages, poverty aggravates lingering tensions. Church groups such as the United Methodist Committee on Relief (UMCOR), funded by deep pockets such as USAID, are encouraging displaced families to start anew with gifts of seeds, tools, bicycles, wheelbarrows, fishing nets, lanterns, and small boats. To prevent hunger crises, they are building food storage bins and training villagers to run maize and sunflower-seed mills.[219] Although the world community has learned that development works best when initiated from within rather than imposed from without, the DRC lacks so many basics that foreigners are very actively intervening. The hope is that widespread health, literacy, and more efficient, democratic governance will empower Congolese to act on their own behalf.

PEACEKEEPING

In the region's healing, however, African leadership is essential. Scholars fear that the tenuous peace in the DRC will not last unless reconstruction also addresses social justice—past human rights abuses and the who-controls-what of land, resources, and political power. Various UN agencies are involved in the "disarmament, demobilization, and reintegration" of fighters from the DRC and surrounding countries, but they lack authority. In the DRC, disarmament is supposed to be voluntary, but when one group complies and another does not, conflict rekindles. Given the DRC's extensive borders and experienced smugglers, international monitors also have difficulty enforcing an arms embargo.[220]

At the local level, combatants and families of those killed or raped must somehow knit themselves back together into a functioning community. As part of the peace accords leading to the transition to democratic government, rebel groups demanded amnesty for all offenses, but many Congolese feel that the DRC cannot move forward until it confronts its past. From Sierra Leone to Ghana to Rwanda, other African countries have experimented with public forums to air pain and guilt. Most celebrated has been South Africa's Truth and Reconciliation Commission, founded on the Christian principle of forgiveness and the Xhosa concept of *ubuntu*, the oneness of humanity. In theory, as victims testified and human-rights abusers confessed, the latter's repentance would lead to the former's forgiveness, and truth would bring about nationwide reconciliation. In the DRC, difficult questions remain about whom to punish and whom to pardon—and how, in order to prevent an escalating cycle of revenge and retribution.[221]

HIV/AIDS

HIV, the virus that causes AIDS, likely crossed from chimpanzees to humans in central Africa, perhaps in the DRC. A blood sample reveals the presence of HIV in the DRC in 1959, and researchers have traced the strain behind the current AIDS pandemic back to Kinshasa, which registered its first HIV case in 1983. Despite this early start, the prevalence of HIV infection in the DRC falls only in the mid-range of sub-Saharan African countries. HIV/AIDS is nonetheless spreading and has had a similarly devastating effect in the DRC as elsewhere on the continent. The past decade's turmoil has made statistics educated guesstimates, but likely more than 1 million and perhaps more than 2.5 million Congolese are living with the disease, which kills about 100,000 adults and children a year.[222]

War accelerated HIV infection in the DRC. With rape a common weapon in a campaign of terror and humiliation, foreign and indigenous troops transmitted the virus—mostly to women, but also to men and children. As a result, HIV infection in the eastern provinces is running at more than 20 percent, and nationwide, young women with the virus outnumber young men three to one. Often injured, often disowned by husbands and families, rape survivors bear a double burden of stigma when living with HIV. Conflict abetted the epidemic in other ways, too. On the move, soldiers spread the disease among sex workers. They destroyed clinics and sterile supplies, making injections and blood transfusions, when available, much riskier. War interrupted HIV education and prevention, from testing to condom giveaways. As the DRC's public health system collapsed, malaria, tuberculosis, diarrhea, and malnutrition so weakened immune systems that HIV met little resistance.

The destruction of the economy has left the Congolese with almost nothing to spend on treatment for AIDS and its associated illnesses—a problem throughout Africa but especially acute in the DRC. Less than 3 percent of Congolese with HIV receive antiretroviral (ARV) combination therapy, the most effective drug "cocktail" for full-blown AIDS, versus 19 percent of Kenyans. ARV treatment costs $30–$40 per month—about 10 times the $3.60 the DRC spends per year for each person with HIV/AIDS.[223]

Without ARV drugs, AIDS is a death sentence, but few Congolese can afford them. Some get conned into buying sham drugs on the black market. At the end of the 20th century, most countries wrote off the HIV infected:

With so many pressing needs, expensive and complex drug therapy seemed an "inefficient" use of scarce antipoverty resources. But the loss of people and their "human capital" in Africa prompted many to rethink that assessment. In the DRC alone, fields lie uncultivated as women die, and at least 680,000 children are growing up without parents because of AIDS. NGOs like Médecins Sans Frontières (Doctors Without Borders) demonstrated in small field trials that even the least educated can manage and benefit from a multifaceted drug-and-wellness regimen—as long as they can afford regular doses. Activists have pressured pharmaceutical companies to provide discounted drugs and to speed cheaper generics on the market. With a $102 million World Bank loan, the DRC has promised to make ARV drugs available to 25,000 citizens by 2009.[224]

International donors are also funding both prevention and treatment. The U.S. President's Emergency Fund for AIDS Relief, for instance, enlisted 14 Congolese musicians to write songs for an AIDS education CD, *ABCD—Rien Que la Vérité* (Nothing but the Truth). Given out to bus drivers, cabbies, truckers, and clients at mobile counseling centers, it sings up the virtues of abstinence, sexual fidelity, AIDS testing, and condom use.[225] Proposed by the UN secretary general, Kofi Annan, in 2002, the public-private Global Fund to Fight AIDS, Tuberculosis and Malaria gives grants to agencies and governments for health initiatives: Of the more than $6 billion committed to date, $34 million has headed to the DRC. Among the beneficiaries have been Congolese NGOs such as Foundation Femme Plus and Amocongo, which assists AIDS orphans and their caregivers.[226] Partnering with local agencies, the U.S.-based Doctors on Call for Service (DOCS) runs a private hospital in Goma for sexual violence survivors, including those with HIV, but such comprehensive programs are rare because of lack of funds and infrastructure.[227] Still, they give people hope, a key asset for Congo or any undeveloped nation striving against poverty.

Conclusion

Small outposts of comfort and relief contrast with widespread insecurity in the DRC. Fighting in the capital in March 2007 prompted foreign governments such as the United States to warn away travelers and evacuate nonessential diplomatic personnel. In May, clashes between Congolese government forces and Rwandan rebels in eastern South Kivu Province displaced more than 6,000 civilians, who fled on foot. Days later, rebels killed 17 villagers in their beds; a UN military patrol found about a dozen more bodies in the forest.[228] Even as UN troops continued to disarm local militias and integrate fighters into the national army, investigators looked into charges that the peacekeepers themselves were trafficking arms and gold.[229] On the economic front, prices were rising in 2007 as the value of the currency was falling, leading IMF officials to underscore "the urgency of taking measures to strengthen macroeconomic stability."[230]

At the same time, then World Bank president Paul Wolfowitz and his EU counterpart urged swift and dramatic help from the international community, with the bank promising about $1.4 billion in grants and loans over three years.[231] To convince Congolese to support their fragile democracy, the UNDP planned to invest $200 million over five years to improve governance, from the integrity of local elections to the delivery of public services.[232] Once war- and poverty-weary Congolese see a peace dividend, the theory goes, militias will lay down their weapons, and citizens will rally to rebuild their country. "No matter how long the night," notes one Congolese proverb, "the day is sure to come."

---

[1] United Nations Development Programme. Human Development Reports. Available online. URL: http://hdr.undp.org/. Downloaded May 18, 2007.

[2] UN Development Programme. Human Development Report 2005, pp. 1–7. Available online. URL: http://hdr.undp.org/reports/global/2005/pdf/HDR05_overview.pdf. Downloaded May 18, 2007.

[3] UNDP. Human Development Report 2005, p. 8.

[4] Organisation for Economic Co-operation and Development. "OECD Review of United States Development Assistance Programmes." Available online. URL: http://www.oecd.org/document/27/0,2340,en_33873108_33873886_37838171_1_1_1_1,00.html. Downloaded May 18, 2007.

[5] UNDP. Human Development Report 2005, p. 8.

[6] Quoted in Narayan, I. *Voices of the Poor: Can Anyone Hear Us.* New York: Oxford University Press for the World Bank, 2000, p. 61. Available online. URL: http: www.worldbank.org/prem/poverty/voices/reports/crying/cry.pdf. Downloaded May 11, 2007.

[7] United Nations Development Programme. "Human Development Index." Human Development Report 2007/2008. Available online. URL: http://hdrstats.undp.org/indicators/1.html. Downloaded January 28, 2008.

[8] UNDP. "Regional Fact Sheet: HRD 2005 Central and Eastern Europe and the CIS." Available online. URL: http://www.undp.bg/uploads/documents/1196_636_en.pdf. Downloaded August 10, 2007.

[9] Central Intelligence Agency. "Ukraine." CIA Factbook. Available online. URL: http//www.cia.gov/cia/publications/factbook/print/up.html. Downloaded May 11, 2007.

[10] Dana Dalrymple. "The Great Famine in Ukraine 1932–33." *Soviet Studies* (January 1964). Reprinted in *Ukraine Weekly.* Available online. URL: http://www.ukrweekly.com/Archive/1983/128312.shtml. Downloaded May 11, 2007.

[11] Yaroslav Lukov. "Ukraine Marks Great Famine Anniversary." BBC News (November 22, 2003). Available online. URL: http://news.bbc.co.uk/1/hi/world/Europe/3229000.stm. Downloaded May 11, 2007.

[12] Andrew Gregorovich. "World War II in Ukraine." Available online. URL: http://www.infoukes.com/history/ww2/. Downloaded May 11, 2007.

[13] "New Rich, New Poor: Wealth and Morality in Ukraine." Summary of talk by Catherine Wanner. Woodrow Wilson International Center for Scholars Web site. February 23, 2004. Available online. URL: http://www.wilsoncenter.org/index.cfm?fuseaction=events.event_summary&event_id=54218. Downloaded May 17, 2007.

[14] Chernobyl.info. "Geographical information and extent of radioactive contamination." Chernobyl.info Web site. Available online. URL: http://www.chernobyl.info/index.php?userhash=25090654&navID=2&lID=2. Downloaded August 10, 2007; Richard Rhodes. *Nuclear Renewal.* New York: Penguin Books, 1993. Available online. URL: http://www.pbs.org/wgbh/pages/frontline/shows/reaction/readings/chernobyl.html. Downloaded August 10, 2007.

[15] Chernobyl.info. "Managing the distaster." Chernobyl.info Web site. Available online. URL: http://www.chernobyl.info/index.php?userhash=17756386&navID=37&lID=2. Downloaded August 10, 2007.

[16] "Ukrainian Government Yields to Students' Demands." *Nonviolent Sanctions,* vol. 2, no. 3 (Winter 1990–91). Albert Einstein Institute Web site. Available online. URL: http://www.aeinstein.org/organizations5929.html. Downloaded August 10, 2007.

[17] UNESCO Institute for Statistics. "Education in Ukraine." UIS Web site. URL: http://www.uis.unesco.org/profiles/EN/EDU/countryProfile_en.aspx?code=8070. Updated June 2006.

[18] Albert Berry and Karin Schelzig. "Economic Collapse, Poverty, and Inequality during Ukraine's Difficult Transition." Report by Development Alternatives, Inc., for USAID (January 2005), pp. 11–13. Available online. URL: http://www.povertyfrontiers.org/ev_en.php?ID=1528_201&ID2=DO_TOPIC. Downloaded May 18, 2007. U.S. Department of Agriculture. "Ukraine: Agricultural Overview." Available online. URL: http://www.fas.usda.gov/pecad/highlights/2004/12/Ukraine%20Ag%20Overview/index.htm. Updated October 21, 2005.

[19] Oleksiy Kryvtsov. "Hyperinflation in Ukraine, 1993–1994." Available online. URL: http://www.econ.umn.edu/~oksana/1102H/Guest%20Lectures/Hyperinflation%20in%20Ukraine%20_slides_.pdf. Downloaded April 16, 2007.

[20] Berry and Schelzig. "Economic Collapse, Poverty, and Inequality during Ukraine's Difficult Transition," pp. 14–15.

[21] Berry and Schelzig. "Economic Collapse," p. 15.

[22] Berry and Schelzig. "Economic Collapse," p. 25.

[23] Ministry of Economy and European Integration of Ukraine. "Millennium Development Goals—Ukraine," p. 8. Available online. URL: http://www.undp.org.ua/download.php?id=1108721530&cm=doc&fn—dg_ukraine_2003_eng.pdf&l=e. Downloaded May 18, 2007. "New Rich, New Poor." Summary of talk by Wanner.

[24] Yaro Bihun. "Ukrainian activist honored in D.C. for anti-trafficking efforts." *Ukrainian Weekly* 70, no. 21 (May 26, 2002). Available online. URL: http://www.ukrweekly.com/Archive/2002/210204.shtml. Downloaded May 11, 2007.

[25] United Nations Children's Fund. "Poverty in Ukraine Leads to Abandoned Babies." Available online. URL: http://www.unicef.org/infobycountry/ukraine_25468.html. Downloaded May 11, 2007.

[26] Berry and Schelzig. "Economic Collapse," p. 35.

[27] JDC-Brookdale Institute. "The Social and Economic Situation in Countries of the FSU: Case Studies of Ukraine, Russia & Moldova. Highlights of the International Literature and Source Documents," p. 8. August 20, 2003. Available online. URL: http://www.claimscon.org/forms/allocations/The%20Social%20and_FSU%20JDC_.pdf. Downloaded August 9, 2007.

[28] Adrian Karatnycky. "Ukraine's Orange Revolution." *Foreign Affairs* (March–April 2005). Available online. URL: http://www.foreignaffairs.org/20050301faessay84205/adrian-karatnycky/ukraine-s-orange-revolution.html. Downloaded May 11, 2007.

[29] Berry and Schelzig. "Economic Collapse," p. 41.

[30] Berry and Schelzig. "Economic Collapse," p. 42.

[31] Simon Clarke. "Poverty in Ukraine." Available online. URL: http://www.warwick.ac.uk/fac/soc/complabstuds/russia/Poverty_Ukraine.doc. Downloaded August 9, 2007; UNDP, Government of Ukraine, International Labour Organization. "Measuring Poverty: Development of Socio-economic Security Indicators in Ukraine." Available online as project document 2005. URL: http://www.undg.org/unct.cfm?module=JointProgramme&page=JointProgrammeView&CountryID=Ukr&&JointProgrammeID=138&. Downloaded August 9, 2007.

[32] Edmundo Murrugarra. "Ukraine Poverty Assessment." World Bank. December 2005. Available online. URL: http://web.worldbank.org/WBSITE/EXTERNAL/COUNTRIES/ECAEXT/UKRAINEEXTN/0,,contentMDK:20810635~pagePK:141137~piPK:141127~theSitePK:328533,00.html. Downloaded May 11, 2007.

[33] Ministry of Economy and European Integration of Ukraine. "Millennium Development Goals—Ukraine," p. 6.

[34] Berry and Schelzig. "Economic Collapse," pp. 45–61.

[35] USAID. "Small Farmers Sell to Supermarkets," USAID Web site. Available online. URL: http://www.usaid.gov/stories/ukraine/fp_ua_farmer.html. Downloaded August 9, 2007; USAID, "Creating Energy Solutions for Ukraine's Industry," USAID Web site. Available online. URL: http://www.usaid.gov/stories/ukraine/ss_ukraine_energyefficiency.html. Downloaded August 9, 2007.

[36] World Bank. "Pension Reform in Ukraine." February 14, 2005. Available online. URL: http://siteresources.worldbank.org/INTECAREGTOPSOCPRO/Resources/UkrainePensionsReform.pdf. Downloaded May 11, 2007.

[37] Chernobyl.info. "Overview of health consequences." chernobyl.info Web site. Available online. URL: http://www.chernobyl.info/index.php?userhash=17756386&navID=21&lID=2. Downloaded August 10, 2007.

[38] Voldymyr Boreyko. "The Environment: Pollution plagues large areas of Ukraine," *The Ukrainian Weekly* LXI, no. 6, February 7, 1993. Available online. URL: http://www.ukrweekly.com/Archive/1993/069303.shtml. Downloaded August 9, 2007.

[39] Irina Kalachova. "Poverty and Welfare Trends in Ukraine over the 1990s." Background paper prepared for the Social Monitor, Florence, Italy: UNICEF Innocenti Research Centre, 2002, pp. 3–32. Available online. URL: http://www.unicef-irc.org/research/ESP/Country Reports2001_02/Ukraine01.pdf. Downloaded August 9, 2007.

[40] Chernobyl.info. "Overview of health consequences." Available online. URL: http://www.chernobyl.info/index.php?userhash=17756386&navID=21&lID=2. Downloaded August 10, 2007.

[41] Svetlana Kravchenko. "Citizen's Environmental Enforcement in Ukraine," pp. 145–148. Available online. URL: http://www.inece.org/5thvol1/kravchenko.pdf. Downloaded August 9, 2007.

[42] MAMA-86. "Environmental Democracy in Ukraine." Available online. URL: http://www.mama-86.org.ua/ecodemocracy/democracy_e.htm. Downloaded August 9, 2007.

[43] Institute for Sustainable Communities. Available online. URL: http://www.iscvt.org/where_we_work/Ukraine/. Downloaded December 4, 2007.

[44] Kravchenko. "Citizen's Environmental Enforcement," p. 148.

[45] World Bank. "Ukraine—Economic Update." April 2007. Available online. URL: http://siteresources.worldbank.org/INTUKRAINE/Resources/EconomicUpdateEngAprilFinal.pdf. Updated April 6, 2007.

[46] World Bank. "The International Bank for Reconstruction and Development and the International Finance Corporation Country Assistance Strategy Progress Report for Ukraine for 2004–07," p. 2. May 19, 2005. Available online. URL: http://siteresources.worldbank.org/INTUKRAINE/147271-1089983407712/20574748/CAS_PR_eng_final.pdf. Downloaded May 18, 2007.

[47] Ministry of Economy and European Integration of Ukraine. "Millennium Development Goals—Ukraine," p. 8.

[48] United Nations Development Programme and Ukraine Ministry of Economy. "Ukraine. Poverty Alleviation," p. 3. 2006. Available online. URL: http://www.undp.org.ua/download.php?id=1161153260&cm=doc&fn—dgp%20poverty%20alleviation%20ukraine%20%202006%20engl%20edited%20october.pdf&l=e. Downloaded May 18, 2007.

[49] UNDP and Ukraine Ministry of Economy. "Ukraine. Poverty Alleviation," pp. 3–11.

[50] United Nations Office for the Coordination of Humanitarian Affairs. Syria: Child Laborers Operate in Legal Loophole, Say Aid Workers." IRIN News. July 13, 2006. Available online. URL: http://www.irinnews.org/Report.aspx?ReportId=27130. Downloaded April 3, 2007.

[51] Library of Congress, Federal Research Division. "Country Profile: Syria." Library of Congress. April 2005. Available online. URL: http://lcweb2.loc.gov/frd/cs/profiles/Syria.pdf. Downloaded May 15, 2007.

[52] United Nations Development Programme. "English Translation of Speech by Dr. Rima Khalaf Hunaidi . . . on the Occasion of the Launch of the Arab Human Development Report 2002," p. 4. July 2, 2002. Available online. URL: http://cfapp2.undp.org/rbas/ahdr/Launch_Speeches2002/rimas.pdf. Downloaded May 15, 2007.

[53] Heba El-Laithy and Khalid Abu-Ismail. "Poverty in Syria: 1996–2004: Diagnosis and Pro-Poor Policy Considerations," p 1. United Nations Development Programme. June 2005. Available online. URL: http://www.undp.org.sy/publications/national/Poverty/Poverty_In_Syria_en.pdf. Downloaded September 12, 2006.

[54] Syrian Ministry of Tourism. "Incomparable Role in History." Available online. URL: http://www.syriatourism.org/index.php?module=subjects&func=viewpage&pageid=708. Downloaded August 9, 2007; Afaf Sabeh McGowan. "Ancient Syria." Library of Congress. 1987. Available online. URL: http://lcweb2.loc.gov/frd/cs/sytoc.html. Downloaded August 9, 2007.

[55] U.S. State Department. "Background Note: Syria." Available online. URL: http://www.state.gov/r/pa/ei/bgn/3580.htm. Downloaded August 9, 2007; Afaf Sabeh McGowan.

"Muslim Empires." Library of Congress. 1987. Available online. URL: http://lcweb2.loc.gov/cgi-bin/query/r?frd/cstdy:@field(DOCID-sy0013). Downloaded August 9, 2007.

[56] Giovanna Calasso. "Universal history, local history, national history: Recent theoretical and methodological contributions in Islamic historiography." In *The East and the Meaning of History*. Rome: Bardi Editore, 1994, pp. 199ff; Steven Bowman. "Twelfth-Century Jewish Responses to Crusade and Jihad." In L. J. Andrew Villalon and Donald J. Kagay, eds. *Crusaders, Condotierri, and Cannon: Medieval Warfare in Societies around the Mediterranean*. Leiden: Brill, 2002.

[57] Afaf Sabeh McGowan. "Succeeding Caliphates and Kingdom." Library of Congress. 1987. Available online. URL: http://lcweb2.loc.gov/frd/cs/sytoc.html. Downloaded August 9, 2007.

[58] Mine Ener. *Managing Egypt's Poor and the Politics of Benevolence, 1800–1952*. Princeton, N.J.: Princeton University Press, 2003. Summary available online. URL: http://press.princeton.edu/chapters/s7640.html. Downloaded August 9, 2007.

[59] Elizabeth Thompson. *Colonial Citizens: Republican Rights, Paternal Privilege, and Gender in French Syria and Lebanon*. New York: Columbia University Press, 2000, pp. 19–23.

[60] Thompson. *Colonial Citizens*, pp. 155, 285. Afaf Sabeh McGowan. "The French Mandate." Available online. URL: http://countrystudies.us/syria/9.htm. Downloaded August 9, 2007.

[61] Thompson. *Colonial Citizens*, p. 284.

[62] Ronald Bruce St. John. "Syria's Baath Party Congress a Watershed for President Assad." *Foreign Policy in Focus* (June 2, 2005). Available online. URL: http://www.fpif.org/fpiftxt/892. Downloaded August 9, 2007.

[63] Anthony Shadid. "Death of Syrian Minister Leaves a Sect Adrift in Time of Strife." *Washington Post*, October 31, 2005, A1. Available online. URL: http://www.washingtonpost.com/wp-dyn/content/article/2005/10/30/AR2005103001270_pf.html. Downloaded August 9, 2007.

[64] Kate Seelye. "Lebanon's History of Occupation." Public Broadcasting System. Available online. URL: http://www.pbs.org/frontlineworld/dispatches/lebanon.syria/seelye1.html. Downloaded August 9, 2007.

[65] Pete W. Moore and Bassel F. Salloukh. "Struggles under Authoritarianism: Regimes, States, and Professional Associations in the Arab World." *IJMES* 39, no. 1 (February 2007): 61.

[66] Gary C. Gambill. "Dossier: The Syrian Muslim Brotherhood." *Mideast Monitor* 1, no. 2 (April–May 2006). Available online. URL: http://www.mideastmonitor.org/issues/0604/0604_2.htm. Downloaded August 9, 2007; Thomas L. Friedman. "Hama Rules." *New York Times*, September 21, 2001. Available online. URL: http://www.mafhoum.com/press2/63P58.htm. Downloaded August 9, 2007.

[67] Council on Foreign Relations. "State Sponsors: Syria." Available online. URL: http://www.cfr.org/publication/9368/ Updated July 2006; "Israel." In Thomas Collelo, ed. *Syria: A Country Study*. Washington, D.C.: GPO for the Library of Congress, 1987. Available online. URL: http://countrystudies.us/syria/62.htm. Downloaded August 9, 2007.

[68] United Nations Development Programme. "Summary of Syria's National Development Report 2005." Available online. URL: http://www.undp.org.sy/publications_national.php#NHDR2005. Downloaded August 9, 2007.

[69] Paul Sullivan. "Globalization: Trade and Investment in Egypt, Jordan and Syria since 1980." *Arab Studies Quarterly* (Summer 1999): 9. Available online. URL: http://findarticles.com/p/articles/mi_m2501/is_3_21/ai_57476491/pg_9. Downloaded May 15, 2007. Peter Wehrheim. "Agricultural and Food Policies in Syria: Financial Transfers and Fiscal Flows." Chapter 4 of *Syrian Agriculture at the Crossroads.* FAO Agricultural Policy and Economic Development Series, no. 8. 2003. Available online. URL: http://www.fao.org/docrep/006/y4890e/y4890e0c.htm. Downloaded May 15, 2007.

[70] International Crisis Group. "Syria Under Bashar (II): Domestic Policy Challenges," *Middle East Report* no. 24, February 11, 2004. Available online. URL: http://www.crisisgroup.org./home/index. Downloaded August 8, 2007.

[71] Thomas R. Stauffer. "The Costs to American Taxpayers of the Israeli-Palestinian Conflict: $3 Trillion." *Washington Report on Middle East Affairs* (June 2003): 20–23. Available online. URL: http://www.wrmea.com/archives/june2003/0306020.html. Downloaded December 4, 2007.

[72] Sami Moubayad. "Damascus Holds Its Ground." *Al-Ahram Weekly* 733 (March 10–16, 2005). Available online. URL: http://weekly.ahram.org.eg/2005/733/re2.htm. Downloaded December 4, 2007.

[73] Sherifa Shafie. Palestinian Refugees in Syria, Forced Migration Online Research Guide, August 2003. Available online. URL: http://www.forcedmigration.org/guides/fmo017/. Downloaded August 9, 2007.

[74] "UNHCR Syria update on Iraqi refugees Feb. 2008," ReliefWeb Web site, February 4, 2008. Available online. URL: http://www.reliefweb.int/rw/RWB.NSF/db900SID/EGUA7BJPPL?OpenDocument. Downloaded on February 7, 2008.

[75] U.S. Department of State. "Country Reports on Terrorism," April 28, 2006. Available online. URL: http://www.state.gov/s/ct/rls/crt/2005/64337.htm. Downloaded August 9, 2007.

[76] BBC News. "US Slaps Trade Sanctions on Syria." May 11, 2004. Available online. URL: http://news.bbc.co.uk/2/hi/middle_east/3705783.stm. Downloaded August 9, 2007.

[77] UNDP Syria. "UNDP Syria Contributions to MDGs." Available online. URL: http://www.undp.org.sy/MDGs.php. Downloaded August 9, 2007.

[78] Sarah Hegland. "The Colours of Social Change," UNDP Syria Web site. Available online. URL: http://www.undp.org.sy/index.php?action=fullnews&id=32. Downloaded August 9, 2007.

[79] SOS Children's Villages. "SOS in Syria." Available online. URL: http://www.soschildrensvillages.org.uk/sponsor-a-child/asian-child-sponsorship/syria.htm. Downloaded August 9, 2007.

[80] United Nations Office for the Coordination of Humanitarian Affairs. "Syria: Among rising poverty, local charity helps the poor." IRIN News. Available online. URL: http://www.irinnews.org/report.asp?ReportID=53260&SelectRegion=Middle_East. Downloaded August 9, 2007.

[81] Human Rights Association in Syria. "About HRAS." HRAS Web site. Available online. URL: http://www.hrassy.org/english/about.htm. Downloaded August 9, 2007.

[82] Abid Aslam. "300,000 Syrian Kurds 'Buried Alive,'" One World U.S. Web site, February 15, 2006. Available online. URL: http://us.oneworld.net/article/view/127600/1/. Downloaded August 9, 2007.

[83] Library of Congress, Federal Research Division. "Country Profile: Syria," p. 12. Library of Congress. April 2005. Available online. URL: http://lcweb2.loc.gov/frd/cs/profiles/Syria.pdf. Downloaded May 15, 2007. El-Laithy and Abu-Ismail. "Poverty in Syria," p 18.

[84] European Commission. "The EU's relations with Syria," External Relations Web site. Available online. URL: http://ec.europa.eu/comm/external_relations/syria/intro/index.htm. Downloaded August 9, 2007.

[85] European Commission. External Relations Web site. Available online. URL: http://ec.europa.eu/comm/external_relations/syria/images/02_syria.pdf. Downloaded August 9, 2007.

[86] U.N. Modern Technologies for Employment Creation and Poverty Reduction in the ESCWA Region. "ACTIVITIES IN THE PIPELINE : : SCP : : Syria : : Qusaybeh." Available online. URL: http://www.escwa.org.lb/mtecpr/initcentre.asp?Title=SCP&country=Syria&Name=Qusaybeh. Downloaded August 9, 2007.

[87] Hegland, "The Colours of Social Change."

[88] UN Office for the Coordination of Humanitarian Affairs, "SYRIA: Women's group to provide assistance to female divorcees," IRIN news Web site, March 19, 2006. Available online. URL: http://www.irinnews.org/report.asp?ReportID=52305&SelectRegion=Middle_East&SelectCountry=SYRIA. Downloaded August 9, 2007.

[89] Angela Melchiorre, "At What Age are school-children married, employed or taken to court?" Right to Education Web site, second edition, April 20, 2004. Available online. URL: http://www.right-to-education.org/content/age/syria.html. Downloaded August 9, 2007.

[90] CIA. "Syria." El-Laithy and Abu-Ismail. "Poverty in Syria."

[91] IRIN News. "Syria: 'Child-Friendly' Schools Help Boost Enrollment." November 1, 2006. Available online. URL: http://www.irinnews.org/report.asp?ReportID=56148&SelectRegion=Middle_East&SelectCountry=SYRIA. Downloaded August 9, 2007.

[92] International Labour Organization. "Equality of Opportunity in Education and Training—Ministry of Education—Syria," Available online. URL: http://www.ilo.org/public/english/employment/gems/eeo/edu/inst/syrme.htm. Updated March 7, 2005.

[93] UNDP, "The Gender and Citizenship Initiative: Country Profiles: Syria." Available online. URL: http://gender.pogar.org/countries/gender.asp?cid=19. Downloaded August 9, 2007.

[94] International Labour Organization, "Equality of Opportunity in Education and Training—Government Education and Training Programmes—Syria." Available online. URL: http://www.ilo.org/public/english/employment/gems/eeo/edu/programme/sygov.htm. Updated March 3, 2005.

[95] "Syrian Women's Union," Mediterranean Women Web site. Available online. URL: http://www.mediterraneas.org/article.php3?id_article=201. Updated September 30, 2004.

[96] United Nations in Syria Web site. "UN and Syria Sign Landmark Development Plan." September 14, 2006. Available online. URL: http://www.un.org.sy/UNDAF_story.html. Downloaded May 19, 2007; "Syrian Arab Republic UN Development Assistance Framework 2007–2011," pp. 3–4. Available online. URL: http://www.un.org.sy/UNDAF2007-2011.pdf. Downloaded May 19, 2007.

[97] BBC News. "Syrian Democracy Activists Jailed." Available online. URL: http://news.bbc.co.uk/1/hi/world/middle_east/6651257.stm. Updated May 13, 2007.

[98] Quoted in Narayan. *Voices of the Poor*, p. 87.

[99] World Bank. *Poverty in Guatemala*. Washington, D.C.: World Bank, 2004, pp. 2–4. Central Intelligence Agency. "Guatemala." *CIA Factbook*. Available online. URL: https://www.cia.gov/library/publications/the-world-factbook/geos/gt.html. Downloaded August 9, 2007; U.S. Department of State, "Background Note: Guatemala," http://www.state.gov/r/pa/ei/bgn/2045.htm; International Research Institute for Climate and Society. "Latin America and the Caribbean Regional Program." Available online. URL: http://iri.columbia.edu/america/background.html. Downloaded August 9, 2007.

[100] Ing. Luis Dumois. "The Maya Civilization." Mexicoconnect Web site. Available online. URL: http://www.mexconnect.com/mex_/travel/ldumois/ldcmmaya1.html. Downloaded August 9, 2007; Glenn Walker. "Mayan Civilization," Indians.org Web site. Available online. URL: http://www.indians.org/welker/maya.htm. Updated September 9, 1998.

[101] World Bank. *Poverty in Guatemala*, p. 56.

[102] World Bank. *Poverty in Guatemala*, p. 57.

[103] "History of Guatemala," Historyworld Web site. Available online. URL: http://www.historyworld.net/wrldhis/PlainTextHistories.asp?historyid=ac12. Downloaded August 9, 2007; Lisa Viscidi, "A History of Land in Guatemala: Conflict and Hope for Reform," International Relations Center Americas Program Web site, September 17, 2004. Available online. URL: http://americas.irc-online.org/citizen-action/focus/2004/0409guatland.html. Downloaded August 9, 2007.

[104] World Bank. *Poverty in Guatemala*, p. 61.

[105] Marcelo Bucheli. "Good Dictator, Bad Dictator: United Fruit Company and Economic Nationalism in Central America in the Twentieth Century," pp. 14–15. University of Illinois at Urbana-Champaign. 2006. Available online. URL: http://www.business.uiuc.edu/Working_Papers/papers/06-0115.pdf. Downloaded August 9, 2007; P. Landmeier. "Banana Republic." Available online. URL: http://www.mayaparadise.com/ufc1e.htm. Updated October 5, 2003.

[106] Bucheli. "Good Dictator, Bad Dictator," pp. 6, 20. World Bank. *Poverty in Guatemala*, p. 62.

[107] Bucheli. "Good Dictator, Bad Dictator," p. 20.

[108] World Bank. *Poverty in Guatemala*, pp. 62–63.

[109] Douglas W. Trefzger. "Guatemala's 1952 Agrarian Reform Law: A Critical Reassessment." *International Social Science Review* (Spring–Summer 2002): 5. Available online. URL: http://www.findarticles.com/p/articles/mi_m0IMR/is_2002_Spring-Summer/ai_92615711/pg_5. Downloaded August 9, 2007.

[110] Bucheli. "Good Dictator, Bad Dictator." Landmeier. "Banana Republic."

[111] World Bank. "Robert Strange McNamara." World Bank Archives Web site. Available online. URL: http://go.worldbank.org/44V9497H50. Downloaded May 23, 2007. United Nations Children's Fund. "The 1970s: Era of Alternatives." *The State of the World's Children 1996* report. Available online. URL: http://www.unicef.org/sowc96/1970s.htm. Downloaded May 23, 2007. Trushna Patel. "Part I: New Directions at the World Bank." Making a Difference Web site. Available online. URL: http://www.open2.net/makingadifference/world_bank.htm. Downloaded May 23, 2007.

[112] "Guatemala, Economy," Countries Quest Web site. Available online. URL: http://www.countriesquest.com/central_america/guatemala/economy.htm. Downloaded August 9, 2007

[113] Paul Kobrak. "Chapter 7: 1973–77, the Social Struggle." In *Organizing and Repression in the University of San Carlos, Guatemala, 1944 to 1996.* Science and Human Rights Program, AAAS. Available online. URL: http://shr.aaas.org/guatemala/ciidh/org_rep/english/part2_7.html. Downloaded August 13, 2007.

[114] Kobrak. "Chapter 7"; World Bank. *Poverty in Guatemala,* p. 63.

[115] World Bank. *Poverty in Guatemala,* pp. 63–65. *News Hour.* "Guatemala's Future." December 30, 1996. Public Broadcasting System. Available online. URL: http://www.pbs.org/newshour/bb/latin_america/december96/guatemala_12-30.html. Downloaded August 9, 2007.

[116] World Bank. *Poverty in Guatemala,* pp. 63–67.

[117] U.S. Agency for International Development. "Central America and Mexico Gang Assessment: Annex 2—Guatemala." Available online. URL: http://www.usaid.gov/locations/latin_america_caribbean/democracy/guatemala_profile.pdf. Downloaded August 9, 2007.

[118] World Bank. *Poverty in Guatemala,* p. 56.

[119] Quoted in Bucheli. "Good Dictator, Bad Dictator," p. 15.

[120] Quoted in Simeon Tegel. "A Nation Yearning: Peace, Equality, and Justice in Guatemala." Center for Latin American Studies, University of California–Berkeley. Updated December 30, 2004 Available online. URL: http://socrates.berkeley.edu:7001/Events/fall2004/11-19-04-menchu/index.html. Didou Diene. "Racism, Racial Discrimination, Xenophobia and All Forms of Discrimination," p. 16. March 11, 2005. United Nations Economic and Social Council Commission on Human Rights. Available online. URL: http://www.nyiha.com/documents/racism_guatemala_002.pdf. Downloaded August 9, 2007.

[121] Diene. "Racism, Racial Discrimination," pp. 16–17.

[122] "Assessment for Indigenous Peoples in Guatemala," Center for International Development and Conflict Management, December, 31, 2003. URL: http://www.cidcm.umd.edu/inscr/mar/assessment.asp?groupId=9002 May 10, 2002. Downloaded February 17, 2007.

[123] Diene. "Racism, Racial Discrimination," pp. 9–10.

[124] Peace Brigades. "Organizations in Guatemala." Available online. URL: http://www.peacebrigades.org/guate.html. Downloaded August 9, 2007.

[125] World Bank. *Poverty in Guatemala,* p. 63.

[126] U.S. State Department. "Guatemala." *International Religious Freedom Report 2005.* Available online. URL: http://www.state.gov/g/drl/rls/irf/2005/51641.htm. Downloaded August 9, 2007.

[127] Catholic Relief Services. "Our Work: Guatemala." Available online. URL: http://www.crs.org/our_work/where_we_work/overseas/latin_america_and_the_caribbean/guatemala/index.cfm. Downloaded February 25, 2007.

[128] Hillsborough Presbyterian Church. "Sayaxche Center." Available online. URL: http://hillsboropresbyterian.org/content/view/47/163/1/2/. Downloaded January 31, 2008.

[129] "SANK starts new education-oriented NGO in Guatemala," press release, Peace Corps Online Web site, April 17, 2002. Available online. URL: http://peacecorpsonline.org/messages/messages/2629/1007711.html. Downloaded August 9, 2007.

[130] World Bank. *Poverty in Guatemala*, pp. 113–116, 120.

[131] World Health Organization. "Maternal Mortality in 2000: Estimates Developed by WHO, UNICEF, UNFPA." 2004. Available online. URL: http://www.who.int/reproductive-health/publications/maternal_mortality_2000/mme.pdf. Downloaded May 24, 2007.

[132] World Bank. *Poverty in Guatemala*, pp. 128–129.

[133] UNICEF. "The 1970s: Era of Alternatives."

[134] Carol Miller. "Investigating Health in Guatemala." Global Health Council Web site Available online. URL: http://www.globalhealth.org/reports/text.php3?id=5. Downloaded August 9, 2007; World Bank. "Improving Health and Nutrition of Mothers and Young Children in Guatemala," April 2006. Available online. URL: http://web.worldbank.org/WBSITE/EXTERNAL/COUNTRIES/LACEXT/GUATEMALAEXTN/0,,contentMDK:20903253~pagePK:1497618~piPK:217854~theSitePK:328117,00.html. Downloaded August 9, 2007.

[135] Save the Children. "Guatemala." Available online. URL: http://www.savethechildren.org/countries/latin-america-caribbean/guatemala.html#. Downloaded August 13, 2007.

[136] World Bank. *Poverty in Guatemala*, p. 119.

[137] Chuck Haren, "2005 News from Plenty Austin & Plenty International." Available online. URL: http://www.plentyaustin.org/latestnews05.htm. Downloaded August 9, 2007.

[138] World Bank. *Poverty in Guatemala*, p. 119.

[139] U.S. State Department. "President Bush and President Berger Participate in Joint Press Availability." March 12, 2007. Available online. URL: http://www.state.gov/p/wha/rls/rm/07/q1/81656.htm. Downloaded May 24, 2007.

[140] World Bank. "Guatemala," World Bank Web site. Available online. URL: http:go.worldbank.org/B7GGO8VXK1. Downloaded August 7, 2007.

[141] Peter Baker. "In Guatemala, Bush Vows to Push Immigration Changes." *Washington Post*, March 13, 2007, A10. Available online. URL: http://www.washingtonpost.com/wp-dyn/content/article/2007/03/12/AR2007031200079.html. Downloaded May 24, 2007.

[142] Inez Benitez. "Guatemala: Indigenous Women Last in Line for MDGs," Inter Press Service News Agency, May 7, 2007. Available online. URL: http://www.ipsnews.org/news.asp?idnews=37642. Downloaded May 24, 2007.

[143] Jeremy Shiffman. "Generating Political Priority for Maternal Mortality Reduction in Five Developing Countries." *American Journal of Public Health* 97 (May 2007): 796–803.

[144] Amnesty International. "Guatemala." *AI Report 2007: The State of the World's Human Rights*. Available online. URL: http://thereport.amnesty.org/eng/Regions/Americas/Guatemala. Downloaded May 25, 2007.

[145] Quoted in Narayan. *Voices of the Poor*, p. 135.

[146] Central Intelligence Agency. "India." *CIA Factbook.* Available online. URL: http://www.cia.gov/cia/publications/factbook/print/in.html. Downloaded U.S. State Department. "Background Note: India." Available online. URL: http://www.state.gov/r/pa/ei/bgn/3454. Downloaded February 7, 2008.

[147] City Mayors. "The World's Largest Cities and Urban Areas in 2006." Available online. URL: http://www.citymayors.com/statistics/urban_2006_1.html. Downloaded August 9, 2007.

[148] United Nations Statistical Institute for Asia and the Pacific. Available online. URL: http://www.unsiap.or.jp/participants_work/cos03_homepages/group4/boon-india-present.htm. Downloaded August 9, 2007.

[149] Richard Hooker. "Ancient India: The Aryans." Available online. URL: http://www.wsu.edu:8080/~dee/ANCINDIA/ARYANS.HTM. Downloaded February 7, 2008; Porter Wiseman. "The Context of Vedic India." Available online. URL: http://www.astronomy.pomona.edu/archeo/india/india1.html. Downloaded February 7, 2008; Religion Facts. "The History of Hinduism." Available online. URL:http://www.religionfacts.com/hinduism/history. htm. Downloaded February 7, 2008.

[150] National Campaign on Dalit Human Rights. "Who are Dalits?" 1995. Available online. URL: http://www.dalits.org/whoaredalits.htm. Downloaded August 9, 2007.

[151] Richard Hooker. "The Historical Siddhartha." Available online. URL: http://www.wsu.edu/~dee/BUDDHISM.SIDD.HTM. Downloaded August 9, 2007. Richard Hooker. "Reaction and Rebellion: Jainism and Buddhism." Available online. URL: http://www.wsu.edu/~dee/ANCINDIA/REACTION.HTM. Downloaded August 9, 2007.

[152] Nupam Mahajan. "Gupta Dynasty, India's Golden Age." Available online. URL: http://www.med.unc.edu/~nupam/Sgupta1.html. Downloaded August 9, 2007.

[153] Richard Hooker. "The Mughals: The Europeans and the Decline of the Mughal Empire," 1996, Available online. URL: http://www.wsu.edu:8080/~dee/MUGHAL/SIKH.HTM. Downloaded August 7, 2007; Shishir Thadani "From Trade to Colonization—History Dynamics of the East India Trading Companies," excerpt from *History of India: The British East India Company and Colonization,* South Asia History Web site. URL: http://india_resource.tripod.com/eastindia.html. Downloaded August 9, 2007; Vinay Lal, "The East India Company," Manas Web site. Available online. URL: http://www.sscnet.ucla.edu/southasia/History/British/EAco.html. Updated February 7, 2007.

[154] Nilish Patel. "The Sepoy War of 1857." Available online. URL: http://www.english.emory.edu/Bahri/Mutiny.html. Downloaded August 13, 2007.

[155] J. M. Blaunt. *The Colonizer's Map of the World,* p. 203.

[156] Hooker. "The Mughals."

[157] Gideon Polya. "The Forgotten Holocaust: The 1943/44 Bengal Famine." Global Avoidable Mortality blog. July 11, 2005. Available online. URL: http://globalavoidablemortality.blogspot.com/2005/07/forgotten-holocaust-194344-bengal.html. Downloaded August 13, 2007; Michael Massing. *New York Times, Books & Arts* (March 1, 2003). Available online. URL: http://folk.uio.no/danbanik/NYTarticle2003.htm. Downloaded August 13, 2007. *News Hour.* "The Economics of Poverty." October 15, 1998. Public Broadcasting System. Available online. URL: http://www.pbs.org/newshour/bb/economy/july-dec98/sen_10-15.html. Downloaded August 13, 2007.

[158] Shishir Thadani, "The Colonial Legacy: Myths and Popular Beliefs." Available online. URL: http://india_resource.tripod.com/colonial.html. Downloaded August 13, 2007. Blaunt. *Colonizer's Map of the World*, pp. 275–284.

[159] Scott Graham, "The Salt March to Dandi." Available online. http://www.english.emory.edu/Bahri/Dandi.html. Downloaded August 13, 2007.

[160] Library of Congress. "Mahatma Gandhi." Available online. URL: htttp://lcweb2.loc.gov/cgi-bin/query/r?frd/cstdy:@field(DOCID+in0026). Downloaded August 13, 2007. National Campaign on Dalit Human Rights. "Who are Dalits?" 1995. Available online. URL: http://www.dalits.org/whoaredalits.htm. Downloaded August 9, 2007.

[161] Shirin Keen "The Partition of India." Available online. URL: http://www.english.emory.edu/Bahri/Part.html. Downloaded August 13, 2007.

[162] Judith E. Walsh. *A Brief History of India*. New York: Facts On File, 2006, pp. 204–205. Paola Bacchetta. "Reinterrogating partition violence: Voices of women/children/Dalits in India's partition." *Feminist Studies* 26, no. 3 (Fall 2000): 567 ff.

[163] "Indian Constitution of 1955," India Code Web site. Available online. URL: http://indiacode.nic.in/coiweb/fullact1.asp?tfnm=00. Downloaded August 13, 2007.

[164] John D. Rogers. "India: Structure of the Economy." Library of Congress. Available online. URL: http://lcweb2.loc.gov/cgi-bin/query/r?frd/cstdy:@field(DOCID+in0097). Downloaded August 13, 2007. John J. Paul. "Nehru's Legacy." Library of Congress. Available online. URL: http://lcweb2.loc.gov/frd/cs/intoc.html. Downloaded August 13, 2007.

[165] R. Sooryamoorthy and K. D. Gangrade. *NGO in India: A Cross-Sectional Study*. Westport, Conn.: Greenwood Press, 2001, pp. 3, 48–49.

[166] Sooryamoorthy and Gangrade. *NGOS in India*, pp. 47–48. Walsh. *Brief History of India*, pp. 214–215. Usha Thakkar, "Vinoba Bhave: a life sketch," Bombay Sarvodaya Mandal Web site. Available online. URL: http://www.mkgandhi-sarvodaya.org/vinoba/bio.htm. Downloaded August 13, 2007.

[167] Ashok Bhargava. "Economic Development: Evolution of Policy." Library of Congress. Available online. URL: http://lcweb2.loc.gov/cgi-bin/query/r?frd/cstdy:@field(DOCID+in0133). Downloaded August 13, 2007. Walsh. *Brief History of India*, pp. 214–215, 218–224.

[168] Walsh. *Brief History of India*, pp. 219–224. John J. Paul. "The Rise of Indira Gandhi." Library of Congress. Available online. URL: http://lcweb2.loc.gov/cgi-bin/query/r?frd/cstdy:@field(DOCID+in0029). Downloaded August 13, 2007.

[169] Walsh. *Brief History of India*, pp. 227–232, 264–267.

[170] Mark Hertsgaard. "Bhopal's Legacy." *The Nation* (May 24, 2004). Available online. URL: http://www.thenation.com/doc/20040524/hertsgaard. Downloaded August 13, 2007. Union Carbide. "The Incident, Response, and Settlement." Available online. URL: http://www.bhopal.com/irs.htm. Downloaded August 13, 2007. Bhopal Medical Appeal and Sabhavna Trust. "What Happened in Bhopal." Available online. URL: http://www.bhopal.org/whathappened.html. Downloaded August 13, 2007; Mike McPhate. "Bhopal Disaster Continues to Be a Plague." *Washington Times*, November 20, 2004. Available online. URL: http://www.washtimes.com/world/20041119-102440-8732r.htm. Downloaded August 13, 2007.

[171] John D. Rogers. "India: Growth since 1980 and Liberalization in the early 1990s." Library of Congress. Available online. URL: http://lcweb2.loc.gov/cgi-bin/query/r?frd/cstdy:@

field(DOCID+in0098). Downloaded August 13, 2007. Walsh. *Brief History of India*, pp. 233, 238, 267–268.

[172] CIA. "India." Scott Baldauf. "India's next test: spreading prosperity." *Christian Science Monitor* (June 26, 2006). Available online. URL: http://www.csmonitor.com/2006/0626/p01s02-wosc.html?s=widep. Downloaded August 13, 2007.

[173] Walsh. *Brief History of India*, p. 240. Arjun Adlakha. "India: Population Trends." U.S. Department of Commerce. April 1997. Deepti Gudipati. "Healthcare Delivery Systems in Rural India Meeting the Changing Needs of Rural Populations." *Heinz School Review*. Available online. URL: http://journal.heinz.cmu.edu/articles/healthcare-delivery-systems-rural- india/. Downloaded August 13, 2007.

[174] Amy Waldman. "Distrust Reopens the Door for Polio in India." *New York Times*, January 19, 2003. Available online URL: http://query.nytimes.com/gst/fullpage.html?sec=health&res=9C03E5D81430F93AA25752C0A9659C8B63. Downloaded August 13, 2007.

[175] Adlakha. "India: Population Trends." Gudipati. "Healthcare Delivery Systems."

[176] Gudipati. "Healthcare Delivery Systems." World Bank, "Safe Motherhood Moving Closer to Center Stage in India" press release, May 8, 1997. Available online. URL: http://go.worldbank.org/TSBRTGWIE0. Downloaded August 13, 2007. Population Council. "Despite Efforts, Maternal Deaths in India Remain Common." *Safe Motherhood* (September 2001) 7, no. 3. Available online. URL: htttp://www.popcouncil.org/publications/popbriefs/pb7(3)_3.html. Downloaded August 13, 2007. P. K. Dutta. "Scope of health systems research in child survival and safe motherhood programme." In *Indian Journal of Maternal and Child Health* 4, no. 2 (1993): 38–41. Available online. URL: http://www.ncbi.nlm.nih.gov/entrez/query.fcgi?cmd=Retrieve&db=PubMed&list_uids=12318484&dopt=Abstract. Downloaded August 13, 2007.

[177] Saroj Pachauri. "NGO Efforts to Prevent Maternal and Infant Mortality in India." *Social Change* 26, nos. 3–4 (September–December 1996): 30–44. Subash Mohapatra. "Child Marriages Persist in Rural India." *Asia Tribune*, August 29, 2006. Available online. URL: http://www.asiantribune.com/index.php?q–ode/1763. Downloaded August 13, 2007. Azad India Foundation Web site. Available online. URL: http://azadindia.org/azad-hind.html. Downloaded August 13, 2007.

[178] United Nations Population Fund, "UNFPA's Contribution to Meeting the MDGs: Findings from the United Nations Millennium Project." Available online. URL: http://www.unfpa.org/icpd/gender.htm. Downloaded August 13, 2007.

[179] Kumar Thangamuthu. "Microcredit in the Rural South." *India Together* (July 1999). Available online. URL: http·//www.indiatogether.org/stories/asa.htm. Downloaded August 13, 2007.

[180] Thelma Kay, "Empowering Women through Self-Help Microcredit Programmes." Available online. URL: http://www.unescap.org/pdd/publications/bulletin2002/ch6.pdf. Downloaded August 13, 2007. Cris Prystay. "Microcredit Helps Women Entrepreneurs in India with Loans, Poor South Asian Women Turn Entrepreneurial." *Wall Street Journal*, May 25, 2005, B1. Available online URL: http://news.mongabay.com/2005/0525a-poverty.html. Downloaded August 13, 2007.

[181] Quoted in "'Our Mission Is Giving Loans to the Poor.'" *Tribune*, August 12, 2006. Available online. URL: http://www.tribuneindia.com/2006/20060812/saturday/main2.htm. Downloaded August 13, 2007.

[182] Thelma Kay, "Empowering Women." Stacey Cordeiro. "Microcredit and Women's Empowerment." Independent Media Center India. January 22, 2004. Available online. URL: http://india.indymedia.org/en/2004/01/208932.shtml. Downloaded August 13, 2007.

[183] Embassy of India. "Child Labor and India." Available online. URL: http://www.indianembassy.org/policy/Child_Labor/childlabor.htm. Downloaded August 13, 2007. Human Rights Watch. "Small Change: Bonded Labor in India's Silk Industry." Summary 15, no. 2 (January 2003). Available online. URL: http://www.hrw.org/reports/2003/india/India0103.htm#P169_20786. Downloaded August 13, 2007; Mitesh Badiwala. "Child Labor in India." Available online. URL: http://www.geocities.com/CollegePark/Library/9175/inquiry1.htm. Downloaded August 13, 2007.

[184] Embassy of India. "Child Labor and India." "Child Labor Act." Available online. URL: http://www.indialawinfo.com/bareacts/cla.html#_Toc502063153. Downloaded August 13, 2007.

[185] Human Rights Watch. "Small Change." "The Exploitation of Child Labor in India." Testimony of Dan Burton, U.S. Representative, Indiana. *Congressional Record*, July 25, 1995. Available online. URL: http://pangaea.org/street_children/asia/carpet.htm. Downloaded August 13, 2007.

[186] Oxfam. Available online. URL: http://www.oxfam.org.uk/coolplanet/kidsweb/world/india/indioxf3.htm. Downloaded August 13, 2007. Concerned for Working Children. "India." Available online. URL: http://www.workingchild.org/intro.htm. Downloaded August 13, 2007.

[187] India Committee of the Netherlands. "Monsanto, Unilever Use Child Labor in India." May 14, 2003. Available online. URL: http://www.indiaresource.org/issues/agbiotech/2003/monsantounilever.html. Downloaded August 13, 2007.

[188] Sunil Raman. "Ten-year-old Divya sits in a low-roofed hut hunched over a six feet high and six feet wide pit loom." BBC News. August 29, 2005. Available online. URL: http://news.bbc.co.uk/1/hi/world/south_asia/4183600.stm. Downloaded August 13, 2007.

[189] Pratham Web site. Available online. URL: http://www.pratham.org/. Accessed February 7, 2008.

[190] "Poorest of poor Dalit children get a world-class education." InfoChange News & Features. May 2004. Available online. URL: http://www.infochangeindia.org/EducationIstory.jsp?recordno=3045&section_idv=5. Downloaded August 13, 2007.

[191] Baldev Raj Nayar. "India: Poverty Retreats with Globalization's Advance." *YaleGlobal* (February 1, 2007). Available online. URL: http://yaleglobal.yale.edu/display.article?id=8701. Downloaded May 29, 2007.

[192] Kirsty Hughes. "India's Poverty: Help the Poor Help Themselves." *International Herald Tribune*, May 9, 2005. Available online. URL: http://www.iht.com/articles/2005/05/08/opinion/edhughes.php. Downloaded May 29, 2007.

[193] Government of India Press Information Bureau. "Poverty Estimates for 2004–2005." March 2007. Available online. URL: http://planningcommission.nic.in/news/prmar07.pdf. Downloaded May 29, 2007. Dilip D'Souza. "A Thin Indian Line." India Together Web site. March 17, 2006. Downloaded May 29, 2007.

[194] Cait Murphy. "India the Superpower? Think Again." *Fortune* (February 9, 2007). Available online. URL: http://money.cnn.com/2007/02/08/news/international/pluggedin_murphy_india.fortune/index.htm. Downloaded May 29, 2007.

[195] Refugees International. "Refugee Voices: One Female Child Soldier's Story in the Democratic Republic of Congo." November 7, 2005. URL: http://www.refugeesinternational.org/content/article/detail/7211/. Downloaded April 3, 2007.

[196] Central Intelligence Agency. "Congo, Democratic Republic of." *CIA Factbook.* Available online. URL: https://www.cia.gov/cia/publications, factbook/print/cg.html. Downloaded August 13, 2007. U.S. Department of State. "Background Notes: Democratic Republic of the Congo." Available online. URL: http://www.state.gov/r/pa/ei/bgn/2823.htm. Downloaded August 13, 2007. Jay Heale. *Democratic Republic of the Congo.* New York: Marshall Cavendish, 1999. CIA. "Rank Order—GDP." *CIA Factbook.* Available online. URL: https://www.cia.gov/cia/publications/factbook/rankorder/2004rank.html. Downloaded August 13, 2007. U.S. Mission to the UN Agencies for Food and Agriculture. "Songs of Sorrow, Rhythms of Hope: Conflict and Hunger in the Congo." U.S. Ambassador Tony Hall's Fact-Finding Visit to the Democratic Republic of the Congo. September 23–30, 2003. Available online. URL: http://usunrome.usmission.gov/files/Congo.htm. Downloaded August 13, 2007. World Bank. "Interim Poverty Reduction Strategy Paper." March 2002. Available online. URL: http://povlibrary.worldbank.org/files/DRC_IPRSP.pdf. Downloaded August 13, 2007. United Nations Development Programme. "Country Fact Sheet: Congo." *Human Development Report 2006.* Available online. URL: http://hdr.undp.org/hdr2006/statistics/countries/data_sheets/cty_ds_COG.html. Down loaded August 13, 2007.

[197] World Bank. "DRC Country Brief." Available online. URL: http://web.worldbank.org/WBSITE/EXTERNAL/COUNTRIES/AFRICAEXT/CONGODemocratICEXTN/0,,menuPK:349476~pagePK:141132~piPK:141107~theSitePK:349466,00.html. Downloaded August 13, 2007.

[198] U.S. Mission to UN Agencies for Food and Agriculture. "Songs of Sorrow." UNDP. "Country Fact Sheet: Congo."

[199] Rene LeMarchand. "Zaire: Human Origins." Library of Congress. Available online. URL: http://lcweb2.loc.gov/cgi-bin/query/r?frd/cstdy:@field(DOCID+zr0015). Downloaded August 13, 2007.

[200] Heale. *Democratic Republic of the Congo,* p. 63. African Development Fund. "Agriculture and Rural Sector Rehabilitation Project in Bas-Congo and Badundu Provinces." *Democratic Republic of Congo Appraisal Report,* p. 2. March 2004. Available online. URL: http://www.afdb.org/pls/portal/docs/PAGE/ADB_ADMIN_PG/DOCUMENTS/OPERATIONS INFORMATION/ADF_BD_WP_2004_35_E.PDF. Downloaded August 13, 2007.

[201] Alistair Boddy-Evans. "Trade Across the Sahara." Available online. URL: http://african history.about.com/library/dyk/bltimbuktumap.htm. Downloaded August 13, 2007. Alexander Ives Bartolot. "Trade Relations among European and African Nations." Available online. URL: http://www.metmuseum.org/toah/hd/aftr/hd_aftr.htm. Downloaded August 13, 2007.

[202] Didier Gondola. *The History of the Congo.* Westport, Conn: Greenwood Press, 2002, pp. 26–31.

[203] Gondola. *History of the Congo,* pp. 32–35. Rene LeMarchand. "Zaire: External Pressures."Library of Congress. Available online. URL: http://lcweb2.loc.gov/cgi-bin/query/r?frd/cstdy:@field(DOCID+zr0019). Downloaded August 13, 2007.

[204] Gondola. *History of the Congo,* pp. 35–39, 43, 46. Alexander Ives Bartolot. "Kingdoms of the Savanna: The Kuba Kingdom." Available online. URL: http://www.metmuseum.org/toah/hd/kuba/hd_kuba.htm. Downloaded August 13, 2007. Alexander Ives Bartolot.

"Kingdoms of the Savanna: the Luba and Lunda Empires." Available online. URL: http://www.metmuseum.org/toah/hd/luba/hd_luba.htm. Downloaded August 13, 2007.

205 Rene LeMarchand. "Zaire: The Colonial State." Library of Congress. Available online. URL: http://lcweb2.loc.gov/cgi-bin/query/r?frd/cstdy:@field(DOCID+zr0020). Downloaded August 13, 2007. Gondola. *History of the Congo*, pp. 50–66.

206 Gondola. *History of the Congo*, pp. 64–75. Martin Ewans. *European Atrocity, African Catastrophe: Leopold II, the Congo Free State and Its Aftermath*. New York: RoutledgeCurzon, 2002, pp. 161–165.

207 Martin Ewans, *European Atrocity, African Catastrophe*, pp. 161–165 Rene LeMarchard. "Zaire: The Leopoldian Legacy." Library of Congress. Available online. URL: http://lcweb2.loc.gov/cgi-bin/query/r?frd/cstdy:@field(DOCID+zr0021). Downloaded August 13, 2007.

208 Gondola. *History of the Congo*, pp. 19, 88–98. Rene LeMarchand. "Zaire: Postwar Reforms." Library of Congress. Available online. URL: http://lcweb2.loc.gov/cgi-bin/query/r?frd/cstdy:@field(DOCID+zr0024). Downloaded August 13, 2007. Ewans. *European Atrocity*, pp. 238–242.

209 Gondola. *History of the Congo*, pp. 19–20, 98–114, 241–245. LeMarchand "Zaire: The Leopoldian Legacy."

210 Gondola. *History of the Congo*, pp. 19–20, 115–123. Ewans. *European Atrocity*, pp. 243–245.

211 Gondola. *History of the Congo*, pp. xxvii, 139–154. Heale. *Democratic Republic of the Congo*, pp. 32, 41. Michael Nest with Francois Grignon and Emizet F. Kisangani. *Democratic Republic of Congo: Economic Dimensions of War and Peace*. Boulder, Colo.: Lynne Rienner Publishers, 2006, p. 20.

212 Gondola. *History of the Congo*, pp. 8, 155–162. Heale. *Democratic Republic of the Congo*, pp. 55.

213 Gondola. *History of the Congo*, pp. 163–180. BBC News. "Quick Guide: Congo." Available online. URL: http://news.bbc.co.uk/nol/shared/spl/hi/pop_ups/quick_guides/04/africa_dr_congo/html/3.stm. Downloaded August 13, 2007. U.S. State Department. "Background Notes: Democratic Republic of Congo." Armed Conflict Database. "DRC." International Institute for Strategic Studies. Available online. URL: http://acd.iiss.org/armedconflict/MainPages/dsp_ConflictTimeline.asp?ConflictID=160&YearID=912&DisplayYear=2002. Downloaded August 13, 2007.

214 Nest et al. *Democratic Republic of Congo: Economic Dimensions*, pp. 12–13, 17–24. United Nations High Commissioner for Refugees. "Democratic Republic of Congo: State Protection," pp. 14, 99. February 2005. Available online. URL: http://www.unhcr.org/home/RSDCOI/430601354.pdf. Downloaded August 13, 2007.

215 Nest et al. *Democratic Republic of Congo: Economic Dimensions*, pp. 99–107. Michael Lasalandra. "Congo War Invisible and Deadly Crisis, Says Speaker." *Harvard Public Health Now* (February 17, 2006). Available online. URL: http://www.hsph.harvard.edu/now/feb17/. Downloaded August 13, 2007.

216 International Committee of the Red Cross, "Congo-Kinshasa: ICRC distributes aid to 11,000 displaced people in South Kivu," press release, July 20, 2006. Available online. URL: http:www.icrc.org/web/eng/siteeng0.nsf/html/news-congo-kinshasa-170706. Downloaded August 14, 2007; UN News Center, "DR of Congo: As the country moves boldly towards historic vote, humanitarian concerns continue to demand attention." Available online. URL:

http://www.un.org/events/tenstories_2006/story.asp?storyID=2300. Downloaded August 14, 2007.

[217] Michael Lasalandra. "Congo War Invisible and Deadly Crisis."

[218] Andrea Lari and Rick Neal. "Democratic Republic of Congo: Aid and UN Leadership Needed in Return Areas." *Refugees International* (December 12, 2006). Available online. URL: http://www.refugeesinternational.org/content/article/detail/9731/?PHPSESSID=5cfliegen3C. Downloaded August 13, 2007.

[219] Nest et al. *Democratic Republic of Congo: Economic Dimensions*, pp. 107–109. United Methodist Committee on Relief. "Democratic Republic of Congo." Available online. URL: http://gbgm-umc.org/umcor/ngo/drcongo/. Downloaded August 13, 2007.

[220] Nest et al. *Democratic Republic of Congo: Economic Dimensions*, pp. 113–116.

[221] Lyn Graybill and Kimberly Lanagram. "Truth, Justice, and Reconciliation in Africa: Issues and Cases." *African Stuaies Quarterly* 8, no. 1 (Fall 2004). Available online. URL: http://www.africa.ufl.edu/asq/v8/v8i1a1.htm. Downloaded August 13, 2007. Theodore Kasongo Kamwimbi. "The DRC Elections, Reconciliation, and Justice." International Center for Transitional Justice. July 27, 2006. Available online. URL: http://www.ictj.org/en/news/coverage/article/986.html. Downloaded August 13, 2007.

[222] Centers for Disease Control and Prevention. "The HHS/CDC Global AIDS Program in Democratic Republic of Congo." January 8, 2007. Available online. URL: http://www.cdc.gov/nchstp/od/gap/countries/drcongo.htm. Downloaded August 13, 2007. United Nations. *2006 Report on the Global AIDS Epidemic*, p. 505. Annabel Kanabus, Sarah Allen, and Bonita de Boer. "The Origins of HIV and the First Cases of AIDS." AVERT. October 23, 2006. Available online. URL: http://www.avert.org/origins.htm. Downloaded August 13, 2007.

[223] United States Agency for International Development. "Health Profile: Democratic Republic of the Congo." November 2001. Available online. URL: http://www.usaid.gov/our_work/global_health/aids/Countries/africa/drocongo_04.pdf. Downloaded August 13, 2007. Amnesty International. "Democratic Republic of Congo: HIV—the longest lasting scar of war." Available online. URL: http://news.amnesty.org/mavp/news.nsf/print/ENGAFR620262004. Downloaded August 13, 2007.

[224] IRINnews. "DRC: ARV Distribution Hindered by War." March 4, 2005. Available online. URL: http://www.plusnews.org/AIDSreport.asp?ReportID=3115&SelectRegion=Great_Lakes. Downloaded August 13, 2007.

[225] PEPFAR. "Congolese Musicians Raise HIV/AIDS Awareness in the DRC." January 2007. Available online. URL: http://www.pepfar.gov/press/78951.htm. Downloaded August 13, 2007.

[226] IRINnews. "DRC: Solidarity against AIDS." October 10, 2006. Available online. URL: http://www.irinnews.org/report.asp?ReportID=55895&SelectRegion=West_Africa. Downloaded August 13, 2007.

[227] Global Fund. "Congo Portfolio." Available online. URL: http://www.theglobalfund.org/programs/Portfolio.aspx?CountryId=ZAR&Component—alaria&lang=en. Downloaded. August 13, 2007. AVERT. "What Is the Global Fund?" Available online. URL: http://www.avert.org/global-fund.htm. Downloaded August 13, 2007. Refugees International. "DRC: Local NGO Works to Heal Victims of Gender-Based Violence." Available online. URL: http://www.refugeesinternational.org/content/article/detail/7310/?mission=7133&PHPSESSID=5cfliegen3C. Downloaded August 13, 2007. Family Health International. "FHI's

Collaboration Boosts Access to Critical Health Services, Builds Local Capacity in DRC." Available online. URL: http://www.fhi.org/en/HIVAIDS/country/DRCongo/res_DRC_GF_USAID.htm. Downloaded August 13, 2007. IRINnews. "DRC: Solidarity against AIDS."

[228] IRIN Africa. "DRC: Thousands More Flee Ongoing Clashes in Kivu." United Nations Office for the Coordination of Humanitarian Affairs. May 24, 2007. Available online. URL: http://www.irinnews.org/Report.aspx?ReportId=72346. Downloaded August 13, 2007. IRIN Africa. "Massacred Villagers Found Dead in Their Bed." UN Office for the Coordination of Humanitarian Affairs. May 28, 2007. Available online. URL: http://www.irinnews.org/Report.aspx?ReportId=72402. Downloaded May 30, 2007.

[229] IRIN Africa. "DRC: Probe into MUNOC Gold, Arms Trafficking Well Advanced." United Nations Office for the Coordination of Humanitarian Affairs. May 25, 2007. Available online. URL: http://www.irinnews.org/Report.aspx?ReportId=72373. Downloaded May 30, 2007. IRIN Africa. "DRC: Demobilisation of Ex-Militias Slowly Taking Root in Northeast." UN Office for the Coordination of Humanitarian Affairs. May 25, 2007. Available online. URL: http://www.irinnews.org/Report.aspx?ReportId=72406. Downloaded May 30, 2007.

[230] International Monetary Fund. "Statement at the Conclusion of an IMF Mission to the Democratic Republic of the Congo." Press release no. 07/55 (March 19, 2007). Available online. URL: http://www.imf.org/external/np/sec/pr/2007/pr0755.htm. Downloaded May 30, 2007.

[231] World Bank. "World Bank and European Union Call for International Support for Democratic Republic of Congo." March 10, 2007. Available online. URL: http://go.worldbank.org/5B3K09C0M0. Downloaded May 30, 2007.

[232] United Nations Development Programme. "UNDP Associate Administrator Visits Democratic Republic of Congo." April 27, 2007. Available online. URL: http://content.undp.org/go/newsroom/2007/april/melkert-drc-20070427.en. Downloaded May 30, 2007.

PART II

Primary Sources

4

United States Documents

The primary sources in this chapter are arranged in chronological order. Documents that have been excerpted are identified as such; all others are reproduced in full.

Isaac Goodwin: "Overseers of the Poor" (1834) (excerpt)

In the early 19th century, local authorities had responsibility to care for the indigent within their jurisdictions. In his popular manual for Massachusetts town officers, attorney Isaac Godwin summarized the duties of the overseer of the poor and cited relevant decisions from the state Supreme Court.

Much discussion focused on how to determine a citizen's "settlement," place of legal residence, since that town had to pay for his or her upkeep in times of need. Some people established settlement by birth or marriage; others acquired it through property ownership or by a vote of the local council. Increasing mobility complicated poor relief because people did not necessarily live where they had settlement. Couples sometimes married across borders. Workers moved to find jobs, dragging wives and children with them. Although a man was expected to provide for his dependents, sometimes couples separated, or injury or death deprived a family of a breadwinner. Many municipalities viewed strangers, immigrants, and out-of-state visitors as potential burdens; should they fall sick or go into debt, they had no deep pockets behind them.

If someone needed aid, the overseer of the poor tried to charge the family first and then the town of settlement—a financial battle sometimes fought in court. As Goodwin noted, overseers had the right to hire out the poor to pay for their room and board.

(. . . .)

Overseers shall relieve and support, and in case of their decease, decently bury all poor persons residing or found in their towns, having no lawful settlements within this Commonwealth, when they stand in need, and may employ them as other paupers may be; the expense whereof may be recovered of their relations, if they have any chargeable by law for their support; otherwise it shall be paid out of the treasury of the Commonwealth, by warrant from the Governor, by and with the advice of Council, an account thereof having been first exhibited to, and examined and allowed by, the General Court. And upon complaint of such Overseers, any Justice of the Peace in their county may, by warrant directed to, and which may be executed by, any constable of their town, or any particular person by name, cause such pauper to be sent and conveyed, by land or water, to any other State, or to any place beyond sea, where he belongs, if the Justice thinks proper, if he may be conveniently removed, at the expense of the Commonwealth; but if he cannot be so removed, he may be sent to and relieved and employed in the house of correction, or work-house, at the public expense.

(. . .)

Overseers of the Poor are empowered, from time to time, to bind out, to any citizen of this Commonwealth, by deed indented or poll, as apprentices, to be instructed and employed in any lawful art, trade or mystery, or as servants, to be employed in any lawful work or labour, any male or female children, whose parents are lawfully settled in, and become actually chargeable to their town; also, whose parents, so settled, shall be thought by said Overseers to be unable to maintain them, (whether they receive alms, or are so chargeable or not:) . . . provision to be made in such deed for the instruction of male children, so bound out, to read, write and cypher, and of females to read and write, and for such other instruction, benefit and allowance, either within or at the end of the term, as to the Overseers may seem fit and reasonable.

It shall be the duty of said Overseers, to inquire into the usage of children so bound out, and to defend them from injuries.

(. . .)

Overseers shall have power to set to work, or bind out to service, by deed as aforesaid, for a term not exceeding one whole year at a time, all such persons residing and lawfully settled in their respective towns, or who have no such settlement within this Commonwealth, married or unmarried, upwards of twenty-one years of age, as are able of body, but have no visible means of support, who live idly, and use and exercise no ordinary or daily lawful trade or business to get their living by, and also all persons who are liable by any law to be sent to the house of correction.

(...)

By stat. of 1830, ch. 150, every master of a vessel coming from any place without the commonwealth, with alien passengers on board who may become chargeable as paupers, is required to give to the selectmen of the towns complete list of such passengers before they leave the vessel, with the names of the places from which they were taken on board, and give bond with sufficient sureties in the penal sum not exceeding two hundred dollars for each alien passenger, with condition to indemnify the inhabitants of said town and also the commonwealth from all manner of expense which may arise from providing for such alien passengers for three years then next coming.

Source: Goodwin, Isaac. *Town Officer; or, Laws of Massachusetts relative to the duties of municipal officers together with a digest of the decisions of the Supreme Judicial Court upon those subjects*. 3rd edition. Worcester, Mass.: Dorr, Howland and Co., 1834.

Populist Party Platform (1892)

The concentration of wealth and power in the hands of industrialists during the Gilded Age produced a popular backlash. Disgruntled and debt-ridden rural Americans, particularly in the West and South, voiced their grievances through farmers' alliances. These groups joined with the Knights of Labor, a workers' organization founded by Philadelphia tailors, to give birth to the Populist Party at a convention in Omaha, Nebraska, in 1892.

Written by novelist and lawyer Ignatius Donnelly, the preamble to the Omaha Platform blamed the country's economic woes on the collusion of politicians, bankers, railroad tycoons, and other business interests. The party proposed numerous remedies, such as an end to corporate subsidies and direct election of senators, and labor rights initiatives included an eight-hour day and a graduated income tax so that those who earned more would pay more. To help the cash strapped poor, Populists argued that the government should mint silver coins freely to expand the money supply. The "people's party" nominated Iowa lawyer James K. Weaver for president.

Although Democrat Grover Cleveland won the election with more than 5 million votes, Weaver collected more than a million and carried Colorado, Kansas, Idaho, and Nevada. Thanks to this strong showing, populist ideas gained more currency. Success—and infighting—proved the party's undoing, however: Democrats coopted much of the platform, and infighting undermined the coalition of urban East and rural South and West. After 1896, the Populist Party ceased to be a major political force although its principles helped shape the New Deal of the 1930s.

NATIONAL PEOPLE'S PARTY PLATFORM

Assembled upon the 116th anniversary of the Declaration of Independence, the People's Party of America, in their first national convention, invoking upon their action the blessing of Almighty God, put forth in the name and on behalf of the people of this country, the following preamble and declaration of principles:

PREAMBLE

The conditions which surround us best justify our co-operation; we meet in the midst of a nation brought to the verge of moral, political, and material ruin. Corruption dominates the ballot-box, the Legislatures, the Congress, and touches even the ermine of the bench. The people are demoralized; most of the States have been compelled to isolate the voters at the polling places to prevent universal intimidation and bribery. The newspapers are largely subsidized or muzzled, public opinion silenced, business prostrated, homes covered with mortgages, labor impoverished, and the land concentrating in the hands of capitalists. The urban workmen are denied the right to organize for self-protection, imported pauperized labor beats down their wages, a hireling standing army, unrecognized by our laws, is established to shoot them down, and they are rapidly degenerating into European conditions. The fruits of the toil of millions are boldly stolen to build up colossal fortunes for a few, unprecedented in the history of mankind; and the possessors of those, in turn, despise the republic and endanger liberty. From the same prolific womb of governmental injustice we breed the two great classes—tramps and millionaires. . . .

We have witnessed for more than a quarter of a century the struggles of the two great political parties for power and plunder, while grievous wrongs have been inflicted upon the suffering people. We charge that the controlling influences dominating both these parties have permitted the existing dreadful conditions to develop without serious effort to prevent or restrain them. Neither do they now promise us any substantial reform. . . .

Assembled on the anniversary of the birthday of the nation, and filled with the spirit of the grand general and chief who established our independence, we seek to restore the government of the Republic to the hands of "the plain people," with which class it originated....

We believe that the power of government—in other words, of the people—should be expanded (as in the case of the postal service) as rapidly and as far as the good sense of art intelligent people and the teachings of experience shall justify, to the end that oppression, injustice, and poverty shall eventually cease in the land....

PLATFORM

We declare, therefore—

First.—That the union of the labor forces of the United States this day consummated shall be permanent and perpetual; may its spirit enter into all hearts for the salvation of the Republic and the uplifting of mankind.

Second.—Wealth belongs to him who creates it, and every dollar taken from industry without an equivalent is robbery. "If any will not work, neither shall he eat." The interests of rural and civic labor are the same; their enemies are identical.

Third.—We believe that the time has come when the railroad corporations will either own the people or the people must own the railroads, and should the government enter upon the work of owning and managing all railroads, we should favor an amendment to the Constitution by which all persons engaged in the government service shall be placed under a civil-service regulation of the most rigid character, so as to prevent the increase of the power of the national administration by the use of such additional government employees.

FINANCE.—We demand a national currency, safe, sound, and flexible, issued by the general government only, a full legal tender for all debts, public and private, and that without the use of banking corporations, a just, equitable, and efficient means of distribution direct to the people, at a tax not to exceed 2 per cent. per annum, to be provided as set forth in the sub-treasury plan of the Farmers' Alliance, or a better system; also by payments in discharge of its obligations for public improvements....

TRANSPORTATION—Transportation being a means of exchange and a public necessity, the government should own and operate the railroads in the interest of the people. The telegraph, telephone, like the post-office system, being a necessity for the transmission of news, should be owned and operated by the government in the interest of the people.

LAND.—The land, including all the natural sources of wealth, is the heritage of the people, and should not be monopolized for speculative purposes, and alien ownership of land should be prohibited. All land now held by railroads and other corporations in excess of their actual needs, and all lands now owned by aliens should be reclaimed by the government and held for actual settlers only.

EXPRESSION OF SENTIMENTS

Your Committee on Platform and Resolutions beg leave unanimously to report the following:

Whereas, Other questions have been presented for our consideration, we hereby submit the following, not as a part of the Platform of the People's Party, but as resolutions expressive of the sentiment of this Convention.

1. RESOLVED, That we demand a free ballot and a fair count in all elections and pledge ourselves to secure it to every legal voter without Federal Intervention, through the adoption by the States of the unperverted Australian or secret ballot system.
2. RESOLVED, That the revenue derived from a graduated income tax should be applied to the reduction of the burden of taxation now levied upon the domestic industries of this country.
3. RESOLVED, That we pledge our support to fair and liberal pensions to ex-Union soldiers and sailors.
4. RESOLVED, That we condemn the fallacy of protecting American labor under the present system, which opens our ports to the pauper and criminal classes of the world and crowds out our wage-earners; and we denounce the present ineffective laws against contract labor, and demand the further restriction of undesirable emigration.
5. RESOLVED, That we cordially sympathize with the efforts of organized workingmen to shorten the hours of labor, and demand a rigid enforcement of the existing eight-hour law on Government work, and ask that a penalty clause be added to the said law.

6. RESOLVED, That we regard the maintenance of a large standing army of mercenaries, known as the Pinkerton system, as a menace to our liberties, and we demand its abolition. . . .

7. RESOLVED, That we commend to the favorable consideration of the people and the reform press the legislative system known as the initiative and referendum.

8. RESOLVED, That we favor a constitutional provision limiting the office of President and Vice-President to one term, and providing for the election of Senators of the United States by a direct vote of the people.

9. RESOLVED, That we oppose any subsidy or national aid to any private corporation for any purpose.

10. RESOLVED, That this convention sympathizes with the Knights of Labor and their righteous contest with the tyrannical combine of clothing manufacturers of Rochester, and declare it to be a duty of all who hate tyranny and oppression to refuse to purchase the goods made by the said manufacturers, or to patronize any merchants who sell such goods.

Source: "Populist Party Platform, 1892." *The World Almanac*, 1893 (New York: 1893), 83–85. Reprinted in George Brown Tindall, ed., *A Populist Reader, Selections from the Works of American Populist Leaders* (New York: Harper & Row, 1966), 90–96. Available online. URL: http://historymatters.gmu.edu/d/5361/. Downloaded August 6, 2007.

Letter to Mrs. Roosevelt (March 29, 1935)

In the 1930s, many Americans wrote to President Franklin Roosevelt and his wife, Eleanor, often seeking help in this time of hardship. Despite their privileged upbringings, the Roosevelts projected concern for the common citizen. The first lady wrote a newspaper column, "My Day," and hosted a radio talk show, and as historian Richard Cohen observed in his book, Dear Mrs. Roosevelt: Letters from Children of the Great Depression, *her very public sympathy for the plight of the poor invited letters—300,000 alone during her husband's first year in office. The FDR Library in Hyde Park, New York, houses a collection of them.*

Many children sent her mail. They explained more than they complained about torn pants and aching teeth. They confided about angry bill collectors, ailing mothers, and out-of-work fathers who drank too much. Asking for bicycles and bathtubs and Easter dresses, many writers begged Mrs. Roosevelt not to reveal their identity. They feared that their parents would not approve of their letters, so full of dollar-and-cents details about their difficulties, and that their family's shame would be splashed across the local newspaper.

Dear Mrs. Roosevelt. I am writing you a little letter this morning. Are you glad it is spring I am. For so manny poor people can raise some more to eat. You no what I am writing this letter for. Mother said Mrs. Roosevelt is a God mother to the world and I though mabe you had some old clothes You no Mother is a good sewer and all the little girls are getting Easter dresses. And I though you had some you no. papa could wear Mr. Roosevelt shirts and cloth I no. My papa like Mr. Roosevelt and Mother said Mr. Roosevelt carry his worries with a smile You no he is always happy. You no we are not living on the relief we live on a little farm. papa did have a job And got laid on 5 yrs ago so we save and got two horses and 2 cows and a hog so we can all the food stuff we can ever thing to eat some time we don't have eni thing but we live. But you no it so hard to get cloth. So I though mabe you had some. You no what you though was no good Mother can make over for me I am 11 yr old. I have 2 brother and a sister 14 yr old. I wish I could see you. I no I would like you both. And shoes Mother wears 6 or 6 1/2. And papa wear 9. We have no car or no phone or Radio papa he would like to have a radio but he said there is other thing he need more. papa is worried about his seed oats. And one horse is not very good. But ever one has't to worrie, I am send this letter with the pennie I get to take to Sunday school Mother give me one So it took 3 week. Cause mother would think I better not ask for things from the the first Lady. But mother said you was an angle for doing so much for the poor. And I though that would be all rite this is some paper my teacher gave for Xmas. My add is

C.V.B.
Rushsyhania, Ohio

Reply to the letter:

April 3, 1935

My dear Miss V. B.:

Mrs. Roosevelt asks me to acknowledge your letter and to express her regret that because of the great number of similar requests, she has found it impossible to comply with them, much as she would like to assist all those who appeal to her.

Assuring you of Mrs. Roosevelt's sympathy, I am

entities, dependent on the United States for support and protection. In exchange for land and in compensation for forced removal from their original homelands, the government promised through laws, treaties, and pledges to support and protect Native Americans. However, funding for programs associated with those promises has fallen short, and Native peoples continue to suffer the consequences of a discriminatory history. Federal efforts to raise Native American living conditions to the standards of others have long been in motion, but Native Americans still suffer higher rates of poverty, poor educational achievement, substandard housing, and higher rates of disease and illness. Native Americans continue to rank at or near the bottom of nearly every social, health, and economic indicator.

Small in numbers and relatively poor, Native Americans often have had a difficult time ensuring fair and equal treatment on their own. Unfortunately, relying on the goodwill of the nation to honor its obligation to Native Americans clearly has not resulted in desired outcomes. Its small size and geographic apartness from the rest of American society induces some to designate the Native American population the "invisible minority." To many, the government's promises to Native Americans go largely unfulfilled. Thus, the U.S. Commission on Civil Rights, through this report, gives voice to a quiet crisis.

Over the last 10 years, federal funding for Native American programs has increased significantly. However, this has not been nearly enough to compensate for a decline in spending power, which had been evident for decades before that, nor to overcome a long and sad history of neglect and discrimination.

Thus, there persists a large deficit in funding Native American programs that needs to be paid to eliminate the backlog of unmet Native American needs, an essential predicate to raising their standards of living to that of other Americans. Native Americans living on tribal lands do not have access to the same services and programs available to other Americans, even though the government has a binding trust obligation to provide them.

In preparing this report, the Commission reviewed the budgets of the six federal agencies with the largest expenditures on Native American programs and conducted an extensive literature review.

Department of the Interior [DOI]

The Bureau of Indian Affairs (BIA), within DOI, bears the primary responsibility for providing the 562 federally recognized Native American tribes with federal services. The Congressional Research Service found that between 1975 and 2000, funding for BIA and the Office of the Special Trustee declined by $6 million yearly when adjusted for inflation.

BIA's mismanagement of Individual Indian Money trust accounts has denied Native Americans financial resources that could be applied toward basic needs that BIA programs fail to provide. . . .

In December 2002, the deferred maintenance backlog of BIA schools was estimated at $507 million and increasing at an annual rate of $56.5 million due to inflation and natural aging and deterioration of school buildings. . . .

Department of Health and Human Services

Native Americans have a lower life expectancy than any other racial/ethnic group and higher rates of many diseases, including diabetes, tuberculosis, and alcoholism. Yet, health facilities are frequently inaccessible and medically obsolete, and preventive care and specialty services are not readily available.

Most Native Americans do not have private health insurance and thus rely exclusively on the Indian Health Service (IHS) for health care. The federal government spends less per capita on Native American health care than on any other group for which it has this responsibility, including Medicaid recipients, prisoners, veterans, and military personnel. Annually, IHS spends 60 percent less on its beneficiaries than the average per person health care expenditure nationwide. . . .

Department of Housing and Urban Development [HUD]

The availability of safe, sanitary housing in Indian Country is significantly less than the need. Overcrowding and its effects are a persistent problem. Furthermore, existing housing structures are substandard: approximately 40 percent of on-reservation housing is considered inadequate, and one in five reservation homes lacks complete plumbing. Native Americans also have less access to homeownership resources, due to limited access to credit, land ownership restrictions, geographic isolation, and harsh environmental conditions that make construction difficult and expensive.

While HUD has made efforts to improve housing, lack of funding has hindered progress. Funding for Native American programs at HUD increased only slightly over the years (8.8 percent), significantly less than the agency as a whole (62 percent). After controlling for inflation, HUD's Native American programs actually lost spending power. . . .

Department of Justice [DOJ]

All three components of law enforcement—policing, justice, and corrections—are substandard in Indian Country compared with the rest of the nation. Native Americans are twice as likely as any other racial/ethnic group to be the victims of crime. Yet, per capita spending on law enforcement in Native American communities is roughly 60 percent of the national average. Correctional facilities in Indian Country are also more overcrowded than even the most crowded state and federal prisons. In addition, Native Americans have long held that tribal court systems have not been funded sufficiently or consistently, and hence, are not equal to other court systems.

Law enforcement professionals concede that the dire situation in Indian Country is understated. While DOJ should be commended for its stated intention to meet its obligations to Native Americans, promising projects have suffered from inconsistent or discontinued funding. Native American law enforcement funding increased almost 85 percent between 1998 and 2003, but the amount allocated was so small to begin with that its proportion to the department's total budget hardly changed.... Additionally, many Native Americans have lost faith in the justice system, in part due to perceived bias. Many attribute disproportionately high incarceration rates to unfair treatment by the criminal justice system, including racial profiling, disparities in prosecution, and lack of access to legal representation....

Department of Education

As a group, Native American students are not afforded educational opportunities equal to other American students. They routinely face deteriorating school facilities, underpaid teachers, weak curricula, discriminatory treatment, outdated learning tools, and cultural isolation. As a result, achievement gaps persist with Native American students scoring lower than any other racial/ethnic group in basic levels of reading, math, and history. Native American students are also more likely to drop out....

Department of Agriculture [USDA]

The USDA is largely responsible for rural development and farm and business supplements in rural communities. Native Americans rely on such programs to foster conditions that encourage and sustain economic investments. However, insufficient funding has limited the success of development programs and perpetuated unstable economies. Poor economic conditions have resulted in food shortages and hunger. Native Americans are more than twice as likely as the general population to face hunger and food insecurity at any given time. . . .

Source: U.S. Commission on Civil Rights. "A Quiet Crisis: Federal Funding and Unmet Needs in Indian Country," pp. ix–xi. July 2003. Available online. URL:http://www.usccr.gov/pubs/na0703/na0204.pdf. Downloaded April 20, 2007.

Maureen Berner, Trina Ozer, and Sharon Payneter: "A Portrait of Hunger, the Social Safety Net, and the Working Poor" (September 2006) (excerpt)

According to the U.S. Department of Labor, in 2003, 7.3 million Americans qualified as the "working poor," meaning that they spent more than 27 hours a week working or looking for work but still did not earn enough to cross the poverty threshold. Almost a third held service jobs, and occupations of high poverty included farming, forestry, and fishing. Expand the definition to include "low income"—up to double the poverty level—and the number of working poor grows. One in four families with a full-time, full-year worker experienced food and housing "insecurity." Many turned to food banks.

This excerpt comes from a September 2006 policy brief by Maureen Berner, a professor of government and public administration, and graduate students Trina Ozer and Sharon Paynter. They studied two food banks—one in Iowa and one in North Carolina—and suggest that hunger is a widespread problem for the working poor, one insufficiently addressed by government programs.

Introduction and Summary of Results

Millions of Americans turn to soup kitchens and other non-profit hunger relief services to feed themselves and their families. According to the U.S. Department of Agriculture, in 2004 more than 38 million Americans lived in food insecure households where there was not enough food for everyone living in the home (Nord, Andrews & Carlson, 2004). Contrary to common perception, many of these families are working and yet their incomes are still insufficient to meet their basic needs. We highlight two examples to illustrate this point. In Iowa, 25 percent of clients surveyed were employed. At the Food Bank of Central and Eastern North Carolina, an even higher number of clients work. More than 37 percent of all clients at this agency are employed (FBCENC, 2005).

Increasingly, non-profit organizations are asked to fill gaps that government is unable or unwilling to close. Nonprofits often operate as a low-cost alternative to big government social service programming (Alexander,

1999). Given our federally supported social safety net, why is there such a great need for non-profits to step in and feed the hungry, especially if many of those people are working? To answer this question, this paper presents the results of a detailed two year (2004–2006) survey of all the clients at the largest food pantry in Northeast Iowa, the Cedar Valley Food Pantry (CVFP), and places them in a national context. Furthermore, the data used for this paper are rich. Gathering valid and reliable data on this population is extremely difficult.

This study gives academics, practitioners, and others an opportunity to better understand the interaction of food assistance programs with other programs through survey data gathered from a full population.

In particular, we describe the working population who rely on Iowa's CVFP for food assistance. Those who work must meet certain criteria to be classified as poor, and different organizations may use different criteria. To be eligible for food assistance at CVFP, a family's income must be at or below 185 percent of the US Department of Health and Human Services' poverty guidelines. Over the two-year span of this study, 185 percent of the average guideline meant an income of $35,890 a year for a family of four (US Department of Health and Human Services).

A sizable portion of clients at the pantry already work (25 percent) or are on government support (49 percent), including Social Security. Surprisingly, working does not appear to alleviate the need for regular food assistance. Job related demands, such as transportation, child care, and uncovered health care costs force choices between food and other necessities more often for working people than for the unemployed. Working individuals are just as likely to need supplemental food assistance on a regular basis as the unemployed.

In addition, this paper suggests government support programs such as Social Security and Food Stamps are an insufficient guard against hunger, and thousands of Americans turn to nonprofits to fill the gap. The policy ramifications of these findings are clear. First, while this study can not be broadly generalized beyond this population, the findings suggest that policies encouraging work among the poor should recognize the standard of living for these individuals may become less stable, rather than more so, as a result of gaining employment. To more fully understand this relationship, a longitudinal analysis of employment and food assistance data should be undertaken. Second, our national social support structure is inadequate. If we wish to maintain the government responsibility to alleviate hunger in our country, benefits for eligible citizens must be increased or food assistance non-profits need greater government support. Otherwise we should face the fact that as an undeclared public policy, our society tolerates hunger.

Source: Maureen Berner, Trina Ozer, and Sharon Paynter. "A Portrait of Hunger, the Social Safety Net, and the Working Poor," pp. 5–7. Center on Poverty, Work and Opportunity, School of Law, University of North Carolina at Chapel Hill. September 1, 2006. Available online. URL: http://www.law.unc.edu/pdfs/poverty/BernerPolicyBrief.pdf. Downloaded April 20, 2007.

Children's Defense Fund Action Council: "Stand Up for Children *Now!*" (2006) (excerpts)

In the late 1960s, the civil-rights movement was heading into a second phase. Although activists had succeeded through the courts in overturning the most egregious discriminatory laws and practices, they recognized that black Americans faced far more insidious barriers to equal opportunity. To Martin Luther King, Jr., the battle against the three big social evils—racism, violence, and poverty—had just begun.

King and the Southern Christian Leadership Conference (SCLC), a civil-rights organization he helped found, planned a Poor People's Campaign in 1968 to draw attention to economic injustice. King called for a guaranteed national income. One activist the campaign drew to Washington, D.C., was lawyer Marian Wright Edelman. Although the Poor People's Campaign fizzled in the wake of King's assassination, Edelman started the Washington Research Project to monitor hunger, education, and other federal programs for low-income families. Out of that emerged the Children's Defense Fund (CDF), a nonprofit that has been gathering data and advocating on behalf of disadvantaged children since 1973.

Among its publications, the CDF releases an annual "State of America's Children" report. The lobbying wing, the CDF Action Council, then uses that information in an "action guide," excerpted below. Since kids lack voting power, CDF gives them a voice, making a case to the public and to lawmakers for policies that benefit children, particularly poor and minority children and those with disabilities.

One Day in the Life of America's Children

1 mother dies in childbirth.

4 children are killed by abuse or neglect.

5 children or teens commit suicide.

8 children or teens are killed by firearms.

77 babies die before their first birthday.

181 children are arrested for violent crimes.

367 babies are born to mothers who received late or no prenatal care.

380 children are arrested for drug abuse.

888 babies are born at low birthweight.
1,154 babies are born to teen mothers.
1,701 babies are born without health insurance.
1,900 public school students are corporally punished.
2,252 babies are born to mothers who are not high school graduates.
2,447 babies are born into poverty.
2,482 children are confirmed abused or neglected.
2,756 high school students drop out.
3,879 babies are born to unmarried mothers.
4,356 children are arrested.
16,964 public school students are suspended.

. . .

The United States, the most militarily powerful and materially rich nation in the world, is so spiritually poor it chooses to let children be the poorest age group and to suffer multiple preventable deprivations. Millions of children lack health care when they are sick, lack enough food to stave off hunger, are homeless when their parents cannot find or afford housing, and lack safe and quality child care and afterschool programs when parents have to work. Millions of poor children are denied an early Head Start and quality preschool experience to help them get ready for school. Millions more children in our schools cannot read or write and are dropping out or being pushed out of school into a cradle to prison pipeline of hopelessness and despair that routes them to juvenile detention and adult jail rather than to jobs or college. And millions of children are struggling to grow up in working poor families who are playing by America's rules but still cannot earn fair wages from their employers or get enough support from their government to escape poverty or better themselves.

How America Stands in the World in Protecting Children

Among industrialized countries, the United States ranks:
1st in military technology
1st in military exports
1st in Gross Domestic Product
1st in the number of millionaires and billionaires
1st in health technology
1st in defense expenditures
1st in the number of persons in prison or jail
12th in living standards among our poorest one-fifth of children

13th in the gap between rich and poor children
14th in efforts to lift children out of poverty
18th in the percent of children in poverty
22nd in low birthweight rates
25th in infant mortality
Next to last among donor nations in the proportion of GDP devoted to international aid to impoverished peoples
Next to last among 16 industrialized countries in the proportion of GDP devoted to income support for non-elderly families
Last among 16 industrialized countries in the proportion of children living in poverty after all income supports are counted
Last in protecting our children against gun violence

According to the Centers for Disease Control and Prevention, U.S. children under age 15 are:
9 times as likely to die in a firearm accident,
11 times as likely to commit suicide with a gun,
12 times as likely to die from gunfire, and
16 times as likely to be murdered with a gun,
as children in 25 other industrialized countries combined.

Of the 191 members of the United Nations, the United States of America and Somalia (which has no legally constituted government) are the only two nations that have failed to ratify the U.N. Convention on the Rights of the Child.

Black infant mortality rates in our nation's capital exceed those of 55 nations, including the Bahamas, Barbados, and Libya.

Twenty-six major industrialized countries provide paid parental leave; the United States is not one of them.

The United States is the only industrialized nation that does not provide guaranteed prenatal care for every pregnant woman.

...

CDF Action Council Priorities

In 2006, the CDF Action Council seeks to:

1. **Stop the revenue hemorrhage from massive tax cuts for the wealthiest Americans, prevent already enacted tax cuts for the top 2**

percent from being accelerated, extended or made permanent, and commit to ending child poverty in our rich nation. . . .

2. **Resist all legislative budget cuts, caps, freezes, block grants, and regulatory erosion of child health, child welfare, early education, education and after-school investments.** At a time when the gap between rich and poor and our nation's budget and trade deficits are at all time highs; child poverty, including extreme child poverty, has increased among all groups of children; infant mortality has increased for the first time in 44 years; and costly wars in Iraq and Afghanistan are raging, it is time to correct course and stop asking poor children to subsidize rich and powerful special interests and a war of choice in Iraq.

3. **Insist on immediate child health coverage for all uninsured children and resist all efforts by governors, state legislatures, the Bush Administration, and Congress to undermine Medicaid coverage for children and CHIP (the Children's Health Insurance Program) under the false guises of flexibility and controlling health costs. . . .**

These children who are left behind come from every race, place and family type in America. Contrary to popular perception, there are more White than Black or Brown poor and uninsured children. More White than Black or Brown children get pregnant and have children each year, and more White than Black or Brown children die from gunfire. But minority children are disproportionately denied a fair chance in life and are disproportionately poor. An unlevel playing field from birth contributes to too many poor minority children getting pulled into a cradle to prison to death pipeline that we must dismantle if the clock of racial and social progress is not to turn backwards. Current national tax and budget policies and political choices will worsen these threats to child well-being unless we reverse them.

- A Black child is 4 times as likely as a White child to have a mother die in childbirth and is twice as likely to die in the first year of life.
- A Black preschool boy born in 2001 has a 1 in 3 chance of going to prison during his lifetime; a Black preschool girl has a 1 in 17 chance. Today, 580,000 Black males and 250,000 Latino males are serving sentences in state or federal prison while fewer than 40,000 Black males and 33,000 Latino males earn a bachelor's degree each year.
- 1 in 3 Black men, 20–29 years old, is under correctional supervision or control. Minority youths represent 34 percent of our adolescent

population but 62 percent of youths in detention. Girls are the fastest growing group of detained juveniles. . . .

- Nearly 70 percent of Blacks in prison never completed high school. When Black children do graduate from high school, they have a greater chance of being unemployed and a lower chance of going directly on to full-time college than White high school graduates.

These figures add up to a national catastrophe. . . .

These facts are not acts of God. These are our moral, political and economic choices as a people. They also represent the lives of real children whose suffering we could and are morally bound to prevent or alleviate with a sense of urgency. Meet a few of them below.

. . .

Homeless, Sick and Poor Children

. . .

Jenna

Jenna is a slight five-year-old girl with big brown eyes, a shy smile and the determination of a mountaineer scaling Everest. Her parents are homeless, forced to abandon their Section 8 apartment in fear for their children's health. Their landlord, despite court orders, refused to make repairs to their apartment, which had holes in the floor, a broken toilet, no heat or hot water for two winters and, most disastrously, dangerously high levels of lead. As a result, Jenna suffered lead poisoning that caused brain damage and developmental delays. This is most noticeable in her almost unintelligible speech. Jenna explains herself over and over again in an attempt to communicate her needs and thoughts. Often tears squeeze out in frustration. Her older sister, Felicia, 8, keeps a close eye, piping up to translate Jenna's muddled words when someone doesn't understand.

. . .

Francie

Nine-year-old Francie is very quiet and shy and still peers anxiously out from her blankets each morning. She remembers when rats were everywhere, burrowing in the walls and running freely through her apartment at night. She and her family became homeless after a rat attacked her foot, biting through her skin. Francie's family has applied for housing and is awaiting approval along with a very long list of others in New York City.

Samantha

Lydia's 4-year-old daughter Samantha has congenital blindness but can no longer get vision or dental services under her state's Children's Health Insurance Program (CHIP) since these services were removed from the

Texas CHIP benefits package. Lydia charged her daughter's $1,800 MRI on her credit card and owes $2,840 in dental fees for Samantha's four cavities and a root canal. Lydia earns $9 an hour cleaning apartments and has been with the same company for the last 10 years. She brings home about $580 every two weeks and does not know how she will pay for these expenses on her limited budget. . . .

Source: "Stand Up for Children *Now!* State of America's Children Action Guide," Washington, D.C.: Children's Defense Fund Action Council, 2006. Available online. URL: http://www.cdfactioncouncil.org/minigreenbook.pdf. Downloaded July 12, 2007.

5

International Documents

This chapter draws together international primary source documents organized into the following sections:

International Documents

Ukraine

Syria

Guatemala

India

Democratic Republic of the Congo

The documents are arranged in chronological order within each section. Documents that have been excerpted are identified as such; all others are reproduced in full.

INTERNATIONAL DOCUMENTS

The 16 Decisions of Grameen Bank (1984)

Founded by Muhammad Yunus in 1976, Grameen Bank offers collateral-free loans to the poor, who are usually denied credit by banks and other lending institution. As of December 2006, this pioneering microfinance institution in Bangladesh had 6.91 million borrowers, 97 percent of them women. For $2 or so, borrowers can buy a share of the bank, and roughly 2 million have done so. They own about 90 percent of the bank and share in decision making about policies and profit.

Unlike a conventional bank, Grameen Bank aims for social transformation. In the Grameen equation, credit leads in small, positive steps to investment, then higher income, then more access to credit, then higher income, then better health and living standards—the measure of success. To instill discipline, Grameen relies heavily on peer pressure. A villager cannot borrow alone; she or he joins a group of five that contracts to pay back all the individual loans. Eight groups form a center, and 60 centers constitute a branch. Each branch has five or six field workers who visit each center every week. Grameen charges about 20 percent interest on its loans—much less than profiteering local money lenders—which helps fund the bank's management and close supervision.

At a 1984 workshop with representatives from 100 centers, the bank developed its "16 decisions." Prospective members must pass a test on them, and borrowers often recite some or all at center meetings.

1. We shall follow and advance the four principles of Grameen Bank—Discipline, Unity, Courage and Hard work—in all walks of our lives.
2. Prosperity we shall bring to our families.
3. We shall not live in dilapidated houses. We shall repair our houses and work towards constructing new houses at the earliest.
4. We shall grow vegetables all the year round. We shall eat plenty of them and sell the surplus.
5. During the plantation seasons, we shall plant as many seedlings as possible.
6. We shall plan to keep our families small. We shall minimize our expenditures. We shall look after our health.
7. We shall educate our children and ensure that they can earn to pay for their education.
8. We shall always keep our children and the environment clean.
9. We shall build and use pit-latrines.
10. We shall drink water from tube-wells. If it is not available, we shall boil water or use alum.
11. We shall not take any dowry at our sons' weddings, neither shall we give any dowry at our daughters' wedding[s]. We shall keep our centre free from the curse of dowry. We shall not practice child marriage.
12. We shall not inflict any injustice on anyone, neither shall we allow anyone to do so.
13. We shall collectively undertake bigger investments for higher incomes.
14. We shall always be ready to help each other. If anyone is in difficulty, we shall all help him or her.

15. If we come to know of any breach of discipline in any centre, we shall all go there and help restore discipline.

16. We shall take part in all social activities collectively.

Source: Grameen Bank. "The 16 Decisions of Grameen Bank." Available online. URL: http://www.grameen-info.org/bank/the16.html. Updated June 12, 2006.

Muhammad Yunus, "Ten Indicators to Assess Poverty Level" (1998, 2006)

Every year Grameen Bank staff evaluate their work and check whether the socioeconomic situation of bank members is improving. Grameen Bank evaluates poverty level of the borrowers using 10 indicators. A member is considered to have moved out of poverty if her family fulfills the following criteria.

1. The family lives in a house worth at least Tk.[Bangladeshi taka] 25,000 . . . [about $375] or a house with a tin roof, and each member of the family is able to sleep on [a] bed instead of on the floor.

2. Family members drink pure water of tube-wells, boiled water or water purified by using alum, arsenic-free, purifying tablets or pitcher filters. [A frequent, unfortunate effect of drinking water from the tube-wells that Grameen Bank and other development agencies recommend has been arsenic poisoning since this metal occurs naturally in groundwater in parts of Bangladesh and neighboring countries.]

3. All children in the family over six years of age are all going to school or [have] finished primary school.

4. Minimum weekly loan installment of the borrower is Tk. 200 [about $3] or more.

5. Family uses sanitary latrine.

6. Family members have adequate clothing for every day use, warm clothing for winter, such as shawls, sweaters, blankets, etc, and mosquito-nets to protect themselves from mosquitoes.

7. Family has sources of additional income, such as vegetable garden, fruit-bearing trees, etc, so that they are able to fall back on these sources of income when they need additional money.

8. The borrower maintains an average annual balance of Tk. 5,000 [about $75] in her savings accounts.

9. Family experiences no difficulty in having three square meals a day throughout the year, i.e. no member of the family goes hungry any time of the year.

10. Family can take care of the health. If any member of the family falls ill, family can afford to take all necessary steps to seek adequate healthcare.

Source: Muhammad Yunus. "Ten Indicators to Assess Poverty Level." Grameen Bank Web site. Available online. URL: http://www.grameen-info.org/bank/tenindicators.htm. Updated September 28, 2006.

United Nations Millennium Declaration (September 8, 2000) (excerpts)

The largest meeting of world leaders in history, the 2000 UN Millennium Summit opened with a moment of silence for four UN workers killed in West Timor and then a plea from U.S. president Bill Clinton and Russian president Vladimir Putin for world peace. The three-day gathering drew representatives from 187 countries, including 99 heads of state and 47 heads of government, many of whom addressed the world body. At the end of the summit, the General Assembly adopted the United Nations Millennium Declaration affirming faith in the United Nations and renewed commitment to fighting poverty worldwide.

In 2002, UN secretary-general Kofi Annan commissioned the UN Millennium Project, an independent advisory group led by Jeffrey Sachs, to develop a strategy for realizing the specific targets of the lofty Millennium Development Goals: 1) eradicate extreme poverty and hunger; 2) achieve universal primary education; 3) promote gender equality and empower women; 4) reduce child mortality; 5) improve maternal health; 6) combat HIV/AIDS, malaria, and other diseases; 7) ensure environmental sustainability; and 8) develop a Global Partnership for Development. Although most people refer to the MDGs as a product of the summit, they actually emerged from a series of international summits throughout the 1990s.

I. Values and principles

1. We, heads of State and Government, have gathered at United Nations Headquarters in New York from 6 to 8 September 2000, at the dawn of a new millennium, to reaffirm our faith in the Organization and its Charter as indispensable foundations of a more peaceful, prosperous and just world.

2. We recognize that, in addition to our separate responsibilities to our individual societies, we have a collective responsibility to uphold the principles of human dignity, equality and equity at the global level. As leaders we have a duty therefore to all the world's people, especially

the most vulnerable and, in particular, the children of the world, to whom the future belongs. . . .

6. We consider certain fundamental values to be essential to international relations in the twenty-first century. These include:

- **Freedom.** Men and women have the right to live their lives and raise their children in dignity, free from hunger and from the fear of violence, oppression or injustice. Democratic and participatory governance based on the will of the people best assures these rights.
- **Equality.** No individual and no nation must be denied the opportunity to benefit from development. The equal rights and opportunities of women and men must be assured.
- **Solidarity.** Global challenges must be managed in a way that distributes the costs and burdens fairly in accordance with basic principles of equity and social justice. Those who suffer or who benefit least deserve help from those who benefit most.
- **Tolerance.** Human beings must respect one other, in all their diversity of belief, culture and language. Differences within and between societies should be neither feared nor repressed, but cherished as a precious asset of humanity. A culture of peace and dialogue among all civilizations should be actively promoted.
- **Respect for nature.** Prudence must be shown in the management of all living species and natural resources, in accordance with the precepts of sustainable development. . . .
- **Shared responsibility.** Responsibility for managing worldwide economic and social development, as well as threats to international peace and security, must be shared among the nations of the world and should be exercised multilaterally. As the most universal and most representative organization in the world, the United Nations must play the central role.

7. In order to translate these shared values into actions, we have identified key objectives to which we assign special significance.

II. Peace, security and disarmament

8. We will spare no effort to free our peoples from the scourge of war, whether within or between States, which has claimed more than 5 million lives in the past decade. We will also seek to eliminate the dangers posed by weapons of mass destruction. . . .

WORLD POVERTY

III. Development and poverty eradication

11. We will spare no effort to free our fellow men, women and children from the abject and dehumanizing conditions of extreme poverty, to which more than a billion of them are currently subjected. We are committed to making the right to development a reality for everyone and to freeing the entire human race from want. . . .

13. Success in meeting these objectives depends, *inter alia*, on good governance within each country. It also depends on good governance at the international level and on transparency in the financial, monetary and trading systems. We are committed to an open, equitable, rule-based, predictable and non-discriminatory multilateral trading and financial system. . . .

15. We also undertake to address the special needs of the least developed countries. . . . We call on the industrialized countries:

- To adopt, preferably by the time of that Conference, a policy of duty- and quota-free access for essentially all exports from the least developed countries;
- To implement the enhanced programme of debt relief for the heavily indebted poor countries without further delay and to agree to cancel all official bilateral debts of those countries in return for their making demonstrable commitments to poverty reduction; and
- To grant more generous development assistance, especially to countries that are genuinely making an effort to apply their resources to poverty reduction.

. . .

19. We resolve further:

- To halve, by the year 2015, the proportion of the world's people whose income is less than one dollar a day and the proportion of people who suffer from hunger and, by the same date, to halve the proportion of people who are unable to reach or to afford safe drinking water.
- To ensure that, by the same date, children everywhere, boys and girls alike, will be able to complete a full course of primary schooling and that girls and boys will have equal access to all levels of education.
- By the same date, to have reduced maternal mortality by three quarters, and under-five child mortality by two thirds, of their current rates.

- To have, by then, halted, and begun to reverse, the spread of HIV/AIDS, the scourge of malaria and other major diseases that afflict humanity.
- To provide special assistance to children orphaned by HIV/AIDS.
- By 2020, to have achieved a significant improvement in the lives of at least 100 million slum dwellers as proposed in the "Cities Without Slums" initiative.

20. We also resolve:

- To promote gender equality and the empowerment of women as effective ways to combat poverty, hunger and disease and to stimulate development that is truly sustainable.
- To develop and implement strategies that give young people everywhere a real chance to find decent and productive work.
- To encourage the pharmaceutical industry to make essential drugs more widely available and affordable by all who need them in developing countries.
- To develop strong partnerships with the private sector and with civil society organizations in pursuit of development and poverty eradication.
- To ensure that the benefits of new technologies, especially information and communication technologies, in conformity with recommendations contained in the ECOSOC 2000 Ministerial Declaration, are available to all.

IV. Protecting our common environment

21. We must spare no effort to free all of humanity, and above all our children and grandchildren, from the threat of living on a planet irredeemably spoilt by human activities, and whose resources would no longer be sufficient for their needs. . . .

V. Human rights, democracy and good governance

. . .

25. We resolve therefore: . . .

- To strengthen the capacity of all our countries to implement the principles and practices of democracy and respect for human rights, including minority rights.

- To combat all forms of violence against women and to implement the Convention on the Elimination of All Forms of Discrimination against Women.
- To take measures to ensure respect for and protection of the human rights of migrants, migrant workers and their families, to eliminate the increasing acts of racism and xenophobia in many societies and to promote greater harmony and tolerance in all societies.
- To work collectively for more inclusive political processes, allowing genuine participation by all citizens in all our countries.
- To ensure the freedom of the media to perform their essential role and the right of the public to have access to information.

VI. Protecting the vulnerable

26. We will spare no effort to ensure that children and all civilian populations that suffer disproportionately the consequences of natural disasters, genocide, armed conflicts and other humanitarian emergencies are given every assistance and protection so that they can resume normal life as soon as possible.

. . .

VII. Meeting the special needs of Africa

27. We will support the consolidation of democracy in Africa and assist Africans in their struggle for lasting peace, poverty eradication and sustainable development, thereby bringing Africa into the mainstream of the world economy.

28. We resolve therefore:

- To give full support to the political and institutional structures of emerging democracies in Africa.
- To encourage and sustain regional and subregional mechanisms for preventing conflict and promoting political stability, and to ensure a reliable flow of resources for peacekeeping operations on the continent.
- To take special measures to address the challenges of poverty eradication and sustainable development in Africa, including debt cancellation, improved market access, enhanced Official Development Assistance and increased flows of Foreign Direct Investment, as well as transfers of technology.

- To help Africa build up its capacity to tackle the spread of the HIV/AIDS pandemic and other infectious diseases.

VIII. Strengthening the United Nations

29. We will spare no effort to make the United Nations a more effective instrument for pursuing all of these priorities: the fight for development for all the peoples of the world, the fight against poverty, ignorance and disease; the fight against injustice; the fight against violence, terror and crime; and the fight against the degradation and destruction of our common home. . . .

Source: Resolution adopted by the United Nations General Assembly [without references to a Main Committee (A/55/L.2)], September 8, 2000. Available online. URL: http://www.un.org/millennium/declaration/ares552e.htm. Downloaded February 6, 2008.

Remarks by Muhammad Yunus, Founder of Grameen Bank (May 19, 2004) (excerpts)

In May 2004, Muhammad Yunus gave a talk at the Global Business and Global Poverty Conference at Stanford Graduate School of Business outlining the history and new initiatives of Grameen Bank. Two years later, he and the bank won the Nobel Peace Prize.

Back in the mid-[19]70s when Bangladesh was going through a difficult time, I was teaching economics at one of the universities in Bangladesh and we were going through a finance situation that sparked something which gradually led to the creation of Grameen Bank. The idea that hit me was that people were dying of hunger and here we are teaching elegant fields of economics that didn't do much good in the situation of starvation. I thought I should be personally trying to be useful to dying people around me. Chittagong University where I was teaching is right in the middle of the villages, it is surrounded by villages, so that is exactly what I did, and along the way I found out how people suffered for tiny bits of money. I went around and made a list of people who borrowed from money lenders, and when my list was completed, there were 42 names on that list and the total money needed was $27. So I thought things are beyond the comprehension of anybody who has gone through the courses in economics; you never talk about $27 and 42 people. And I also thought, this is within the realm of my capability to solve the problem.

So I gave this money, the $27, and got them kind of liberated from the clutches of the money lenders, and that created such an excitement among the people in the village I wanted to continue this because I asked myself, if you can make so many people so happy with such a small amount of money, why shouldn't you do more of it? So that led me to go to the local banker and try to argue with him to lend money to the poor people. The more I argued the more he became defensive of his rules. I didn't succeed, but it led me to start a debate with the higher officials in the bank, and ultimately I resolved this after several months of negotiation by offering myself as a guarantor. So I said, I'll become the guarantor, I'll sign all your papers, take the risk, and you get the money. And that was the beginning of the whole thing. . . .

Gradually, we aimed at the women, extremely poor women, and still it didn't work very well with the banks because every time they asked many questions, they were hesitant about the viability of the whole thing. So I said, why don't they just set up a separate bank? And it was again a long process, but in 1983 we succeeded, we became a bank, Grameen Bank, and we continued to expand our work through the country. Today Grameen Bank works all over the country, and 95 percent of our borrowers are women. Right now we have 3.5 million borrowers, mostly women. Sizes of loans are really small. An average loan would be $200, and with that money people invest in businesses and change their lives.

One of the things we insisted right from the beginning is that families send their children to school. In the Grameen families most of the borrowers are illiterate, but we wanted to create a second generation within the families who would be literate. It worked, and today almost 100 percent of the children of Grameen families are in school. And that also led to something else. At that time our intention was to make sure they were going to school and staying for at least five years to finish primary school. Now we see that they are not only finishing primary school, they are going to colleges and universities. So about eight years back we introduced the student loan, so that for those who were going to medical school, engineering schools, universities, their entire financing is done from Grameen Bank. . . .

The kind of activities we have are basically things they are familiar with, but something came that is dramatically different. We set up a mobile telephone company called Grameen Phone, which has nothing to do with Grameen Bank. The government wanted to liberalize the telecommunications sector; they wanted to give licenses and the thought came to us—why don't we apply? Our intention was to bring telephones into the villages of Bangladesh because Bangladesh villages don't have electricity to begin with; 70 percent of the people in Bangladesh don't have access to electricity. We thought they should at least have some telephone service so they can communicate with each other, and we calculated that it should work as a good business. Our intention was to bring those with phones to be borrowers of the Grameen Bank and finance them to buy a handset and start a telephone business, selling the service of a telephone. Everybody thought it was a crazy idea. This was about six years back. We got the license and we started doing that, and it became a roaring success.

Today Grameen Phone is the largest mobile telephone company in the country. We brought those mini telephones, about 55,000 telephones, into the villages for the Grameen borrowers, so there are 55,000 telephone ladies all around Bangladesh. You can go anywhere in Bangladesh and you can now connect to the whole world and, since there is no electricity, we brought the solar panels to connect to the wire phones so that their batteries are charged. . . .

Over the years we have given more than $4 billion worth of loans and had a perfect recovery (at least 99 percent recovery), and it makes good sense because it makes profit. The borrowers own the bank itself; it is not something that is owned by somebody else. So it's a bank owned by the women, works for the poor women, and at the end of the day it makes a profit. In 2003 it made over $11 million of profit and it continues to make profit all the time. So if you want to address poverty, one way to do that is to go the business route. It can be done in a business way and once you design it in a business way, you can expand it as much as you want and the sky's the limit. . . .

One criticism is that micro business is very good to poor people, but it's good only for the top layer of the poor people; it cannot go all the way to the bottom. And that surprises us because, all too oddly, we had been working only with the bottom layer of poor people. So this year we want to address it once and for all, and in order to do that we are addressing exclusively the beggars. There are plenty of beggars in Bangladesh. . . . The idea was that we go and talk to the beggar women.

You go house to house to do the begging, get some rice, get some food, and then at the end of the day you can bring all the food and share it with all the family members and survive. We can't change all this over night, but we can offer you an alternative, or an option. While you go house to house begging, would you care to carry some merchandise with you, some food items, some toys, some little knickknacks for the kids and so on? You have both options: you can beg or you can sell, whichever way you find convenient. . . . We thought throughout the year we would have about 3,000 or so beggars in our program, but by the end of April we already had 9,000 beggars in the program, all taking little money, the typical loan is $10. With $10 she feels like she's a businesswoman.

Then we added one more place, we said we'd take the beggars to the local business owner in the marketplace and tell the business owner that she's our member, a Grameen Bank member and we gave out an identity card, so that people start looking at her in a different way, with a name and address and Grameen logo saying that she is a Grameen Bank member. And we introduce to the business owner that we guarantee up to 2,000 Taka [about $35], so she can take any amount, anything from your shop that she likes, total amount not exceeding 2,000 Taka. If she doesn't pay you a penny, we'll guarantee and pay for her. The deal is between us and the member, not with the shop owner. The shop owner gets her money back. So we tell the person, you choose whatever you think you can sell, and during the day you sell, and whatever unsold product you have you return and settle the account, and that's it. Then you go house to house, you ask everybody what is it that they'd like for you to bring, so the next day you can bring it, because the whole shop is yours. So you become the liaison between the household and the market, because in Bangladesh women can't go out and do the shopping—so even if you needed a match she has to ask the husband to bring the match and the husband always forgets. . . .

Some beggars don't have limbs, they are blind, they are stationary, they don't go house to house, so questions are asked. What do you do with them, our staff was asking me. I said that is very simple. As we said, we don't want to disturb their livelihood, so let them do the begging with the beggar's bowl. We ask them would they like to keep some soft drinks, some bananas, some cookies next to them, and since he or she sits in a very strategic place, she knows or he knows the way to sit to get more attention from people. So it's a good strategic place for selling too, and people have a choice whether they want to throw a coin or buy a soft drink or buy a banana. So, as the business part picks up she can get as much business as she wants. All we need to do is put a roof on top and she turns into a businesswoman right there. Just because one cannot move it doesn't mean one is totally incapable. . . .

There are two kinds of business in the world and we pay attention to one kind and don't pay much attention to another kind. There are businesses for making money and there are businesses for doing good, but the world is made up of mostly businesses for making money. So I am trying to remind people that more businesses could be for doing good, and the people who want to go into businesses for doing good could be called social business entrepreneurs. . . .

Question: . . . How do you see the far reaching effects of microfinance . . . ?

Yunus: The impact of microfinance on people's lives comes in many ways. When you talk about microfinance we think about the money amount, but as you see, gradually the money part becomes the smaller part of the whole thing. It's almost like getting a tool to explore yourself. Money becomes the first reason why you started finding out who you are, how good you are in business, how good you are in taking responsibility for yourself.

The first women who took the first loan, a $30 loan or $35, she was a very shaky woman. She was not sure because everyone said you are not good, you have no capacity to do anything. Ever since she was born she was told she brought misery to the family, difficulties for the family, but once she started paying her first installment and she sees that she can do it and feels that it is not all black, she has some capacity to handle her life. By the time she finishes her last installment she feels delighted; she felt she was nobody, now she feels she is somebody, and she can conquer the whole world. This is a transformation process, so the money becomes the first step in that transformation process. . . .

Question: . . . My question is specifically with regard to women's improved position in Bangladesh: How much of a backlash has there been against that, and how have you tried to prevent that specifically?

Yunus: There is always backlash when you try to do something new.

So one backlash you get from the traditional way of doing banking and another backlash comes from development. You're just giving money. No development is building roads; development is big investment. You give a $30 loan, $50 loan, $100 loan—that's not development, so that's another backlash. Another one is you're giving money to women. That is totally unacceptable. Women should be staying home, they shouldn't get themselves involved in businesses or anything; this is the traditional way. Then the main opposition transforms into religious opposition, saying that it is unacceptable from a religious point of view. There is political opposition. The extreme left thought this is an American conspiracy brought to the country to bring capitalism to the country at the very grass-roots level, at the very bottom level, so that the revolution never take place in this country. The extreme right thought this was a Communist movement, organizing the poor people. Today they get money and tomorrow they will be looking for political power, and so on. These are the kinds of backlashes, but the important thing is no matter what they say, the people see genuine benefits coming to the people. . . .

Source: "Remarks by Muhammad Yunus." Global Business and Global Poverty Conference, May 19, 2004. Stanford Graduate School of Business. Available online. URL: http://www.gsb.stanford.edu/news/headlines/2004global conf_yunus_speech.shtml. Downloaded April 20, 2007.

International Nongovernmental Organizations Accountability Charter (June 2006) (excerpts)

At the end of the 20th century, nongovernmental organizations proliferated. Some operate domestically; others work across borders. Surveys suggest that the public trusts NGOs more than governments and corporations.

But as NGOs have grown in influence, so too have complaints about how they operate. Sometimes the challenge they present to the status quo draws government fire. Accusing international NGOs of meddling in internal affairs, Russia, for instance, passed a tough NGO registration law in 2006 that suspended the operation of many human-rights groups. Conservative associations such as Washington, D.C.–based NGOWatch monitor NGO activities. While most organizations stake out the moral high ground in the fight against global ills, their staffers sometimes make mistakes, give in to temptation, or assume they know better than the people they serve. Accusations of sexual harassment, improper spending, or mere arrogance can hamper and may destroy an NGO.

To defend their good names, a loose network of international NGOs collaborated on a voluntary code of conduct, endorsed in June 2006 by the heads of 11 leading organizations, from Amnesty International to the World YWCA. By signing on, NGOs pledged to regulate their own operations and to set an example for the industries and governments whose practices they aim to improve.

Who we are

We, international non-government organisations (INGOs) signatory to this Charter, are independent non-profit organisations that work globally to advance human rights, sustainable development, environmental protection, humanitarian response and other public goods.

Our organisations are proud and privileged to work across a wide range of countries and cultures, with a diverse range of peoples and in varied eco- and social and political systems. . . .

Our legitimacy is also derived from the quality of our work, and the recognition and support of the people with and for whom we work and our members, our donors, the wider public, and governmental and other organisations around the world.

We seek to uphold our legitimacy by responding to inter-generational considerations, public and scientific concerns, and through accountability for our work and achievements.

By signing this Charter we seek to promote further the values of transparency and accountability that we stand for, and commit our INGO to respecting its provisions.

How we work

INGOs can complement but not replace the over-arching role and primary responsibility of governments to promote equitable human development and wellbeing, to uphold human rights and to protect ecosystems.

We also seek to promote the role and responsibilities of the private sector to advance human rights and sustainable development, and protect the environment.

We can often address problems and issues that governments and others are unable or unwilling to address on their own. Through constructive challenge, we seek to promote good governance and foster progress towards our goals. . . .

The Charter's purpose

This Charter outlines our common commitment to excellence, transparency and accountability. To demonstrate and build on these commitments, we seek to:

- identify and define shared principles, policies and practices;
- enhance transparency and accountability, both internally and externally;
- encourage communication with stakeholders; and
- improve our performance and effectiveness as organisations.

. . .

Our stakeholders

Our first responsibility is to achieve our stated mission effectively and transparently, consistent with our values. In this, we are accountable to our stakeholders.

Our stakeholders include:

- Peoples, including future generations, whose rights we seek to protect and advance;
- Ecosystems, which cannot speak for or defend themselves;
- Our members and supporters;
- Our staff and volunteers;
- Organisations and individuals that contribute finance, goods or services;
- Partner organisations, both governmental and non-governmental, with whom we work;
- Regulatory bodies whose agreement is required for our establishment and operations;
- Those whose policies, programmes or behaviour we wish to influence;
- The media; and
- The general public.

In balancing the different views of our stakeholders, we will be guided by our mission and the principles of this Charter.

Principles

Respect for Universal Principles

INGOs are founded on the rights to freedom of speech, assembly and association in the Universal Declaration of Human Rights. We seek to advance international and national laws that promote human rights, ecosystem protection, sustainable development and other public goods.

Where such laws do not exist, are not fully implemented, or abused, we will highlight these issues for public debate and advocate appropriate remedial action.

In so doing, we will respect the equal rights and dignity of all human beings.

Independence

We aim to be both politically and financially independent. Our governance, programmes and policies will be non-partisan, independent of specific governments, political parties and the business sector.

Responsible advocacy

We will ensure that our advocacy is consistent with our mission, grounded in our work and advances defined public interests.

We will have clear processes for adopting public policy positions, (including for partners where appropriate,) explicit ethical policies that guide our choices of advocacy strategy, and ways of identifying and managing potential conflicts of interest among various stakeholders.

Effective Programmes
We seek to work in genuine partnership with local communities, NGOs and other organisations aiming at sustainable development responding to local needs.

Non-Discrimination
We value, respect and seek to encourage diversity, and seek to be impartial and non-discriminatory in all our activities. To this end, each organisation will have policies that promote diversity, gender equity and balance, impartiality and non-discrimination in all our activities, both internal and external.

Transparency
We are committed to openness, transparency and honesty about our structures, mission, policies and activities. We will communicate actively to stakeholders about ourselves, and make information publicly available. . . .

Source: "International Non Governmental Organizations: Accountability Charter." Amnesty International Web site. Available online. URL: http://web.amnesty.org/library/Index/ENGIOR800062006. Updated June 6, 2006.

Statement from African Civil Society Organizations at the World Social Forum (January 25, 2007)

Many opponents of globalization gather at the World Social Forum, conceived as an alternative to the World Economic Forum, a much more mainstream international nonprofit organization that meets annually in Davos, Switzerland. Sometimes participants of the two overlap. Founded by Brazilian trade unions, charities, and left-wing NGOs in 2001, the World Social Forum represents a loose coalition of organizations that often contest prevailing economic and development paradigms.

At the World Social Forum in January 2007, more than 80,000 grass-roots activists from around the world gathered in Nairobi, Kenya, under the banner "People's struggles, people's alternatives—Another world is possible." At free-flowing seminars, workshops, debates, and other get-togethers, participants questioned the merits of economic partnership agreements between the European Union and developing countries and discussed landlessness, HIV/AIDS, debt relief, housing, and more.

At the end of the five-day assembly, representatives of 70 organizations from 12 African countries issued a statement objecting to the Gates and Rockefeller Foundations' plan to spur a second "Green Revolution." The foundations' Program for Africa's Seed Systems will improve "the availability and variety that can produce higher yields in the often harsh conditions of sub-Saharan Africa," according to the donors, but some activists worry that the environmental costs, especially of introducing genetically altered plants, will outweigh the agricultural benefits.

> Africa is the source of much of the world's agricultural knowledge and biodiversity. African farming represents a wealth of innovation: for example, Canada's main export wheat is derived from a Kenyan variety called "Kenyan farmer"; the US and Canada grow barley bred from Ethiopian farmers' varieties; and the Zera Zera sorghum grown in Texas originated in Ethiopia and the Sudan. This rich basis of biodiversity still exists in Africa today, thanks to the 80% of farmers in Africa that continue to save seed in a range of diverse eco-systems across the continent.
>
> The future of agriculture for Africa and the world will have to build on this biodiversity and farmers' knowledge, especially in the current context of climate change. The diversity of seed varieties continually developed by African farmers will be vital to ensure that they have the flexibility to respond to changing weather patterns. With the challenges that climate change will bring, only a wealth of seed diversity maintained by farmers in Africa can offer a response to prevent severe food crises.
>
> However, new external initiatives are putting pressure on these agricultural systems. A new initiative from the Bill Gates/Rockefeller Foundation partnership, called the "Alliance for a Green Revolution for Africa" (AGRA) is putting over $150 million towards shifting African agriculture to a system dependent on expensive, harmful chemicals, monocultures of hybrid seeds, and ultimately genetically modified organisms (GMOs). Another initiative funded by the G8 is pushing biotechnology in agriculture through four new major Biosciences research centres in Africa. And GM companies such as Monsanto and Syngenta are entering into public-private-partnership agreements with national agricultural research centres in Africa, in order to direct agricultural research and policy towards GMOs. These initiatives under-represent the real achievements in productivity

through traditional methods, and will fail to address the real causes of hunger in Africa. . . .

This push for a so-called "green revolution" or "gene revolution" is being done once again under the guise of solving hunger in Africa. Chemical-intensive agriculture is, however, already known to be outmoded. We have seen how fertilisers have killed the soil, creating erosion, vulnerable plants and loss of water from the soil. We have seen how pesticides and herbicides have harmed our environment and made us sick. We know that hybrid and GM seed monocultures have pulled farmers into poverty by preventing them from saving seed, and preventing traditional methods of intercropping which provide food security. We vow to learn from our brothers and sisters in India, where this chemical and genetically modified system of agriculture has left them in so much debt and hunger that 150,000 farmers have committed suicide.

The push for a corporate-controlled chemical system of agriculture is parasitic on Africa's biodiversity, food sovereignty, seed and small-scale farmers. Farmers in Africa cannot afford these expensive agricultural inputs. But these new infrastructures seek to make farmers dependent on chemicals and hybrid seeds, and will open the door to GMOs and Terminator crops. Industrial breeding has in fact been driven by the industry's demand for new markets—not to meet the needs of farmers.

We know, however, that the agroecological approach to farming, using traditional and organic methods, provides the real solutions to the crises that we face. Studies show that a biodiversity-based organic agriculture, working with nature and not against it, and using a diversity of mixed crops, produces higher overall yields at far lower costs than chemical agriculture. A 2002 study by the International Centre for Research on Agroforesty (ICRAF) showed that Southern African farms using traditional agroforestry techniques did not suffer from the drought that hit the region so severely that year.

We reject these new foreign systems that will encourage Africa's land and water to be privatised for growing inappropriate export crops, biofuels and carbon sinks, instead of food for our own people. We pledge to intensify our work for food sovereignty by conserving our own seed and enhancing our traditional organic systems of agriculture. . . .

Source: "Statement from African Civil Society Organisations at the World Social Forum 2007," Nairobi, Kenya, January 25, 2007. Food First Web site. Available online. URL: http://www.foodfirst.org/node/1610. Downloaded April 20, 2007.

UKRAINE

Ivan Kasiianenko, "Testimony on the Ukrainian Famine of 1932–33" (February 10, 1987) (excerpts)

To prove the superiority of communism, Joseph Stalin, dictator of the Soviet Union, set out in 1928 to "bypass the capitalist world" through rapid industrialization. To enable this, he needed food—to sell and to feed factory workers. He ordered the collectivization of agriculture, seizing holdings large and small and forcing now landless peasants to produce for the state. Many Ukrainians resisted, sometimes killing off their livestock rather than ceding them to the Communist regime. Stalin's henchmen shot or deported opponents to the icy wastes of Siberia and the Arctic. Demanding that collective farms meet government grain quotas first, Stalin not only funded his economic initiative but broke Ukrainian nationalist resistance through starvation: 6 or 7 million people died. The world had little inkling of the unfolding famine—largely because of Stalin's news blackout but also because of the collusion of New York Times *reporter Walter Duranty, who won a 1932 Pulitzer Prize for his rosy reporting on the Soviet Union, which was later discredited.*

In 1984, Congress authorized the U.S. Commission on the Ukraine Famine to investigate this tragedy. Besides studying documents, it traveled across the United States gathering eyewitness testimony. At the commission's 1987 regional hearing in California, Ivan Kasiianenko recounted the horrors he had seen as a boy.

.. In 1932 the harvest (in Kovalivka, Hrebinka raion, Kiev province) was a normal one. It was brought in before anyone suspected what was to happen. It was winter when they came in to take the grain that had already been ground into flour and was stored in bags. They came and seized all of this grain, not only from us but from all the villagers. And ours was a large village—6,000 people lived there.

The sound of crying was everywhere. Those who seized the grain carried out their orders without mercy. I remember as if it were yesterday how a man ran away, leaving behind a wife and three children. They took absolutely everything: cows, pigs, everything. There was nothing left for the wife to do. She sent her children away to fend for themselves, set fire to the house and hanged herself.

Things were a little different in my family. My father was always on the run during the day and would only come at night. We had nothing; they had taken everything from us. They came with their pikes, poked around, asked questions and grabbed my mother by the hair. They tore off my mother's earrings and her cross. We children cried, but nothing helped. No one paid any attention to our tears.

They locked our mother in the basement. So there we were, five of us children with me the oldest, and our father nowhere to be found. They came back to see if they had missed anything and found one egg that had not been taken. They took it away.

Father would sometimes be able to bring us a little flour, sometimes a little grain, anything that had not been seized. But protecting the food was impossible because our house was under constant surveillance, and he could not get to us every night. They took everything, even our clothes. We did not even have a blanket. We were poor as church mice. We huddled together at night to keep warm.

After two weeks they let mother out of the basement. But what could she do when there was nothing to eat? In March or April 1933 they took our cow. The first to die was my youngest sister, then another sister. Then my brother and a third sister died at the same time. Father died and was buried on Holy Thursday. Mother died two days later, and they threw her in a hole on Easter Sunday. I remember how a neighbor came and comforted me, saying that although my parents had gone, they had died on holy days, Holy Thursday and Easter. It was a terrible time for me. I was starving myself, to such an extent that I could not walk.

Before he died, my father had asked one of the teachers to take me under his wing. I was only in the first grade at the time, and it was only thanks to this teacher that I survived. He took me to a hospital. I don't remember who the doctor was or anything about the place. I only remember that my skin was shiny and transparent like glass. The doctor cut me open in several places and let the liquid under my skin run out. It smelled like dead flesh. When I left the hospital, I had no strength to walk and sat in the sun. The teacher picked me up and saved my life.

... A horrifying silence settled over the village. I can still remember going to my neighbors' houses to see if anyone was alive. I remember going into one house and seeing the blind son sitting in one corner. His skin was grey. He had been dead perhaps a week or two. And he wasn't the only one. Starving people on the verge of death, sometimes even mothers, sometimes lost their sanity and turned into animals who smothered their own children and ate them. It happened, for example, to one of my acquaintances. His name was Ivan Ostapenko. His mother put a noose around his neck and tried to strangle him, but he was stronger than she was and managed to break her hold. But he kept the marks the ropes left on his throat for a long time.

I went to another neighbor's house. They were young people. I looked in the window and saw the mother and father lying dead on the floor. Their infant son was lying in the middle, still alive, and sucking it's [sic] mother's dry breast. I took him to a retention place for such children, and he was saved. As long as I stayed in the village, he was like a brother to me, and I watched over him. When they took us to the orphanage, we went together. Children whose parents had died of starvation were not treated well. They were not allowed to light the stove to keep warm or to wear warm clothing. We were told that we were parasites, capitalists, vestiges of the kulaks [relatively wealthy peasants] and exploiting classes.

These weren't orphanages; they were houses of torture. The children had nothing to eat. It was impossible to keep clean. We were literally eaten by lice. But nobody cared. We were the progeny of the defeated class enemy. . . .

Source: "For the Record: Eyewitness Testimony before Commission on Famine," San Francisco, February 10, 1987. *The Ukrainian Weekly* 55, no. 21 (May 24, 1987). Available online. URL: http://ukrweekly.com/Archive/1987/218716.shtml. Downloaded April 20, 2007.

"Ten Years after Chernobyl" (1996) (excerpts)

On the 10th anniversary of the 1986 accident at the Chernobyl nuclear plant in Ukraine, the international NGO Greenpeace gathered memoirs from those affected. Many workers, such as bus driver Alexander Motornov, lived in the nearby town of Pripyat, which was evacuated the day after the radiation leak. Although the Soviet authorities resettled some evacuees—building, for instance, New Martinovichi for former residents of Martinovichi—many found it hard to adjust because of the loss of familiar social networks and the stigma of being "contaminated." Some residents refused to leave the exclusion zone (a 30-kilometer [18.6-mile] ring around the contaminated plant), and others returned.

After a decade, long-term health effects were surfacing from radiation exposure. In 2006, the World Health Organization took another look at the affected population and estimated that 5,000 youths at the time of the accident had developed thyroid cancer, with more cases likely brewing. Over the years, Ukrainian officials relocated more than 346,000 people. Yet, 5 million still live in areas with radioactive material, and they suffer from anxiety and a variety of unexplained physical symptoms.

Alexander Motornov [a pseudonym], aged 47, was a bus driver at the time of the accident and then became a clean-up worker.

I began my work here a few years before the accident and from the first day I became a liquidator. Almost immediately after the accident we began to use "armoured carriers"—ordinary buses produced by Lvov bus plant, but equipped with lead armour sealed doors and a specially design of passenger section. Air to the buses was supplied through air conditioners with filters. We used these vehicles till October 1986 and then we switched to other armour-free vehicles. I can say from first-hand experience that there was no proper decontamination of people and no dose control. Most of us knew how it should be done—all of us had served in the Armed Forces and had attended civil defence courses. I also worked in the fire emergency unit, which was first on the scene at the reactor fire and we also studied these things. . . . I understand there were definite guidelines from Moscow that the real doses should be concealed.

It was like a thriller. Just before the accident I had a party for my eldest son who was about to enter the Armed Forces. Then in the night I heard the loud noise which shook the windows. Nobody paid attention to this until the next morning when my neighbour asked me if I had heard the atomic explosion. We could not believe the reactor had exploded. . . .

It was a terrible picture in Pripyat that day. People walked in the streets, and children played in the gardens. Nobody acted according to the guidelines for such situations. Even Pripyat market was open, although the market place was in a direct line with the burning reactor. Radiation is still heavy at that place near the bridge, so what was it 10 years ago? Absolutely nobody controlled either background radiation, or population dose loads in these first days, when people faced the heaviest exposure. People were not told what was happening or how to tackle the situation. Later even the dose counters they supplied were out of order. . . .

Natalia works in the kindergarten at New Martinovichi.

They built the kindergarten in our village a year ago. We have 54 children in three groups. They are like any other children, but they are special—they are Chernobyl children. All of them have certificates verifying their status. They are weak and they are often sick. Naturally, we do all we can. We feed them with vitamins to try to eliminate the deadly stuff and make them healthy. They especially suffer from respiratory diseases in cold seasons. Strong winds are frequent here and the climate is different. Our children are used to the Polissya climate. Maybe they are sick because their bodies are not used to it. But there may also be some effects from Chernobyl. Children are more affected by radiation than adults.

We are afraid to have children, but it is impossible to be without them. A woman without children is not really a woman. Who would give you a glass of water in your old age, who would close your eyes after your death? So the Polissya women have children anyway and bring them up as well as we can under the circumstances. . . .

The following story of one old woman from Ilnitsy village in the Polissya district explains why some of the evacuees went back to their homes.

We were evacuated at the first day of Easter (4 May 1986). First they transferred us to the Makarievsky region (Kiev oblast) and settled us among local residents. Our cattle were collected and evacuated first, we were evacuated the next day. Four months we lived among strangers and then after five months they transferred to new housing in the Yagotin region. We stayed there over the winter. The new houses were constructed badly, they were cold and wet. They were built on water-logged soil and the land was not levelled properly. The winter was acute: a lot of snow and frosts. In spring when the snow has melted we faced a new disaster: the water did not flow away. The wells caved in and the houses collapsed. Fortunately the head of the local collective farm from Dibrovy helped us and managed to re-evacuate people. So we returned home. . . .

Ilnitsy is also home to Ganna, aged 77, one of a hundred people still living in the village.

We can live here mainly because of our harvests. No one can survive just on their pension. . . . If we buy bread, there is no money left for other purposes. We have to cut spending for about five months to buy something more. We live by collecting berries and mushrooms, and we sow some crops. I have planted five acres of potatoes this year. . . . We plant different crops here—onions, cucumbers, poppies. Cakes with poppy seeds taste very good. But the flour they deliver is expensive, so we can buy one sack for two people. . . .

Of course there are less residents now than before the disaster. Ilnitsy was a large village, with about 700 houses. Those of use who don't work meet together in the holidays and relax as best we can. There is no church but we have a prayer house. The priest lives in Chernobyl. Those of use who are not ill gather in the prayer house. We wear out old clothes—we cannot afford to buy new clothes. We cook our meals in stoves using firewood. Either we collect it nearby or the boys deliver it in exchange for a bottle of drink. We have no other option. There is no coal or gas supplied to us. Even if they did supply it, where can we get money to pay for it? From our pensions?

Illness is natural, we are elderly and we have had hard lives—the war, famine, German occupation. We have survived all these troubles and reared out children here. Now we want to spend the rest of our lives here and be buried near our ancestors. . . .

Anatoly Mateyko is chief doctor of the Ukrainian Diagnostic Parental Centre. At the time of the accident he was also a deputy in the parliament and became a member of an ad hoc parliamentary committee set up to study the situation. He spent several months in the Chernobyl zone investigating medical problems in regions contaminated with radioactivity.

It was my experience in this working group which made me decide to dedicate my life to patients suffering from the effects of radiation. Even while we were still part of the Soviet Union our Committee pushed Ukraine into becoming the first Soviet republic to diagnose Chernobyl-related illness as radiation disease. This decision caused problems for us and for our Health Minister, Yury Spizhenko, and we came under pressure from the Moscow leadership. At that time there was an official ban on diagnosing Chernobyl-related disease. We were the first to show that there are two types of radiation disease: acute and chronic. Patients who had been engaged in the clean-up operations in the Chernobyl area from 1986 to 1987 and had suffered acute radiation disease subsequently developed chronic illnesses. In those who lived in less severely contaminated areas we find that various organs are gradually affected.

Treating patients today, 10 years after the accident, is especially hard. We are paying the price for that earlier censorship. We should have told the world at the very beginning that the Chernobyl accident was an unprecedented complex disaster, unique in the history of the humankind. That was not comparable to Hiroshima or Nagasaki but much more complicated. But because of the ban we lost vital experience and valuable scientific information that would have helped us. . . .

The treatments developed by Ukrainian doctors have called into question traditional ways of treating radiation disease and refuted some classical theories. Ukrainian doctors were first to forecast a sharp increase in central nervous system diseases due to low doses of ionising radiation. Now we have experience and statistics to prove this. It is also clear that the social situation has a great impact on the rate of disease. Children suffer the most. The risk that a newborn will have an affected central nervous system increases substantially if the mother is under stress. So there are medical and social aspects.

Our research shows that illness among children and women of reproductive age in contaminated areas is 1.5–2 times higher than average for Ukraine. . . . Even common diseases are showing some nev properties and changing their patterns. Stomach ulcer is an example. There is marked increase in its incidence, especially for heavily contaminated regions. . . . We are now advising close monitoring to make possible early diagnosis of stomach ulcer in contaminated zones. However the reality is quite different—our economic problems are seriously compromising the medical services.

We are now beginning to see the long-term effects of Chernobyl. Today children who were 6–8 years in 1986 are having their own children. Preliminary studies suggest that these babies are likely to have various central nervous system pathologies, especially if their mothers live in contaminated areas. . . .

Malignant tumours among children also show an upward trend, especially affecting the thyroid gland, blood and respiratory organs. Diseases of the blood are also increasing. This applies to the children born in contaminated areas a long time after the accident. . . .

As for a humanitarian aid, I am aware of the proverb that "One should not look a gift horse in the mouth." But a lot of people in the West seem to be making capital out of our misfortunes. I will not mention any names, but there are plenty of them. Several times I have seen loads of foreign aid containing out-of-date medicines and obsolete equipment or medical instruments. Maybe some citizens of the West have confused a zone of human disaster with a rubbish dump. However this is not true of all donors. I would like to express my sincere gratitude to Japan for sending aid which always contains what we need—not only medicines but also special instruments and equipment. . . .

Source: Greenpeace. "Testimony Report, Ten Years after Chernobyl." Available online. URL: http://archive greenpeace.org/comms/nukes/chernob/read13.html. Downloaded April 20, 2007.

Oksana Daragushak "Children's Radio Program Summary" (c. 2003) (excerpts)

Young journalists, ages 10–18, cover children's rights for the Independen. Children's Media-Center in Kiev, Ukraine. They pick topics, conduct inter-

views, write scripts, and air their concerns in an FM-radio program, on a Web page, and in children's pages in adult newspapers. Along the way, budding citizens of the newly independent nation learn the questioning skills required in a democracy.

The Ukraine-based international NGO Foundation of Youth Culture and Education created the Children's Voice project, which beat out other social entrepreneurial projects at the World Bank and UNICEF's "Day of Innovative Ideas" competition for recognition and funding. The young Ukrainian producers, editors, reporters, presenters, and writers then won an award of their own, the 2002 OneWorld/UNICEF award for outstanding radio produced by and for children. Their winning program focused on the lives of street children. Summaries of some programs are available at the center's Web site—most in Ukrainian, but a few in English on gender, happiness, and, as seen below, juvenile crime.

> ... A child and a crime. From the first sight these two things are just incompatible. But life is an unpredictable thing. And that's why more and more often we hear information about crimes, committed by children. Today more and more often we face the fact that children become active participants of robberies, rapes and even murders.
>
> Who are they, teenagers, who had broken the law,—cruel criminals or victims of the society? What drives them to crime? Do they understand they do wrong? With the purpose to look into the problem we decided to talk to a child who has met this situation in his life.
>
> **Why are you here [in jail]?**
> **Child 1:** I and my friend attacked one man; we took away his shoes and jacket. Then we saw another man. We beat him, took his bag and ran away. And we were arrested right away.
>
> **Child 2:** We—I and my friend—were returning from a birthday party. It was late already. We saw a man and we misunderstood each other. And we started a fight. My friend hit him a hard blow, the man fell and beat his head on asphalt, lost consciousness. My friend said that we had to kill him because if he regained consciousness he would have reported the incident to the police. I was drunk at that time; I didn't understand what he was doing. Nevertheless I told him not to do it. But my friend was older and stronger than me, so I—to tell the truth—didn't insist strongly. He took out his knife and killed him. And then in a month we were arrested.
>
> **Child 3:** I am here because I committed a robbery. I with my friend attacked a man, took away his money, cigarettes, watch. And I was sentenced

to 2-years imprisonment for the previous crime I had made and to 4-years imprisonment for this crime according for the 142 article.

What forced you to commit a crime?
Child 1: I wanted to buy some shoes. It has been for 6 years that we hadn't received farm wages.

Do you regret [w]hat you have done?
Child 1: Only here I begin to understand what liberty is, what this word means, and what a Mother is.

Child 2: I have dreams about life at liberty, recalling events of the past. . . .

Child 3: My life is broken. Not my whole life—my youth, the best years are broken. What about conscience? I have a great dark spot on it, the spot is on my family, unfortunately it couldn't be removed even if my reference from here would be good, if it would be good after discharge—this dark spot will remain at any case. . . .

Please, introduce yourself.
I am Maksimova Natalia Yuryivna, the president of the Committee for Assistance to Child's Rights Protection, Doctor of Psychology.

In your opinion, why have children broken a law?
There a lot of reasons. Firstly, in case when children are of small ages—1–2 form; instead of attending school lessons he begs—it is breaking of the law; but he doesn't think about it, he doesn't understand that he has broken the law. Secondly, the children—especially teenagers—have the tendency to search the bounds of permissibility; they investigate which of their actions would be punished and which of them would be not; so the child sets the bounds of his behavior—what is permitted and what is prohibited. In the period of those investigations the child breaks the law very often.

What kinds of crimes are mostly committed by children?
Mostly it is thefts, hooliganism, robberies. But the colony for juvenile offenders contains mostly teenagers, especially those of 16 years old, who have committed a murder or a rape. That is because, in accordance with the legislation, persons under 16 can be prosecuted only for serious crimes.

What is an age for criminal responsibility?
A person undergoes complete criminal responsibility at the age of 16, in case of a serious crime—at the age of 14.

Which rights have the arrested children?
First of all they have a right to call their parents or tutors.

What is the system of punishment for juvenile offenders?
There are different types of punishment—arrests, fines, liberty limitations, corrective labor, and suspended sentence and for the end imprisonment—it has been decide by courts.

What is known about released juvenile offenders, what part of them has broken the law again?
About 10%.

What is the mean term of children's imprisonment?
It is impossible to say about the mean term because every term is set in accordance with an article of the criminal law which has been broken. But the term doesn't exceed 15 years.

Does the state system of juvenile offenders' rehabilitation exist in our country?
It is difficult to say about the system because it doesn't exist although we need it. But today we have social service for youth where you can certainly find a person who is responsible for the work with released young people.

How many children are behind bars today?
Of course, the number changes, about 3,000 children.

In your mind what we have to do to reduce the level of children's criminality?
There are a lot of works to do. Firstly, we have to change our economical situation that will give us the possibility not to leave every child out. . . .

Source: Oksana Daragushak. "Programmes' Summary/Criminality." Children's Voice Web site. Available online. URL: http://fyce.org/mediacenter/mediacenter_eng/statti/radio_zlochyn.htm. Download April 20, 2007.

SYRIA

Bashar al-Assad, Speech at Damascus University (November 10, 2005) (excerpts)

In November 2005, Syrian president Bashar al-Assad gave this speech at his alma mater, Damascus University, and the official Syrian Arab News Agency posted an English translation online. As always, talk of politics overshadowed discussion of poverty and economic reform.

Assad's speech alludes to world pressure on his regime. Since taking office, U.S. president George W. Bush had repeatedly vilified Syria and in 2005 continued his drumbeat, accusing Syria of "destabilizing Lebanon, permitting terrorists to use its territory to reach Iraq, and giving safe harbor to Palestinian terrorist groups." Although Syria had supported the Persian Gulf War in 1991, it opposed the U.S. invasion of neighboring Iraq in 2003. Just days before Assad's speech, U.S. and Iraqi forces were battling insurgents near the Syrian border, and a marine spokesman confirmed a U.S. bomb there had killed at least five civilians.

In his speech, Assad also mentions the Association Agreement between Syria and its major donor and trading partner, the European Union. Although both sides initialed the agreement in 2004, as of 2006, it had still not been finalized, in part because of EU demands for human-rights protection as a condition of economic cooperation. Implying that the West has a double standard in requiring nations to fulfill promises, Assad refers to UN Security Council Resolution 242, which calls for Israel to withdraw from territories occupied in the 1967 Six Day War, and Resolution 338, which reiterates that demand as a step toward peace negotiations.

Esteemed professors, dear students,

. . . It is a great opportunity for me to be in the university in which I spent some of my most beautiful and energetic days. . . .

The fast pace of developments in our region and the incumbent tragic consequences of these developments made Arab citizens pay a high price in terms of their livelihood, security and dignity. The confused vision and the loss of direction among some people violently shocked the convictions, ideas and values of the Arab people, particularly young people. A number of international circles, and their agents in our Arab establishment, have been trying to promote their destructive political schemes under exciting names which touch people's feelings and emotions and have been targeting people's minds and souls before targeting their countries and invading their cultural identity and national existence before invading their national borders. They have been doing this in an orchestrated media campaign which has met a partial success thanks to the high technology it possesses, the money it spends, and because of the dubious trumpets it hires in order to promote this campaign of deceit with unparalleled shallowness. The campaigns which have been waged on the Arab nation, and Syria in particular, in recent years, are extremely dangerous. The danger lies in the fact that they target the intellectual, psychological and moral structure of Arabs, within the framework of a media, cultural and scientific war which targets our young generations in particular with the aim of separating them from their identity, heritage and history and making them lose confidence in themselves and their capabilities, and consequently pushing them to surrender to the illusion of certain defeat at the first attempt to confront and stand fast before outside pressure put on the whole region, and on Syria in particular....

A quick look at the issues raised at present on the political arena with a great deal of noise against Syria and her stances, will show that all of them have one root which is our absolute rejection to bargain over independence versus subordination, sovereignty versus submission and dignity versus submission....

The problem of certain powers with Syria, or Syria's problem with certain powers is its pan-Arab national identity. Arab nationalism is our identity and our history; and history is our memory which enables us to go to the heart of the present and the future. They want us without a memory so that they can plan our future for us, and without an identity so that they can identify our role for us.

Here I [c]ite a few examples to illustrate this point. We read and hear from some foreign envoys that the cause of the anger of some officials in certain countries, and you know whom I mean, against Syria is that President Bashar al-Assad committed himself before them to internal reform, and he has not implemented that reform. We did not know that the Syrian people have elected these foreign officials as representatives of their members of parliament in order to represent them; and that President Bashar has to express commitment to those foreign officials. We did not know that they cared more for us than we cared for ourselves. We did not know that they were appointed as our guardians. This, in fact, shows a great deal of contempt, not for Syria, I am speaking in general about the Arab countries. They look at us as if we were non-existent, as if we have no people, no resources and no owners; as if Syria were a farm. And the same applies to other countries.

What are the reforms they want us to implement so that we check their credibility. Is it political reform? What kind of political reform are they talking about? They want the country without controls so that they could blackmail any regime from the inside.

Is it economic reform? They want us to open our markets before them regardless of our interests, in return for some charity and left-overs which will be offered to us.

As to cultural reform, they want us to get out of our skin and become a copy of them. If they want to prove the credibility of their propositions, since they always express concern for our internal situation, let them come forward and support us in the political framework to restore our occupied land and to prevent aggression against us if they are truthful.

In the economic context, let them come forward and support us so that we improve our economic situation and consequently the living conditions of our citizens. We want real support, not imaginary or partial support that does not achieve the desired objectives.

A couple of days ago there was a statement that the European Union did not invite the Syrian President. Of course we responded in a clear manner. This shows that they do not accept any Arab to decline an invitation. It is incomprehensible for them that anyone might say no, even to an invitation to a conference. . . .

Ladies and gentlemen,

Our region, as you can see, has witnessed bloody events. And Syria was at the heart of these events. And by virtue of its position and historical role, it faced its fare [sic] share of similar challenges which were accompanied by direct threats which depended on dubious political and media campaigns based on falsifying conceptions and twisting the truth in order to achieve their objectives.

The political scene consisted of a number of hot spots whose elements converged in order to lead to changing the political, cultural and human face of the region and redrawing its map in a manner that meets the new tasks and functions of this region and serves the strategies interests of some foreign powers, particularly Israel. The Israeli factor has had always a dubious presence on all these arenas. Developments have in fact shown that that Israel was the most prominent actor and the greatest beneficiary. . . .

What is happening in Iraq is cause for concern for every Arab. This Arab country is in the process of fragmentation and disintegration. And no one knows when the big explosion that will throw the region into the vortex of the unknown and lead to dangerous repercussions that could affect regions far beyond the boundaries of the Middle East will happen.

The first danger threatening Iraq is eliminating its Arab identity under a number of pretexts and implications which are at odds with the history of Iraq and its people. The second danger is the political and security chaos which pervades the Iraqi arena and which is directly related to the question of Iraq's territorial integrity. The more chaos prevails, the greater the possibility for internal strife, which increases the danger on Iraq and leads to shedding more of the blood of innocent Iraqis. Both dangers pave the way before the disintegration of Iraq with its incumbent direct dangers for Iraq's neighbors. . . .

We supported international legitimacy and did not support international disorder. International legitimacy is the UN charter, while international disorder is basing resolutions on the interests and moods of certain officials in this world. Those countries, those forces and everybody in this region and in the world should know that the era of tutelage which existed at the beginning of the last century is over, and now the region is in front of two choices, either resistance and steadfastness or chaos. There is no third choice. Resistance prevents chaos. Resistance has a price and chaos has a price, but the price of resistance is much less than the price of chaos. We need to know these things. . . .

Despite the difficult situation we are going through, we continue to implement our development plans in order to improve the living conditions of our citizens, and in the process of political, economic and administrative reform. We are also going ahead in our anti-corruption campaign and in widening the circle of accountability to involve all those who harm the interests of the people and the country. . . .

The world is moving very fast. And there are challenges produced by these changes. There have been new opportunities for achievement. Since at the heart of these changes lie information, communications and the digital revolution, we have all to work in order to integrate young people into this information age and to provide the integration mechanisms in all our institutions starting from the school, whether material mechanisms like laboratories, the internet, or activating the institutional, educational, cultural and media structures, in a manner that allows for embracing their creative energies and guarantee confidence in their capabilities on which we pin great hopes, because they are the real guarantee for the greatness and progress of our country. . . .

Since we have not talked today about resolutions 338 and 242 because they have become self evident for us, and because we know that we waste our time when we talk about the non-implementation of international legitimacy resolutions and the double standards and all that; I still want to greet, on your behalf and on behalf of every Syrian citizen, our steadfast Syrian brothers and sisters in the occupied Golan. . . . So, we salute those who prove everyday the truthfulness of their loyalty to their people and their homeland and prove their deep belonging to the causes and dignity of their people and defy with their strong will the Israeli oppression machine. . . .

National cohesion will remain, God willing, as powerful as ever. This country is protected by its people, by its state and above all, as the popular saying has it, "Syria is protected by God."

Source: "Speech of President Bashar al-Assad at Damascus University." November 10, 2005. Syrian Arab News Agency Web site. Available online. URL: http://www.sana.org/eng/21/2005/11/10/pr-1546.htm. Downloaded April 20, 2007.

Refugees International, "Buried Alive: Stateless Kurds in Syria" (2006) (excerpts)

In 2006, Refugees International, an NGO based in Washington, D.C., published the report "Buried Alive: Stateless Kurds in Syria." Through interviews and a 2005 trip to the region, researchers gathered details about the hardships of roughly 300,000 Kurds denied citizenship in Syria.

In 1962, the Syrian government conducted a census in al-Hasaka, one of 14 governates and a Kurdish stronghold. It aimed to identify "alien infiltrators" who had crossed the border from Turkey and to Arabize the resource-rich northeast by stripping citizenship from any Kurd who could not prove residency in Syria prior to 1945. Reports gathered by human-rights groups, however, reveal an arbitrary process that at times accorded a different status to two brothers in the same village or denied Syrian citizenship to army veterans. About 120,000 people lost their rights and sometimes their property. Because children inherit their parents' status, through the generations, the number of stateless Kurds has grown. According to the report, they fall into two categories: ajanib, *"foreigners" issued a red identity card stating that they are not Syrian nationals, and* maktoumeen, *"the unregistered," who have no ID at all. Those lacking citizenship cannot vote or obtain a passport to travel; they also face discrimination in school and in the workplace.*

Fundamental Human Rights Denied

The difficulties faced by stateless Kurds in Syria are numerous, despite Syria's obligations as a signatory to the Universal Declaration of Human Rights, the International Covenant on Civil and Political Rights, the Convention on the Rights of the Child, and the International Convention on the Elimination of All Forms of Racial Discrimination. Individuals have irregular access to education, health care, livelihoods, travel, property ownership, judicial and political systems, and registration of businesses, marriages, and children. They cannot vote or run for public office.

Statelessness affects every part of daily life. "Our condition is worse than that of a criminal," a man from Qamishli said. "They can own a car or house. We can't." A young woman told RI [Refugees International], "When I was young, I was not sensitive to my status. Now I know it will affect my education, my job, and my marriage." The births and deaths of some Maktoumeen (individuals lacking identity documents; the term is defined as "hidden" by some and "unregistered" by others) go unrecorded and their murders are reportedly not investigated or prosecuted as a result of their status. They are people who never existed. One young stateless man summed up this treatment in a single statement: "The Syrian government wants to erase us." . . .

The Right to a Nationality & an Identity

Most denationalized Kurds and their descendents are labeled Ajanib ("foreigners") and issued red identity cards by the Ministry of Interior, stating they are not Syrian nationals and are not entitled to travel. Even some children listed on red cards are listed under the statement, "His name was not in the survey of 1962," an irony given that they were born long after the date of the census. Replacing such documents or obtaining them for the first time poses particular problems, as they often involve paying large bribes. . . .

A significant number of stateless Kurds in Syria do not possess even this identity document and are effectively invisible. Maktoumeen now number between 75,000 and 100,000. . . .

The Right to Education

The Syrian government recognizes the right of Kurdish children to primary education, but not to primary education in their native Kurdish. Stateless Kurds face difficulties enrolling in secondary schools and universities, and Ajanib were reportedly not permitted to enroll in universities until after 1978. Enrolling in university proves nonetheless to be an arduous task, as Ajanib are required to obtain a report from state security in order to attend university and again upon graduation. This report contains information about the student's parents, travels, friends, and political involvements. Maktoumeen sometimes use the name of a national or foreigner so they can study, albeit illegally.

Kurdish students study with Syrian Arab textbooks and are compelled to recite versions of history that contribute to their invisibility in the country. Stateless university students generally do not have the right to participate in school activities such as athletics teams, social clubs, or competitions or to pursue their professions after graduation. Even those Ajanib who do manage to enroll, find it impossible to obtain employment in many of their fields of expertise. Ajanib are restricted from government jobs and the practice of law, pharmacy, or medicine and practice other professions such as teaching or engineering in severely restricted ways.

It is next to impossible for Maktoumeen to access higher education. . . . Maktoumeen children do not receive a diploma from secondary school, preventing their university enrollment. Some parents even report listing their children under the names of relatives who have nationality in order to facilitate their access to school.

No stateless Kurds, even those at the top of their class, can access government scholarships for post-graduate education abroad, and unlike Syrian nationals, they cannot receive government loans or stipends for their undergraduate university education. In addition, stateless Kurds with a disability cannot obtain state-funded special education. . . .

The Right to Employment

With limited access to employment, a majority of stateless Kurds in Syria works two to three jobs at any given time in the informal sector or practices professions without a license or in an extremely limited capacity. They cannot practice agriculture on the land which was taken from them. Moreover, most stateless Kurds are not permitted to become members of professional labor unions, with the exception of the Engineers' union on a limited basis. "I work night and day, but still have nothing," a Maktoumeen man told RI. "Because our life is hard, we think only of how to eat." . . .

Unlike the Maktoumeen, Ajanib can obtain drivers licenses and cash checks, but neither are permitted to open bank accounts or obtain commercial drivers licenses. One Maktoumeen man reported receiving paychecks or entering into contracts for work under the name of a friend who has nationality in order to be able to receive and cash paychecks at banks. Another Maktoumeen man described how companies often exploit Maktoumeen labor due to lack of documentation. He stated, "I had contracted with a government-owned company to do a construction job laying telephone lines with a crew of men that I hired. . . . but after we finished the work, the company refused to pay me. They said that I do not possess an identity card and therefore cannot receive a paycheck. . . ."

Economic consequences of limited access to the labor market and lack of trust in the education system compel many Maktoumeen children to work picking cotton, selling cigarettes or lottery tickets, cleaning windows, shining shoes, working as porters, and helping in mechanic shops. Many child laborers are exploited in the market and forced to pay the police bribes in order to continue their work. A number of these children suffer from ailments connected with poor nutrition, such as anemia and rickets.

Many stateless Kurds residing in the northeast have also been compelled to move into larger urban centers such as Damascus, Homs, Hama, or Latakia to find work in the informal sector. In the neighborhood of Wad El Mashariya Zor Ava, on the outskirts of Damascus, for example, nearly 2,000 stateless Kurdish families, many of whom work in construction, are living in settlements constructed without legal building permits. Most of these families have relatives and close family members still living in the northeastern region of Syria. Unemployment in this neighborhood has been associated with increasing levels of petty crime, poor academic performance, isolation, and depression amongst Kurdish youth.

The Right to Health

Stateless Kurds are prohibited from accessing Syrian public health services or hospitals as either employees or patients, although in some rare emergency cases, they may be granted limited admission. They are instead forced to seek the services of private doctors and health clinics, where costs can be prohibitive and the numbers of which are limited. . . .

There is also concern about psychological problems developing amongst stateless Kurdish youth. One parent said, "The youth see the Arabs and see themselves. They don't have money. There is no place for the children to play. They stay at home. Their study is not good." . . .

The Right to Marry

Official marriage registration is a particularly painful point for many stateless Kurds. Male nationals who marry women who are Ajanib may register their marriages and pass their status to their children. All other marriages, such as those between Ajanib and Maktoumeen or a marriage between a stateless man and a woman who is a Syrian national, cannot be registered officially, even if a court decree is obtained recognizing the marriage. One man reported that he was only able to legalize his marriage after twelve years of approaching different branches of security and obtaining a court decree recognizing the marriage.

Married couples in such families are listed on their identity cards as "single," which poses problems for the registration of children on family identity cards and even prevents husband and wife from sharing a room in a hotel. . . . Many Kurdish families who have Syrian nationality refuse to allow their children to marry Ajanib or Maktoumeen for these reasons. . . .

The Right to Own Property

Ownership and registration of businesses and property is also difficult. With no nationality, Kurds cannot obtain property deeds or register cars or businesses.

Ironically, they are still required to pay property taxes to the government on the land they do not legally own. Some register their property under the names of friends or relatives who are nationals to circumvent these issues. Yet this arrangement forces them to rely upon the good faith of such persons, and the problem still remains that they cannot pass on ownership of property to their children. . . .

The Right to Freedom of Movement

Stateless Kurds are unable to obtain travel documents for purposes of travel outside of Syria, regardless of whether it is for study, travel, attending funerals or family gatherings, or obtaining urgent medical treatment. One example cited was that of two Kurdish musicians who were prevented from traveling with their troupe to attend a music festival outside of Syria. . . .

There are additional problems for Ajanib who wish to change their residence. Unlike Syrian nationals, they must obtain permission from state security in order to change their place of residence. One young university student in Aleppo was required to do this when he wished to move out of the student dormitory. The restrictions on movement are a grave disadvantage, preventing possible economic, academic, cultural, and civil society projects within the Kurdish community and in Syria as a whole. Furthermore it contributes to the culture of frustration that has characterized a large portion of the Kurdish population in Syria. The obstacles to free movement have enhanced the risk of regional discontent and instability.

Source: Refugees International. "Buried Alive: Stateless Kurds in Syria." Available online. URL: http://www.refintl.org/section/publications/syria_human_rights/. Downloaded April 20, 2007.

Joshua Landis, "Syria Shuts Out Iraqi Refugees. Is Arabism Over?" (2007) (excerpts)

It is difficult for Americans to get accurate information about Syria. The U.S. government considers Syria a rogue state, limiting contacts, and the Syrian government stifles public speech.

In many countries living under authoritarian rule, the Internet has opened a new channel of communication that often skirts state censorship because of its free flow and anonymity. But in the early 2000s, Syria had only one computer for every 56 people, according to the U.S. Library of Congress, and the fees charged by the two government Internet service providers (ISPs) made Web access too expensive for most Syrians. Moreover, the government ISPs barred users from Arabic-language opposition sites. While computer-savvy Syrians have found ways to stay one step ahead of the state—connecting with a long-distance call to a server in neighboring Lebanon, for instance—

many bloggers nonetheless fear that what they say will get them in trouble. In a small survey of bloggers in Syria, Lebanon, and Jordan, 80 percent said they practiced self-censorship. According to Reporters without Borders, an NGO dedicated to press freedom, Syria ranks as "the Middle East's biggest prison for cyber-dissidents."

One of the liveliest English-language blogs about Syria belongs to Joshua Landis, an assistant professor of Middle Eastern studies and codirector of the Center for Peace Studies at the University of Oklahoma. In this post, he surveys the political and economic impact of Iraqis seeking refuge in Syria from the sectarian strife unleashed by the American invasion and occupation of Iraq. Bastion of Pan-Arab nationalism, Syria long allowed Arabs to enter the country without visas, but on January 20, 2007, it imposed new requirements.

> ... Iraqis were previously granted renewable three-month residency permits but Syria now issues two-week permits that can be renewed just once, upon presentation of documents including a rental contract. Otherwise, Iraqis must return home for a month before they can apply again. This change does not extend to non-Iraqi Arab visitors, but it is a first step. Following the withdrawal of the Syrian army from Lebanon, Syria also imposed a visa regime of sorts on visitors to and from Lebanon, who must now pay a fee for crossing the border. Arabism, the central tent poll of the Baathist regime, is now being dismantled as Syria ends the free passage of Arab visitors across its borders.
>
> Official Syrian sources on Sunday said the measures introduced by the Syrian government on the Iraqi newcomers were taken for security and economic purposes....
>
> The cause of this reversal are many. First and foremost, The flood of Iraqi refugees, which is approaching one million, has overburdened the constrained Syrian economy and provoked an anti-Iraqi backlash among the Syrian population. Housing prices in greater Damascus have risen by 300% over the last three years, in part, due to refugee pressure. Food prices have also risen dramatically. Syrians complain about overcrowding at some schools in the Damascus area, which have reportedly admitted up to 28,000 Iraqi children. In areas where Iraqis have settled, residents say some classes have swollen from 30 pupils to 50. Most Syrians blame the rampant inflation in the economy of the Iraqis. Another worry is the dramatic rise in crime rates, which is blamed on Iraqis....
>
> The United States for the last three years has been demanding that Syria impose a visa regime on Arab visitors to the country in order to allow for background checks and heightened security. Washington has asked Syria to build a counterpart to America's Homeland Security

regime in order to stanch the flow of Muslim Jihadists headed for Iraq through Syria. Iraq and Washington have also demanded that Syria expel Iraqi Baathists residing in Syria, who they accuse of directing the Sunni resistance based in Anbar province. In some ways, Syria's crackdown of Iraqis is a perverse response to this pressure. Although it is not uniquely directed against Baathist Iraqis, it will allow Syria to claim that it does not protect them and has taken positive measures to restrict the open access of Iraqis to Syria.

Another reason for the refugee policy reversal is Syrian peevishness at being continually isolated by the US and Saudi Arabia. It is tired of being blamed for the lamentable level of violence in Iraq. Syria does not believe it is responsible for the steady deterioration of Iraq, rather, it sees itself as the victim of others misguided policies. Syrians believe they have been more generous than any other Iraqi neighbor in taking in Iraqi refugees and bearing the burden of Washington's failed policies. There is merit to Syrians' sense of frustration at being punished for their help. Refugees International president Kenneth H. Bacon wrote in a recent op-ed:

Syria is the last country in the Middle East to leave its borders open to Iraqi refugees. The United Nations estimates that 1.8 million Iraqis have sought refuge in the region, and Syria and Jordan host the largest concentration. It can't maintain its open-door policy without international support. Refugees already strain social services. Yet, the international response to the Iraqi refugee crisis has been dismal. Despite numbers that rival the displacement in Darfur, there has been scant media attention and even less political concern. The Office of the U.N. High Commissioner for Refugees is doing little.

Unfortunately, the price of this spitting match between Syria, on the one hand, and the US and its allies, on the other, will be paid by the vulnerable refugees who do not deserve more suffering. . . .

The UNHCR reported that the number of Iraqis registered with the organization was at more than 46,000 and increasing daily. . . .

Syria can see that there is no future course but to hope that the American surge can help the Iraqi government to survive. . . .

All the same, Syria will not cut off its links to the Sunni leadership of the opposition in Iraq. Syria will continue to cover all bets on Iraq's future. It does not believe it can afford to alienate any group so long as the future of the country is in such doubt. If the US government is pessimistic about the outcome of its present policy, as demonstrated in the recent intelligence estimate on Iraq, the Syrian government is doubly pessimistic. . . .

Syria's recent policy shift toward Iraq underlines how futile and self-destructive Washington's policy of excluding Syria has become. US prospects of stabilizing the situation in Iraq are not good, but without cooperating from Syria, they are surely worse than they have to be. Syria shares many of Washington's objectives in Iraq—not all, to be sure, but enough to make cooperation the only wise policy.

addendum:
UNHCR offices in Damascus have been mobbed by Iraqis since the new visa requirement was imposed. The UNHCR registered very few of the Iraqis in Syria prior to the visa requirement because it could offer them no protection or value. Now that they will be forced to return to Iraq every 15 days, they need official refugee status to go elsewhere. Some journalists are beginning to speculate that America will have to welcome many more Iraqis as refugees.

Carolyn Lochhead writes this:

When the South Vietnamese government collapsed, the United States initially accepted 130,000 Vietnamese, including 65,000 fearing their lives because of their collaboration with Americans. Many conferences later, 1.4 million Vietnamese, Cambodians and Laotians had been admitted, according to U.S. Citizenship and Immigration Services.

Bill Frelick, refugee policy director at Human Rights Watch and author of an extensive report on the situation. "As it turns out, many of the people who are fleeing Iraq are fleeing because of their associations with the United States. . . ."

[One of more than a dozen comments posted on the blog] **qunfuz** said: (February 5th, 2007, 7:52 pm / #)

My mother-in-law thinks there are four million Iraqis in Syria. You hear such stories, but they surely aren't true. About a million is a very visible number in a city the size of Damascus. Yes, there's lots of Iraqi prostitution, including child prostitution. A sign of the desperation of often very conservative families who've run out of cash. Of course the visa moves don't mean that Arabism is dead. It means there's a crisis, and one which could soon become much worse. Iraq seems to be heading for total collapse. Syria urgently needs international help with the refugee crisis. It is appalling that the rich nations which triggered the whole disaster are not talking about it. I think the Americans should be talking to the Syrians about the region anyway. And given the refugee crisis, even if Bashaar [President Bashar al-Asad] were Hitler the US should be dealing with him.

Source: Joshua Landis. "Syria Shuts Out Iraqi Refugees. Is Arabism Over?" Syria Comment blog. Available online. URL: http://joshualandis.com/blog/?p=152. Uploaded February 4, 2007.

GUATEMALA

Interview with Rigoberta Menchú Tum (March 20, 1993) (excerpts)

Daughter of a conservative peasant farmer and a midwife, Rigoberta Menchú Tum grew up in the middle of Guatemala's civil war and became active in social reform through the Catholic Church. Although researchers have questioned the details of her autobiography, her story dramatizes the suffering of indigenous Guatemalans. Guerrilla activity in the northern highlands soon drew in her family. In 1979, when Menchú was 20, the army arrested, tortured, and killed her younger brother, and after demanding an accounting, her mother was kidnapped, raped, and murdered. In the meantime, her father died in a fire when government security forces confronted rebels occupying the Spanish embassy.

In 1981, Menchú went into hiding, then fled to Mexico City, where she became an outspoken critic of Guatemalan oppression and an advocate for the rights of the indigenous. In 1993—after winning the Nobel Peace Prize and on the eve of becoming the official spokesperson for the UN International Decade of Indigenous Peoples—she gave this interview to Global Vision, an educational media NGO sponsored by UN agencies. The text has been translated from Spanish. Menchú has since returned to Guatemala and now directs the Rigoberta Menchú Tum Foundation. She had two sons, one of whom died shortly after birth, and continues to campaign worldwide on behalf of peace, justice, and indigenous rights.

What is your message to humankind?

We are living in a troubled world, in a time of great uncertainty. It's a time to reflect about many things, especially about humankind as a whole, and the balance between collective values and individual values.

The world right now is preoccupied with business, buying and selling and making money. But solutions can be found in our community, among the indigenous peoples who are the victims of terrible repression and violations of the law in many parts of the world. You can find experience, self-educated people, and a whole side of science which is not well known.

There is a big change going on in the way people see the world: change in the concept of development, in the way people live together. But for this change to bear fruit, we need education on a global scale. Humankind will not recover from its mistakes without global education. The United Nations, human rights organisations, indigenous peoples, and all the countries of the world should concentrate their efforts on education. . . .

We have to focus on solutions in this time of great challenges. If we just wait around, the problems will overwhelm us. We need to take the initiative, to launch local, regional and global projects, to unite our efforts, and really listen to indigenous peoples. We have to listen to people to find out what they want, to discover the solutions they have to offer for the future.

What should be done to protect indigenous peoples?

It is very important to understand that we indigenous peoples don't need "protection." What we do need is simply to be allowed to exist, to live, to let our own culture develop, and to recover the meaning of our own history. Indigenous peoples have always depended on their traditional wisdom and culture. Our cosmological vision, our way of thinking, our lifestyle have empowered us to survive through many difficult times in the past. Now that we stand at the close of the twentieth century, this fact should send a very clear message to the conscience of the world. We indigenous people reaffirm our struggle to survive!

To me, the most important thing is that indigenous people still possess a balance, an equilibrium with Mother Nature, a balance between human life and the earth itself. For us, the Earth is the source of knowledge, of historical memory, of life! But the rest of the world does not share this vision, and so they keep on destroying Mother Earth. Indigenous people aren't strange. We may be special, but we are also part of the modern world in which we all live. We are part of the diversity of cultures, the plurality of races, the mixture of societies on all the continents where we live today. Indigenous people are not some myth from the past, a myth that survives only in legends and in ruins!

You should find out what indigenous people can contribute toward a global vision, a vision of nature, of development, of community based on the oral transmission of our ancestors' knowledge from generation to generation. You should also look at the way we think about nature. Around the world, there have been many struggles in which indigenous peoples have played an important role. But their names are never mentioned, their contributions have been ignored. Others have given new names to these concerns which indigenous peoples have always cared about.

The fact that indigenous people are among the most marginalised of the marginalised people on Earth, among those whose rights have been violated for so long, is a call to conscience. I hope this call will be answered in the new millennium which now awaits us.

The time has come now to stop feeling sorry for all the wrongs that have been done to indigenous people. The time has come to go beyond blame, beyond sympathy with our cause, beyond identifying with our world-view. It's time to implement programmes—alternative projects and technologies that combine the benefits of science and the benefits of nature, that respect the traditional ethno-botanical knowledge of peasants and the age-old experience through which they have survived—and to combine these with the advances of technology and science. We indigenous peoples have nothing against the innovations of technology and science when they are shown to be appropriate. But we are against such innovations if they are applied in opposition to the values which indigenous people protect, which are those of life, nature, and historical memory. . . .

What do you feel about human rights?

Among the nations which have suffered the most widespread human rights abuses, unpunished atrocities, murders, terror and fear, is Guatemala. The recent historical events in Guatemala have fragmented the culture of the Mayas in many places. Displacement, refuge, exile are daily facts of life in my country. However, these things have also allowed us to learn something more in our experience of the world. In Guatemala today, there are some very courageous women who are making a stand, indigenous women, who are leading the struggle! We believe the war in Guatemala is no disgrace for the Mayas. It's a disgrace for the people of Guatemala. . . .

Unfortunately, the rest of the world has turned a blind eye on the situation. Atrocities still go unpunished, and many governments have helped to cover up the problem. . . .

What is going on in Guatemala now?

It's a very complex situation. The war is officially over, yet there are continuous assassinations, enormous suffering and grinding poverty. But the greatest problem in Guatemala is that most people cannot participate in the political negotiations, because they don't speak Spanish! An emergency parliament needs to be formed immediately to address the problem. Blatant disregard for the law is rampant. We must put an end not only to these violations of law, but also to the suppression of truth, to the repression and persecution of over a million civilians who take part in our self-defence patrols.

About a million people have been displaced within the country. Some have sought refuge in the mountains, where they suffer a great deal of bombing. Over two hundred thousand Guatemalans are refugees. Many people have been forced to permanently abandon their farms or leave their towns. In other words, the war is not just the armed conflict which occurs every day, but it's also the general persecution which afflicts the whole economy and society, and which also--as a routine matter—limits our freedom of speech. In the end, the people of Guatemala are paying a very high price for all of this. If we don't recognise the magnitude of the problem in Guatemala, we will never come to grips with the whole issue of development both in Central America and throughout the continent. . . .

Source: Global Visions. "A Plea for Global Education." Interview with Rigoberta Menchú Tum, March 20, 1993. Available online. URL: http://www.global-vision.org/interview/menchu.html. Updated December 3, 2004.

Agreement on Socioeconomic Aspects and the Agrarian Situation (May 16, 1996) (excerpts)

In December 1996, after 36 years of devastating civil war in Guatemala, representatives of opposing sides finalized a series of peace accords negotiated over the previous few years. One of the last completed accords, the Agreement on Socioeconomic Aspects and the Agrarian Situation addresses some of the inequalities that have long divided a rich elite from the poor masses in Guatemala and that underlay the violent conflict. The agreement calls for political and educational enfranchisement, improved health care, and land reform. It was signed in Mexico City on May 6, 1996.

Among its many specific provisions, the agreement charged the government with making available at least three years of schooling to all children between the ages of seven and 12 by the year 2000. In the health system, the government had the same deadline for cutting the infant and maternal mortality rate in half—which it had to accomplish by devoting half of health spending to preventive care. On the legal front, the agreement called for revising and/or passing laws to eliminate discrimination against women, to stiffen penalties for tax evasion and fraud, and to regulate a land trust fund that would buy up land and allocate it to rural men and women.

Observers report that while the international community and Guatemala's powerful generally endorsed the agreement, labor and peasant groups objected to both its process and content, feeling that they had made the greater concessions. A decade after the peace accords' passage, many provisions remain unfulfilled.

Agreement on Social and Economic Aspects and Agrarian Situation

Whereas:

A firm and lasting peace must be consolidated on the basis of social and economic development directed towards the common good, meeting the needs of the whole population,

This is necessary in order to overcome the poverty, extreme poverty, discrimination and social and political marginalization which have impeded and distorted the country's social, economic, cultural and political development and have represented a source of conflict and instability,

Socio-economic development requires social justice, as one of the building blocks of unity and national solidarity, together with sustainable economic growth as a condition for meeting the people's social needs,

Rural areas require an integral strategy that facilitates access by small farmers to land and other production resources, offers juridical security and promotes conflict resolution,

It is essential, both for the realization of the production potential of Guatemalan society and for the achievement of greater social justice, that all sectors of society participate effectively in finding a way to meet their needs, particularly in setting public policies that concern them,

The State should pursue democratisation in order to expand those possibilities for participation and strengthen its role as a leader of national development, as a legislator, as a source of public investment and a provider of services and as a promoter of consensus-building and conflict resolution,

This Agreement seeks to create or strengthen mechanisms and conditions to guarantee the effective participation of the people and contains the priority objectives for Government action to lay the foundations of this participatory development. . . .

The Government of Guatemala and the Unidad Revolucionaria Nacional Guatemalteca (hereinafter referred to as "the Parties") have agreed as follows:

I. Democratisation and Participatory Development

A. Participation and consensus-building

1. In order to pursue a true, functional and participatory democracy, the process of social and economic development should be democratic and participatory and include: (a) consensus-building and dialogue among agents of socio-economic development; (b) consensus-building between these agents and State bodies in the formulation and implementation of development strategies; and (c) effective citizen participation in identifying, prioritising and meeting their needs.

2. Expanded social participation is a bulwark against corruption, privilege, distortions of development and the abuse of economic and political power to the detriment of society. Therefore, it is an instrument

for the eradication of economic, social and political polarization in society.

3. In addition to representing a factor in democratisation, citizen participation in economic and social development is essential in order to promote productivity and economic growth, achieve a more equitable distribution of wealth and train human resources. It ensures transparency in public policies and their orientation towards the common good rather than special interests, the effective protection of the interests of the most vulnerable groups, efficiency in providing services and, consequently, the integral development of the individual. . . .

B. Participation of women in economic and social development

11. The active participation of women is essential for Guatemala's economic and social development, and the State has a duty to promote the elimination of all forms of discrimination against women. . . .

Education and training

(b) Ensuring that women have equal opportunities for education and training in the same conditions as men, and that any form of discrimination against women that may be found in school curricula is eliminated; . . .

Health

(d) Implementing nationwide comprehensive health programmes for women, which involves giving women access to appropriate information, prevention and health care services;

Labour

(e) Guaranteeing women's right to work, which requires:

(i) Using various means to encourage vocational training for women;

(ii) Revising labour legislation to guarantee equality of rights and opportunities between men and women;

(iii) In rural areas, recognizing women as agricultural workers to ensure that their work is valued and remunerated;

(iv) Enacting laws to protect the rights of women who work as household employees, especially in relation to fair wages, working hours, social security and respect for their dignity;

. . .

II. Social Development

... State responsibilities

16. The State has inescapable obligations in the task of correcting social inequities and deficiencies, both by steering the course of development and by making public investments and providing universal social services. Likewise, the State has the specific obligations, imposed by constitutional mandate, of ensuring the effective enjoyment, without discrimination of any kind, of the right to work, health, education and housing, as well as other social rights. The historical social imbalances experienced in Guatemala must be corrected, and peace must be consolidated, through decisive policies which are implemented by both the State and society as a whole....

A. Education and training

21. Education and training have a fundamental role in the country's economic, cultural, social and political development. They are central to the strategy of equity and national unity, and vital for economic modernisation and international competitiveness....

22. In response to the country's needs in the field of education, the Government undertakes to:

Spending on education

(a) Implement significant increases in the resources allocated to education. By the year 2000, the Government proposes to step up public spending on education as a proportion of gross domestic product by at least 50 per cent over its 1995 level. These targets will be revised upwards in the light of future developments in State finances; ...

Coverage

(c) Expand, as a matter of urgency, the coverage of education services at all levels, and in particular the provision of bilingual education in rural communities, by means of:

(i) The integration of children of school age into the educational system, ensuring that they complete the pre-primary and primary levels and the first level of secondary school; in particular, by the year 2000, the Government undertakes to provide access, for all those between ages 7 and 12, to at least three years of schooling;

(ii) Literacy programmes in as many languages as is technically feasible, with the participation of suitably qualified indigenous organizations;

the Government undertakes to raise the literacy rate to 70 per cent by the year 2000; and

(iii) Education, training and technical courses for adults....

B. Health

23. The Parties agree on the need to promote a reform of the national health sector....

Low-income population

(c) The system would create the conditions for ensuring that the low-income population has effective access to quality health services. The Government undertakes to increase the resources it allocates to health. By the year 2000, the Government proposes to step up public spending on health as a proportion of gross domestic product by at least 50 per cent over its 1995 level. This target will be revised upwards in the light of future developments in State finances;

Priority care

(d) The system would give priority to efforts to fight malnutrition and to promote environmental sanitation, preventive health care and primary health care, especially maternal and child care. The Government undertakes to allocate at least 50 per cent of public health expenditure to preventive care and undertakes to cut the 1995 infant and maternal mortality rate in half by the year 2000. In addition, the Government undertakes to maintain the certification of eradication of poliomyelitis, and to eradicate measles by the year 2000; ...

Indigenous and traditional medicine

(f) The system would enhance the importance of indigenous and traditional medicine, promoting its study and renewing its concepts, methods and practices; ...

E. Work

26. Work is essential for the integral development of the individual, the well-being of the family and the social and economic development of Guatemala....

Protective labour legislation

(c) Promote, in the course of 1996, legal and regulatory changes to enforce the labour laws and severely penalise violations, including violations in respect of the minimum wage, non-payment, withholding and delays in wages, occupational hygiene and safety and the work environment;

(d) Decentralize and expand labour inspection services, strengthening the capacity to monitor compliance with the labour norms of domestic law and those derived from the international labour agreements ratified by Guatemala, paying particular attention to monitoring compliance with the labour rights of women, migrant and temporary agricultural workers, household workers, minors, the elderly, the disabled and other workers who are in a more vulnerable and unprotected situation; . . .

III. Agrarian Situation and Rural Development

27. It is essential and unavoidable to solve the problems of agrarian reform and rural development in order to address the situation of the majority population, which live in rural areas and is most affected by poverty, extreme poverty, injustice and the weakness of State institutions. The transformation of the structure of land use and ownership must have as its objective the incorporation of the rural population into economic, social and political development so that the land constitutes, for those who work it, the basis of their economic stability, the foundation of their progressive social well-being and the guarantee of their freedom and dignity.

28. Land is central to the problems of rural development. From the conquest to the present, historic events, often tragic, have left deep traces in ethnic, social and economic relations concerning property and land use. These have led to a situation of concentration of resources which contrasts with the poverty of the majority and hinders the development of Guatemala as a whole. It is essential to redress and overcome this legacy and promote more efficient and more equitable farming, strengthening the potential of all those involved, not only in terms of productive capacity but also in enhancing the cultures and value systems which coexist and intermingle in the rural areas of Guatemala. . . .

Access to land ownership: land trust fund

(a) Establish a land trust fund within a broad-based banking institution to provide credit and to promote savings, preferably among micro-, small and medium-sized enterprises. The land trust fund will have prime responsibility for the acquisition of land through Government funding, will promote the establishment of a transparent land market and will facilitate the updating of land development plans. The fund will give priority to the allocation of land to rural men and women who are organized for that purpose, taking into account economic and environmental sustainability requirements; . . .

E. Legal framework and juridical security

37. Guatemala is in need of reform of the juridical framework of agriculture and institutional development in the rural sector so that an end can be put to the lack of protection and dispossession from which small farmers, and in particular indigenous peoples, have suffered, so as to permit full integration of the rural population into the national economy and regulate land use in an efficient and environmentally sustainable manner in accordance with development needs. To this end, and taking into account in all cases the provisions of the Agreement on Identity and Rights of Indigenous Peoples, the Government undertakes to:

Legal reform

(a) Promote a legal reform which will establish a juridical framework governing land ownership that is secure, simple and accessible to the entire population. This reform will need to simplify the procedures for awarding title and registering ownership and other real estate rights, as well as to simplify administrative and judicial formalities and procedures; . . .

(d) Protect common and municipal land, in particular by limiting to the strict minimum the cases in which it can be transferred or handed over in whatever form to private individuals;

(e) With respect to community-owned land, to regulate participation by communities in order to ensure that it is they who take the decisions relating to their land; . . .

I. Environmental protection

40. Guatemala's natural wealth is a valuable asset of the country and mankind, in addition to being an essential part of the cultural and spiritual heritage of the indigenous peoples. The irrational exploitation of Guatemala's biogenetic and forest resource diversity endangers a human environment that facilitates sustainable development. Sustainable development is understood as being a process of change in the life of the human being through economic growth with social equity, involving production methods and consumption patterns that maintain the ecological balance. . . .

IV. Modernisation of Government Services and Fiscal Policy

A. Modernisation of government services

43. Government services should become an efficient tool of development policies. To this end, the Government undertakes to:

Decentralization and redistribution

(a) Deepen the decentralization and redistribution of the powers, responsibilities and resources concentrated in the central Government in order to modernise, render effective and streamline government services. Decentralization should ensure the transfer of decision-making power and sufficient resources to the appropriate levels (local, municipal, departmental and regional) so as to meet the needs of socio-economic development in an efficient way and promote close cooperation between government bodies and the population. . . .

Fiscal commitment

50. As a step towards a fair and equitable tax system, the Government undertakes to address the most serious issue relating to tax injustice and inequity, namely, evasion and fraud, especially on the part of those who should be the largest contributors. . . .

Source: "The Socio-Economic Accord." Conciliation Resources Web site. Available online. URL: http://www.c-r.org/our-work/accord/guatemala/socio-economic-accord.php. Downloaded April 20, 2007.

Bishop Álvaro Ramazzini's Testimony before a U.S. House Subcommittee (April 13, 2005) (excerpts)

In Guatemala, as elsewhere in Latin America, clergy often take a lead role in advocating for the disadvantaged. On April 13, 2005, Catholic bishop Alvaro Ramazzini testified against the Dominican Republic–Central American Free Trade Agreement (DR-CAFTA) before the International Relations Subcommittee on the Western Hemisphere of the U.S. House of Representatives. Proponents of the agreement argued that it would integrate Guatemala into the global marketplace, benefiting the country's economy. Ramazzini countered that it overlooked the rural poor and turned a blind eye to harmful U.S. immigration policy.

Signed by the United States, Costa Rica, the Dominican Republic, El Salvador, Guatemala, Honduras, and Nicaragua in August 2004, DR-

CAFTA provoked massive demonstrations by Guatemalans opposing its ratification. Just a month before Bishop Ramazzini's testimony, police and soldiers in Guatemala City fired tear gas, rubber bullets, and water hoses at protesters. According to a Gallup poll in Guatemala, 65 percent of respondents feared CAFTA would hurt the country. Groups such as the Indigenous, Peasant, Union and Popular Movement demanded a voice in trade negotiations, handled privately by government and business leaders, and a shift to policies more weighted toward social justice and sustainable development. Nonetheless, Guatemala—and every party but Costa Rica—ratified the treaty.

> ... Mr. Chairman, the rural poor today make up 70 percent of poor people across the globe. In Latin America, two-thirds of those who live in rural areas are poor. In Guatemala, 56 percent of the population is poor and 16 percent is extremely poor with 93 percent of those living in extreme poverty living in rural areas in my country. Almost one quarter of Guatemala's GDP comes from the agricultural sector. Our farmers are hardworking and will continue to find ways to compete with their northern neighbors. But they cannot compete against the United States Treasury and the $170 billion subsidies granted in your Farm Bill of 2002.
>
> And when they can no longer farm and support their families, because of cheap commodity imports or restricted access to seeds and fertilizers because of stringent intellectual property restrictions, where do my people go? What do they do when they are no longer on the land, growing corn, rearing cattle, raising their family, going to church and building communities? The older people mostly stay on the land, while our young head to industrial centers in search of jobs. This is good, some say, as we enter more and more the industrial age.
>
> As you know, Mr. Chairman, many come to the United States, lured by a dream that is shared by all people of the Americas: to build a life, earn a decent wage, be treated well and to raise a family. Some call them "illegals". But according to our market model, they are better described as entrepreneurs without assets, pursuing the American dream. They are not free-loaders. They work hard, often in several jobs, supporting a way of life that many have come to take for granted. They earn minimum wage in large part, can go to your local emergency room when sick, enroll their children in school, and enjoy a relatively safe working environment. Their relatives, meanwhile, who are U.S. citizens or permanent residents, have jobs with paid health care, have a voice in the workplace, receive on-going training to become more skilled and can plan for their future and their

children's future. This resembles the culture of life that Pope John Paul spoke eloquently about.

But what about those who move to the cities and industrial areas to work in the *maquilas* [foreign-owned factories]? As is the case in the rest of Latin America, most of them are women, who have children and who are the only wage-earner in the family. Many of them face an uncertain future. I know of repeated instances where workers were treated in a way that would be against basic labor law in the United States. Employment is at the heart of development. We know that poor working conditions make for bad economics. Without enforceable labor rights that are part of trade agreements with sanctions for non-compliance applied to them, you will not raise standards of labor, you will not raise standards of living, wages will not go up and jobs will continue to hemorrhage from the United States. . . .

We will only approach long-term solutions to these problems when we begin to place the dignity of the human person, especially the poor, at the center of our discussion. I do so in light of other testimony you will hear today. I recognize that we are all people of good will. We all want the best for the people of our hemisphere. But the hearing this afternoon is exploring vital questions about our future with serious consequences for all of us.

Some see increased trade as the solution to all economic problems; others see it as the source of major economic distress. In fact it is neither. I echo once again the concerns of John Paul II: "If globalization is ruled merely by the laws of the market applied to suit the powerful, the consequences cannot but be negative." (Ecclesia in America, 20) These include, for example, "unemployment, the reduction and deterioration of public services, the destruction of the environment and natural resources, the growing distance between rich and poor, unfair competition which puts the poor nations in a situation of ever increasing inferiority." (Ecclesia in America, p. 20). The terms of trade that will be enshrined in law through these various agreements—laws that constitute a treaty between our countries—will impact more than the movement of goods and services across our borders; more than the private property rights of investors and corporations. These agreements will define the kind of relationship we wish to establish between our countries. As such they should reveal an understanding of human dignity and interdependence between the people of our hemisphere that is marked by solidarity and mutual concern. . . . The current model is deficient—and I am confident that we can repair it so that trade works for all, and especially the poor. . . .

To do so, we must all look at trade policies from the bottom up—from their impact on the lives and dignity of poor families and vulnerable workers across the hemisphere.

In the case of CAFTA, the United States is entering into a comprehensive trade agreement with some of the poorest countries in the hemisphere. Our hemisphere has some of the largest inequality in the region. It is easy to understand why our national leaders in poor countries such as Guatemala may seem enticed by the prospect of favorable access to the mighty market of the United States. But we must ask the question: will any short-term gains envisaged by such bilateral agreements be far out-weighed by the loss of bargaining power in other forums. . . .

A one-sided approach to economic integration that focuses only on liberalizing trade barriers makes it difficult for nations to focus on other vital ways of promoting social development. . . . You are perhaps aware that Guatemala ranked among the 10 worst nations in Latin America in the level of income inequality. These nations desperately need a growing middle class. Industrial workers, equipped with the basic rights to have a say in the workplace, were key to the growth of a middle class in our nation. It was a key element in making the United States the economic powerhouse it is today. This is not happening in Central America and it will not happen as long as hundreds of thousands of workers are suppressed, not empowered, at the workplace.

. . . Upbeat predictions regarding the positive impact of these trade agreements must be evaluated carefully. During my meeting with Assistant United States Trade Representative Padilla, in June, 2004, we both recognized that attempts at developing a broad consultative process about trade in Guatemala—ones envisaged by the USTR—were unsuccessful. This experience of exclusion does nothing to further democratic reforms in my country and across the region.

Many voices, including some we have heard today, address the limits of any trade agreement. They highlight the fact that a trade agreement is only a part of the solution to poverty, exclusion, lack of education and integral development. "Trade is not a panacea," we are told, and that is correct. For that very reason, trade policies need to be complemented by institutional reform and a broader development framework that affords each person their right to participate in a market that is fair and compassionate. However, in my experience, trade agreements run the risk of further entrenching inequality in our societies. . . .

We are also assured by proponents of current trade policies that these agreements will lead to transparency, participation and a strengthening of democracy in a region that has seen significant unrest. And here I would like to tell you of the large public demonstrations that have been taking place across the hemisphere against ratification of current trade agreements. Mr. Chairman, the people, who are exercising their fundamental rights in a democracy to have their voices heard. They are ordinary people. They understand their livelihoods and what it means to daily struggle to support themselves and their families. They are not a privileged group afraid of losing what they have come to expect. If they were, then the rich elites in our country would be marching. Instead the elites are in Washington, DC trying to hurry this process along. I bring those people before this hearing today, I hope that my words reflect their hopes and aspirations. . . .

Currently, trade discussions begin by asking how policies will be good for business and economic growth. We need to ask how trade policies will be good for those who live in situations of poverty. It is not enough to rush ahead with so-called "state of the art" trade agreements, while our development policies languish behind. Financial assistance to the region has been steadily decreasing and will fall by another again by 10 percent in Fiscal Year 2006. Without a concerted effort to complement trade and development in a serious way, by putting our most talented trade experts with our most talented development experts in the same room, to solve the same problems with contributions from their own specific field of competence—then the rights of workers to decent wages, small farmers to a fair price, access to health care and education for the young will be cruelly denied and the promise of democratic reforms and a just participation in the global market will be frustrated. . . .

Source: "Testimony of Bishop Alvaro Ramazzini before the House International Relations Committee Subcommittee on the Western Hemisphere." April 13, 2005. Transcript posted by the Office of Senator Tom Harkin of Iowa. Available online. URL: http://harkin.senate.gov/documents/pdf/RamazziniTestimony.pdf. Downloaded April 20, 2007.

INDIA

Mohandas Gandhi, Letter to Lord Irwin (March 2, 1930) (excerpts)

With the British Empire rebuffing Indian demands for home rule, Mohandas Gandhi helped Congress Party leaders draft an Indian declaration of independence in January 1930. He followed that with a simple but inspired act of civil disobedience: a march to the sea to protest the British monopoly on the production and sale of salt.

Civil disobedience is an act of political theater, enlisting the power of public opinion to counter the powers that be. Before his march, Gandhi publicized his intent to break the law, including sending this letter to British viceroy Lord Irwin. On March 12, Gandhi set out with about 80 disciples on a 240-mile walk. All along the route, Indians turned out to watch the procession. When he reached the coastal village of Dandi three weeks later, Gandhi picked up a handful of sand and boiled up a batch of salt. He urged Indians to do likewise, to break this and other unjust laws and to boycott British goods. As Gandhi expected, the British arrested and jailed him—again. But his "soul force" helped unify the "voiceless millions" in their struggle for independence and subdue, at least temporarily, fighting between Hindus and Muslims. His creative and inclusive nonviolent challenge to British rule "spoke truth to power."

Satyagrha Ashram, Sabarmati,
March 2, 1930

Dear Friend,

Before embarking on civil disobedience and taking the risk I have dreaded to take all these years, I would fain approach you and find a way out.

My personal faith is absolutely clear. I cannot intentionally hurt anything that lives, much less fellow human beings, even though they may do the greatest wrong to me and mine. Whilst, therefore, I hold the British rule to be a curse, I do not intend harm to a single Englishman or to any legitimate interest he may have in India.

I must not be misunderstood. Though I hold the British rule in India to be a curse, I do not, therefore, consider Englishmen in general to be worse than any other people on earth. I have the privilege of claiming many Englishmen as dearest friends. Indeed much that I have learnt of the evil of British rule is due to the writings of frank and courageous Englishmen who have not hesitated to tell the unpalatable truth about that rule.

And why do I regard the British rule as a curse?

It has impoverished the dumb millions by a system of progressive exploitation and by a ruinously expensive military and civil administration which the country can never afford.

It has reduced us politically to serfdom. It has sapped the foundations of our culture. And, by the policy of cruel disarmament, it has degraded us spiritually. Lacking the inward strength, we have been reduced, by all but universal disarmament, to a state bordering on cowardly helplessness. . . .

Let me put before you some of the salient points.

The terrific pressure of land revenue, which furnishes a large part of the total, must undergo considerable modification in an independent India. Even the much vaunted permanent settlement benefits the few rich zamindars [landholders responsible for collecting taxes], not the ryots [peasants]. The ryot has remained as helpless as ever. He is a mere tenant at will. Not only, then, has the land revenue to be considerably reduced, but the whole revenue system has to be so revised as to make the ryot's good its primary concern. But the British system seems to be designed to crush the very life out of him. Even the salt he must use to live is so taxed as to make the burden fall heaviest on him, if only because of the heartless impartiality of it incidence. The tax shows itself still more burdensome on the poor man when it is remembered that salt is the one thing he must eat more than the rich man both individually and collectively. . . . If the weight of taxation has crushed the poor from above, the destruction of the central supplementary industry, i.e., hand-spinning, has undermined their capacity for producing wealth. . . .

The iniquities sampled above are maintained in order to carry on a foreign administration, demonstrably the most expensive in the world. Take your own salary. . . . It is over Rs. [rupees] 21,000 per month, besides many other indirect additions. The British Prime Minister gets £ 5,000 per year, i.e., over Rs. 5,400 per month at the present rate of exchange. You are getting over Rs. 700 per day against India's average income of less than annas 2 per day. The Prime Minister gets Rs. 180 per day against Great Britain's average income of nearly Rs. 2 per day. Thus you are getting much over five thousand times India's average income. The British Prime Minister is getting only ninety times Britain's average income. On bended knees I ask you to ponder over this phenomenon. I have taken a personal illustration to drive home a painful truth. I have too great a regard for you as a man to wish to hurt your feelings. I know that you do not need the salary you get. Probably the whole of your salary goes for charity. But a system that provides for such an arrangement deserves to be summarily scrapped. What is true of the Viceregal salary is true generally of the whole administration. . . .

Not one of the great British political parties, it seems to me, is prepared to give up the Indian spoils to which Great Britain helps herself from day to day, often, in spite of the unanimous opposition of Indian opinion. . . .

And the conviction is growing deeper and deeper in me that nothing but unadulterated non-violence can check the organized violence of the British Government. Many think that non-violence is not an active force. My experience, limited though it undoubtedly is, shows that non-violence can be an intensely active force. It is my purpose to set in motion that force as well against the organized violent force of the British rule as [against] the unorganized violent force of the growing party of violence. . . .

I know that in embarking on non-violence I shall be running what might fairly be termed a mad risk. But the victories of truth have never been won without risks, often of the gravest character. Conversion of a nation that has consciously or unconsciously preyed upon another, far more numerous, far more ancient and no less cultured than itself, is worth any amount of risk.

I have deliberately used the word "conversion". For my ambition is no less than to convert the British people through nonviolence, and thus make them see the wrong they have done to India. I do not seek to harm your people. I want to serve them even as I want to serve my own. . . . If the people join me as I expect they will, the sufferings they will undergo, unless the British nation sooner retraces its steps, will be enough to melt the stoniest hearts. . . .

If the British commerce with India is purified of greed, you will have no difficulty in recognizing our independence. I respectfully invite you then to pave the way for immediate removal of those evils, and thus open a way for a real conference between equals, interested only in promoting the common good of mankind through voluntary fellowship and in arranging terms of mutual help and commerce equally suited to both. . . . But if you cannot see your way to deal with these evils and my letter makes no appeal to your heart, on the 11th day of this month, I shall proceed with such co-workers of the Ashram as I can take, to disregard the provisions of the salt laws. I regard this tax to be the most iniquitous of all from the poor man's standpoint. As the independence movement is essentially for the poorest in the land the beginning will be made with this evil. The wonder is that we have submitted to the cruel monopoly for so long. It is, I know, open to you to frustrate my design by arresting me. I hope that there will be tens of thousands ready, in a disciplined manner, to take up the work after me, and, in the act of disobeying the Salt Act to lay themselves open to the penalties of a law that should never have disfigured the Statute-book. . . .

This letter is not in any way intended as a threat but is a simple and sacred duty peremptory on a civil resister. Therefore I am having it specially delivered by a young English friend who believes in the Indian cause and is a full believer in non-violence and whom Providence seems to have sent to me, as it were, for the very purpose.

I remain,
Your sincere friend,
M. K. Gandhi

Source: Mohandas Gandhi. "380. Letter to Lord Irwin." March 2, 1930. In *Collected Works of Mahatma Gandhi*, 100 volumes published in various editions by the government of India, pp. 362–367. Available online. URL: http://www.gandhiserve.org/cwmg/VOL048.PDF. Downloaded April 20, 2007.

International Confederation of Free Trade Unions, Observations on Child Labour in India as Included in "The Effective Abolition of Child Labour" (2003) (excerpts)

The ILO, a UN agency, monitors labor policies and practices around the world. In the ILO's 2003 global report, "The Effective Abolition of Child Labor," the government of India reiterated its commitment to that goal, pointing to its comprehensive Child Labor (Prohibition and Regulation) Act of 1986. The Indian Supreme Court added force to that law in 1996 by issuing a number of specific directions, such as requiring employers that break the law to pay a fine of about $455 to a child welfare fund. Employers must also hire in the child's place an adult from the same family. The court charged the Indian government with conducting a survey to identify working children.

While the Supreme Court decision raised public awareness, many local NGOs and international agencies have faulted the Indian government for failing to enforce its child labor laws and policies. In the ILO report, two labor organizations—the Hind Madoor Sabha, a confederation of Indian trade unions, and the International Confederation of Free Trade Unions (ICFTU), which links labor organizations from 156 countries—echoed those concerns. The ICFTU's comments, excerpted here, were followed in the report by a rebuttal from the Indian government.

Observations submitted to the Office by the International Confederation of Free Trade Unions (ICFTU)

India has neither ratified the ILO Minimum Age Convention, 1973 (No. 138), nor the ILO Worst Forms of Child Labour Convention, 1999 (No. 182).

There is no universal minimum age for employment and primary school education is not compulsory, free or universal. Child labour is not illegal in India except in hazardous sectors. The Child Labour (Prohibition and Regulation) Act, 1986, prohibits the employment of children in some occupations and processes that are considered hazardous—notably, railways; carpet weaving; cement manufacturing; building and construction; cloth printing; dyeing and weaving; matches, explosives, and fireworks; cigarette making; printing; and soldering processes in electronics industries. The Act regulates the employment of children in other areas, providing for six hours' daily work and one day's rest per week. Forced and bonded labour by children is prohibited, but this law is not effectively enforced. . . .

The implementation of the Child Labour (Prohibition and Regulation) Act, 1986, which is the responsibility of state governments, is very poor as reflected by the lack of convictions under the Act. Industries that utilise a large degree of child labour include many which are defined as hazardous under the Act. The main sectors using child labour include: agriculture; hand-knotted carpets; gemstone polishing; brass and base metal articles; glass and glassware; footwear; textiles; silk; fireworks; bidi cigarettes; domestic service; and sporting goods.

Estimates of the numbers of working children in India vary between 22 million and 50 million—indeed, some estimates have put the figure as high as 100 million. Due to the clandestine nature of much child labour, accurate figures are hard to obtain. The ILO estimates the number as at least 44 million, while the Government in 1999 estimated 11 million child workers. . . . Most, if not all, of the 85 million children not in school do housework; work on family farms; work alongside their parents as paid agricultural labour; work as domestic servants; or are otherwise employed.

Perhaps half of India's child labourers are engaged in dangerous professions. Many of them do not survive the harsh environment or are left physically or mentally scarred. The other half are employed elsewhere in the vast informal sector where they are deprived of minimum wages, regular working hours and any measure of job security. Some of the sectors where children are employed are closely related to exports, particularly gemstones and jewellery (which accounted for 17 per cent of India's exports in 1994/95) carpets, textiles and sporting goods. A research survey by Christian Aid in 1997 revealed that Indian children as young as seven were routinely stitching footballs for export to Britain and that there are about 30,000 children employed in India's sportinggoods industry. In the carpet industry, human rights organizations estimate that there may be as many as 300,000 children working, many of them under conditions that amount to bonded labour. The Government of India has now indicated support for fair labeling initiatives.

In the diamond cutting and polishing industry in India, at least ten per cent of the 800,000 workers are less than 14 years old. They work for 12 hours a day and are paid a wage that is at a maximum 60 per cent of the normal average daily wage of an adult.... Conditions for other gemstone industries are worse still than in the diamond sector and many children work up to two years for no income under the pretext that they are "learning the trade". About 200,000 child labourers are employed in Jaipur where some 95 per cent of gemstones processed in India are cut, shaped, polished and carved....

A plan to eliminate child labour from hazardous industries by the year 2000, and from all industries by 2010, has so far touched only a small fraction of children in the workplace. The current Government has carried on with the programme, but has dropped the time bound targets....

A constitutional provision to provide free and universal primary education has never been implemented, and school enrolment rates remain low notwithstanding recent commitments to a 300 per cent increase in the education budget. The Government has informed the ILO that changes to child labour laws are being considered, which would include a universal minimum age for employment of 14 years, and a minimum age for hazardous employment of 18 years. There has however been no progress in this regard for the last two years.

India has been involved with the ILO's International Programme on the Elimination of Child Labour (IPEC) since the early 1990's, and some estimates suggest 90,000 child labourers have been rehabilitated in that time. There is also the National Child Labour Project (NCLP) that rehabilitates children in hazardous work through education and small family stipends. Government figures suggest that over 200,000 children were involved in the NCLP over the course of the year 2000, but no figures are available to suggest how many of these children were actually removed from hazardous employment. There are also numerous non-governmental organizations (NGOs) active in rehabilitating working children, in particular the South Asian Coalition on Child Servitude (SACCS).

Given the scale of the problem of child labour in India, the measures undertaken so far stand to be inadequate to achieve their objectives. Trade unions, social organizations and the Government have initiated programmes to work together to achieve the elimination of child labour. Such programmes need to be supported through a much greater commitment of resources from the Government of India. Such an effort stands to yield substantive results. In this regard, the example of the relatively poor Indian state of Kerala continues to be extremely instructive. Kerala's consistent high level of spending on education as a share of the state budget, well above the average level in India, has achieved spectacular successes in terms of the highest school retention rate in India; by far the lowest gender disparity; almost double the national figure for literacy; and a far lower work participation rate of children, at a third or less of the average level for India. . . .

Source: International Labour Organization. "The Effective Abolition of Child Labor," pp. 100–103. 2003 report. Cornell University's School of Industrial and Labor Relations Digital Commons Web site. Available online. URL: http://digitalcommons.ilr.cornell.edu/cgi/viewcontent.cgi?article=1001&context=child. Downloaded April 20, 2007.

Palagummi Sainath: "How the Better Half Dies" (2004)

Since 1997, tens of thousands of Indian farmers have committed suicide—as well as uncounted numbers of their relatives. Particularly distressed has been the southern state of Andhra Pradesh, India's third largest, home to the high-tech boom town of Hyderabad. Observers blame a combination of drought, unintended consequences of the Green Revolution, and economic policies linked to globalization for driving farm families deeper into debt. The despairing have taken their own lives, often by drinking pesticides.

The Green Revolution promoted biotechnology, and critics charge that the expensive machinery, fertilizers, pesticides, and genetically modified seeds pushed by multinational companies deliver far less than promised. Seeds have a lower germination rate, for instance, and chemicals have compromised the soil. Under international pressure to balance the budget and compete in the world market, the Indian government has cut subsidies and urged farmers to grow cash crops, such as cotton, rather than the traditional mix of food and other agricultural products. When the harvest fails in a dry year, farmers borrow even more from moneylenders.

Journalist Palagummi Sainath has won many international awards for his muckraking coverage of Indian poverty. He wrote this piece as rural affairs editor of The Hindu *newspaper. Spurred by media coverage of the agricultural crisis, federal and state officials launched inquiries and proposed relief packages that included irrigation projects, crop loans, interest waivers, and rural employment opportunities. But the plans do not address most of the underlying problems, according to Sainath and other reporters, and corruption often prevents aid from reaching the poor,*

ANANTAPUR (ANDHRA PRADESH), JULY 31—When Pedda Narsamma hanged herself in Pandi Parthi village, her eight-member household was shattered. For decades, it was Narsamma, 50, who kept both farm and family going. Two years later, the Government has taken note of this suicide.

And an inquiry process seems to be on. But her family is unsure of any compensation.

Pedda Narsamma was a Dalit. And a woman. And women are not accepted as "farmers." Which means this may not finally go down as a "farmer's suicide."

"Our mother ran everything," says her son, Narasimhalu. "My father is mentally unsound and has not worked in a long time. She did most of the work at home, brought up the children and even looked after her grand children. She also planned and did much of the work on our five acres. And often worked on the fields of others to make ends meet."

By 2002, the ends would not meet. And Narsamma planned her own end. "It was too much for her that the crops kept failing," says Narasimhalu.

Just farmers' wives

That thousands of farmers have committed suicide in Andhra Pradesh in the past seven years is now known. Far less known is that women farmers, too, have taken their lives in no small number.

It is only in recent months that—in a few cases—their suicides are being counted at all. "In both social and official perception," says a senior Government officer, "the farmer is a landed male with a patta. Women do not fit in that category. Their property rights do not exist in practice. And men do not accept them as farmers. They are seen, at best, as farmers' wives."

Though close to a fifth of all rural households in India are female-headed, few women hold titles to land. Even in land-owning households, they do most of the work on the farm, but are not seen as farmers. In one estimate, women account for 90 per cent of all those engaged in transplantation.

They also make up 76 per cent of those sowing seeds and 82 per cent of people transporting crops from field to home. They are a third of the work force that prepares the land for cultivation. And between 70 and 90 per cent of those involved in dairying.

In districts like Anantapur and Mahbubnagar, the numbers of women-headed households are even higher. Lakhs [hundreds of thousands] of people migrate from these regions each year in search of work. With men usually going first.

Working against odds

In recent times landed farmers have joined the same landless labourers they used to employ, in large-scale distress migrations out of the State. This leaves still more women running farms, families and finances alone and against huge odds.

Those odds proved too much for Kovurru Ramalamma in Digumari village. "The only thing I ever saw her do was work," says Sudhamani, her daughter. "My father never did. The two acres of land we had leased kept her busy every moment that she was not running the home. She worried about my marriage and that of my sister."

By 2000, the family's debts touched Rs. 1.5 lakhs [about $3,659] as crops failed. Over Rs. 30,000 [$732] went in medical costs. A broken Ramalamma, 46, consumed pesticides and took her life. After her death, her family gave up the leased land. They have none of their own. That makes compensation claims sticky. How do they prove they were farmers when it happened?

. . .

There have also been suicides among women farmers whose husbands have migrated. Swaroopa Rani, vice-president of the All-India Democratic Women's Association in the State, explains why.

Many responsibilities

"To begin with, they were doing the bulk of the work. Now they have to face the banks, the moneylenders. They have to bring up the children and send them to school. Raising and spending money for the needs of the household becomes their job. And, on top of it all, they have to run the farm. Sometimes, the pressure becomes too much."

And sometimes, one suicide swiftly follows another. As in Choutapalli village in Krishna district. "Madduri Anasuya killed herself three days after her husband Mohan Rao took his own life," points out AIDWA's Swaroopa Rani. . . .

How many women's suicides have there been in these years of farmer distress? "We may never know," says Dr. Rama Devi. Now based in Hyderabad, she was teaching at the Government Medical College, Anantapur, in 2001 when she noticed the number of women's suicides being brought in or reported.

"In a single year from August 2001," says Dr. Rama, "there were 311 women's suicides in just Anantapur district alone. And these were only the recorded ones. There must have been a lot more that went unreported. Close to 80 per cent of these 311 were from villages. And most of the women were from a farming background.

"The links with the farm disaster were clear and many. For instance, the worse the farm crisis got, the more the dowry problems grew. This was a factor in quite a few suicides. The crisis also had another serious fallout for families. Many weddings were delayed for lack of money. And I came across cases where the girl committed suicide because she felt she was a burden on her family."

Hit in other ways too

"The women were also hit in other ways. As farming floundered, many families came to the towns. The men sought work as auto drivers or daily wage labour. Often without success. In this struggle against poverty, the stress on their wives was enormous. Drunkenness and beatings were on the rise. Some of these women, too, took their own lives. Whichever way you look at it, the collapse of farming in Anantapur was closely linked to the suicides of hundreds of women in the district."

Source: Palagummi Sainath. "How the Better Half Dies," *The Hindu*, July 31, 2004. Available online at the India Together website. URL: http://indiatogether.org/2004/aug/psa-womenfarm.htm. Downloaded July 13, 2007.

DEMOCRATIC REPUBLIC OF THE CONGO

King Afonso I of Kongo, Letters to King João III of Portugal (1526) (excerpts)

Upon contact with the Portuguese at the end of the 15th century, the king of Kongo sent emissaries to Lisbon. When they returned in 1491 in the company of Portuguese priests and artisans, they brought with them stories, goods, and a printing press. That year, the king converted to Catholicism, as did his son, Nzinga Mbemba, christened Afonso. Afonso's devotion to his new faith prompted one Franciscan missionary to remark, "He is not a man, but an angel, sent by the Lord in this kingdom to convert it."

Ascending to the throne in 1506, Afonso I admired much of European culture. He made Catholicism the state religion, adopted Portuguese as the court language, and sent noble sons to Portugal to study. His own son, Henrique, became the first black Catholic bishop in West Africa. But Afonso was not blind to the deleterious effects of the slave trade on his kingdom. In letters dictated to his secretaries in Portuguese, he complained to one Portuguese king after another about the abuses of merchants.

About two dozen of Afonso's letters survive. They cover a variety of topics. In 1526, he appealed to King João III of Portugal as a fellow royal and Christian to curb slaving, which was undermining political stability. João did not—or perhaps could not. Although Afonso later survived an assassination attempt by Portuguese in his midst, the Kingdom of Kongo could not withstand the voracious exploitation by Portuguese and rival European, Arab, African, and mixed-race opportunists.

> [**1526**] Sir, Your Highness [of Portugal] should know how our Kingdom is being lost in so many ways that it is convenient to provide for the necessary remedy, since this is caused by the excessive freedom given by your factors and officials to the men and merchants who are allowed to come to this Kingdom to set up shops with goods and many things which have been prohibited by us, and which they spread throughout our Kingdoms and Domains in such an abundance that many of our vassals, whom we had in obedience, do not comply because they have the things in greater abundance than we ourselves . . .
>
> And we cannot reckon how great the damage is, since the mentioned merchants are taking every day our natives, sons of the land and the sons of our noblemen and vassals and our relatives, because the thieves and men of bad conscience grab them wishing to have the things and wares of this Kingdom which they are ambitious of; they grab them and get them to be sold; and so great, Sir, is the corruption and licentiousness that our country is being completely depopulated, and Your Highness should not agree with this nor accept it as in your service. And to avoid it we need from those [your] Kingdoms no more than some priests and a few people to teach in schools, and no other goods except wine and flour for the holy sacrament. That is why we beg of Your Highness to help and assist us in this matter, commanding your factors that they should not send here either merchants or wares, because it is *our will that in these Kingdoms there should not be any trade of slaves nor outlet for them*. . . . I kiss your hands many times.

The Origins of Slaving

[**1526**] . . . Moreover, Sir, in our Kingdoms there is another great inconvenience which is of little service to God, and this is that many of our people, keenly desirous as they are of the wares and things of your Kingdoms, which are brought here by your people, and in order to satisfy their voracious appetite, seize many of our people, freed and exempt men; and very often it happens that they kidnap even noblemen and the sons of noblemen, and our relatives, and take them to be sold to the white men who are in our Kingdoms; and for this purpose they have concealed them; and others are brought during the night so that they might not be recognized.

And as soon as they are taken by the white men they are immediately ironed and branded with fire, and when they are carried to be embarked, if they are caught by our guards' men the whites allege that they have bought them but they cannot say from whom, so that it is our duty to do justice and to restore to the freemen their freedom, but it cannot be done if your subjects feel offended, as they claim to be.

And to avoid such a great evil we passed a law so that any white man living in our Kingdoms and wanting to purchase goods in any way should first inform three of our noblemen and officials of our court . . . who should investigate if the mentioned goods are captives or free men, and if cleared by them there will be no further doubt nor embargo for them to be taken and embarked, But if the white men do not comply with it they will lose the aforementioned goods, And if we do them this favor and concession it is for the part Your Highness has in it, since we know that it is in your service too that these goods are taken from our Kingdom, otherwise we should not consent to this. . . .

A Call for Aid

[**1526**] Sir, Your Highness has been kind enough to write to us saying that we should ask in our letter for anything we need, and that we shall be provided with everything, and as the pace and the health of our Kingdom depend on us, and as there are among us old folks . . . , it happens that we have continuously many and different diseases which put us very often in such a weakness that we reach almost the last extreme; and the same happens to our children, relatives and natives owing to the lack in this country of physicians and surgeons who might know how to cure properly such diseases. And as we have got neither dispensaries nor drugs which might help us in this forlornness, many of those who had been already confirmed and instructed in the holy faith of Our Lord Jesus Christ perish and die; and the rest of the people in their majority cure themselves with herbs and breads and other ancient methods, so that they put all their faith in the mentioned herbs and ceremonies if they live, and believe that they are saved if they die; and this is not much in the service of God.

. . . we beg of you to be agreeable and kind, enough to send us two physicians and two apothecaries and one surgeon, so that they may come with their drug-stores and all the necessary things to stay in our kingdoms, because we are in extreme need of them all and each of them. We shall do them all good and shall benefit them by all means, since they are sent by Your Highness, whom we thank for your work in their coming. . . .

Source: Basil Davidson, ed. *The African Past*. Boston: Little, Brown, 1964, pp. 191–194.

Democratic Republic of the Congo, Interim Poverty Reduction Strategy Paper (March 2002) (excerpts)

Countries receiving aid from the IMF and World Bank must prepare Poverty Reduction Strategy Papers (PRSPs), which "describe the country's macroeconomic, structural and social policies and programs over a three year or longer horizon to promote broad-based growth and reduce poverty, as well as associated external financing needs and major sources of financing." The reports should include input from domestic stakeholders and international donors. An Interim PRSP (I-PRSP) lays the groundwork for the fuller report.

Civil war imploded antipoverty programs in the Democratic Republic of the Congo, but in 2001, the DRC declared a commitment to "transform its shame . . . into an opportunity to eradicate once and for all the virus and the endemic disease of poverty in our country . . . to involve everyone, every Congolese woman and every Congolese man." This I-PRSP reveals the formidable challenges the DRC faces, but the international voice narrating the report applauds the government's attempt to include the private sector, NGOs, universities, and professional and religious groups in the planning—and the state's willingness to invest its own, albeit limited, funds in producing the I-PRSP.

CHAPTER I: CONTEXT AND IMPORTANCE OF THE PRSP

1.1. Introduction

1. The Democratic Republic of the Congo (DRC) is located in Central Africa, in the sub-region of the Great Lakes. It covers an area of 2,350,000 square kilometers with a population of approximately 52 million, growing at a rate of between 3 percent and 3.2 percent a year. At least 60 percent of the population inhabit rural areas and survive on traditional farming, hunting, and fishing. . . .

2. The country is divided into 11 provinces, including Kinshasa, the administrative and political capital. The Eastern provinces, Kasaï Oriental and Katanga, have extensive mineral deposits (including copper, cobalt, diamonds, and gold). The other provinces, whose mineral potential has yet to be exploited, are best known for their farming, livestock, and fishing activities.

3. In spite of these vast human and natural resources, the DRC ranks as one of the poorest countries in the world. Some indicators place it amongst the most destitute countries in sub-Saharan Africa. About 80 percent of its 52 million inhabitants live at the brink of what human dignity can endure, on less than US$0.20 a day.

4. For over 30 years the country was run by a corrupt, predatory dictatorship. The transition from dictatorship to democracy has been poorly handled since 1990. The resulting institutional instability, pillaging, and inter-ethnic fighting have plunged the DRC into an ongoing multi-faceted crisis, one of the effects of which is the increase of poverty.

5. The DRC is the only country in Africa sharing borders with nine other countries (Angola, Burundi, Central African Republic, Congo, Rwanda, Sudan, Tanzania, Uganda, and Zambia). The longstanding economic and institutional crisis has kindled the greed of certain countries, which have pounced on the DRC's rich land and minerals. Under the cover of rebel movements, foreign armies occupy part of its territory. This situation has triggered one of the most complex crises in the Great Lakes sub-region.

6. The economic, social, political, and environmental cost of this conflict has been huge. More than three million human lives have been lost. Almost four million people are estimated to have been displaced in the sub-region and some 10,000 to 15,000 children are being used as soldiers. The extent and complexity of the conflict have seriously undermined institutional stability and eroded grassroots socio-economic infrastructure.....

1.2. Rebuilding the DRC: window of opportunities and actions under way

7. Since the first quarter of 2001, the government has been firmly committed to restoring peace and rebuilding a modern State, correcting macroeconomic imbalances, and relaunching growth, while addressing the urgent needs generated by conflicts and natural disasters....

8. The willingness to restore peace and rebuild the State was expressed first in support of the signing of the Lusaka agreements and then by implementation of a ceasefire agreement (Security Council Resolution No. 1341), and its reinforcement by the troops of the UN Organization Mission in Congo (MONUC). Numerous financial, diplomatic, and political initiatives

are under way to try and ensure that the inter-Congolese dialogue reaches a successful conclusion, enabling the country to put in place legitimate and credible institutions and a democratic, modern State that respects human rights and freedom: the sole guarantee for sound political, administrative, and judicial governance. Following the example of other countries in the sub-region of the Great Lakes, the DRC has put in place a disarmament and reintegration program for former combatants, especially child soldiers. . . .

9. At the same time, the international community focusses its assistance on macroeconomic stabilization and resumption of economic growth. The World Bank (WB), the International Monetary Fund (IMF), the African Development Bank (AfDB), the European Union (EU), and the specialized agencies of the United Nations System (WHO, UNICEF, and UNDP) support the reform programs adopted by the government of the DRC. To break the hyperinflation cycle, the WB and the IMF have provided substantial technical support for implementation of the Interim Program (IP) and Enhanced Interim Program (EIP). The US$50 million IDA grant to finance urgent activities, including technical capacity building for the public administration and the rebuilding of the highway between Kinshasa and the sea port of Matadi, bears ample witness to the international community's commitment to support the DRC. . . .

2.3.1. Education

28. It is worth noting the deterioration of public sector education, in particular the inadequacy of facilities, the dilapidated infrastructure, the dearth of pedagogical materials, the lack of motivation of teachers, the poor returns reflected in high drop-out rates, the poor performance of students at every level, and the mismatch between the training imparted and the skills required by the labor market. The percentage of children entering school at the legally required age (6 years) has plummeted from 22.5 percent in 1995 to 13.9 percent in 2001. . . .

2.3.2. Health

30. Most of the health districts are in a state of complete abandonment. Conservative estimates of health facilities coverage show that at least 37 percent of the population or approximately 18.5 million people, have no access to any kind of health care.

31. The high mortality rate affects especially the poor and the vulnerable: people in rural and suburban areas, women of child-bearing age, and children under five, and is associated with the deterioration of the main health indicators (life expectancy at birth, all forms of malnutrition, and the prevalence of HIV/AIDS).

32. Between 65 percent and 85 percent of births are not attended by skilled health personnel and result in a high maternal mortality rate. The infant mortality rate in 2001 was 129 deaths per 1,000 births (138 per 1,000 births in rural areas), while the mortality rate for children under 5 years of age was 213 per 1,000 in 1998. The maternal mortality rate (870 per 100,000 births in 1995), which was already too high, rose steeply to 1,289 per 100,000 births in 2001.

33. Immunization coverage is very low. . . .

34. Financial constraints are the main reason hampering the development of routine vaccination activities, and vaccination coverage of children from 0 to 5 years is only 29 percent. In June 2001, a joint WHO and UNICEF mission estimated that the minimum investment required to stem the deterioration in the mortality rate and reverse trends in health indicators on a lasting basis would be US$350 million a year. In reality, contributions by donors and creditors between 1998 and 2001 amounted to only US$82.19 million. The percentage of the population infected with the HIV virus also continues to rise for lack of the resources needed for awareness and prevention campaigns. In 2001, the contraceptive usage rate was 31.4 percent.

2.3.3. Nutrition

35. Malnutrition is a major public health problem. In November 2000, the World Food Program (WFP) calculated that 16 million people (33 percent of the population) suffered from serious malnutrition following prolonged displacement, isolation, lack of access to markets, disruption of supply routes, and inflation.

36. In the occupied territories, the overall malnutrition rates for children under 5 recorded for the last 12 months were as high as 41 percent, with a severe malnutrition rate of up to 25.79 percent.

2.3.4. Employment

37. Unemployment has increased steeply as a result of the State's inability to manage public enterprises, and absence of a policy of joint-ventures and incentives to invest. In 2000, 2 percent of the total population, 4 percent of the labor force, and 8 percent of the male work force were employed, compared with 8, 18, and 35 percent, respectively, in 1958. The social and political crisis of the 1990s and the conflicts have only exacerbated this downward spiral to a point at which unemployment and the lack of vocational training have become one of the root causes of grave social unrest. The result is a worsening of poverty, increased vulnerability of the population, and the proliferation of urban unemployment.

38. As a result of the generalized crisis in the country, the economy is dominated by the informal sector. The formal sector is characterized by pathetically low wages and benefits and by a universal lack of motivation. Working conditions have in fact become inhuman, especially in the public sector, where the average monthly salary is US$15. In the private sector, in the absence of a Guaranteed Minimum Wage (SMIG) and of a coherent wage policy, firms have only paid subsistence wages. . . .

2.5. HIV/AIDS and other endemic diseases

46. The prevalence rate at end-1999 was 5.07 percent, causing 300,000 deaths a year, of which 80 percent are persons of 15.45 years of age. In 1999, 8 percent of pregnant women were estimated to have HIV/AIDS. This ratio has increased rapidly in the combat zones in the eastern part of the country. Thus, Ministry of Health statistics showing a decline in life expectancy from 52.4 years in 1994 to 50.8 percent in 1997 are quite credible. . . . UNSIDA estimates that at least 90 percent of people who are HIV positive are unaware of the fact. Some refuse to take a test because of its cost (US$10) and the unaffordability of treatment, others because they prefer not to know.

47. As regards malaria, the Ministry of Health's report for 2000 on potentially endemic diseases indicates that, of 12 diseases kept under surveillance, malaria accounts for most cases (92.3 percent of registered medical consultations) and most deaths (52.4 percent of registered deaths) especially among children under five. . . . In 2001, it was estimated that only 6.3 percent of the child population uses insecticide-treated anti-malarial mosquito nets.

48. Tuberculosis is the principal killer disease for adults, implying that it also impoverishes both families and the country. The HIV/AIDS pandemic and the conflicts increase the incidence of the disease. Indeed, 30 to 50 percent of those suffering from tuberculosis are also infected with HIV and therefore constantly having relapses. Medical statistics show that 40 percent of deaths of individuals with HIV/AIDS are attributed to tuberculosis.

2.6. Recent developments in urban poverty

49. The crisis that has engulfed the DRC since the 1970s, the failure of the stabilization and structural adjustment programs of the 1980s, the plundering of the country twice during the 1990s, and the wars of 1996 and 1998 induced massive displacements of people to the big towns and thereby altered the patterns of urban poverty. In twelve recently surveyed provinces, urban poverty is estimated at 75 percent. . . .

50. In these towns, access to basic socio-economic services is far from adequate; for every hundred households, only 44 have access to potable water, and just under three households have sanitary garbage disposal facilities. At the start of the 2000–01 school year, only about 20 percent of pupils were able to attend school in Kinshasa. Repeated strikes paralyze schools. . . . Those pupils that do get to school, frequently study under appallingly insalubrious conditions. Finally, the number of people sharing one bedroom is high, that is to say more than three persons per room, and most of the urban workforce is unemployed. To survive, it engages in informal sector activities.

51. With respect to public transportation, the roads are full of potholes and puddles, or simply gaping holes. Above all, at rush hour there is a severe shortage of vehicles. The concentration, especially in Kinshasa, of economic activities downtown forces people to come a long way either to get to or return from work, to take supplies to a store or stand, or to procure essential goods or services. The jostling is a dismal spectacle in most Congolese towns. Moreover, frequent urban flooding often affects entire districts.

2.7. Conflict and poverty: the destitution of the victims

52. Ongoing warfare since 1996 has exacerbated poverty in the country, particularly in provinces occupied by rebel forces. The impact of war will be assessed using consumption budget surveys under the final PRSP. In addition, the recent eruption of the Nyiragongo volcano destroyed more than half the town of Goma and plunged its inhabitants into a state of utter destitution.

53. Several sources observed that in the east and center of the country, rape is used as a tactic to prevent women from working in the fields. Also, children cannot be vaccinated because their mothers are not wearing decent clothing. Some men, too, only work at night for lack of clothes. Prostitution and sexual enslavement are widespread. Plunder and theft of harvests by (unpaid) armed groups are commonplace. This situation has added to the disruption of subsistence farming and increased the already severe malnutrition.

54. In the eastern part of the country, war has aggravated the poverty of both the displaced population and the local host communities. In certain isolated areas that can be reached only by plane (Shabunda, Kindu, and Sankuru, for example), the cost of staple items such as salt, oil, soap, and clothing has risen to a point at which the population can no longer afford them. . . .

56. The war has destroyed hospitals, medical centers, and health posts. Medicine is scarce and routine vaccination programs have been interrupted. The budget for health services is nonexistent and the cost of health care and medicine is prohibitive. . . .

3.3.3. Priority actions and preliminary lessons

77. A summary of the participatory consultations indicates that Congolese communities consider that poverty affects, in order of importance, health, education, and general welfare (access to safe water, electricity, a clean environment), and hygiene (housing, household refuse disposal, etc.). . . .

79. Other areas, such as job creation, equal treatment of women, nutrition, and socioeconomic infrastructure, were also emphasized, but constitute second order priorities. . . .

Source: Democratic Republic of the Congo. "Interim Poverty Reduction Strategy Paper." Kinshasa, March 2002. Translated from the French. Available online. URL: http://www.imf.org/External/NP/prsp/2002/cod/01/033102.pdf. Downloaded November 14, 2007.

Amnesty International, A Rape Survivor's Testimony, as Included in "DRC: Mass rape—time for remedies" (October 2004)

Bullets cost money; rape is cheap. Although women have long suffered sexual violence during war, civil and international conflicts in poor countries like the DRC have unleashed particularly vicious assaults on women—and children. Especially in the eastern provinces, soldiers often kidnap victims, keeping them in sex camps and subjecting them to repeated and gang rapes. Some militiamen cut off women's feet to keep them from running away or gouge out their eyes to prevent them from identifying their attackers. Aid workers report that Congolese women are suffering long-term health problems from injuries and mutilations, in addition to psychological distress, which may never diminish. With experts estimating that perhaps 60 percent of combatants carry HIV, AIDS is a well-grounded fear for rape victims, but many never seek treatment, out of shame or worry that travel to a distant health center may expose them to another assault. Labeled "infected" and "dishonored," they often face ostracism in their villages and rejection by their families.

In October 2004, the human-rights NGO Amnesty International published the report "DRC: Mass rape—time for remedies." Researchers interviewed rape victims and with their permission published some of their testimony, with names and details changed to protect their identity.

The Market Trader

Florence is 28 years old and describes herself as *une petite commerçante*, a small trader. In September 2003 she was one of several people travelling on a minibus through the Rusizi plain in South-Kivu province when they were stopped at a roadblock put in place by an armed political group.

AI [Amnesty International] researcher: Can you tell me what happened?
Florence: That day we were coming from Bukavu. When we reached N., some soldiers stopped the vehicle and made us get out. When soldiers stop vehicles like that, it's to rob the passengers, but they often take the opportunity to rape the women too. I was with five other women, and we were all raped, there at the side of the road. Then they gathered us together again and told us that they were taking us to their commander. So, like that, we were led off to their camp in the forest. Since there were six of us, when we were presented to the commander, he made the first choice of which woman he would take. Then the other officers made their choice: each officer took a woman. When it's the commander who chose you, the others can't touch you. But when he's had enough of you, he hands you on to others to rape you.

Q: How long were you there?
F: I spent two months there.

Q: Every day like that?
F: Every day. Each day I was raped by two soldiers.

Q: And then?
F: Well, when the soldiers were tired with me, I was put into a hut which they used as a kind of prison. There, the prison guards would rape us.

Q: How long were you in this prison for?
F: We spent about one month in there.

Q: Did they feed you?
F: They gave us haricot beans. We had to cook them ourselves. Only at night time; not during the day.

Q: Why was that?
F: So that no smoke could be seen. They were frightened of being spotted and attacked. Most nights, too, some of the soldiers went off, and sometimes they brought back cattle. They might give us the head or the hooves. The meat they kept for themselves. So we ate only once a day. They had their own women with them, too, "free" women you could say, who followed them into the forest and prepared the food for them, but not for us.

Q: Did those women try to help you in any way?
F: The women who were there couldn't help us, since they would have been killed on the spot. Even our clothes. They stole our clothes and gave them to their women. There were some women with babies who had been abducted like us. They even stripped the babies of clothing.

Q: There are children held there?
F: Yes. Then there are also children they've had with their own women. There was a whole mix of people there, from almost all the countries [of the region].

Q: How was your health? Did you fall ill during that time?
F: I fell ill. I was bleeding from my vagina. And the water there smelt really bad. They told me I had an infection.

Q: What was the most difficult?
F: For me, the most difficult was each time to be raped by so many different soldiers, every day. And then I was almost entirely naked throughout that time: I had only my panties. For two months. So I had to use a piece of cloth here [over her breasts] to cover myself.

Q: So you were kept naked. And the others you were with, did they all manage to get away?
F: I think so. I think they were released. But it was on condition of payment. Someone had to bring them money or goods before they let you go.

Q: Are you married?
F: My husband threw me out as soon as I got home. Divorced me. For the moment, I'm on my own.

Q: How is that? Why did he decide to throw you out?
F: When I came out from the forest, when I reached the house, he decided to abandon me that same day. Now he has another wife.

Q: And in the community? your neighbourhood?
F: There's no respect. Every one of them, even if they see you are on the large side, like me, in good health, they say, "But you've got AIDS, you slept with the soldiers." But I'm worried too: I ask myself, perhaps I have got AIDS. And I've deep pains here, in my lower stomach. I couldn't bear to sleep with a man now. It's as if I have wounds inside me. It hurts so much.

Q: Florence, would you like to tell us anything else?

F: What I would ask is to see how you can help us; to see how you can help us just to stay alive. Because when you don't have a husband, it's as if you are shamed, despised, not considered. For example, I made my living by buying and selling. But now I can't do anything. My children suffer; I have problems. We don't even have a house where we can spend the night. I am asking you to support us morally, to give us courage, to help us have hope once more in life.

Source: Amnesty International. "Democratic Republic of Congo Surviving rape: Voices from the east." Part of the report "DRC: Mass rape—time for remedies," October 2004. Available online. URL: http://web.amnesty.org/library/print/ENGAFR620192004. Downloaded April 20, 2007.

PART III

Research Tools

6

How to Research World Poverty

As a topic of study, poverty first poses a problem of abundance rather than deprivation. There is a mind-boggling amount of information available. In 2006, the *New York Times* alone ran 339 articles that mentioned the subject, according to its online database. Under the key word "poverty," the Library of Congress online lists 10,000 titles. A Google search turns up 63.3 million Web pages. Where do you start?

NARROWING YOUR TOPIC

As with any research and writing project, defining the boundaries of your inquiry will make the task less daunting. What angle will you explore?

The purpose of this book and other general studies of poverty is to give you a feel for complex terrain. You gather by now that experts measure poverty in different ways, that historical perspectives shape present debates, and that economists, policy makers, activists, and impoverished people have different stakes and opinions. Another way to reconnoiter the field is to skim widely. Allow yourself some roaming time.

In the library catalog, try a few different search words, such as *poverty* or *development.* If you find a likely title, see if the entry includes "subject" terms at the bottom: *Poor—United States* or *Economic assistance* or *Millennium Development Goals.* Use these words the next time you cast your net.

After summoning a few call numbers from the library catalog, eyeball what is on the shelves in that vicinity. Browse the table of contents in a handful of books. On the Internet, click on some of the most popular pages and then dip deeper, perhaps 10 or 20 pages into the hit list. Note titles, section breaks, and headlines—ways other writers have chosen to divide a mammoth subject.

Your assignment or your interests may guide you to a point of entry. Are you going to tackle U.S. poverty or global poverty? Within that, geography may help you narrow your topic. You might decide to focus on a particular region—the American Southwest, for instance, or sub-Saharan Africa—and then within that locale you might select an even smaller area, say a Navajo reservation in New Mexico or a particular country, such as Chad. Demographics suggests other divisions: location (urban or rural poverty), gender (male or female poverty), age (child or elder poverty), or occupation. So many issues compound to create hardship that you can tame the topic by concentrating on a single component: food, housing, education, health care, or political enfranchisement, among other issues.

Even with parameters on poverty, you will likely unearth a mountain of information. Your mission is to discard irrelevant material. First, commune with your assignment. Likely you will be asked to communicate some of what you have learned about poverty. Who is your audience, and what is the nature of your task? Will you be describing (what) or analyzing (how) or arguing (why this and not that)? Phrasing your assignment as specific questions will turn groping into a more manageable, targeted search for answers.

VETTING YOUR SOURCES, PART I

Evaluation of your sources is such an important task that you should have it in mind right from the start. No document is neutral. Sometimes opinions marble a piece like fat in a slab of meat, and the writer's agenda is obvious, but many documents aspire to a professional, objective tone. The journalist or scholar or policy expert parades "hard" facts—numbers, quotes from experts, maps, photographs—but facts are not value-free, as historian Howard Zinn always warns his readers. Reality is messy, complicated, and often riddled with contradictions. A writer, like a photographer framing an image, chooses what to include and what to leave out. Be aware of the creative (subjective) process at work.

To better understand your sources, always ask yourself, Who is presenting this? For what audience? For what purpose? Who else agrees or disagrees?

Gathering Information

Start gathering information early. Locate resources. Likely your public library offers more than paperbacks and hardcovers on the shelves. Perhaps it has e-books that you can read online or skim through with a keyword search, or maybe it subscribes to databases, such as the popular

ProQuest. With ProQuest, you type in a search word or two, indicate the dates you want to cover, and then call up a host of article titles, some with abstracts and some with full text. Many libraries have databases for American newspapers "of record" such as the *New York Times* and the *Washington Post.* Do you, or does someone you know, have access to a university library? That will expand your catalog of books and database options. The best shortcut of all sits at the reference desk: Make the librarian your new best friend.

Of course, much up-to-the-minute information about poverty and policy lies not in books but on the World Wide Web. So easy—just click! Many news organizations post abbreviated content online. For background information on specific countries, the British Broadcasting Corporation (BBC), for instance, offers country profiles that include modern-era time lines and BBC audio and video clips. The U.S. Public Broadcasting System (PBS) posts historical material related to its educational programming.

But the Web poses particular perils related both to volume (overload) and to reliability (authenticity) of information. Build up your context before you surf the Internet widely. The more background knowledge you have, the more efficiently you will gather information and the more effectively you will evaluate it.

Experts versus Eyewitnesses

As your mound of information grows shovelful by shovelful, start sorting it into primary and secondary sources. A good researcher uses both, but differently.

Much of your pile will consist of secondary sources, works that analyze or interpret or comment. A professor's tome is the quintessential secondary source, but biographies, textbooks, television documentaries, journal articles, and think-tank policy reviews also qualify. How so? They maintain a distance in time or perspective from the topic under consideration. Often they synthesize opinions and evidence from many places.

While the mark of a secondary source is digested material, primary sources are information in the raw: firsthand accounts by participants or observers. They range from letters to diaries, poems to plays, speeches to courtroom testimony, surveys to statistics, photographs to newspaper accounts. Although primary sources usually originate close to the event at hand, they may also look back with hindsight, as with autobiographies or oral histories. Even though secondary sources often reference primary sources, primary sources rarely return the favor; primary sources rarely discuss other works in depth.

Some sources, particularly by journalists, fall into a gray area between primary and secondary. Because most reporters aspire to objectivity, their writing usually sounds impartial and expert. Because of long experience or academic training, they may bring outside knowledge to the topic. Allotted space, they may quote at length from many interviews and highlight contradictions among different sources. Sometimes they reflect on historical events. In these cases, articles may cross into secondary territory. Yet, more important than tone or knowledge to "secondariness" is that distance in time and space and emotion. If a journalist creates a sense that "you are there," then you are probably dealing with a primary source.

Because of their immediacy, primary sources usually make strong impressions. Often they convey voices of the down and out, refreshing and rare because the poor are so often silent. Among dense and often muddy academic works, primary sources glitter like gems. But for all their sparkle, they often confuse readers. They lack context. They cannot stand alone to explain a multilayered issue such as poverty. In a paper or a presentation, they serve as vivid examples—of themes, issues, or problems that you introduce. You need to provide the overview, and for that, the analysis in secondary sources usually offers a more fruitful place to start.

Although scholarly or bureaucratic jargon may make your eyes cross, selective reading will help you mine them for what you need. Do not get distracted by the meat; go straight to the skeleton. With a book, browse the table of contents, the index, and the introduction, where many social scientists lay out a road map that summarizes their arguments or their findings chapter by chapter. Follow this pattern as you move to the center of the book. Peruse the first and last few paragraphs of any chapter that sounds relevant to decide if you need to read more. Do not dwell on every word. If this source looks promising, add it to your bibliography in progress, in the correct format. This will save you time later. Jot a few notes with page numbers so you don't have to scope out the book twice.

If a scholar covers ground relevant to your project, hunt with that name for other titles. Does the book strike you as interesting but dense? Use the author's name in database and online searches. Sometimes professors condense their arguments in an article or present them in a conversational tone in a lecture.

With government reports, writers usually open the briefing with an "executive summary" for busy policy makers. As you light upon information relevant to your project, follow footnotes to find out where the author located it, which is where you might also look. Next, flip to the back. In addition to the index, most documents include a bibliography (sometimes annotated) that suggests other relevant titles. You may also find a list of acronyms and/or several appendices or annexes. Sometimes researchers include the full text of a primary source there or elaborate on their methodology. Approach a publication as something not so much to be read as to be dissected.

Government Sources

Budget and space limit the collections of school and regional libraries, which often have little material about countries other than the United States. Do not limit your search for sources to the library stacks, and do not limit it to books.

Government agencies, both in the United States and abroad, produce voluminous reports about poverty-related issues at home and abroad. The United States makes many research documents available to the people who fund it—taxpayers—at special repositories open to the public. There is one near you, probably located within a university library. But to spare researchers a trek, agencies post much of their most general material online.

ABOUT THE WORLD

The Library of Congress, for instance, has a "global gateway" on its Web site. Under "Portals to the World," the library staff recommends links to electronic resources on individual countries. Also useful for context are its Country Studies. Note, however, that the library published these studies between 1988 and 1998, so most do not include the most recent developments.

Much more up to date are the U.S. State Department's Background Notes. Each country narrative lists statistics on geography, people, government, and the economy before delving a little more deeply into history, economic and political conditions, and foreign relations. The U.S. Central Intelligence Agency also publishes a frequently revised *World Factbook*. Be forewarned that the State Department and the CIA may present slightly different information (as they do about many issues). In profiles of Yemen updated in the same month, one agency listed Yemen's 2006 per-capita GDP at $720 and the other at $900. Remember that statistics often approximate and that agencies may use different methods to arrive at a result.

Wealthy donor nations all run development agencies, which lay out the challenges they face even as they tout their successes. The U.S. Agency for International Development details its $9.3 billion poverty-fighting operations region by region and country by country. It reports not only on U.S. projects but on cooperative ventures with local partners. Canada, Australia, Great Britain, Norway, the European Union—all discuss their global humanitarian efforts. If you read more than one language, you have an advantage, but on the Internet, English often poses no language barrier. Even Japan's International

Cooperation Agency maintains an English version of its Web site that presents news from the field.

USAID is not the only American agency working internationally. Within the U.S. Department of Agriculture, the Foreign Agricultural Service publishes information about trade agreements, food aid programs, and much more. At the U.S. Environmental Protection Agency, the Office of International Affairs cooperates with multilateral organizations and provides and receives technical assistance from the Americas to Asia. Because poverty touches upon so many facets of life, global initiatives reside in almost every cabinet department, from commerce to energy, justice to transportation.

Embassies also make poverty-related information, some primary, some secondary, available online. If you are looking for background information about a foreign country or its policy makers, try a phone call to the public affairs officer at the country's embassy in Washington, or search the Internet for the corresponding American embassy abroad. Also, do not overlook the head of state's Web site. Just as the White House presents the U.S. president's stance on issues such as education, immigration, and Social Security, chief executives of countries such as Ukraine also maintain Web sites promoting their policy initiatives. Some states, such as Syria, maintain a government "news" agency that disseminates presidential speeches and select information about social welfare. Bear in mind that being "official" does not make a publication or piece of data fact.

In the United States, thanks to the checks-and-balances relationship between the executive and legislative branches, federal officials are often presenting information to a skeptical Congress. The Trade and Development Act of 2000, for example, requires the U.S. Department of Labor to submit an annual report on the worst forms of child labor around the world. Both the House of Representatives and the Senate gather and evaluate information through committees and more focused subcommittees. When considering a bill or resolution, the committee solicits written statements and holds hearings. Both the House Committee on Foreign Affairs and the Senate Committee on Foreign Relations consider issues of U.S. policy, aid, and outreach to developing nations, and each has a Web site that links to testimony from experts inside and outside government. Subcommittees may focus on specific regions, such as Africa. Much of this testimony surfaces on the Internet.

ABOUT THE UNITED STATES

The U.S. government delves even more deeply into domestic poverty. The topic arises before many different congressional committees: Veteran Affairs; Health, Education, Labor, and Pensions; Indian Affairs; Banking, Housing, and Urban Affairs; Appropriations. Subcommittees and special committees (the names of which change over the years) tackle specific issues, from migrant labor to Social Security.

Like global poverty, American poverty concerns almost every U.S. Cabinet office. If you are researching homelessness and public housing, for example, you will find leads at the Department of Housing and Urban Development. Should you want to know more about the No Child Left Behind Act, consult the Department of Education. For statistics and crunched numbers try the census and economic analysis bureaus within the Department of Commerce or the Bureau of Labor Statistics, within the Department of Labor. The lead agency for social welfare, the Department of Health and Human Services (HHS) coordinates the government's most direct assistance to the needy. It oversees subagencies ranging from the Indian Health Service to the Office of Refugee Resettlement. Its sprawling Web site guides consumers to benefits for which they might be eligible, such as Medicare, and gives access to the department's annual report to Congress on Temporary Assistance to Needy Families.

International Associations and Nongovernmental Organizations

Governments fight poverty out of national interest, which encompasses a variety of motives, from compassion to concern about a country's standing in the world community. International associations, such as the United Nations, juggle the competing concerns of nations across the political and economic spectrum, from rich to poor, capitalist to communist, democratic to authoritarian. In a delicate diplomatic dance, the United Nations encourages collaboration and tries to build consensus.

NGOs, on the other hand, are more often free agents. Sometimes they work closely with government agencies and the United Nations, accepting grants and sharing experts. Sometimes they strike an antagonistic stance. Regardless, associations and NGOs (also known as private voluntary organizations, civil society organizations, and citizen associations) are go-to places for information.

ABOUT THE WORLD

The United Nations coordinates much global antipoverty activity. Through the Web sites of its many agencies, you can download oceans of primary and secondary material. One source is the UN Development Programme's annual Human Development Report, as well as its country and regional reports, which you can search by date or theme. Another source is the annual report about schooling produced by a special rapporteur (data collector) on the right to education for the UN Commission on Human Rights. The Joint United Nations Programme on HIV/AIDS publishes an epidemic update with the World Health Organization every year. So vast is the sea of UN material that the University of Wisconsin has collaborated on a resource guide to help Web surfers navigate the world body (http://www.uwm.edu/Dept/CIS/unguide/index.html).

International financial institutions like the World Bank and IMF, with field offices all over the world, also generate voluminous amounts of information—books, newsletters, forecasts, reports, policy briefs, working papers, and so on. The World Bank employs more than 10,000 people, from anthropologists to economists to engineers, and much of their research surfaces online and in libraries.

The millions of NGOs around the globe produce data as eclectic as the organizations. Some specialize in research, others in service. Some employ only volunteers; others hire professional staff. Some operate locally; some operate locally but affiliate with international organizations; some operate worldwide. Since anyone with an idea can start an NGO, these organizations spring up and sometimes disappear quickly. While many NGOs with shoestring budgets may provide valuable assistance and understand poverty firsthand, they may not have cash or time to spare for publicity and publication.

Look to large NGOs when first gathering facts about global poverty. Later trails may lead you to smaller agencies in countries of interest. Duke University has made an alphabetical list of some of the heavyweights, designating their subject and continent of focus (http://docs.lib.duke.edu/igo/guides/ngo/).

ABOUT THE UNITED STATES

U.S. wealth translates into an abundance of NGOs that work to improve the lives of the American poor. Captains of industry have emblazoned their names on the charitable foundations their fortunes endowed: Carnegie, Ford, Gates, Johnson, Pew, Rockefeller, and so on. So generous are Americans that philanthropy itself has become an industry, matching donors and seekers. The Foundation Center, for instance, helps grant seekers identify funding sources and posts a list of the top 100 givers. The nonprofit world even shares a biweekly newspaper, *The Chronicle of Philanthropy.*

Most foundations, charities, and organizations have carved a niche within poverty relief. Some aim to transform the lives of the disadvantaged at an individual or neighborhood level, through a transfer of goods, such as food or clothing, or of knowledge, such as tips on finding jobs or filling out Medicaid applications. If you are trying to generate your own primary sources, that is, to conduct interviews or take photos, these front-line agencies can introduce you to the community you want to study.

Other nonprofits fund research alongside community development projects. Think tanks, which employ academics and former government officials, trade in information and opinions, seeking to effect social change through the legislative process. You can connect to scores of public policy organizations through C-Span, the cable channel that films Congress.

People Sources

Another way to learn about and present poverty is through stories of people, both the people who endure it and the people who combat it. Their experiences illuminate problems as no numbers can. Keep an eye out for quotes, for testimony, and for obituaries, which often distill remarkable lives into a score of paragraphs.

VOICES OF THE POOR

The disadvantages that trap people at the bottom of the economic pyramid conspire to deprive them of their say. If a woman does not know how to read, she cannot send a letter to the governor complaining about corrupt officials demanding bribes. If a man has no electricity, he will not be blogging about toxic waste from the nuclear power plant next door. Obviously, those thrust suddenly into poverty because of a natural or financial disaster are more likely to have the resources to describe their adversity than people who have known nothing but severe hardship all their lives.

As mentioned, if you are studying poverty next door, you might consider face-to-face research: serving dinner at a soup kitchen, observing preschoolers in a Head Start class, interviewing a homeless person at a shelter, photographing day laborers outside a paint store, or writing a school newspaper article about a local charity. If you do that, make sure that you have the permission of both the agency and the people quoted or photographed. To learn more about building trust and avoiding exploitation, consult with a teacher and check out the ethical guidelines for interviewers developed by the Oral History Association.

You may also tap primary sources housed in the archives of many university libraries or state and local historical societies. You will likely find firsthand descriptions of American poverty in oral history collections or the papers of people who lived through the Great Depression or participated in the civil rights movement. A trove of material resides at the Library of Congress, much of it available online through the American Memory project. Among its treasures are depression-era photos and narratives collected by the Federal Writers' Project from African Americans born into slavery.

Much more difficult to access will be the unmediated words of impoverished people living abroad. Again, international NGOs sometimes translate interviews with their constituencies. And you will find witness accounts from Americans who served in the foreign service (part of American Memory) or the Peace Corps.

EYE ON THE PRIZES

Most of the world's poverty fighters, and their work, go unrecognized. But the few plucked from obscurity by an award committee offer both a window on poverty and an inspiring example.

Nobel Prizes give scholars and activists a world-class platform. The economics prize occasionally honors scholars whose work has deepened the world's understanding of poverty. The peace prize frequently goes to anti-poverty activists. On its Web site, the Nobel Foundation lists all the peace prize laureates since 1901, and links lead to biographies, presentation speeches, the laureates' Nobel lectures, and often much more.

Other honors also point to noteworthy individuals and groups, with useful information accompanying the money and fanfare. The Conrad Hilton Foundation bestows a $1.5 million Humanitarian Prize. The Goldman Environmental Prize spotlights eco-action heroes. Dubbed the "alternative Nobel Prize," Right Livelihood Awards have been saluting grass-roots organizers since 1980. The Gleitsman Foundation also honors international activists. Holding an annual awards ceremony in Washington, D.C., Vital Voices, a global partnership, builds the capacity of "emerging women leaders." Prizes big and small may open new avenues of research.

VETTING YOUR SOURCES, PART 2

Likely you are accruing more information than you ever imagined and wondering how to make sense of it all. Remember Howard Zinn? No matter how neutral-sounding your assignment, your decisions about what to keep and what to toss amount to an interpretation.

A Balancing Act

If there were one right way to address poverty, likely no one would be poor anymore. The world would have solved the problem. But the perpetuation of hardship has generated a lot of controversy, and you have to deal with it. Do not ignore a source just because you personally disagree with it. Whatever your presentation—even something as bland as a description—you will need to acknowledge contrary points of view. Like a good debater, you will want to acknowledge your opponents' points well taken before mustering the more powerful evidence for your opinion.

Reports abound, but you must read between the lines. Diplomacy sometimes blunts UN frankness, for instance. Without alienating rich and powerful nations like the United States (whose financial and moral support it needs), it must heed all its members' diverse and sometimes divergent concerns. While major NGOs often follow the UN consensus-building approach, others strike out on their own. Mounting an effective argument requires understanding the strengths, weaknesses, and orientation of your sources, whether an organization or an individual.

BOOKS AND ARTICLES

Always find out as much as you can about the author. With books, read the jacket copy or biographical note on the back cover. Track down a book review (which often provides a useful summary and evaluation, too). With an article, see if a footnote at the beginning or end adds more identifying information. If you're still unsure, try typing the author's name into a search engine such as Google.

Every occupation and affiliation presents certain advantages and disadvantages. If authors teach at a college or university, likely they earned a Ph.D., which takes years of study. If an academic press or a scholarly journal published their work, it likely passed through a peer-review process in which other experts read the manuscript and found the scholarship sound. Likely they earn a living from teaching and researching, so probably they are not trying to earn a fast buck from a flashy book. On the other hand, writing for a scholarly audience, they may use off-putting jargon.

Think tanks employ researchers with and without Ph.D.s. Unlike universities, whose mission is simply to increase knowledge, think tanks often combine research with advocacy. They hire policy specialists and usually skip the "verification" process of teaching and peer review. Experts on staff with the Campaign for America's Future, say, hold and promote liberal views while those at the Heritage Foundation take conservative positions. Think tanks often have a party affiliation or ties to a major benefactor.

Ideology does not necessarily invalidate research, but it does color it (even among academics), so try to suss out where authors stand so you can make sure to have a representative mix of opinion. In poverty debates, where does the writer attribute cause? In international development, does the writer favor capitalism and free trade or find merit in other economic systems? Does the author put American interests above all else or consider indigenous concerns that may differ? Again, a reference librarian can often alert you to the orientation of a writer or an institute. Also helpful is the political science think-tank directory compiled by the University of Michigan library (http://www.lib.umich.edu/govdocs/psthink.html).

Journalists write about poverty as well, for a general audience. What they may lack in scholarly depth they often make up for in approachable language. Major periodicals have their own set of checks and balances, from newspaper editors and lawyers who read over copy (especially with major investigative series) to magazine fact checkers. Since journalists depend on mass appeal for their livelihood, however, critics sometimes accuse them of sensationalizing. Like think tanks, certain periodicals wear their ideology on their covers, so you should expect left-wing coverage in *Mother Jones* and right-wing commentary in the *National Review.* Offering free subscriptions, *Saudi Aramco World,* a beautifully illustrated bimonthly magazine published by the oil company of the same name, has developed into a rich English-language source about the history and culture of the Arab and Muslim world—but only the positive aspects.

ONLINE MATERIAL

While intellectual democracy has bloomed on the Internet, the abundance and diversity of postings have complicated the researcher's task. Any person with access to a server can post documents or blogs. On the one hand, this open forum enfranchises the poor and their advocates. On the other, no gatekeeper with a reputation and an eye for quality (such as a publishing house) screens material. You can strike gold on the World Wide Web—but also turn up pages that are misinformed or deliberately misleading.

As with other sources, learn as much as you can about the author and the context of an Internet posting. Click around the entire Web site, especially links to "about us" or "contact." Domain names provide clues, too: .edu at end of the URL address points to an educational institution, .gov to a U.S. government site, .org to an association, .com to a commercial site, .museum to—surprise!—a museum, .net to a personal site, etc. While .pdf (portable document format) files look authentic because they bear their original format, try to trace them to a parent Web site.

Educational sites tend to provide the most disinterested information, often where to find what. A partnership led by the University of Houston is building a Digital (American) History site that includes links to primary sources such as court cases. The Avalon Project at Yale University makes available a host of American documents from before the 18th century to the present: treaties, congressional resolutions, inaugural addresses, etc. Of particular relevance to contemporary U.S. poverty scholars are national poverty centers. For researchers on international topics, the Internet Modern History Sourcebook sponsored by Fordham University links to many primary sources. For European documents, try EuroDocs at Brigham Young University. Among the many specialized portals, the University of California at Berkeley has mapped online information available about British colonial rule in India. With so many excellent resources, do not get "blogged down" in Web pages of murky origin.

With .gov and .org sites you can expect documents related to national or associational concerns. Do not overlook the papers and photographs the National Archives has gathered at presidential libraries from Herbert Hoover (1929–33) on. While Wikipedia.org, the free online encyclopedia written by volunteers around the world, provides a quick introduction to a myriad of subjects, some of the information is inaccurate. Use it as a point of departure rather than a final destination. Expect a hodgepodge with .com and .net sites.

Newspaper reporters sometimes joke about the professional skepticism required in their profession: "If your mother tells you she loves you, check it out." That is a good rule of thumb for the Internet, and for all sources for that matter. Can you find somebody else to back up what you just read?

7

Facts and Figures

UNDERSTANDING POVERTY

1. Poverty and Prosperity as a Web

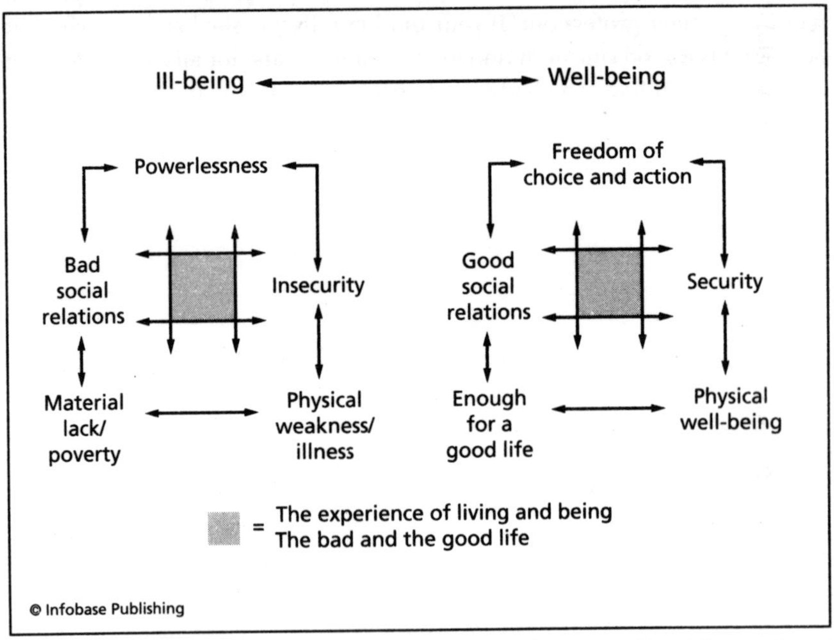

Source: Robert Chambers. "What is Poverty? Who asks? Who answers?" p. 4. *Poverty in Focus*, December 2006. Available online. URL: http://www.undp-povertycentre.org/pub/IPCPoverty_in_Focus009.pdf. Downloaded April 26, 2007.

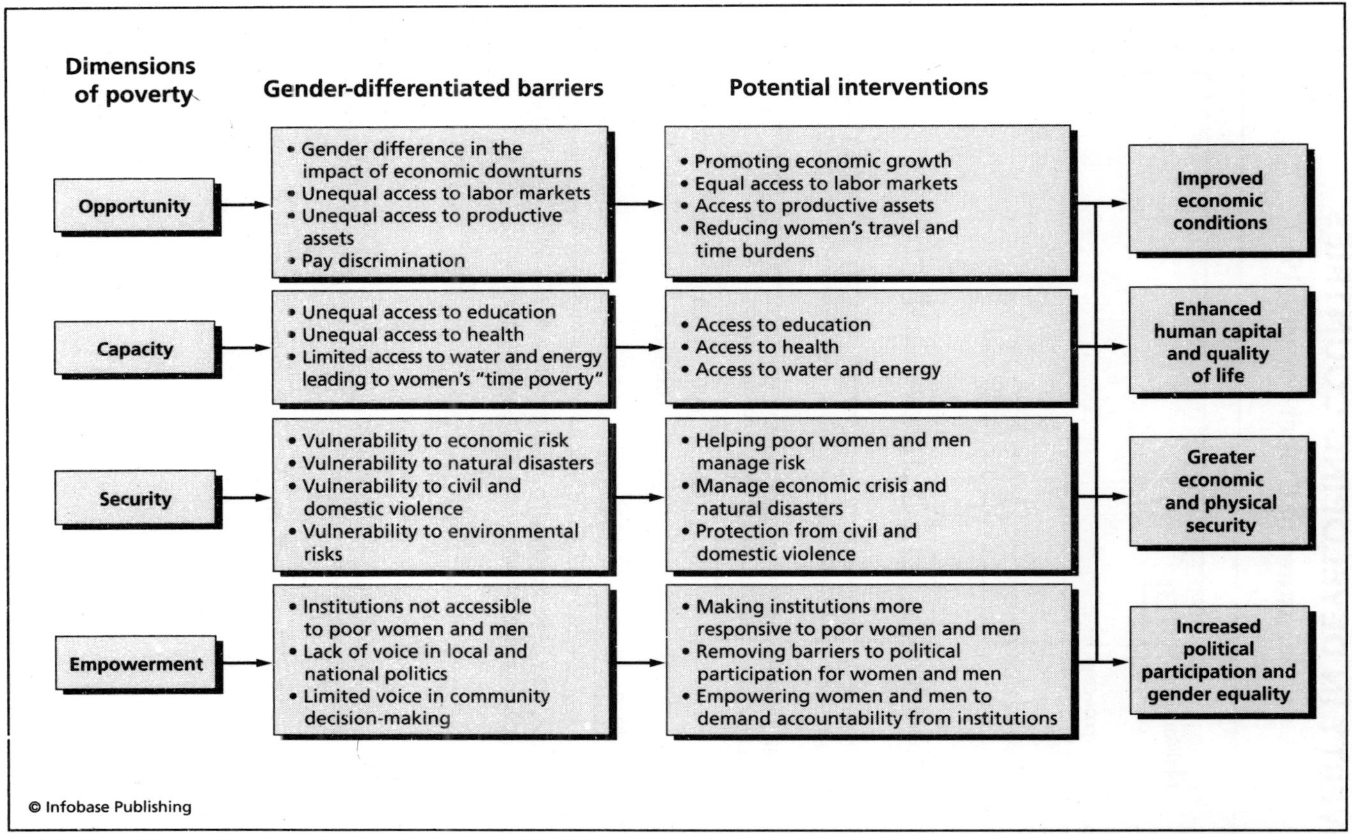

Source: World Bank Gender and Development Group. "Gender Equality and the Millennium Development Goals," p. 8. April 4, 2003. Available online. URL: http://www.mdgender.net/upload/monographs/WB_Gender_Equality_MDGs.pdf. Downloaded April 26, 2007.

POVERTY IN DEVELOPING COUNTRIES

1. Measures of Global Poverty, 1997

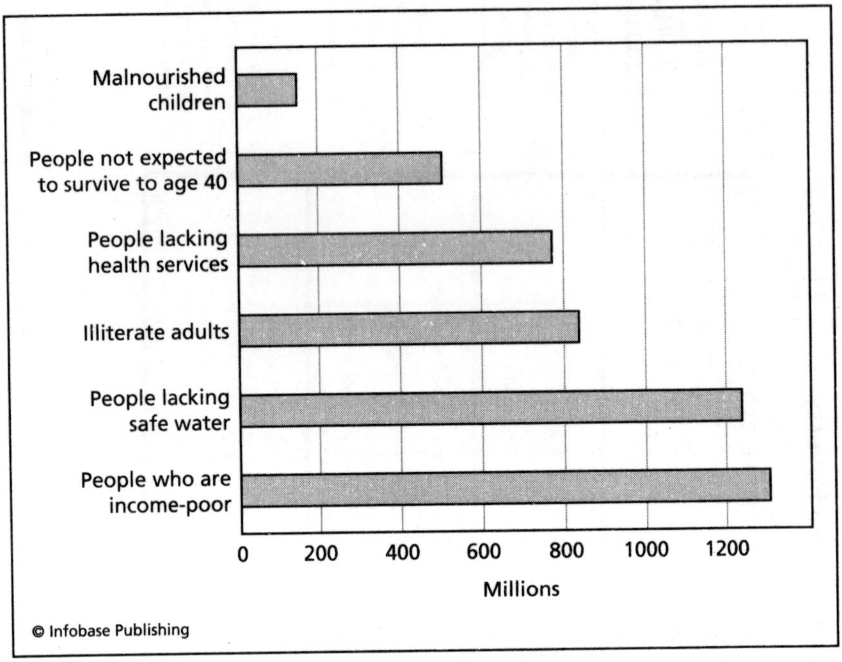

Source: United Nations Environment Programme. "Chapter 1: Global Perspectives—Figure: Measures of Poverty." In *Global Environment Outlook 2000.* Available online. URL: http://www.unep.org/geo2000/english/i15a.htm. Downloaded April 25, 2007.

2. Trends in Severe Poverty

	NUMBER OF PEOPLE (MILLIONS)						
	LIVING ON $1 PER DAY			LIVING ON $2 PER DAY			
	1981	2001	CHANGE SINCE 1981	1981	2001	CHANGE SINCE 1981	POPULATION 2001 (MILLIONS)
East Asia and Pacific	796	271	–66%	1,170	864	–26%	1,823
Eastern Europe and Central Asia	3	18	468%	20	94	363%	474
Latin America and the Caribbean	36	50	40%	99	128	30%	518
Middle East and North Africa	9	7	–22%	52	70	35%	300
South Asia	475	431	–9%	821	1,064	30%	1,378
Sub-Saharan Africa	164	316	93%	288	516	79%	673
Global Total	**1,482**	**1,093**	**–26%**	**2,450**	**2,736**	**12%**	**6,127**

Source: World Resources Institute. "$1 and $2 per day poverty trends, 1981–2001." Table in "World Resources 2005—The Wealth of the Poor: Managing ecosystems to fight poverty." Available online. URL: http://www.wri.org/biodiv/pubs_content_text.cfm?ContentID=3640. Downloaded April 25, 2007.

3. Food Security and Nutrition: Proportion of Undernourished People in Total Population—a Regional Sample

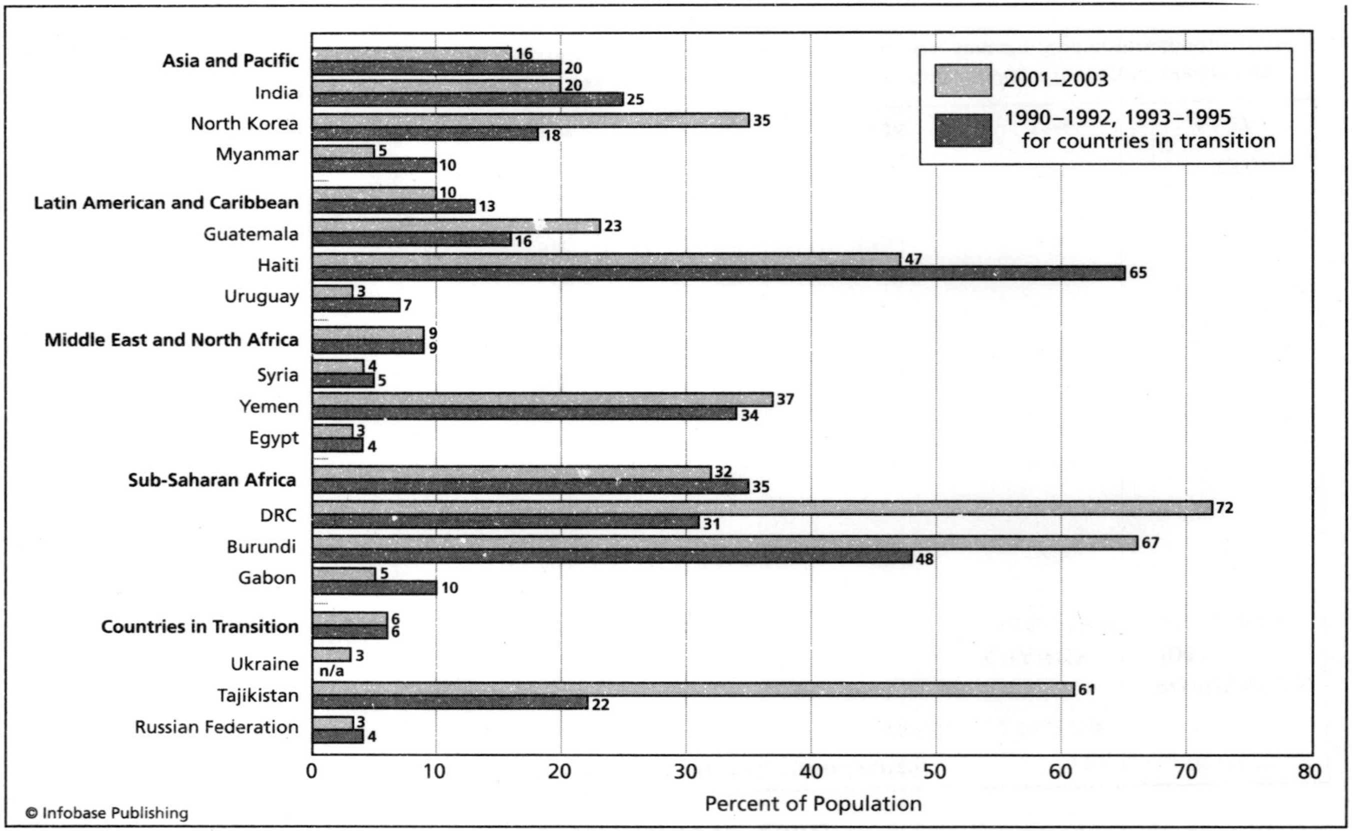

Source: Food and Agriculture Organization of the United Nations. "Food Security and Nutrition." Table in "State of Food and Agriculture 2006." Rome: FAO, 2006, pp. 118–121. Available online. URL: ftp://ftp.fao.org/docrep/fao/009/a0800e/a0800e.pdf. Downloaded April 26, 2007.

4. The Education Gap: Average Years of Schooling by Wealth in Latin America and East Asia, 1996–2002

	AVERAGE YEARS OF SCHOOLING, 1996–2002[1,2]			PER CAPITA INCOME
	POOREST 20% OF HOUSEHOLDS	RICHEST 20% OF HOUSEHOLDS	DIFFERENCE BETWEEN POOREST AND RICHEST 20% (YEARS)	GDP PER CAPITA (CONSTANT US$ 2000)
Colombia	2.4	9.8	7.4	1,970
Guatemala	2.0	8.9	6.9	1,680
Paraguay	4.9	9.6	4.7	1,400
Peru	5.0	9.8	4.8	2,080
Average, above four countries	3.6	9.5	6.0	1,780
Cambodia	2.4	7.4	5.0	300
Indonesia	6.7	10.8	4.1	760
Philippines	6.2	10.2	4.0	1,020
Vietnam	5.2	10.3	5.1	440
Average, above four countries	5.1	9.7	4.6	630

Notes: [1]Average years of formal schooling received by population aged 15–24 years;
[2]Data are for the latest year available during the period 1996–2002.

Source: Nancy Birdsall. "The World Is Not Flat: Inequality and Injustice in Our Global Economy," p. 14. UNU World Institute for Development Economics Research (UNU-WIDER) Annual Lecture 9, 2005. p. 14. Available online. URL: http://www.wider.unu.edu/publications/annual-lectures/annual-lecture-2005.pdf. Downloaded April 27, 2007.

5. Improving AIDS Treatment in Africa: People in Sub-Saharan Africa on Antiretroviral Treatment as Percentage of Those in Need, 2002–2005

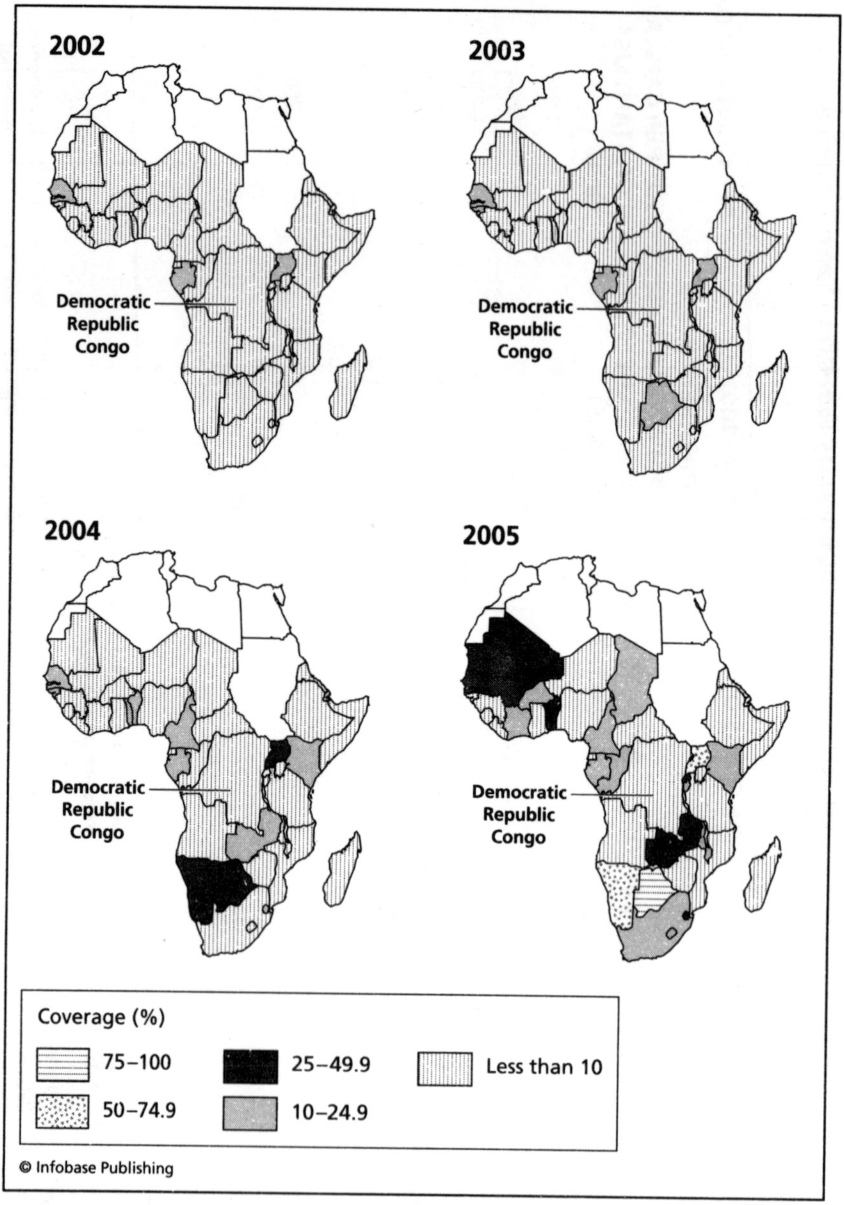

Source: Joint United Nations Programme on HIV/AIDS (UNAIDS). "Chapter 7: Treatment and Care," p. 153. "2006 Report on the Global Aids Epidemic." Available online. URL: http://data.unaids.org/pub/GlobalReport/2006/2006_GR_CH07_en.pdf. Downloaded April 26, 2007.

POVERTY IN THE UNITED STATES

1. United States Poverty Trends, 1959–2006

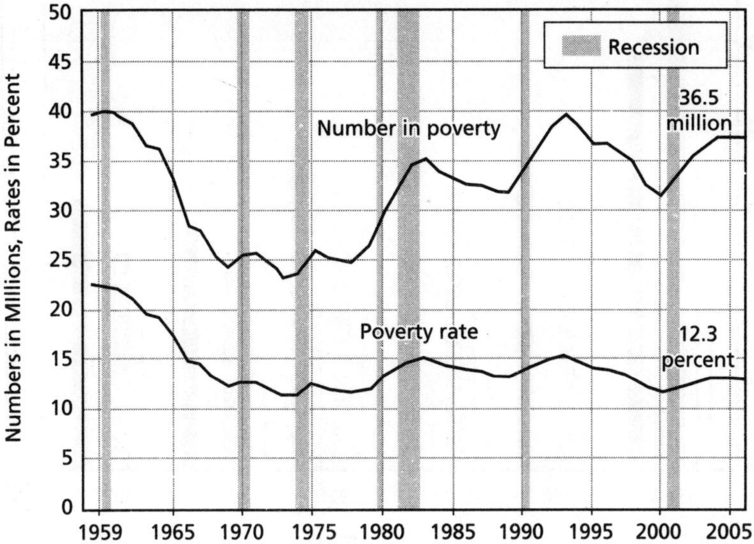

Note: The data points are placed at the midpoints of the respective years.

Source: U.S. Census Bureau. "Number in Poverty and Poverty Rate: 1959 to 2006." Based on U.S. Census Bureau, Current Population Survey, 1960 to 2007 Annual Social and Economic Supplements. Available online. URL: http://www.census.gov/prod/2007pubs/pp60-233.pdf. Downloaded February 28, 2008.

2. Ethnic/Marital Dimensions of American Poverty, 1960–2005

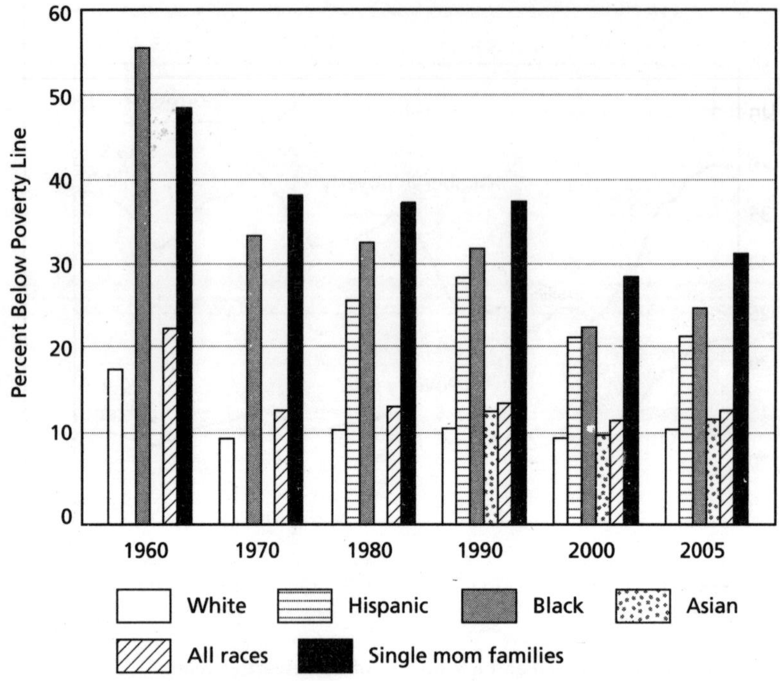

Note: No data is available for Hispanic poverty in 1960 and 1970 and for Asian poverty in 1960, 1970, and 1980. The 1960 figure for Black poverty is taken from 1959.

Source: U.S. Census Bureau. "Historical Poverty Tables." Available online. URL: http://www.census.gov/hhes/www/poverty/histpov/hstpov2.html. Updated September 6, 2006.

3. Child Poverty Rates in 15 Rich Countries in the 1990s

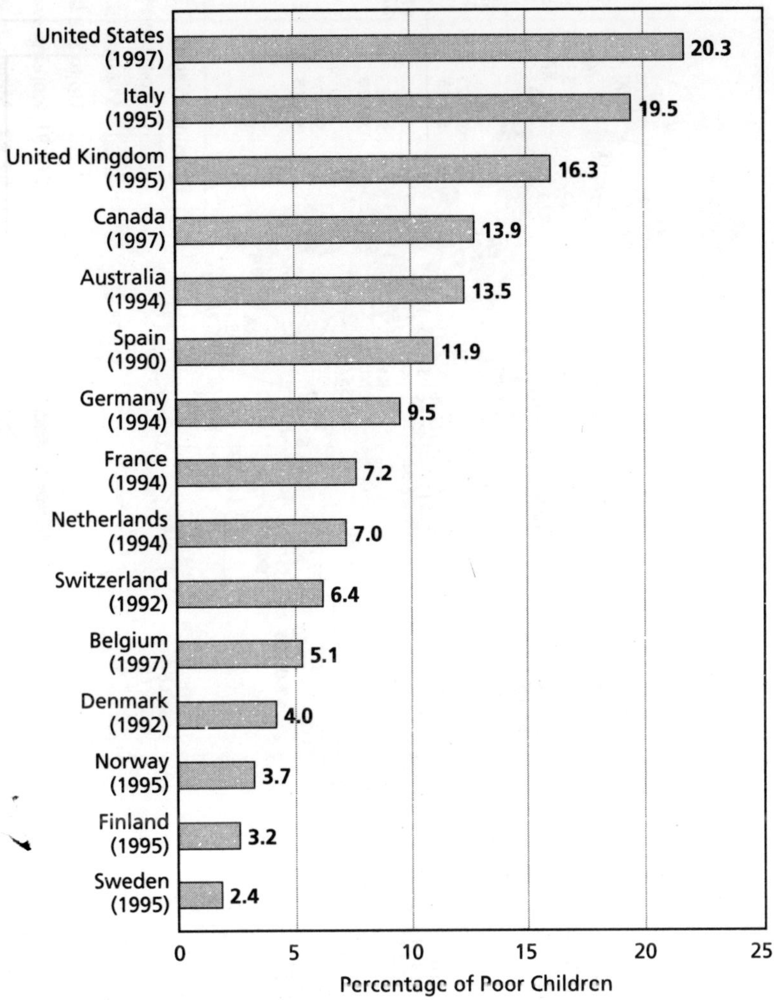

Source: Lee Rainwater and Timothy M. Smeeding. *Poor Kids in a Rich Country: America's Children in Comparative Perspective.* New York: Russell Sage Foundation, 2003, p. 21.

4. Housing Wage, 2006

The Housing Wage represents the hourly wage that a household must earn (working 40 hours a week, 52 weeks a year) in order to afford the Fair Market Rent for a two-bedroom unit at 30 percent of income. The federal minimum wage was $5.15 in 2006.

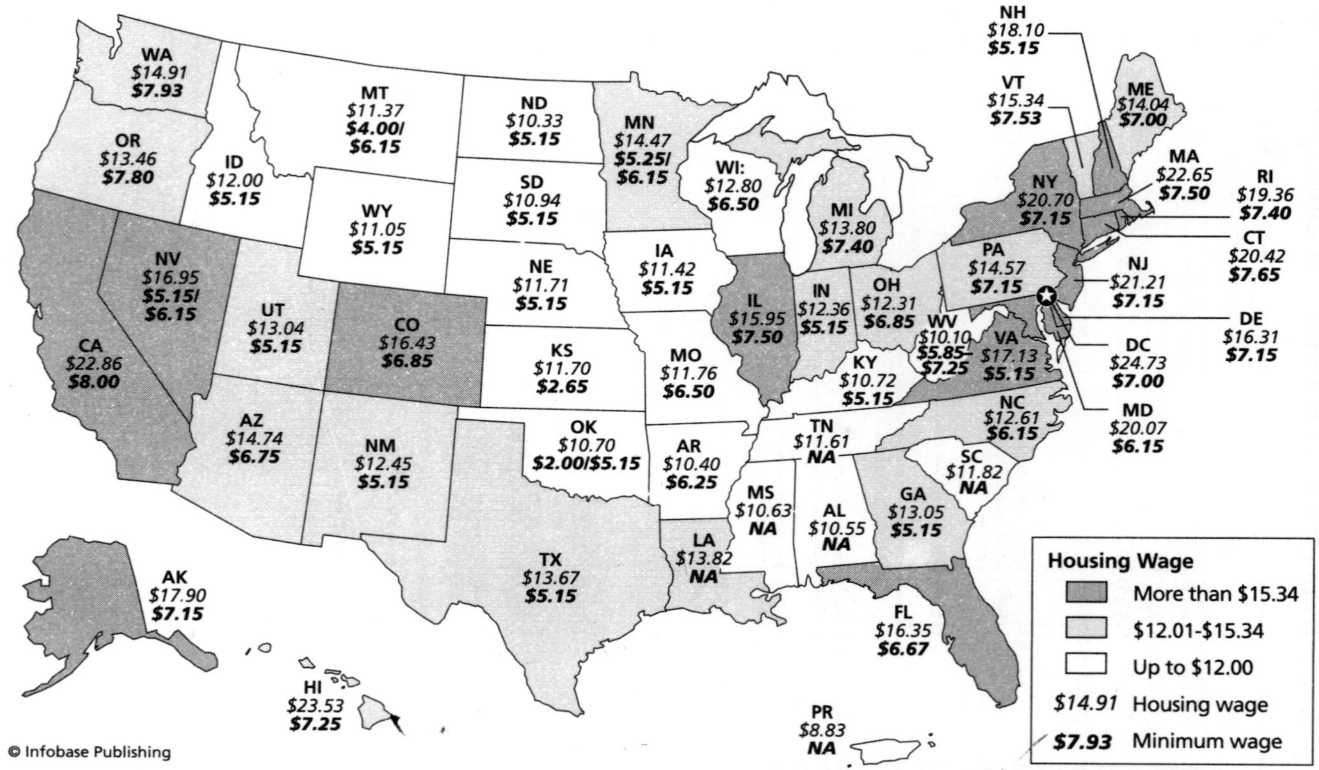

Sources: National Low Income Housing Coalition. "Housing Wage." Map in "Out of Reach 2006." Available online. URL: http://www.nlihc.org/oor/oor2006/housingwagemap.pdf. Downloaded April 24, 2007.

5. Education Pays: Unemployment and Earnings by Educational Attainment, 2006

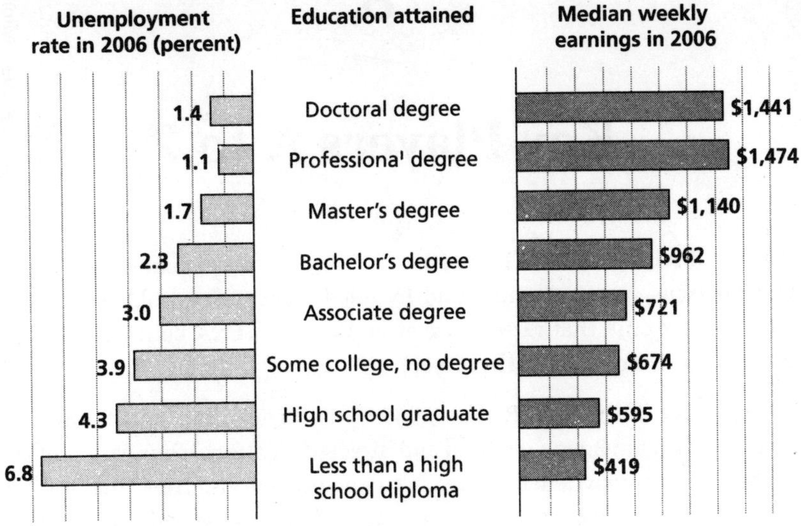

Note: Data are 2006 annual averages for persons age 25 and over. Earnings are for full-time wage and salary workers.

Source: U.S. Bureau of Labor Statistics. "Education and Training Pay." Based on Bureau of Labor Statistics figures for unemployment and U.S. Census Bureau figures about earnings. Available online. URL: http://www.bls.gov/emp/empetab7.htm. Downloaded May 16, 2007.

8

Key Players A to Z

AMMAR ABDULHAMID (1966–) Writer, blogger, and dissident born in Damascus, Syria. Abdulhamid founded DarEmar, a publishing house–NGO–think tank that raises civic awareness in MENA countries and coordinates the Tharwa (Wealth) Project.

JOSÉ ANTONIO ABREU (1939–) Venezuelan economist and composer-organist who inspired and directed a national foundation of youth orchestras with particular outreach to low-income children. The orchestras have been credited with integrating rich and poor Venezuelans and improving participants' academic and social performance.

JANE ADDAMS (1860–1935) Illinois feminist, pacifist, and social-work pioneer who won the 1931 Nobel Peace Prize. With her friend Ellen Starr, Addams visited the famous London settlement house Toynbee Hall, and they returned to Chicago to found Hull-House in 1889. It became the model and inspiration for a nationwide settlement house movement.

MARGARET ALVA (1942–) Indian lawyer and politician. Serving in parliament from 1974 to 2004, Alva championed legislation improving the rights and status of women, including protecting brides from dowry abuse and reserving slots for women on village councils.

KOFI ANNAN (1938–) Ghanaian diplomat and former UN secretary general (1997–2006). He won the 2001 Nobel Peace Prize for revitalizing the United Nations in many ways, including strengthening its ties to civil society organizations, affirming its commitment to defending human rights, and tackling poverty and the AIDS pandemic.

SUSAN B. ANTHONY (1820–1906) Educator, suffragist, and labor activist. Raised a Quaker, Anthony grew up in the abolition and temperance movements, but personal experiences of discrimination prompted her work on behalf of women's rights, particularly the right to vote. In her lectures and writings, she connected women's disenfranchisement with economic disadvantage.

OSCAR ARIAS (1940–) Costa Rican political scientist, politician, and peacemaker. Born into a well-connected, coffee-producing family, he studied law and economics and taught at the University of Costa Rica before entering government service. Committed to democratic socialism, he won the presidency on a platform of "roofs, jobs, peace" and a year later the Nobel Peace Prize for brokering a Central American settlement to the civil war spilling over borders from Nicaragua.

JAYA ARUNACHALAM (c. 1937–) Indian economist, geographer, and advocate for poor working women. Born a Brahman, she married out of caste and in 1978 founded India's Working Women's Forum, a microcredit social movement. She also heads the National Union of Working Women, a grass-roots trade union for vendors, silk weavers, lace makers, fishers, etc.

HANY EL BANNA (c. 1960–) Doctor and development specialist who heads the humanitarian NGO Islamic Relief Worldwide. Born in Egypt, el Banna was studying medicine in Birmingham, England, in 1983, when he was invited to a conference in Sudan, then gripped by famine and civil war. He raised money for that crisis and a year later founded IRW.

WALDEN BELLO (1945–) Philippine sociologist, writer, environmentalist, and globalization critic. For two decades he campaigned against President Ferdinand Marcos and documented how Marcos milked the country's wealth with the support of the World Bank and IMF. After Marcos's ouster, Bello continued exploring alternatives to the Bretton Woods institutions, arguing for a more pluralistic development community with checks and balances. In 1995, he cofounded the NGO Focus on the Global South.

NANCY BIRDSALL (c. 1945–) Widely published development economist and founding president of the Center for Global Development. Her work experience spans the World Bank, the Inter-American Bank, and the Carnegie Endowment for International Peace, where she directed the Economic Reform Project focusing on globalization, inequality, and reform of international financial institutions.

BONO (1960–) Rock star and Afrocentric antipoverty activist. Born Paul Hewson in Dublin, Ireland, Bono is the lead singer-songwriter of U2. In the 1980s, he began to lend his star power to African poverty relief and in 2002 cofounded DATA (Debt Aids Trade Africa) to pressure Western countries to increase aid and forgive debt while calling on African governments to realize democracy, accountability, and transparency.

NORMAN BORLAUG (1914–) Plant pathologist and Green Revolution pioneer. He directed the Cooperative Wheat Research and Production Program in Mexico, which within two decades bred a high-yield, disease-resistant wheat. He went on to lead the International Wheat Improvement Program, work recognized by a 1970 Nobel Peace Prize.

GEORGE WASHINGTON CARVER (1864–1943) Educator and agricultural chemist. A former slave and the first African-American student anc faculty member at Iowa State University, Carver went on to direct the agri culture department at Tuskegee Institute in Alabama. There, he discoverec that nitrogen-producing peanuts, pecans, sweet potatoes, and peas revital ized soil exhausted by cotton growing. His crop rotation system improve the livelihood of poor southern farmers—especially since he also invente more than 300 uses for peanuts.

CESAR CHAVEZ (1927–93) Mexican-American labor and Latino right activist. He cofounded the United Farm Workers of America union (UFW in the 1960s, which he led with spiritual and nonviolent tactics, such as boy cotts and fasts, in the tradition of Mohandas Gandhi and Martin Luthe King, Jr.

ROBERT COLES (1929–) Child psychiatrist, writer, and Harvar professor of social ethics. Awakened to racial injustice when drafted int the military and sent to Mississippi, Coles began interviewing underpriv leged children, particularly those involved in the civil rights movemen Volumes two and three of his *Children of Crisis* series won the 1973 Puli zer Prize, and he became a well-known advocate for volunteerism an service.

DOROTHY DAY (1897–1980) Journalist and founder of the Cathol Worker Movement espousing nonviolence, voluntary poverty, and "hospita ity for the homeless, exiled, hungry, and forsaken." In 1933, Catholic conve Day and Peter Maurin began publishing a newspaper exploring Catho ideas about social justice, *The Catholic Worker.* They also opened their do to those in need, inspiring Catholic Worker community houses across t country and in several Western countries.

EUGENE DEBS (1855–1926) Labor leader and politician. Indiana-bo Debs dropped out of school at 14 to work on the railways, first as a paint and later as a fireman. Elected president of the American Railway Union, was sent to prison during the Pullman strike of 1894 and became a Socialist, in favor of radical reform without the violent means espoused by many Communists. He ran for president on the Socialist Party ticket in 1900, 1904, 1908, 1912, and 1920 on a platform demanding women's right to vote and improved working conditions.

HERBERT JOSÉ DE SOUZA (1935–97) Brazilian sociologist, political scientist, and champion of the poor. De Souza, known as "Betinho" (little buddy), had to flee Brazil's military dictatorship, but he returned from exile in 1979 and founded the NGO IBASE (Brazilian Institute of Social and Economic Analysis). A beloved social gadfly, de Souza led land reform, democracy, human rights, and antihunger campaigns. Through blood transfusions required to treat his hemophilia, he contracted HIV and died of AIDS.

CHARLES DICKENS (1812–70) Journalist and popular novelist who humanized the poor in Victorian England. Although Dickens's family was moderately wealthy, his father spent unwisely, and in 1824, authorities briefly imprisoned the whole family for debt—all but 12-year-old Charles, who supported them by working 10-hour days in a boot-blacking factory. Echoes of those dark days surfaced in Dickens's socially conscious fiction.

DOROTHEA DIX (1802–87) Massachusetts teacher and crusader on behalf of the mentally ill. After surveying jails, prisons, and poorhouses across the state, she presented a report to the legislature in 1843 that galvanized support for expanding the Worcester state hospital for the insane. She later campaigned nationwide for more humane mental hospitals.

MARION WRIGHT EDELMAN (1939–) A civil rights lawyer and child-centered antipoverty activist who founded the Washington Research project, which became the Children's Defense Fund in 1973. Mentor and inspiration to many, she has written several books, including *Families in Peril: An Agenda for Social Change* (1987) and *The Measure of Our Success: A Letter to My Children and Yours* (1992).

PAUL FARMER (1959–) Medical anthropologist and physician who focuses on infectious diseases that disproportionately afflict the poor. Born in Massachusetts and raised on a bus and a houseboat in Florida, Farmer won a full scholarship to Duke University and later graduated from Harvard Medical School. Working in Peru and rural Haiti, he pioneered community-based treatment of AIDS and tuberculosis.

HASSAN FATHY (1900–89) Egyptian architect who pioneered sustainable building and appreciation of indigenous building materials and forms.

He was teaching at the Cairo Faculty of Fine Arts when he began experimenting with mud brick. In the 1950s, he supervised the construction of New Gourna, a government project he envisioned as a prototype for rural housing. Working with residents, he designed houses with traditional features, such as courtyards and vaulted ceilings, and gained international recognition with his book *Architecture for the Poor.*

IRENE FERNANDEZ (1946–) Malaysian labor organizer who founded the NGO Tenaganita in 1991 to protect and promote the rights of marginalized citizens, particularly prostitutes, migrant workers, and people with HIV. For her well-documented 1995 report on the abuse of migrant laborers, the government charged her with "maliciously publishing false news" and has subjected her to intimidation for more than a decade.

JOHN KENNETH GALBRAITH (1908–2006) Influential liberal economist and diplomat. Long an adviser to Democratic presidents, he administered wage and price controls for Franklin Roosevelt during the depression and served as ambassador to India for John F. Kennedy in the 1960s. His most famous book, *The Affluent Society* (1958), warned that Americans were not investing in the public good. In his 1996 follow-up, *The Good Society,* he described the United States as a "democracy of the fortunate."

MOHANDAS "MAHATMA" GANDHI (1869–1948) Indian lawyer, unconventional anticolonial activist, and revered philosopher. Born into a middle-class, middle-caste Hindu family, he was married at 13. After studying in England, he took a position in South Africa, home to a small community of Indians descended from laborers brought to work sugar estates. In response to discrimination, he organized nonviolent resistance and noncooperation that forced the government to negotiate reforms. In 1915, he carried this strategy back to India. Frequently jailed during the struggle for independence, Gandhi used his own suffering and fasts to unite Indians and to draw attention to Hindu discrimination against Dalits, the "untouchables."

BILL GATES (1955–) Computer visionary and global philanthropist. Son of a Seattle lawyer and a schoolteacher, Gates dropped out of Harvard University his junior year to build Microsoft with a childhood friend. In 2006, Gates announced that while remaining Microsoft's chairman, he would step back from day-to-day operations in order to devote more time to the poverty-fighting foundation he and wife had created.

MOHAMMED GHANEM (c. 1955–) Syrian journalist, teacher, and novelist who advocates for human rights in Syria, particularly the political and cultural rights of his country's Kurdish minority. In June 2006, a military court sentenced him to six months in prison for "insulting the Syrian president, discrediting the Syrian government and fomenting sectarian unrest" through his news Web site, Surion.

ERNESTO "CHE" GUEVARA (1928–67) Controversial doctor–turned–Marxist revolutionary who symbolized hope and defiance against oppression for many people around the world. Born to an aristocratic Argentine family, Guevara traveled widely in Latin America while a medical student and young doctor. Visiting mines, villages, and leper colonies, he came to see socialism as the solution to widespread poverty and armed rebellion as the means to achieve it. With Fidel Castro, he led the revolution against Cuban military dictator Fulgencio Batista in the late 1950s. A supporter of guerrilla movements around the world, he led a failed revolt in the Congo in 1965 and was executed two years later by government forces in Bolivia.

ANIL K. GUPTA (?–) Indian professor who catalyzed the international Honey Bee network to recognize, publicize, and reward grass-roots innovation. The poor, he says, are rich in knowledge. Gupta, who holds a master's degree in biochemical genetics and a doctorate in management, builds bridges between indigenous wisdom (in agriculture, say) and academic science.

GUSTAVO GUTIÉRREZ (1928–) A Peruvian Catholic priest and professor who helped pioneer "liberation theology." In *A Theology of Liberation* (1971), he challenged the church to change from bystander to participant in the movement to overturn unjust regimes responsible for the perpetuation of Latin American poverty.

MAHBUB UL-HAQ (1934–98) Pakistani economist who brought to fruition the United Nations Human Development Index as an alternative to income as a measure of well-being. Director of policy planning at the World Bank in the 1970s, he also held posts in Pakistan's government before serving as a special adviser to the UN Development Programme.

EDGAR HELMS (1863–1942) Methodist minister and driving force of Goodwill Industries. Born in a logging camp in northern New York, Helms apprenticed as a printer and worked as a journalist before finishing his theological studies. During the financial collapse of 1902, Helms, pastor of a Boston parish, came up with the idea of employing and training immigrants to mend castoff clothes and repair unwanted furniture, which they later sold.

LEWIS HINE (1874–1940) Documentary photographer whose images of immigrants, child workers, and city tenements fueled Progressive-era reform. On assignment for the National Child Committee, he traveled in the South and the East photographing working children at home, on the street, and in mines, factories, canneries, textile mills, etc. During World War I, he documented the plight of refugees and internally displaced persons for the American Red Cross.

HARRY HOPKINS (1890–1946) New Deal administrator who helped put 7.5 million Americans to work during the depression. Hopkins's social-work experience dispensing Red Cross relief during World War I helped catapult him to the head of the Federal Emergency Relief Administration and later the Works Progress Administration.

JESSE JACKSON (1941–) Minister, politician, freelance diplomat, and civil rights leader. An early disciple of Martin Luther King, Jr., Jackson founded and serves as president of the RainbowPush Coalition, a national social justice organization promoting economic and political empowerment.

LYNDON BAINES JOHNSON (1908–73) Politician and 36th U.S. president (1963–69). Growing up during hard times, Johnson worked his way through Southwest Texas State Teachers College and taught poor Mexican Americans before winning election to Congress in 1937. After a long Senate career, he became president following John F. Kennedy's assassination and declared a "War on Poverty." The public elected him by the widest popular margin in history, and he set out to build a "Great Society," steering through Congress laws barring discrimination, extending health coverage to the poor and elderly through Medicaid and Medicare, and improving education.

MARY HARRIS "MOTHER" JONES (1830–1930) Labor organizer. An immigrant from Ireland, Jones lost her steelworker husband and four children during a yellow fever epidemic in Memphis, Tennessee, in 1867. Four year later, she lost her home and dressmaking business in the Great Chicago Fire. With a gift for theater, she then traveled the country publicizing labor grievances and supporting strikes. She also helped found the Social Democratic Party and the Industrial Workers of the World.

JOHN F. KENNEDY (1917–1963) Politician, 35th U.S. president (1961–1963). Born into a wealthy and well-connected Irish Catholic family, Kennedy survived severe injuries during World War II and returned a hero. As a U.S. senator from Massachusetts, he condemned colonialism and as president launched the Peace Corps to send American volunteers abroad to help developing nations "cast off the chains of poverty." In the months before his assassination he drew attention to inequality in the United States in preparation for a major antipoverty initiative.

ROBERT F. KENNEDY (1925–68) Lawyer, politician, and antipoverty activist. As attorney general in the administration of his older brother, President John F. Kennedy, and later as a New York senator, he supported the civil rights movement and a number of liberal causes. At the time of his assassination, he was running for the Democratic presidential nomination.

ASMA KHADER (1952–) Jordanian teacher, journalist, lawyer, and campaigner against violence against women, particularly "honor killings." Coordinator of the Jordanian branch of the Sisterhood is Global Institute, she also founded the National Network on Poverty Alleviation, for which she won a 2003 UN Development Programme Poverty Eradication Award.

MARTIN LUTHER KING, JR. (1929–68) Baptist minister and charismatic civil rights leader. Beginning with the 1956 bus boycott in Montgomery, Alabama, King led numerous peaceful protests, including the 1963 March on Washington, where he electrified 250,000 demonstrators with his "I Have a Dream" speech. Influenced by Mohandas Gandhi, King embraced nonviolence and won the 1964 Nobel Peace Prize.

SIMON KUZNETS (1901–85) Economist whose meticulous research on national income and the process of development won him the 1971 Nobel Prize. Born to Jewish parents in Russia, he immigrated to the United States at 21 and completed a distinguished academic career as a Harvard professor. Kuznets noticed that economic growth in developing countries first widens rather than narrows the income gap between rich and poor.

FRANCES MOORE LAPPÉ (1944–) Writer and social activist. After graduating from Earlham College, Oregon-born Lappé began researching food issues and in 1971 published *Diet for a Small Planet*, which linked scarcity to the inefficiency of feeding grain to beef cattle and other meat-producing livestock rather than directly to people. Four years later, she cofounded Food First/Institute for Food and Development Policy.

BARTOLOMÉ DE LAS CASAS (1484–1566) A 16th-century Spanish "gentleman priest" turned Indian rights activist. In 1542, he wrote *A Brief Report on the Destruction of the Indies*, which described atrocities in the colonies and prompted short-lived laws to end slavery in the Americas.

JULIA LATHROP (1858–1932) Pioneer social worker. After graduating from Vassar College, she returned to her native Illinois and worked at Hull-House. Appointed by the governor to the state board of charities, she inspected shelters, orphanages, poorhouses, and soup kitchens. From 1912 to 1922, she led the new Children's Bureau in the U.S. Department of Commerce and

Labor, campaigning for better maternal-child nutrition, child labor protection, and juvenile justice.

OSCAR LEWIS (1914–70) American anthropologist who coined the concept of a "culture of poverty." A longtime professor at the University of Illinois, he explored his influential culture-of-poverty thesis in *Five Families: Mexican Case Studies in the Culture of Poverty* (1959) and *The Children of Sánchez: Autobiography of a Mexican Family* (1961).

HUEY LONG (1893–1935) Populist politician from Louisiana who proposed a radical redistribution of wealth during the depression. An ambitious high school dropout self-trained in law, Long courted the rural poor, who elected him governor and in 1930 sent him to the U.S. Senate, where he championed the interests of the "little guy" under the slogan, "Every man a king." Accusing President Franklin Roosevelt of being in cahoots with bankers and businessmen, Long argued for his Share Our Wealth plan, guaranteeing every American a minimum $5,000 annual income.

WANGARI MAATHAI (1940–) Kenyan environmentalist and founder of the grass-roots Green Belt movement. After earning a Ph.D. in veterinary anatomy, Maathai taught at the University of Nairobi. Active in the National Council of Women, Maathai suggested a women's tree-planting campaign to counter deforestation, erosion, and lack of water. It evolved into a national and later Pan-African movement to empower poor women through environmental activism. She won the 2004 Nobel Peace Prize.

NELSON MANDELA (1918–) Lawyer, Nobel Prize winner, and leader of the antiapartheid struggle in South Africa. Born a chief's son, Mandela and other Youth League leaders re-energized the African National Congress, which had opposed the 1913 Land Act and other taxes and laws that forced blacks off their land to work for whites on farms and in mines and then restricted their movement. Mandela spent 26 years in prison, where he became a powerful symbol of resistance. Released in 1990 as apartheid was crumbling, he negotiated for a transition to democracy and won South Africa's first multiracial election. He has campaigned against poverty, discrimination, and AIDS, which killed his eldest son.

WILMA MANKILLER (1945–) Native American activist and first woman chief of the Cherokee Nation. In the 1950s, the Bureau of Indian Affairs relocated her large family from rural Oklahoma to San Francisco as part of a program to urbanize Native Americans. She later returned to live on her grandfather's land and to work in community development. Committed to improving education, health care, and utilities, she served as the

Cherokee's elected chief from 1985 to 1995, when ill health forced her to retire.

RUTH MANORAMA (1952–) Indian social worker, slumdweller organizer, and founder of the National Federation of Dalit Women. Born to Dalit parents who converted to Christianity to escape discrimination, Manorama has mobilized women to fight the triple burden of gender, poverty, and caste discrimination. In the 1980s and 1990s, she helped lead mass protests against eviction and slum demolition in the state of Karnataka.

RUSSELL MEANS (1939–) Oglala Lakota (Sioux) actor and activist. Born on the Pine Ridge reservation in South Dakota, Means founded the American Indian Movement (AIM) in the 1960s with Dennis Banks and served as its first national director. Although both Means and Banks had run-ins with the law, AIM protests asserted Native American sovereignty and pride and drew attention to broken U.S. commitments.

OLYA MELEN (c. 1980–) Ukrainian public-interest lawyer who filed suit on behalf of Environment-People-Law to stop construction on a government canal that would have cut through the Danube Delta, a wetland of international importance. Despite threats and accusations of being a traitor and spy, Melen persevered and won both the court case and a 2006 Goldman Environmental Prize.

RIGOBERTA MENCHÚ TUM (1959–) A Quiché Maya activist from Guatemala and winner of the 1992 Nobel Peace Prize. Although her dictated autobiography *I, Rigoberta Menchú* (1984) has come under fire by scholar David Stoll, among others, for misrepresenting some of the details of her past, she remains a powerful symbol of and tireless campaigner for indigenous rights around the world.

EDMUND DENE MOREL (1873–1924) British journalist and antislavery activist. He was working as a clerk when he noticed that ships from Belgium setting out for the Congo carried mostly guns and ammunition and returned with far more raw rubber and ivory than officially reported. He began publishing articles on Congo exploitation, started his own newspaper (*The West Africa Mail*), and, gathering allies, formed the Congo Reform Association in 1904 that helped end the Leopold regime.

GUNNAR MYRDAL (1898–1987) Nobel Prize–winning Swedish economist and author of a transforming book on race relations, *An American Dilemma: The Negro Problem and Modern Democracy* (1944). It was the culmination of a six-year study for the Carnegie Corporation, which had picked Myrdal as an unbiased "outsider" from a country untainted by a colonial past.

White racism shocked Myrdal, who saw it undermining American ideals. Myrdal later applied his interdisciplinary approach to social problems in Asia.

DADABHAI NAOROJI (1825–1917) Indian math professor, politician, and author of *Poverty and Un-British Rule in India* (1901). An early proponent of *swaraj*, or "self-rule," he argued that foreign domination drained wealth from the colonies. Serving three times as president of the Indian National Congress, he inspired the next generation of nationalists and worked to educate Indians about their rights.

JOHN BOYD ORR (1880–1971) Scottish doctor and nutritionist. His research in the 1930s on malnutrition in Great Britain shaped national food policy. Director-general of the UN Food and Agriculture Organization after World War II, Boyd Orr won the 1949 Nobel Peace Prize for trying to improve the production and fair distribution of food.

MARIA PACHECO RODRÍGUEZ (?–) Guatemalan biologist, organic farmer, and social entrepreneur. In 1993, poor highland villagers asked her help growing trees for firewood, and with them, she developed a lumber business that included making educational wooden toys. She founded and manages Kiej de los Bosques, which nurtures rural businesses and helps Mayas find national and international markets for their products.

ABBÉ PIERRE (1912–2007) Beloved French priest who inspired the international Emmaus movement on behalf of the poor and homeless. Part of the French resistance during World War II, Abbé Pierre founded the Emmaus Society in 1949, gathering donations and shaming the government to offer emergency housing. Emmaus grew into a network of international health and social service centers.

(DOMINIQUE) GEORGES-HENRI PIRE (1910–69) Belgian monk and refugee activist. In the wake of World War II, his open-air camps for children fed the hungry, and he arranged sponsors, old age homes, and small villages for war refugees. He won the 1958 Nobel Peace Prize for his organization, Aid to Displaced Persons. He later founded a peace university and continued his refugee work worldwide through the Heart Open to the World.

FRANCES FOX PIVEN (1932–) Welfare scholar and political reformer. Written with lifelong collaborator Richard Clowland, her classic *Regulating the Poor* (1972) described how welfare policy controls the poor and working class. Her other books include *Poor Peoples' Movements* (1977) and *Why Americans Don't Vote* (1988). She coupled her writing with activism that spurred welfare expansions in the 1960s and the 1993 "motor voter bill" that allowed Americans to register to vote when applying for a driver's license.

FRANKLIN DELANO ROOSEVELT (1882–1945) Lawyer, politician, and U.S. president during the Great Depression and World War II. From a prominent New York family, Roosevelt contracted polio at age 39 and lost the use of his legs but resumed his political career in a wheelchair. Elected to the first of four terms in 1932, he promised swift action to end the economic crisis that had sidelined 13 million American workers. In his first 100 days, he set up scores of agencies that restored confidence as they helped the needy—but also involved the government in economic and social life to an unprecedented degree. His "New Deal" legacy includes Social Security.

JEFFREY SACHS (1954–) Michigan-born professor of sustainable development, professor of health policy, and director at the Earth Institute at Columbia University. Frequently identified as one of the most influential economists and consultants in the world, he has advised governments and international agencies on poverty reduction and environmentally sensitive development. From 2002 to 2006, he directed the UN Millennium Project and served as Secretary General Kofi Annan's special adviser on the Millennium Development Goals. In *The End of Poverty* (2005), Sachs argued that a comprehensive plan coupled with a funding surge from rich nations could quickly pull developing countries out of the "poverty trap."

PALAGUMMI SAINATH (1954–) Prize-winning Indian journalist and author of *Everybody Loves a Good Drought: Stories from India's Poorest Districts* (1996). Through photos as well as well-researched articles and essays, he has rejuvenated mainstream media reporting on rural poverty, bringing to light farmer suicides, rapes of Dalit women, and government inefficiency.

ZAINAB SALBI (c. 1970–) Social entrepreneur empowering women in war-torn societies. A Muslim born and raised in Baghdad during the Iran-Iraq War, Salbi studied and settled in the United States. She and her husband made their first humanitarian foray to survivors of Croatian rape camps during the Bosnian war and returned to found Women for Women International in 1993.

CHÉRI SAMBA (1956–) Congolese popular artist whose paintings confront AIDS, corruption, and other social ills. Born in Kinto-M'Vuila and trained as a sign painter and comic strip artist in Kinshasa, Samba gained international recognition in the 1980s for his art–cum–social commentary. His younger brother, painter Cheik Ledy, trained in his studio and later died of AIDS.

MARGARET HIGGINS SANGER (1884–1966) Nurse and birth control crusader. After tending to immigrant mothers in New York slums, Sanger in

1913 began publishing a monthly newspaper, *Woman Rebel*, advocating birth control—for which she was arrested and charged with mailing "obscene materials." She helped organize the first World Population Conference in Switzerland in 1927 and the international Planned Parenthood movement.

ALBERT SCHWEITZER (1875–1965) Medical missionary who founded a hospital compound at Lambaréné in French Equatorial Africa (now Gabon). Born in Alsace, then part of Germany, he gained prominence as a musician and a theologian before becoming a doctor. His "reverence for life"—communicated both through his work and his writings—inspired many humanitarians. When he won the Nobel Peace Prize in 1952, he used the prize money to build a leprosarium.

AMARTYA SEN (1933–) Economics professor who won a 1998 Nobel Prize for his contributions to "welfare economics." The Nobel committee applauded Indian-born Sen for his research on reconciling majority rule and individual rights, improving the accuracy of poverty indexes, defining well-being, and analyzing famine. According to Sen, income creates opportunities (capabilities), but these are affected by other factors as well, such as health. This thinking led to the UN Human Development Index, among other tools, as a more accurate measure of poverty than income alone.

ROBERT SARGENT SHRIVER, JR. (1915–) Lawyer, diplomat, and public servant. Tapped by his brother-in-law John F. Kennedy to organize the Peace Corps in 1961, Shriver set the agency's tone of rigorous idealism. He then directed the Office of Economic Opportunity, one of the lead agencies in Lyndon Johnson's War on Poverty and had a hand in establishing many long-running programs, including VISTA (Volunteers in Service to America), Head Start, and Indian and Migrant Opportunities.

GEORGE SOROS (1930–) Global financier and philanthropist. Born in Hungary, Soros defected in 1946 during the Soviet takeover of his country. After making his way to the United States and earning billions, he started a network of foundations supporting "open society" projects, from copy machines for Hungarian democracy activists to grants for health initiatives among Ukrainian drug users. In 2006, he announced a $50 million gift to the UN Millennium Villages project in Africa.

RONALD TAKAKI (1939–) Multicultural historian and pioneer in ethnic studies. Takaki's grandfather emigrated from Japan to work the sugarcane fields in Hawaii. A professor at the University of California, Berkeley, Takaki has written almost a dozen books, including *Iron Cages*

(1979), about race and culture in 19th-century America, and *A Different Mirror: A History of Multicultural America* (1993).

MOTHER TERESA (1910–97) Catholic nun from Macedonia who won the 1979 Nobel Peace Prize for her work among the dying and destitute in India. Teaching at a girls' school in Calcutta, she overcame her superiors' resistance and left the convent to serve the "poorest of the poor." She founded the Missionaries of Charity, now an international order.

LOUIS "STUDS" TERKEL (1912–) Radio broadcaster and author who wrote the voices of ordinary people into popular history. Son of a New York tailor and seamstress, Terkel earned a law degree but during the depression began working in the radio division of the WPA Writers' Project. Interviewing both the privileged and the disadvantaged, he compiled oral histories striking for their diversity and honesty. His many books include *Hard Times: An Oral History of the Great Depression* (1970).

BOOKER T. WASHINGTON (1856–1915) Author, educator, and founder of Tuskegee Normal and Industrial Institute in 1881. Born a Virginia slave, Washington first attended school at 16 and paid his own way through college after emancipation by working as a janitor. Believing education to be African Americans' ticket to equality, he emphasized school and work as a route to economic progress rather than legal and political rights—a "realism" that sometimes irritated those who felt blacks should not accommodate an unjust status quo. His books include the autobiography *Up from Slavery* (1901).

MELAKU WOREDE (1936–) Ethiopian agronomist dedicated to preserving Africa's biodiversity. From 1979 to 1993, he directed the Plant Genetic Resources Centre in Addis Ababa, where he trained local plant breeders and created "strategic seed reserves" of traditional varieties of food crops, such as wheat, being replaced by modern cultivars. The center distributed these native seeds to farmers during droughts, when little else could survive, and enhanced them to increase the yield without the addition of expensive chemical fertilizers. Worede now advises the Seeds for Survival program and has helped set up the African Biodiversity Network.

MUHAMMAD YUNUS (1940–) Optimistic Bangladeshi economist and microcredit pioneer. In 2006, he and the Grameen Bank he founded won the Nobel Peace Prize.

KATERYNA YUSHCHENKO (1961–) Ukrainian-American economist, philanthropist, and first lady. Captured and sent to Germany as slave laborers during World War II, her parents immigrated to Chicago, where

Yushchenko was born. She held various diplomatic and financial positions in the United States and Ukraine, where she met her husband, then a banker and now president. She chairs the Ukraine 3000 International Foundation, which encourages charitable activities in fields ranging from the arts to social welfare.

9

Organizations and Agencies

Acción International
URL: http://www.accion.org/
56 Roland Street, Suite 300
Boston, MA 02129
Phone: (617) 625-7080

From a community development organization in Venezuela started by an American law student, Acción has evolved into a major microfinance organization. It offers loans and business assistance to low-income entrepreneurs in Latin America and the Caribbean as well as Africa and Asia.

African Medical and Research Foundation (AMREF)
URL: http://www.amref.org/
Langata Road
PO Box 27691–00506
Nairobi, Kenya
Phone: (254–20) 699-3000

In the 1950s, three Western surgeons began flying their services into remote African communities, and from the "Flying Doctors" was born AMREF, now with a staff 97 percent African. Priorities of this health care, training, and research organization include malaria, HIV, safe water, and family health. The Web site links visitors to an online library, as well as human-interest stories and technical briefing papers.

Africare
URL: http://www.africare.org/contact/contact_us.html
Africare House
440 R Street NW

Washington, DC 20001-1935
Phone: (202) 462-3614

A private U.S. charity founded by Africans and Americans in 1970, during a drought in West Africa. This multiracial agency with a diverse donor base focuses on village-based development.

American Friends Service Committee (AFSC)
URL: http://www.afsc.org/
1501 Cherry Street
Philadelphia, PA 19102
Phone: (215) 241-7000

The pacifist religious sect known as Quakers founded AFSC in 1917 to enable World War I conscientious objectors to serve civilian war victims. With its British counterpart, it won the 1947 Nobel Peace Prize. Its Web site includes links to criminal justice (including U.S. prison reform), economic justice (from international debt to the U.S. minimum wage), humanitarian assistance and education, immigration and migration, peace building and conflict prevention, and youth (from child soldiers abroad to volunteerism in the United States).

Arab Fund for Social and Economic Development
URL: http://www.arabfund.org/index.htm
PO Box 21923 SAFAT
13080 Kuwait, State of Kuwait
Phone: (965) 495-9000

This League of Arab States finance organization funds and gives technical assistance to MENA social and economic development projects.

Asian Development Bank (ADB)
URL: http://www.adb.org
6 ADB Avenue
Mandaluyong City 1550, Philippines
Phone: (632) 632-4444

The 66-member ADB assists developing nations in Asia through grants, loans (about $6 billion per year), technical assistance, policy dialogue, etc. Its Web site links to a handful of recent publications, such as *Curbing Corruption in Public Procurement in Asia and the Pacific.* It also provides statistics and news releases on projects in specific countries.

Association of Community Organizations for Reform Now (ACORN)
URL: http://www.acorn.org/
739 Eighth Street SE
Washington, DC 20003
Phone: (877) 55-ACORN; (202) 547-2500

A grass-roots organization of low- and moderate-income families, ACORN has agitated since the 1970s for better police response in urban neighborhoods, toxic-waste cleanup, public school safety, wider voter registration, and community investment. Current national campaigns focus on Hurricane Katrina relief, living wage ordinances, and health-care access. An international wing works in Peru, Canada, and Mexico.

Casa Alianza Guatemala
URL: http://www.casa-alianza.org/en/news.php
13 Avenida 0-37, Zona 2 de Mixco
Colonia la Escuadrilla
Mixco, Guatemala
Phone: (502) 2433-9600

A nonprofit, nonpartisan organization rehabilitating street children, Casa Alianza Guatemala began in 1981 as an affiliate of New York's Covenant House to shelter and defend children whose lives had been shattered during the civil war. It has extended into Honduras, Nicaragua, and Mexico.

Catholic Relief Services (CRS)
URL: http://www.crs.org/
PO Box 17090
Baltimore, MD 21203-7090
Phone: (410) 625-2220

The humanitarian agency of the U.S. Catholic Church community, CRS educates American Catholics about poverty and injustice overseas and directly serves 99 developing countries. It partners with local agencies in agriculture, community health, education, emergency response, HIV/AIDS, microfinance, peacebuilding, and safety net programming.

Center for Budget and Policy
URL: http://www.cbpp.org/
820 First Street NE, #510
Washington, DC 20002
Phone: (202) 408-1080

A nonpartisan think tank minding the impact of policies and program on low- and middle-income Americans. As responsibility for assisting the poor has shifted somewhat from the federal to state level, so too has the center's focus. "Socially liberal, fiscally conservative, and academically rigorous," the center posts its very readable reports on its Web site.

Center for Global Development
URL: http://www.cgdev.org/
1776 Massachusetts Avenue NW, Third Floor
Washington, DC 20036
Phone: (202) 416-0700

An "independent, not-for-profit think tank that works to reduce global poverty and inequality by encouraging policy change in the U.S. and other rich countries." Its comprehensive Web site publishes links to expert bios, research initiatives, publications, and opinion pieces, including blog posts.

Children's Defense Fund
URL: http://www.childrensdefense.org/
25 E Street NW
Washington, DC 20001
Phone: (202) 628-8787

The Children's Defense Fund advocates for children, especially those poor and disabled, through research, policy analysis, and lobbying. In the United States, it coordinates summer and after-school enrichment programs and aims to break the "Cradle to Prison" pipeline by pulling families out of poverty. Recent initiatives include the Global Women's Action Network for Children.

Chornobyl Union International
URL: http://www.cochems.com/chornobyl/chorn4.html
1 Lesya Ukrainaka Square
252196 Kiev, Ukraine
Fax: (380–044) 296-4734

A self-help organization run by liquidators and those in the fallout zone of the nuclear accident. Affiliates in 15 former Soviet republics provide social services and medical aid to the needy, particularly children suffering radiation contamination.

Deepalaya
URL: http://www.deepalaya.org/

46 Institutional Area
D-Block, Janakpuri
New Delhi 110058, India
Phone: (91–11) 2852-0347

Founded in 1979, this Indian NGO aims to build the self-reliance of "the economically and socially deprived, the physically and mentally challenged—starting with children." Its strategy involves community organizing: In education, for instance, it identifies shortcomings in government schools and organizes pressure groups, such as mothers, to push for improvements. Its Web site includes links to archived newsletters and annual reports.

Department for International Development (DFID)
URL: http://www.dfid.gov.uk/
1 Palace Street
London SW1E 5HE
United Kingdom
Phone: (020) 7023-0000

The United Kingdom is the world's fifth largest donor to developing countries, and DFID channels that aid to the European Commission, the United Nations, international financial institutions, national governments, and civil society organizations. The British counterpart to USAID; DFID works directly in 150 countries, profiled on its Web site. Other links lead to fact sheets, country assistance plans, education documents, case studies, etc.

European Community Humanitarian Aid Department (ECHO)
URL: http://ec.europa.eu/echo/
European Commission Directorate-General for Humanitarian Aid
AN-88, B-1049 Brussels, Belgium
Phone: (32–2) 296-6499

Through ECHO, the European Union funds UN agencies and NGOs in the field in the wake of natural disasters or armed conflict in nonmember countries. It pays for food, medicine, tents, diesel generators—whatever may improve the chances of victims' short-term survival. Its Web site shares reports by country, theme, and partner, as well as eyewitness accounts.

Feinstein International Center
URL: http://fic.tufts.edu/
200 Boston Avenue, Suite 4800

Medford, MA 02155
Phone: (617) 627-3423

Based in the Tufts University School of Nutrition, the center sponsors field research in countries experiencing humanitarian crises not limited to but including famine. The Web site links to center publications and reports and also embraces the Humanitarianism and War project (http://hwproject.tufts.edu/), with its own links to research and training materials.

Food First/Institute for Food and Development Policy
URL: http://www.foodfirst.org/
398 60th Street
Oakland, CA 94618
Phone: (510) 654-4400

Since founders Frances Moore Lappé and Joseph Collins published *Food First: Beyond the Myth of Scarcity* in 1977, this nonprofit has been pushing "to eliminate the injustices that cause hunger." Many of the publications linked to their Web site—fact sheets, backgrounders, policy briefs, etc.—question dominant paradigms in trade and development.

Forced Migration Online
URL: http://www.forcedmigration.org/
University of Oxford
3 Mansfield Road
Oxford OX1 3TB
United Kingdom
Fax: (44–018) 6527-0297

An online information clearinghouse. Resources accessible from its comprehensive Web site include a digital library, discussions lists, blog posts, handbooks, working papers, and an introductory guide for newcomers.

Ford Foundation
URL: http://www.fordfound.org/
320 East 43rd Street
New York, NY 10017
Phone: (212) 573-5000

A charitable foundation chartered in 1936 by Edsel Ford and Ford Motor Company executives. It proclaims four broad goals: strengthen democratic values, reduce poverty and injustice, promote international cooperation, and advance human achievement. In the United States and around the world, the foundation funds "work force development"—helping low-income people build marketable job skills—and reproductive health, among other projects.

Bill & Melinda Gates Foundation
URL: http://www.gatesfoundation.org/
PO Box 23350
Seattle, WA 98102
Phone: (206) 709-3100

Microsoft founder Bill Gates and family launched this charitable foundation "guided by the belief that every life has equal value." Not surprisingly, it promotes access to technology in public libraries around the world. In the United States, it attacks inequality through education, one of its prominent initiatives being the Gates Millennium Scholars Program. In more than 100 developing countries, it focuses on improving health and reducing extreme poverty.

Goodwill Industries International
URL: http://www.goodwill.org/
15810 Indianola Drive
Rockville, MD 20855
Phone: (800) 741-0186

A nonprofit operating through member organizations in 24 countries that provides education, training, and career services for the disadvantaged, including people homeless, on welfare, or coping with disabilities.

Grameen Foundation
URL: http://www.grameenfoundation.org/
50 F Street NW, Eighth Floor
Washington, DC 20001
Phone: (202) 628-3560

Inspired by the original Grameen Bank in Bangladesh, the foundation supports microfinance initiatives in Latin American and the Caribbean, the Middle East and North Africa, Asia, and sub-Saharan Africa. It helps front-line service providers through funding, technical assistance, and training.

Habitat for Humanity International
URL: http://www.habitat.org/
121 Habitat Street
Americus, GA 31709-3498
Phone: (229) 924-6935, ext. 2551 or 2552

This "ecumenical Christian housing ministry" involves volunteers and people served in building and rehabilitating houses, which are then sold at no profit to low-income families. Affiliates work in 92 countries. The main Web site provides links to a few case studies, research papers, and homeowners' stories around the world. Habitat invites visitors to its Global Village and Discovery Center in Georgia, which features life-size Habitat housing types.

Heifer International
URL: http://www.heifer.org/
1 World Avenue
Little Rock, AR 72202
Phone: (800) 422-0474

Antihunger NGO that gives animals such as cows and chickens, as well as "agroecology" training, to poor families around the world. Families improve their food supply and often earn a little extra by selling milk and eggs. Central to Heifer philosophy is "passing on the gift"; recipients must donate female offspring of their livestock to a needy neighbor.

HumanTrafficking.org
URL: http://www.humantrafficking.org/
1825 Connecticut Avenue NW
Washington, DC 20009-5721
Phone: (202) 884-8916

A Web site for NGOs and government officials. The site profiles individual East Asian and Pacific nations notorious for trafficking and links to sites for laws, agencies, and best practices.

InterAction
URL: http://www.interaction.org/
1400 16th Street NW, Suite 210
Washington, DC 20036
Phone: (202) 667-8227

An alliance of more than 160 U.S.-based international development and humanitarian NGOs. Aiming to increase members' effectiveness, coordination, and professionalism, InterAction has developed a set of standards for private voluntary organizations in government, finance, communication, etc. Its Web page "Humanitarian Policy & Practice" links users to UN, U.S., NGO, academic, and military sites.

Inter-American Development Bank (IDB)
URL: http://www.iadb.org/
1300 New York Avenue NW
Washington, DC 20577
Phone: (202) 623-1000

A Latin American development institution launched in 1959 in partnership with the United States, the IDB soon expanded into the Caribbean. These regional members borrow from the bank for development projects and hold a tiny majority of voting power on the IDB board. Nonregional members now stretch from Europe to Asia.

International Federation of Red Cross and the Red Crescent Societies
URL: http://www.ifrc.org/
PO Box 372
CH-1211 Geneva 19, Switzerland
Phone: (41–22) 730-4222

The Red Cross, a Swiss committee to help war wounded that won the 1917 Nobel Peace Prize, went international after World War I. The federation now serves as the umbrella for 181 national societies, which specialize in disaster response and preparedness, as well as health care and promotion of humanitarian values. Its Web site includes an annual report on world disasters and the current issue of *Red Cross Red Crescent Magazine.*

International Indian Treaty Council (IITC)
http://www.treatycouncil.org/
2390 Mission Saint, Suite 301
San Francisco, CA 94110
Phone: (415) 641-4482

Indigenous peoples' rights organization. IITC encourages indigenous networking and participation in the United Nations and seeks recognition for treaties between native peoples and nation-states. The Web site posts links to news and information about vigils, court cases, UN initiatives, and more.

International Monetary Fund (IMF)
URL: http://www.imf.org/
700 19th Street NW
Washington, DC 20431
Phone: (202) 623-7000

With 184 member countries, the IMF aims for economic stability around the world. It publishes newsletters, research bulletins, surveys, statistics, and other data, available from the IMF Web site.

Islamic Relief
URL: http://www.islamic-relief.com/
19 Rea Street South
Birmingham B5 6LB
United Kingdom
Phone: (44–121) 605-5555

The international charity Islamic Relief has field offices in the Muslim world, from Albania to Indonesia, although it funds emergency relief and sustainable development without regard to religion, race, or gender. Projects include water and sanitation, health and nutrition, and education and training, as well as a special focus on sponsoring orphans and organizing *waqfs*, charitable trusts sanctioned by Islamic law.

Madre
URL: http://madre.org
121 West 27th Street, #301
New York, NY 10001
Phone: (212) 627-0444

An international human rights organization led by women. Founded by artists and activists horrified by the consequences of U.S. involvement in the 1980s Nicaragua contra war, Madre has branched out into other areas of Latin America, such as Guatemala and Peru, as well as countries in the Middle East, Africa, and Asia. Madre partners with community-based women's organizations to tackle recovery from war, women's health, trade and aid, environmental stability, indigenous rights, and violence against women.

Médecins Sans Frontières (MSF)/Doctors without Borders
URL: http://www.msf.org/
Rue de Lausanne 78
CP 116–1211
Geneva 21, Switzerland
Phone: (41–22) 849-8400

MSF has provided emergency medical aid in the wake of natural and human-made disasters in about 70 countries. Although the group often collaborates with local authorities to rebuild health infrastructure, such as vaccination programs or water supplies, it also speaks out about human-rights abuses.

National Center for Children in Poverty
URL: ttp://www.nccp.org/
215 West 125th Street, Third Floor
New York, NY 10027
Phone: (646) 284-9600

Nonpartisan research organization at Columbia University's public-health school dedicated to low-income children and their families. The Web site offers links by state and by policy to briefs, reports, and expert testimony before government agencies. "Data wizards" allow users to plug in numbers to build tables that compare welfare benefits across states.

National Low Income Housing Coalition
URL: http://www.nlihc.org/
727 15th Street NW, Sixth Floor
Washington, DC 20005
Phone: (202) 662-1530

An information and advocacy group "dedicated solely to ending America's affordable housing crisis." It publishes an annual report, *Out of Reach,* as well as research reports, an advocates' guide, and an almost weekly "Memo to Members." Its well-linked Web site also features housing-related news.

National Poverty Center
URL: http://www.npc.umich.edu/
Joan and Sanford Weill Hall, Suite 5100
735 South State Street
Ann Arbor, MI 48109-3091
Phone: (734) 615-5312

A federally funded nonpartisan research center based at the University of Michigan. Its Web site includes links to a newsletter, *Poverty Research Insights,* as well as working papers, policy briefs, FAQs, and other antipoverty academic research centers. These include two former national poverty centers, the Joint Center for Poverty Research (Northwestern University and the University of Chicago) and the University of Wisconsin–Madison Institute for Research on Poverty (IRP). Under "About Us," you will also find information about and links to three area poverty research centers: the IRP, which now specializes in Midwestern poverty; the University of Kentucky

Center for Poverty Research, which focuses on Kentucky and the South; and the Rural Poverty Research Center at the University of Missouri.

National Welfare Rights Union
URL: http://www.nationalwru.org/
23 E Adams Street, 4th floor
Detroit, MI 48226
Phone: (313) 964-0618

A coalition of grass-roots organizations. Its site links to welfare advocacy organizations, such as the National Coalition for the Homeless, and to chapters, such as the Kensington Welfare Rights Union in Philadelphia, which has spearheaded the Poor People's Economic Human Rights Campaign (http://www.economichumanrights.org/).

OneWorld United States
URL: http://us.oneworld.net/
3201 New Mexico Avenue NW, Suite 395
Washington, DC 20016
Phone: (202) 885-2679

Part of OneWorld International Foundation, which governs an online network of relief and development agencies, advocacy groups, and individuals worldwide committed to human rights and sustainable development. OneWorld.net produces content in about a dozen languages and invites involvement.

Open Society Institute (OSI) & Soros Foundation Network
URL: http://www.soros.org/
400 West 59th Street
New York, NY 10019
Phone: (212) 548-0600

Philanthropist George Soros launched foundations in the 1980s to help Soviet states make the transition to democracy. An outgrowth, OSI awards grants in more than 60 countries "to support the rule of law, education, public health, and independent media." Initiatives range from the Documentary Photography Project, for photographers with a lens on social justice, to AfriMAP (Africa Governance Monitoring and Advocacy Project), which tries to hold African Union states to their promises on good governance.

Organisation for Economic Co-operation and Development (OECD)
URL: http://www.oecd.org/

2 rue André Pascal
F-75775 Paris Cedex 16
France
Phone: (331) 4524-8200

A policy-monitoring organization of 30 member countries, including the United States, committed to democratic government and a market economy. Besides facilitating trade and scientific cooperation, OECD tracks members' development programs and outreach to nonmember nations. Available from its Web site are OECD's well-regarded publications, including statistical compilations on such topics as aid effectiveness.

Oxfam International
URL: http://www.oxfam.org/en/
Oxfam House
John Smith Drive
Cowley, Oxford OX4 2JY
United Kingdom
Phone: (44–18) 6547-3727

A coalition of 13 NGOs, including a U.S. affiliate, Oxfam International delivers emergency and long-term development assistance with an emphasis on social justice. Working in about 100 countries, it campaigns very publicly for poor people's "right to a sustainable livelihood, right to basic social services, right to life and security, right to be heard, and right to an identity." Its Web site includes links to policy papers and analyses.

People & the Planet (Planet 21)
URL: http://www.peopleandplanet.net/
60 Twisden Road
London NW5 1DN
United Kingdom
Phone: (44–20) 7485-3136

This Internet gateway to information population, poverty, health, consumption and the environment succeeds a magazine of the same name. Sponsored by the United Nations Population Fund, the World Conservation Union, the World Wide Fund for Nature International, the International Planned Parenthood Federation, and the Swedish Development Co-operation Agency, the site has links to articles and fact sheets.

Pew Charitable Trusts
URL: http://www.pewtrusts.com/
2005 Market Street, Suite 1700
Philadelphia, PA 19103-7077
Phone: (215) 575-9050

Independent foundation that conducts research, proposes policy, and supports civic life. Among its top priorities are preschool education, foster-care reform, and retirement security. Its "global attitudes project surveys opinion around the world. The trust's Hispanic center studies Latinos in the United States, tracking wages, remittances sent back to Latin America, educational outcomes, and other measures of well-being and inclusion.

Rockefeller Foundation
URL: http://www.rockfound.org/
420 Fifth Ave
New York, NY 10018
Phone: (212) 869-8500

One of the oldest U.S. charitable foundations. It promotes "well-being" in the United States and abroad, which in the 21st century means helping to "ensure that globalization's benefits are more widely shared." With a historic focus on "global health, agricultural productivity, innovation for development, economic resilience and urban life," the foundation funds initiatives that usually yield some results within three to five years. The Web site details grant summaries (project and amount) as well as information about joint projects, such as the Partnership for Higher Education in Africa.

Sargent Shriver National Center on Poverty Law
URL: http://povertylaw.org/
50 East Washington Street, Suite 500
Chicago, IL 60602
Phone: (312) 263-3830

NGO founded on the belief that "the law can get the poor out of poverty." It focuses on communications and policy development—state-level responses to federal law and policy. The Web site connects to several publications, such as the monthly *Poverty Action Report* newsletter aimed at public officials. An online Poverty Law Library makes available more than 500,000 legal documents on such topics as disability, environmental justice, and food programs.

Save the Children (U.S. headquarters)
URL: http://www.savethechildren.org/
54 Wilton Road
Westport, CT 06880
Phone: (203) 221-4030 or (800) 728-3843

The world's largest independent children's rights organization working in more than 110 countries. Providing both emergency relief and long-term development assistance, Save the Children advocates for food, shelter, health care, education, and freedom from violence, abuse, and exploitation.

Schwab Foundation for Social Entrepreneurship
URL: http://www.schwabfound.org/
Route de la Capite 91-93
CH–1223 Cologny/Geneva, Switzerland
Phone: (41–22) 869-1212

This foundation provides recognition and networking support to social entrepreneurs, people who achieve "large scale, systemic and sustainable social change through a new invention, a different approach, a more rigorous application of known technologies or strategies, or a combination of these."

Southern African Regional Poverty Network
URL: http://www.sarpn.org.za/
PO Box 11615
Hatfield 0028, South Africa
Phone: (27–12) 342-9499

An NGO that "promotes debate and knowledge sharing on poverty reduction processes and experiences" in a 14-country region that runs from the DRC south. Comprehensive Web site includes a country analysis section with links to relevant documents as well as a section on regional themes such as debt, energy, HIV/AIDS, and "poverty reduction frameworks and critiques."

Southern Poverty Law Center
URL: http://www.splcenter.org
400 Washington Avenue
Montgomery, AL 36104
Phone: (334) 956-8200

Born during the civil rights movement, the Southern Poverty Law Center fights discrimination. While its legal department represents vulnerable groups such as migrant workers or Vietnamese-American fishermen, the center also monitors hate crimes and offers antibigotry training to K–12 teachers.

Tharwa Community
URL: http://www.tharwacommunity.org/
Damascus, Syria

A mixed English and Arabic online forum spotlighting diversity-related concerns and issues in the MENA region. This news and blog spot is part of a broader project focused on five initiatives: diversity, gender, environmental issues, youth, and peacebuilding.

Transparency International (TI)
URL: http://www.transparency.org/
Alt Moabit 96
10559 Berlin, Germany
Phone: (49–30) 3438-300

A global NGO fighting corruption. TI works in five areas: politics, public contracting, private sector, international anticorruption conventions, and poverty and development. Its Website offers links to its corruption measurement tools, such the "Bribe Payers Index," as well as to position and working papers.

United Nations (World Headquarters)
URL: http://www.un.org/english/
First Avenue at 46th Street
New York, NY 10017
Phone: (212) 963-4475

An organization of 192 member countries dedicated to establishing international peace and security and fostering cooperation in solving international problems. Links to its many agencies, some headquartered in New York and others abroad, can be found at http://www.unsystem.org.

Many UN agencies are involved in fighting poverty. Based in Rome, Italy, the **Food and Agriculture Organization (FAO)** coordinates information sharing at all levels, from farmers to policy makers, and publishes an annual State of Food and Agriculture Report, available from its Web site, along with fact sheets and links to profiles of food-deficit countries.

The first specialized UN agency, the **International Labor Organization (ILO)** offers technical assistance on issues ranging from working conditions to management development to social security. From its Web site are available factsheets and selected articles from *World of Work* magazine, published three times a year.

The **United Nations Children's Fund** (UNICEF) advocates for children's rights in five areas: child survival and development, basic education and gender equality, HIV/AIDS and children, child protection, and policy advocacy and partnership. Besides extensive information on the state of the world's children, UNICEF features on its Web site profiles of youth leaders, discussion boards for teens and children, and "Voices of Youth" digital diaries.

With staff on the ground in 166 countries, the **United Nations Development Programme** (UNDP) coordinates development efforts around the world. It commissions the annual Human Development Report, accessible through its Web site.

Headquartered in Switzerland, the **United Nations High Commissioner for Refugees** (UNHCR) safeguards the rights and well-being of refugees. Available on its comprehensive Web site are statistics and advocacy reports, as well as issues of *Refugees Magazine*.

Dedicated to reproductive health and choice, the **United Nations Population Fund** (UNFPA) helps countries gather, analyze, and respond to population data. It publishes an annual State of the World Population.

The United Nations established the **United Nations Relief and Works Agency (UNRWA)** for Palestinian refugees as a temporary agency to deal with the humanitarian disaster that followed the UN partitioning of Palestine and establishment of the State of Israel. Because wars continued to destabilize the population and conflicts remain unresolved, UNRWA has served as the overextended mainstay of four generations of Palestinians.

The **World Health Organization** (WHO) tracks health data country by country, monitors disease outbreaks and epidemics, distills research, makes public-health recommendations, and publishes the *Bulletin of the World Health Organization*, a peer-reviewed monthly for researchers and policy makers. Its Web site covers a panoply of topics, from asthma to zoonoses (diseases passed from animals to people).

United States Agency for International Development (USAID)
URL: http://www.usaid.gov/
Ronald Reagan Building
Washington, DC 20523-1000
Phone: (202) 712-4810

Although USAID has roots in the post–World War II Marshall Plan, the Foreign Assistance Act of 1961 established it as an independent federal agency guided by the State Department. It supports U.S. foreign policy by helping more than 100 countries "recovering from disaster, trying to escape poverty, and engaging in democratic reforms." In fiscal year 2006, Congress allocated

USAID more than $9 billion. Its Web site summarizes the policy on USAID outreach in fields ranging from agriculture to education.

Women for Women International
URL: http://www.womenforwomen.org/
4455 Connecticut Avenue NW, Suite 200
Washington, DC 20008
Phone: (202) 737-7705

A nonprofit that aims to turn women in societies ravaged by conflict from victims to survivors. First, the agency pairs women with sponsors outside the country who provide financial aid and emotional support through exchanging letters. Next, Women for Women offers vocational and leadership training, as well as microcredit for entrepreneurial ventures.

Working Women's Forum
URL: http://www.workingwomensforum.org
55 Bhimasena Garden Street
Mylapore
Chennai–600 004, India
Phone: (91–44) 2499-2853

An NGO committed to improving the lot of poor working women through microcredit and microinsurance, reproductive health care, unionization, training, and rehabilitation of child laborers. Its Web site includes links to the forum's newsletter, *Groots*, and articles about the organization and its president, Dr. Jaya Arunachalem.

World Bank
URL: http://www.worldbank.org/
1818 H Street NW
Washington, DC 20433
Phone: (202) 473-1000

Founded near the end of World War II, the bank pursues global poverty reduction by offering low-interest loans, interest-free credit, and grants for development projects. It runs two funds: the International Bank for Reconstruction and Development (IBRD), for middle-income countries or low-income nations with good credit, and the International Development Association (IDA), for the poorest nations. The World Bank's Web site reflects its sprawling operation, providing access to more than 15,000 free, downloadable documents as well as to the bank's historical archives and library.

10

Annotated Bibliography

This sampling from the voluminous publications about poverty falls into eight categories:

The Study of Poverty

Global Poverty

Poverty in the United States

Poverty in Europe

Poverty in the Middle East and North Africa

Poverty in Latin America and the Caribbean

Poverty in Asia

Poverty in Sub-Saharan Africa

Note that under "Poverty in the United States," many of the books about immigrants include information about their home countries. An asterisk (*) marks publications aimed at younger readers.

Each category is further divided into "Books," "Articles, Reports, and Papers," "Web Documents," "Other Media," and "Fiction." Fiction may seem an unlikely source for a research paper, but many creative writers draw upon firsthand experience or observations for realistic details. Recognizing that the poor so often lack a voice, writers often speak up on their behalf. Poems, short stories, and novels sometimes reveal a "truth" about poverty that facts and figures may obscure.

If you are looking for movies about economic and social justice, one place to start is MediaRights (http://www.mediarights.org), a nonprofit organization that produces and distributes independent documentaries and short films. You can browse more than 6,500 films by topic.

THE STUDY OF POVERTY

Books

*Balkin, Karen, ed. *Poverty: Opposing Viewpoints.* Farmington Hills, Mich.: Greenhaven Press, 2004. Juxtaposes point-counterpoint essays about American and global poverty, questioning its seriousness, causes, and solutions. More heavily weighted toward the United States, topics of the opinionated pieces in this collection include hunger, homelessness, welfare reform, faith-based charity, and minimum wage.

Bannerjee, Abhijit Vinayak, Roland Benabou, and Dilip Mookherjee, eds. *Understanding Poverty.* New York and London: Oxford University Press, 2006. Aims to inform educated noneconomists about groundbreaking poverty research since the 1980s. The contributing professors consider geography, colonialism, globalization, agriculture, fertility, and corruption.

*Griffin, Geoff, ed. *How Can the Poor Be Helped?* Farmington Hills, Mich.: Greenhaven Press, 2006. Presents diverse opinions about the effectiveness of aid and government intervention in the United States and abroad.

Hayek, Friedrich. *The Constitution of Liberty.* Chicago: University of Chicago Press, 1960. Crosses history, economics, and political philosophy to explore the nature of freedom and government's role in promoting individual liberty. Although economist Hayek eschews socialism and endorses the free market, he makes a case for judicious intervention.

Vollman, William. *Poor People.* New York: Ecco, 2007. Roams over the globe and over the topic of poverty in a personal meditation rather than an academic study. Novelist and freelance journalist Vollman stops in Thailand, Russia, Yemen, Afghanistan, Iraq, Kazakhstan, and Mexico and asks people why they are poor.

Web Documents

Aslanbeigui, Nahid, and Adele Wigk. "Progress: poverty or prosperity? Joining the debate between George and Marshall on the effects of economic growth on the distribution of income." *American Journal of Economics and Sociology* (Deccember 2001). Available online. URL: http://www.findarticles.com/p/articles/mi_m0254/is_5_60/ai_82469378/pg_1. Accessed March 8, 2007. Contrasts two influential late 19th-century economists—Henry George and Alfred Marshall—troubled by poverty and inequality.

Banerjee, Abhijit Vinayak. "Inside the Machine: Toward a New Development Economics." *Boston Review* (March–April 2007). Available online. URL: http://bostonreview.net/BR32.2/banerjee.html. Downloaded March 27, 2007. Reviews in a conversational tone historic economic ideas about capitalism, from Malthus to Marx. MIT (Massachusetts Institute of Technology) economics professor Banerjee also reports recent theories about the connection between property rights and poverty and conflicting data about investment in education.

Birdsall, Nancy. "Inequality Matters: Why Globalization Doesn't Lift All Boats." *Boston Review* (March–April 2007). Available online. URL: http://bostonreview.net/BR32.2/birdsall.html. Downloaded March 27, 2007. Contrasts Latin America with East Asia to conclude that inequality is not necessarily an inevitable consequence of growth and can be destructive.

Conley, Dalton. "The Geography of Poverty: Rethinking Social Policy." *Boston Review* (March–April 2007). Available online. URL: http://bostonreview.net/BR32.2/conley.html. Downloaded March 27, 2007. Reviews influential ideas about U.S. poverty since the 1960s, from "culture of poverty" to the "underclass" to "workfare versus welfare." Sociologist Conley proposes another theory—that poverty results from segregating the poor, which increases the likelihood that children will attend poor schools and have less supervision from their working, commuting parents.

International Poverty Center in Brazil. "What Is Poverty? Concepts and Measures." Entire issue of *Poverty in Focus* (December 2006). United Nations Development Programme. Available online: URL: http://www.sarpn.org.za/documents/d0002253/IPC_UNDP_Poverty-focus_Dec2006.pdf. Discusses, through 10 articles, differing definitions of poverty and why they matter.

Maxwell, Simon. "The Meaning and Measurement of Poverty." Overseas Development Institute Poverty Briefing, February 3, 1999. Available online. URL: http://www.odi.org.uk/publications/briefing/pov3.html. Accessed November 12, 2006. Outlines the history and fault lines of current poverty debates for generalist readers.

Reddy, Sanjay, and Thomas Pogge. "How Not to Count the Poor." Social Science Research Network. Available online. URL: http://papers.ssrn.com/sol3/papers.cfm?abstract_id=893159. Posted October 29, 2005. Disputes World Bank methods for measuring poverty. Reddy, a development economist, and Pogge, a philosopher, believe the World Bank measure has understated the extent of poverty and overstated its recent decline.

Singer, Peter. "What Should a Billionaire Give—and What Should You?" *New York Times Magazine* (December 17, 2006), pp. 58ff. Available online. URL: http://www.nytimes.com/2006/12/17/magazine/17charity.t.html?ex=1178856000&en=f43dd25b1c1bcc34&ei=5070. Accessed May 9, 2007. Ponders the moral dimension of poverty relief. A Princeton University professor of bioethics, Singer does the math and concludes that the rich could eliminate poverty—if they made that commitment.

GLOBAL POVERTY

Books

*Armstrong, Jennifer, ed. *Shattered: Stories of Children and War.* New York: Alfred A. Knopf Books for Young Readers, 2002. Brings together a dozen first-person stories from around the world of conflicts' impact on children—from the 19th-century U.S. Civil War to the 20th-century Soviet invasion of Afghanistan.

Blaut, J. M. *The Colonizer's Model of the World: Geographical Diffisionism and Eurocentric History*. New York: Guilford Press, 1993. Debunks Western historical and scientific assumptions that have long passed for fact. Geography professor Blaut argues that inequality is not "natural."

Diamond, Jared. *Guns, Germs, and Steel: The Fates of Human Societies*. New York: W. W. Norton, 1997. Contends that environment—not race—accounts for modern differences of prosperity from continent to continent. A professor of geography and physiology, Diamond won the Pulitzer Prize for this long view of history (13,000 years) that considers the variety of plants and animals available for domestication, disease burden, and other geographic variables.

Easterly, William. *The Elusive Quest for Economic Growth*. Cambridge: MIT Press, 2001. Explores international development initiatives in the Global South that have largely failed, from loans and aid to birth control and investment in technology. Drawing on his experience with the World Bank, Easterly argues that people need incentives, and he favors good governance that protects rule of law and encourages free trade.

———. *The White Man's Burden*. New York: Penguin Press, 2006. Questions the effectiveness of massive foreign aid, finding more success in homegrown reform efforts. Economist Easterly recommends higher standards of accountability for aid agency and recipient governments.

*Gerdes, Louise, ed. *Globalization: Opposing Viewpoints*. San Diego, Calif.: Greenhaven Press, 2005. Presents essays with strong and contrasting opinions about the impact of globalization on culture and developing economies. Besides questioning globalization's effects on poverty, democracy, and the environment worldwide, essays also ask if outsourcing hurts or helps U.S. workers.

*Harris, Nancy ed. *AIDS in Developing Countries*. San Diego, Calif: Greenhaven Press, 2003. Samples opinions on why AIDS is spreading and how to contain the pandemic.

*January, Brendan. *Globalize It! The Stories of the IMF, the World Bank, the WTO—and Those Who Protest*. Minneapolis, Minn.: Twenty-First Century Books, 2003. Explains how the Bretton Woods organizations affect the world economy and touches on criticism of their role.

Klein, Naomi. *Fences and Windows: Dispatches from the Front Lines of the Globalization Debate*. New York: Picador USA, 2002. Gathers newspaper reporting on sweatshops, crowd control, and other topics that suggest that capitalism puts up tangible and intangible fences that deny the poor access to everything from education to clean water. Many articles build on Klein's 1999 book, *No Logo: Taking Aim at the Brand Bullies*, which notes that multinational corporations such as Disney, Microsoft, Nike, and others often exploit workers in the United States and the developing world.

McLellan, Elisabeth P., ed. *The World Bank: Overview and Current Issues*. New York: Nova Science Publishers, 2003. Presents basic information about the biggest international development institution.

Mortenson, Greg, and David Relin. *Three Cups of Tea: One Man's Mission to Fight Terrorism and Build Nations... One School at a Time.* New York: Viking Press, 2006. Recounts the adventures of an American "climbing bum" who has a mountainside epiphany that spurs him to found schools, particularly for girls, in remote Pakistan and Afghanistan.

*Parker, David L., with Lee Engfer and Robert Conrow. *Stolen Dreams: Portraits of Working Children.* Minneapolis, Minn.: Lerner Publications, 1998. Profiles with text and photos of child laborers in Mexico, Bangladesh, India, and Nepal—including a chapter on Pakistani child activist Iqbal Masih.

Sachs, Jeffrey. *The End of Poverty.* New York: Penguin Books, 2005. Proposes a solution to poverty through major investments of foreign aid followed by free-market capitalism. Sachs draws on extensive personal experience in developing nations for this passionate argument.

Smith, Stephen. *Ending Global Poverty: A Guide to What Works.* New York: Palgrave Macmillan, 2005. Identifies "poverty traps" and a number of effective grass-roots programs for eliminating them. Economics professor Smith wants to help readers make informed decisions about which aid organizations to support.

World Bank. *World Development Report 2007: Development and the Next Generation.* Washington, D.C.: World Bank, 2006. Focuses on opportunities and risks in the transition to adulthood among 12- to 24-year-olds, touching on topics ranging from job markets to AIDS.

Yunus, Muhammad. *Banker to the Poor: Micro-Lending and the Battle against World Poverty.* Rev. ed. New York: PublicAffairs, 2003. Recounts Yunus's life story and the history of the Grameen Bank.

Articles, Reports, and Papers

Eviatar, Daphne. "Spend $150 Billion per Year to Cure World Poverty." *New York Times Magazine* (November 7, 2004), pp. 44–49. Profiles globe-trotting economist Jeffrey Sachs but tempers his optimistic message about eliminating poverty through comments by skeptics.

Fishman, Ted C. "Making a Killing." *Harper's* 305, no. 1,827 (August 2002), pp. 33ff. Refutes the idea that global trade will defeat terrorism. Editor and former currency trader Fishman explores how globalization has fueled armed conflict in many poor nations.

Hardin, Garrett. "Lifeboat Ethics: The Case against Helping the Poor." *Psychology Today* 8 (September 1974), pp. 38–43. Advocates population control and immigration restrictions. Noted ecologist Hardin describes rich nations as lifeboats surrounded by swimmers in the sea, the poor, who will sink the boats if they board in large numbers.

"Leaders: Rich man poor man: Globalisation and the rise of inequality." *Economist* 382, no. 8,512 (January 20, 2007), p. 12. Contends that inequality is acceptable as long as the overall economy is growing and provides opportunities for the talented.

"Ranking the Rich." *Foreign Policy* 156 (September–October 2006): 68ff. Comments on the Center for Global Development's Commitment to Development Index, which assesses the aid and actions of 21 rich nations. The article faults the United States (number 13) for its tied food aid and wasted assistance to Iraq because of corruption.

Rice, Susan E. "The Threat of Global Poverty." *National Interest* (Spring 2006): 76ff. Lays out the direct and indirect links of poverty to disease, terrorism, and other threats to U.S. and global security. Former U.S. assistant secretary of state for African affairs, Rice argues for a multifaceted campaign against poverty that includes aid, debt cancellation, and good government in developing countries.

Rosenberg, Tina. "The Free-Trade Fix." *New York Times Magazine* (August 18, 2002), pp. 28ff. Concludes that the current free-trade system needs improvement. Foreign policy journalist Rosenberg looks closely at Chile and Mexico and points out how the wealthy and big business worldwide benefit from the wide open market.

Sheehan, Molly O'Meara. "Snapshots of Our Urban Future." *World Watch* 20, no. 2 (March–April 2007): 25ff. Samples from NGO Worldwatch Institute's *State of the World 2007: Our Urban Future,* which considers the increasing urbanization of the world's population and its environmental impact. Researcher Sheehan has selected Los Angeles; Lagos, Nigeria; Loja, Ecuador; Malmö, Sweden; Mumbai, India; Nairobi, Kenya; and Rizhao, China, to represent struggles and successes in sustainable development.

Web Documents

Birdsall, Nancy. "The World Bank of the Future: Victim, Villain, Global Credit Union?" Carnegie Endowment for International Peace Policy Brief 1, no. 1 (October 2000). Available online. URL: http://www.cgdev.org/doc/expert%20pages/birdsall/BirdsallTWB.pdf. Downloaded May 4, 2007. Considers criticism of international financial institutions from the Left and the Right. Economist and reformer Birdsall concludes that those who want "social justice and sensible use of Earth's resources" should support openness and democracy in the Global South.

Bureau of International Affairs, U.S. Department of Labor "The Department of Labor's 2005 Findings on the Worst Forms of Child Labor." Available online. URL: http://www.dol.gov/ilab/media/reports/iclp/tda2005/tda2005.pdf. Downloaded May 4, 2007. Details country by country the work children perform, child labor laws and their enforcement, and government policies and programs. The worst forms of child labor encompass slavery and debt bondage, sex and drug trade, and dangerous occupations.

Cecelski, Elizabeth. "The Role of Women in Sustainable Energy Development." Contractor's report (NREL/SR-550-26889) for the National Renewable Energy Laboratory of the U.S. Department of Energy. June 2000. Available online. URL: http://www.nrel.gov/docs/fy00osti/26889.pdf. Downloaded May 4, 2007. Touches upon the invisible time and labor burdens of women from Latin America to

Africa and underlines the importance of considering women's needs and knowledge in developing any "improved" technology.

Global Fund to Fights AIDS, Tuberculosis and Malaria. "Partners in Impact: Results Report 2007." Available online. URL: http://www.theglobalfund.org/en/files/about/replenishment/oslo/Progress%20Report.pdf Downloaded March 9, 2007. Details the progress of this disease-fighting fund since its 2002 launch with an emphasis on successful country partnerships and results.

La Vina, Antonio, et al. "Agricultural Subsidies, Poverty and the Environment: Supporting a Domestic Reform Agenda in Developing Countries." World Resources Institute Policy Note. January 2007. Available online. URL:http://pdf.wri.org/aspe_domestic_reform.pdf. Downloaded May 4, 2007. Recommends policy changes that wed poverty alleviation to environmental protection.

Multilateral Development Banks and the International Monetary Fund. "Global Poverty Report." Report to the G8 Okinawa Summit, July 2000. Available online. URL: http://www.worldbank.org/html/extdr/extme/G8_poverty2000.pdf. Downloaded May 4, 2007. Summarizes poverty conditions and trends region by region, including "optimistic" and "less optimistic" forecasts.

Narayan, Deepa, et al. *Voices of the Poor: Can Anyone Hear Us?* New York: Oxford University Press for the World Bank, 2000. Available online. URL: http://www1.worldbank.org/prem/poverty/voices/reports/canany/vol1.pdf. Downloaded October 2, 2006. Untangles the web of global poverty with explanations reinforced by qualitative and participatory studies. The World Bank researchers lace the report with poignant observations by poor people from almost 50 countries.

———. *Voices of the Poor: Crying Out for Change.* New York: Oxford University Press for the World Bank, 2000. Available online. URL: http://www1.worldbank.org/prem/poverty/voices/reports/crying/cry.pdf. Downloaded October 2, 2006. Continues with discussion based on fieldwork among the poor. Chapters explore the participatory method and "Places of the Poor," "The Body," and "Gender Relations in Troubled Transition."

Narayan, Deepa, and Patti Petesch, eds. *Voices of the Poor: From Many Lands.* New York: Oxford University Press for the World Bank, 2002. Available online. URL: http://www1.worldbank.org/prem/poverty/voices/reports/lands/full.pdf. Downloaded October 2, 2006. Finishes the Voices of the Poor series with in-depth studies of Ghana, Malawi, Nigeria, Bangladesh, Indonesia, Bulgaria, the Russian Federation, Argentina, Brazil, Ecuador, and Jamaica.

Quillgan, James Bernard. "The Brandt Equation: 21st Century Blueprint for the New Global Economy." Philadelphia: Brandt 21 Forum, 2002. Available online. URL: http://www.brandt21forum.info/BrandtEquation-19Sept04.pdf. Downloaded May 4, 2007. Revisits the much-discussed but unimplemented proposals of the 1980 Brandt report. Writer Quillgan updates proposals for restructuring the international economy.

Shapiro, Alan. "Globalization: Free Trade & Fair Trade, Jobs & Justice." 2004. Teachable Moment, Morningside Center for Teaching Social Responsibility. Available online. URL: http://www.teachablemoment.org/high/globalization.html. Downloaded

August 3, 2007. Offers short readings on the globalization debate in the 2004 presidential election, touching on NAFTA and the outsourcing of U.S. jobs, with references to popular press articles and discussion questions.

United Nations Children's Fund. "The State of the World's Children 2007: Women and Children—the Double Dividend of Gender Equality." New York: UNICEF United Nation's Children's Fund, 2006. Available online. URL: http://www.unicef.org/sowc07/docs/sowc07.pdf. Downloaded March 13, 2007. Links women's empowerment to the well-being of children. In two-thirds of developing countries surveyed, most women lacked a say in household decisions, with adverse effects on child nutrition, health, and education.

Other Media

Dworking, Mark, and Melissa Young. *Another World Is Possible: Impressions of the World Social Forum.* Produced by Melissa Young. 24 min. DVD. Oley, Pa.: Bullfrog Films, 2002. Reports from the 2002 World Social Forum in Brazil, a gathering of grass-roots social and environmental activists.

Hardin, Frances Anne. *How the IMF Tracks Economies and Makes Loans.* Produced and directed by Frances Anne Hardin. 16 min. VHS. Princeton, N.J.: Films for the Humanities & Sciences, 2001. Outlines IMF operations, including loans to developing nations and debt reduction.

Jeffrey Sachs on ESSD and the Millennium Development Goals: What Is the ESSD Contribution and Impact? 56 min. World Bank video, 2005. Available online. URL: http://info.worldbank.org/etools/docs/voddocs/548/1061/hi.htm. Downloaded February, 22, 2007. Blames prolonged poverty on donors who do not provide enough aid and Bretton Woods institutions that force structural adjustment rather than advocating on behalf of the poor.

Kammen, Glenn. *Worlds Apart.* Produced by Glenn Kammen. 17 min. DVD. Pasadena, Calif: Intelecom, 2005. Discusses globalization, neoliberalism, and inequality through the work of Médecins Sans Frontières (Doctors without Borders).

POVERTY IN THE UNITED STATES

Books

*Bartoletti, Susan Campbell. *Kids on Strike!* New York: Houghton Mifflin, 1999. Recounts the labor activism of children toiling in mills, mines, and other workplaces from the 1880s through the beginning of the 20th century.

*Bausum, Ann. *With Courage and Cloth: Winning the Fight for a Woman's Right to Vote.* Washington, D.C.: National Geographic Children's Books, 2004. Reviews late 19th-century suffrage struggles and details the final push from 1900 to 1920, chronicling tensions between the National American Woman Suffrage Association and the National Woman's Party, as well as between activists for women's and African Americans' rights.

Annotated Bibliography

Cohen, Richard, ed. *Dear Mrs. Roosevelt: Letters from Children of the Great Depression*. Chapel Hill: University of North Carolina Press, 2002. Presents almost 200 of the thousands of letters young people wrote to First Lady Eleanor Roosevelt between 1933 and 1941.

*Collins, Tracy Brown. *Living through the Great Depression*. Farmington Hills, Mich.: Greenhaven Press, 2004. Describes everyday American life in the wake of the 1929 stock market crash and worsening hard times.

Conley, Dalton, ed. *Wealth and Poverty in America: A Reader.* Malden, Mass.: Blackwell Publishing, 2002. Draws together classic and contemporary essays, from Adam Smith, Karl Marx, and Max Weber to Michael Katz and William Julius Wilson.

Crow Dog, Mary, with Richard Erdoes. *Lakota Woman*. New York: HarperPerennial, 1991. Recounts a Native American's difficult childhood and awakening as part of the American Indian Movement (AIM) in the late 1960s. Crow Dog, daughter of a "mostly white" trucker and a Sioux nurse, grew up in poverty with her grandparents on the Rosebud Reservation in South Dakota and endured abuse at a Catholic boarding school. After troubles with alcohol and aimlessness, she joined AIM's 1972 march on Washington, D.C., and occupation of the Bureau of Indian Affairs.

Daniels, Roger. *Coming to America: A History of Immigration and Ethnicity in American Life*. 2d ed. New York: Harper Perennial, 2002. Explores sociological explanations for migration before turning to profiles of different ethnic groups. History professor Daniels champions immigration but also documents negative responses to newcomers.

DeParle, Jason. *American Dream: Three Women, Ten Kids, and a Nation's Drive to End Welfare*. New York: Viking, 2004. Looks at the impact of welfare reform on three Milwaukee families. A *New York Times* reporter who covers social policy, DeParle details both the legislative and human drama of the 1996 Personal Responsibility and Work Opportunity Reconciliation (PRWOR) Act.

Dorris, Michael. *The Broken Cord*. New York: HarperPerennial, 1989. Reveals the human and medical dimensions of fetal alcohol syndrome. An anthropologist and creative writer, Dorris adopted a Native American baby boy and broke new ground in discovering the consequences of alcohol abuse among pregnant women.

Dunar, Andrew J., and Dennis McBride. *Building Hoover Dam: An Oral History of the Great Depression*. Reno: University of Nevada Press, 2001. Weaves together first-person accounts of construction workers and other eyewitnesses. History professor Dunar and researcher McBride discuss laborers' hardship living in tents and cardboard boxes in the Nevada desert and many deaths from carbon monoxide poisoning in the tunnels in the rock.

Egan, Tim. *The Worst Hard Time: The Untold Story of Those Who Survived the Great American Dust Bowl*. Boston: Houghton Mifflin, 2006. Charts the rise and fall of the Great Plains from the turn of the 20th century through the 1930s. *New York Times* reporter Egan draws on accounts from elderly survivors of the ecological disaster that impoverished the rural Midwest and Southwest.

Ehrenreich, Barbara. *Nickel and Dimed: On (Not) Getting By in America.* New York: Henry Holt, 2001. Gives a thoughtful, often humorous first-person account of the difficulties of low-wage workers. A maverick writer with a Ph.D., Ehrenreich tried on a series of low-skill jobs by presenting herself as "a divorced homemaker reentering the workforce after many years."

Eitzen, D. Stanley, and Kelly Eitzen Smith. *Experiencing Poverty: Voices from the Bottom.* Belmont, Calif.: Thomson Wadsworth, 2003. Weaves introductory segments on poverty issues with relevant primary sources. Father-daughter sociologists Eitzen and Smith emphasize race and gender as factors in poverty.

Ellingwood, Ken. *Hard Line: Life and Death on the U.S.-Mexico Border.* New York: Pantheon Books, 2005. Describes the face-off between undocumented Mexicans and U.S. Border Patrol agents in the Southwest especially during 1994 Operation Gatekeeper. *Los Angeles Times* reporter Ellingwood has won praise from reviewers for covering immigration issues from many perspectives.

Engel, John. *Poor People's Medicine: Medicaid and American Charity Care since 1965.* Durham, N.C.: Duke University Press, 2006. Characterizes American medical care for the poor as "a story of ambivalence." A professor of health care administration, Engel explores the successes and failures of U.S. health policy as it diverged from the western European model.

Finnegan, William. *Cold New World: Growing up in a Harder Country.* New York: Random House, 1998. Documents the lives of poor teenagers in a Connecticut city, a rural Texas county, a Washington (state) valley, and a California suburb. A *New Yorker* journalist, Finnegan lets details reveal youthful alienation.

Freedman, Jonathan. *From Cradle to Grave: The Human Face of Poverty in America.* New York: Atheneum, 1993. Describes poverty through easy-to-read vignettes organized by the life cycle—babies born to crack addicts, middle-aged workers laid off from steel mills, seniors consigned to nursing homes.

*Gerdes, Louise. *The Homeless: Opposing Viewpoints.* Farmington Hills, Mich.: Greenhaven Press, 2007. Compiles essays that probe causes and potential solutions to homelessness.

Goode, Judith, and Jeff Maskovsky, eds. *The New Poverty Studies: The Ethnography of Power, Politics, and Impoverished People in the United States.* New York: New York University Press, 2001. Assembles academic essays that show the poor have been losing ground since the 1980s. Anthropologists Goode and Maskovsky contend that "market-based solutions to the problems of impoverishment and inequality" actually work against the poor.

Gorn, Elliott. *Mother Jones: The Most Dangerous Woman in America.* New York: Hill & Wang, 2001. Links the early life of labor activist Jones with her reinvention as a grandmotherly firebrand. Professor Gorn points out inaccuracies in Jones's autobiography and documents how both she and others used the persona she created.

*Gourley, Catherine. *Society's Sisters: Stories of Women Who Fought for Social Justice in America.* Minneapolis, Minn.: Lerner/Twenty-First Century Books, 2003.

Profiles such turn-of-the-century Progressive activists as social worker Jane Addams, public-health doctor Alice Hamilton (who investigated workplace toxins), journalist Ida B. Wells, civil-rights lecturer Mary Church Terrell, and suffragists Frances Willard and Alice Paul.

*Haskins, James, and Kathleen Benson. *Out of the Darkness: Blacks Moving North, 1890–1940.* New York: Benchmark Books, 1999. Puts in context the Great Migration, drawing on first-person and newspaper accounts as well as secondary sources. The late Haskins, an English professor, and his wife Benson, a museum curator, wrote many books for young people on African-American history.

Jones, LeAlan, David Isay, and Lloyd Newman. *Our America: Life and Death on the South Side of Chicago.* New York: Scribner, 1997. Expands the National Public Radio documentaries made by Jones and Newman when they were 13. This bottom-up view of the Ida B. Wells Homes, a Chicago public-housing project, focuses on the death of five-year-old Eric Morse, dropped from the top of a high-rise by two preteen boys.

Iceland, John. *Poverty in America: A Handbook.* 2d ed. Berkeley: University of California Press, 2006. Discusses history, measurement, causes, and policy. Sociology professor Iceland draws on research and past experience with the U.S. Census Bureau.

*Kallan, Stuart A., ed. *Are America's Wealthy Too Powerful?* Farmington Hills, Mich.: Greenhaven Press, 2006. Gathers essays on both sides of this issue.

Kotlowitz, Alex. *There Are No Children Here.* New York: Doubleday, 1991. Reports on the dangers and coping strategies of two boys trying to survive childhood in Chicago's violence-plagued Henry Horner housing project. *Wall Street Journal* reporter Kotlowitz befriended Lafayette and Pharoah Rivers when they were 10 and seven, two of six children living with their mother in a decrepit apartment.

*Kowalski, Kathiann M. *Poverty in America: Causes and Issues.* Berkeley Heights, N.J.: Enslow, 2003. Explores U.S. poverty: inequality, absolute versus relative poverty, stereotypes, demographics, government intervention—including welfare, the working poor, and private aid.

Kozol, Jonathan. *Amazing Grace: The Lives of Children and the Conscience of a Nation.* New York: Crown, 1995. Describes the poorest neighborhood in New York, Mott Haven in the South Bronx, through interviews with teachers, ministers, residents, and mostly children, who somehow transcend the misery of their surroundings. Modern muckraker Kozol blames lack of economic opportunity, cutbacks in services, and hopelessness for drug abuse, AIDS, violence, and other ills. He later revisits the resilient black and Hispanic children of Mott Haven in *Ordinary Resurrections: Children in the Years of Hope* (2000).

———. *Death at an Early Age: The Destruction of Hearts and Minds of Negro Children in the Boston Public Schools.* Boston: Houghton Mifflin, 1967. Recounts the author's first teaching experience in Boston, a city that a few years later exploded with resistance to court-ordered busing to end de facto segregation.

———. *Illiterate America*. Garden City, N.Y.: Anchor Press, 1985. Combines statistics on the scope of the problem (one-third of adults cannot read well) with human stories. Drawing on research for previous books and his commission to design a literacy plan for large cities, Kozol critiques existing programs that focus only on narrow functional goals.

———. *Rachel and Her Children: Homeless Families in America*. New York: Crown Publishers, 1988. Humanizes the problem of homelessness by listening to the residents of Hotel Martinique, a temporary shelter in New York City for 400 families, including 1,400 children.

———. *The Shame of a Nation: The Restoration of Apartheid Schooling in America*. New York: Random House, 2005. Reports on the creeping return of de facto segregation in the nearly 60 public schools the author visited in 11 states. Not only are residential patterns separating white students from black, but educators are subjecting minority students to harsh behavior control and rigid instruction. This work builds on Kozol's earlier *Savage Inequalities: Children in America's Schools* (1991), which contrasted stellar public schools in affluent communities with dilapidated schools in minority neighborhoods and rural districts such as Greene County, Mississippi, so poor that children had to bring their own toilet paper.

Lang, Kevin. *Poverty and Discrimination*. Princeton: Princeton University Press, 2007. Evaluates antipoverty and antidiscrimination policies. Economist Lang rigorously roots out faulty research and debunks unsupported assumptions.

Loury, Glenn C. *The Anatomy of Racial Inequality*. Cambridge, Mass.: Harvard University Press, 2002. Describes the evolution of racial stereotypes and the debilitating impact of stigma (as distinct from legal discrimination) on black Americans. Once conservative Loury, an economist and social critic, moves toward a more liberal position about the need for interventions such as affirmative action to overcome the legacy of slavery and Jim Crow.

Lui, Meizhu, et al. *The Color of Wealth: The Story Behind the U.S. Racial Wealth Divide*. New York: New Press, 2006. Explains in easy-to-understand terms the historical roots for inequality in economic assets. "For every dollar owned by the average white family in the United States, the average family of color has less than one dime." The authors, experts affiliated with the social-justice organization United for a Fair Economy, devote separate chapters to Native Americans, blacks, Latinos, and Asians.

*Marrin, Albert. *Sitting Bull and His World*. New York: Dutton Children's Books, 2000. Reveals through a biography of the Lakota warrior the subjugation of the Plains Indians in the late 19th century as the United States conquered the West. Yeshiva University history professor Marrin portrays the Battle of Little Bighorn—Custer's "last stand"—as an Indian act of self-defense.

McElvaine, Robert S. *The Depression and New Deal: A History in Documents*. New York: Oxford University Press, 2000. Presents a wide range of primary sources—diaries, newspaper articles, campaign memos and speeches, political cartoons, songs, poetry, art, advertisements, photographs, and personal letters—along with advice about how to read them and an assessment of their significance. College history professor McElvaine has published widely about the era.

———. *Down and Out in the Great Depression: Letters from the Forgotten Man.* Chapel Hill: University of North Carolina Press, 1983. Gathers nearly 200 letters from men, women, and children out of the thousands sent to the first family and New Deal administrators during the 1930s.

*Meltzer, Milton. *The Black Americans: A History in Their Own Words.* Reprint, New York: HarperTrophy, 1987. Gathers together primary sources—letters, speeches, and other documents—spanning more than three centuries. Prolific children's author Meltzer frequently focuses on the underdogs in American history.

Meyers-Lipton, Scott J., ed. *Social Solutions to Poverty: America's Struggle to Build a Just Society.* Boulder, Colo.: Paradigm Publishers, 2006. Assembles more than 50 poverty-related texts across the political perspective from the colonial period to the present. This collection of primary sources includes Thomas Paine's "Agrarian Justice" (1797), which proposes an old-age pension; Julia Lathrop's presidential address to the National Conference of Social Work (1919), which concerns child welfare and child labor; and one of President George W. Bush's speeches on the role of religion in poverty relief, "Faith-Based Charities Work Daily Miracles" (2002).

Newman, Katherine. *No Shame in My Game: The Working Poor in the Inner City.* New York: Alfred A. Knopf, 1999. Documents the strong work ethic and obstacles to prosperity among black and Latino fast-food workers in Harlem. Harvard cultural anthropologist and urban studies professor Newman interviews more than 200 workers and points to some promising new initiatives to improve their lot.

*Partridge, Elizabeth. *Restless Spirit: The Life and Work of Dorothea Lange.* New York: Viking, 1998. Profiles depression-era photographer Lange through letters, journals, oral history, and images. Partridge is the daughter of Lange's assistant.

Pipher, Mary. *The Middle of Everywhere: Helping Refugees Enter the American Community.* New York: Harcourt, 2002. Describes how oppressed people from countries such as Sudan, Liberia, Vietnam, and Kenya land in Lincoln, Nebraska, and adapt to a new culture. Psychologist and family therapist Pipher shares firsthand stories of their interactions with schools and social-service agencies.

Ramos, Jorge. *The Other Face of America: Chronicles of the Immigrants Shaping our Future.* Trans. by Patricia J. Duncan. New York: HarperCollins, 2002. Collects almost 50 newspaper columns and essays about immigrants, especially Hispanics, and their effect on U.S. culture. Mexican-American journalist Ramos anchors the news on Univisión, the largest Spanish-language TV network in the United States.

Rank, Mark Robert. *One Nation, Underprivileged: Why American Poverty Affects Us All.* Oxford: Oxford University Press, 2004. Disputes the notion that poverty results from "individual inadequacies" and instead points to institutional (structural) failings. Sociologist and social-work professor Rank proposes raising wages and/or increasing tax credits, creating jobs, improving education and health care access, enforcing child support, and building individual and community assets.

Riis, Jacob. *How the Other Half Lives: Studies Among the Tenements of New York.* New York: Penguin Classics: 1890/1997. Alerts readers to the deplorable living conditions in slums at the end of the 19th century. In this successful and now classic work illustrated with his own photographs, the Danish-American police reporter for the *New York Evening Sun* reveals the ethnic stereotypes of his age and anticipates later muckraking journalism and documentary photography.

Rodriguez, Richard. *Hunger of Memory: The Education of Richard Rodriguez.* Reprint, New York: Dial Press, 2004. Reflects on the Mexican-American author's journey from Spanish-speaking child to English literature scholar. Editor and writer Rodriguez has won much acclaim for this autobiographical meditation, but some Hispanics have called him a traitor for opposing bilingual education and affirmative action. He continued to explore cultural identity *in Days of Obligation: An Argument with My Mexican Father.*

Santiago, Esmeralda. *Almost a Woman.* New York: Vintage Books, 1999. Recalls a large, poor Puerto Rican family's transition to life in New York City in the 1960s. The eldest of 11 children, writer and filmmaker Santiago wrote this memoir as a sequel to *When I Was Puerto Rican.*

Schulman, Bruce. *Lyndon B. Johnson and American Liberalism: A Brief Biography with Documents.* 2d ed. New York: Bedford/St. Martin's, 2007. Links Johnson to the New Deal and discusses the triumphs and failures of his 1960s presidency, including the War on Poverty. Boston University professor Schulman includes in the document section critiques and defenses of Johnson's vision of the Great Society.

Schwartz-Nobel, Loretta. *Growing Up Empty: The Hunger Epidemic in America.* New York: HarperCollins, 2002. Expands on her earlier book, *Starving in the Shadow of Plenty,* blending stories of struggling "food-insecure" families with an assessment of government programs, including the 1996 "welfare-to-work" act.

Seccombe, Karen. *So You Think I Drive a Cadillac? Welfare Recipients' Perspectives on the System and Its Reform.* 2d ed. Boston: Allyn & Bacon, 2007. Quotes from research interviews with people receiving and no longer receiving Temporary Aid to Needy Families in Florida and Oregon. Sociology professor Seccombe asks why people need assistance, what they think of reform, how they manage, and what they are dreaming for the future.

*Shein, Lori, ed. *Inequality: Opposing Viewpoints in Social Problems.* San Diego, Calif.: Greenhaven Press, 1998. Stages a debate about the cause of American inequality tied to race, gender, age, and class. The essays by policy makers, activists, and others question the fairness of the justice system and the government's role as problem fixer.

Shipler, David K. *The Working Poor: Invisible in America.* New York: Knopf, 2004. Weaves the personal stories of low-wage workers with the frustrations of teachers and doctors who try to help them. A former *New York Times* reporter, Shipler highlights the diversity of the poor and the many layers of their predicament.

Simon, David, and Edward Burns. *Corner: A Year in the Life of an Inner-City Neighborhood.* New York: Broadway Books, 1997. Observes the characters and problems of a west Baltimore neighborhood infamous for its drug trade. Simon, a crime reporter, and Burns, a 20-year-police veteran, focus on a teenage hustler and his addict parents.

*Sims, Robert, ed. *Is the Gap between the Rich and Poor Growing?* Farmington Hills, Mich.: Greenhaven Press, 2006. Offers a wide range of viewpoints about the U.S. wealth gap.

Washington, Harriet. *Medical Apartheid: The Dark History of Medical Experimentation on Black Americans from Colonial Times to the Present.* New York: Random House, 2007. Uncovers many abuses of African-American vulnerability, including recent forced sterilization of poor black women and drug testing on foster children with HIV. Doctor and ethicist Washington notes that these improper and often hurtful studies sowed distrust of medical authorities in the black community.

*Worth, Richard. *Dolores Huerta.* Philadelphia: Chelsea House Publications, 2006. Profiles the Mexican-American community activist who founded the United Farm Workers union with Cesar Chavez.

Zinn, Howard. *A People's History of the United States, 1492–present.* New York: HarperCollins Publishers, 1999. Retells American history from the underdogs' point of view.

*Zinn, Howard, ed. *The People Speak: American Voices, Some Famous, Some Little Known.* New York: Perennial Books, 2004. Presents many voices from the span of American history, including a farmer and participant in Shays' Rebellion, a Lowell mill worker, a Southern sharecropper, and activists such as abolitionist Frederick Douglass, labor leader Mother Jones, and Socialist Eugene V. Debs.

Articles, Reports, and Papers

Carniero, Pedro, and James Heckman. "Human Capital Policy," in *Inequality in America: What Role for Human Capital?* eds. James Heckman and Alan Krueger. Cambridge, Mass.: MIT Press, 2003. Notes the decline in the quality of the American workforce and the importance of human capital (education and skills). The economist authors favor targeting aid to young children rather than low-skilled adults and to families as well as schools.

Critser, Greg. "Let Them Eat Fat." *Harper's* 300, no. 1,798 (March 2000), pp. 41ff. Explores the obesity epidemic, especially among children, and its relationship to fast food, poverty, and lack of fitness.

Donohue, John J. III and James Heckman. "Continuous Versus Episodic Change: The Impact of Civil Rights Policy on the Economic Status of Blacks," *Journal of Economic Literature* 29, no. 4, December 1991. Contends that the civil rights movement significantly improved black Americans' economic standing once the federal government enacted and enforced antidiscrimination laws and policies. Nobel Prize winner Heckman and economist/lawyer Donohue acknowledge that hard data is limited but draw a strong conclusion nonetheless.

Durlauf, Steven. "Neighborhood Effects," in *Handbook of Regional and Urban Economics* 4, J.V. Henderson and J. F. Thisse, eds. Amsterdam: North-Holland, 2004, pp. 2,173–2,242. Reviews scholarly economics articles about the association of neighborhoods and poverty, especially in inner cities. Economist Durlauf points for the need to link theory and field research.

Edelman, Marian Wright. "Losing the Children, Early and Often." *Crisis* 113, no.6 (November–December 2006): 16ff. Underscores how poverty (from poor schooling to poor health care access) helps create juvenile offenders, nearly 100,000 of whom are incarcerated.

Gertner, Jon. "What Is a Living Wage?" *New York Times Magazine* (January 15, 2006), pp. 38ff+. Charts the evolution of the nationwide living-wage movement, from Baltimore to Albuquerque.

Heckman, James. "Skill Formation and the Economics of Investing in Disadvantaged Children," *Science* 312, no. 5,782, June 2006, pp. 1,900–1,902. Summarizes findings on brain development. Economist Heckman argues that investing in people, especially young children, by improving their environment and education promotes both social justice and economic productivity.

Kenneally, Brenda Ann. "Children of the Storm." *New York Times Magazine* (August 27, 2006), pp. 18ff. Portrays through photos and captions the lingering hardship of Hurricane Katrina in New Orleans.

Samuelson, Robert J. "Trickle-Up Economics? No one should be happy with today's growing inequality. It threatens our social compact, which relies on a shared sense of well-being." *Newsweek* 148, no. 12 (October 2, 2006), p. 40. Reflects with dismay on the 2005 poverty statistics from the U.S. Census Bureau.

Schlosser, Eric. "In the Strawberry Fields." *Atlantic Monthly* 276, no. 5 (November 1995), pp. 80ff. Critiques agribusiness-as-usual through a close look at California farm workers.

Wellington, Darryl Lorenzo. "New Orleans: A Right to Return?" *Dissent* 53, no. 4 (Fall 2006): 23ff. Surveys the long-term effects of 2005 Hurricane Katrina flooding and the difficulties of rebuilding. Culture critic Wellington takes a "disaster tour" and then asks, "What are the rights of victims of natural disasters?"

Web Documents

Friery, Mike. "Poverty in America Bibliography." Available online. URL: http://www.hartwick.edu/x10974.xml. Accessed March 28, 2007. Lists books, articles, and Web sites accompanying the Hartwick College diversity program's "The Politics of Race and Class: Legacies and Visions," 2004–05.

Frontline. "Why Poverty Persists in America: An Interview with Cynthia M. Duncan." Public Broadcasting System. Available online. URL: http://www.pbs.org/wgbh/pages/frontline/countryboys/readings/duncan.html. Posted January 9, 2006. Questions a sociology professor about the chronic poverty of Appalachia as background information for the documentary *Country Boys*, also available online, about two boys struggling to escape their circumstances.

"King Encyclopedia." Martin Luther King, Jr., Research and Education Institute. Available online. URL: http://www.stanford.edu/group/King/encyclopedia/index.htm. Downloaded October 4, 2006. This index to an online encyclopedia offers links to entries on civil rights pioneers, such as Ella Baker, and projects, such as Operation Breadbasket.

"A New Deal for Carbon Hill, Alabama: A Photographic Document by William C. Pryor." New Deal Network, sponsored by the Franklin and Eleanor Roosevelt Institute and the Institute for Learning Technologies at Teachers College, Columbia University. Available online. URL: http://newdeal.feri.org/carbonhill/index.htm. Downloaded March 19, 2007. Collects photos and documents related to a 1938 visit to a coal-mining town. Head of the photo section of the WPA's Division of Information Services, Pryor picked Carbon Hill as a New Deal success story because the town had suffered severe depression losses but had pursued federal funds for improvement projects, such as sewers and schools.

Rector, Robert E., and Kirk A. Johnson. "Understanding Poverty in America." Heritage Foundation Backgrounder #1713. Available online. URL: http://www.heritage.org/Research/Welfare/bg1713.cfm. Posted January 5, 2004. Examines 2002 poverty statistics through a conservative lens to conclude that many Americans categorized as poor enjoy adequate material conditions. Researchers Rector and Kirk assert that more work and marriage—not welfare—are "steady ladders out of poverty."

Runcie, John. "'Hunting the Nigs' in Philadelphia: The Race Riot of August 1834." *Pennsylvania History* 39 (April 1972): 187–218. Available online. URL: http://cip.cornell.edu/DPubS/Repository/1.0/Disseminate/psu.ph/1134399621/body/pdf. Downloaded April 15, 2007. Digs into underlying 19th-century economic tensions between blacks and poor, mostly Irish laborers.

Samuelson, Robert. "The Culture of Poverty." *Washington Post*, April 30, 1997, A21. Available online. URL: http://www.washingtonpost.com/wp-srv/politics/special/welfare/stories/op043097.htm. Downloaded November 12, 2006. Digests a sociologist's study of welfare reform that concludes that parents' character more than income improves children's prospects in life.

Shapiro, Alan. "The Class and Race Divide in New Orleans and in America." Teachable Moment, Morningside Center for Teaching Social Responsibility. Available online. URL: http://www.teachablemoment.org/high/raceclass.html. Posted September 28, 2005. Offers short readings on the aftermath of Hurricane Katrina with references to popular press articles. Although aimed at teachers, this site provides background knowledge and discussion questions useful for paper writers.

"Shays' Rebellion (1786–87) and the Constitution." Calliope Web site. Available online. URL: http://www.calliope.org/shays/shays2.html. Updated February 5, 2007. Charts the clash between New England farmers and merchants during the debt crisis after the Revolutionary War and its impact upon the U.S. Constitution.

Other Media

Dunn, Geoffrey. *Dollar a Day, Ten Cents a Dance: A Historic Portrait of Filipino Farmworkers in America.* Produced by Geoffrey Dunn and directed by Geoffrey Dunn and Mark Schwartz. 29 min. VHS. San Francisco, Calif.: NAATA, 1995. Gathers the reminiscences of immigrants from the Philippines who arrived in the United States in the 1920s and 1930s.

The Faces of Environmental Injustice in Cincinnati: A Presentation by the Cincinnati Communities of Lower Price Hill and Winton Hills. Produced by Sunshine Productions, Sierra Club, Urban Appalachian Council, Communities United for Action. 25 min. DVD. Reedsburg, Wisc.: Sunshine Productions, 2003. Links industrial pollution, poverty, and health problems of two Ohio communities. Onetime state senator and Cincinnati mayor Mark Mallory narrates this call to action.

Kinoy, Peter, ed. *Poverty Outlaw.* Produced and directed by Pamela Yates and Peter Kinoy in association with the Kensington Welfare Rights Union. 60 min. VHS. New York: Skylight Pictures, 1997. Depicts the downside of welfare reform as well as the Kensington Welfare Rights Union's efforts to improve a poor Philadelphia neighborhood.

Wheeler, Charles. *Lyndon Johnson's Great Society?* Produced and directed by David Coxon Taylor. 51 min. VHS. Princeton, N.J.: Films for the Humanities & Sciences, 1998. This documentary originally broadcast by the British Broadcasting Corporation examines the Johnson administration's 1960s initiatives in civil rights, health care, and poverty alleviation.

Wolf, Virginia, Barbara Grazzini, and William Simon. *Building Community in America's Inner Cities Block by Block.* Produced by Virginia Wolf and directed by Frank Maniglia. 60 min. VHS. Alexandria, Va.: PBS Video, 1997. Discusses community activism in poor inner-city neighborhoods.

Fiction

*Gallo, Donald R., ed. *First Crossing: Stories about Teen Immigrants.* Candlewick Press, 2004. Gathers together 10 short stories about young immigrants from a range of economic backgrounds, including, for instance, a Mexican boy smuggled across the border.

*Hesse, Karen. *Out of the Dust.* New York: Scholastic Press, 1997. Describes the Great Depression through poems by a 15-year-old girl on an Oklahoma wheat farm.

*Jiménez, Francisco. *The Circuit: Stories from the Life of a Migrant Child.* Boston: Houghton Mifflin, 2001. Describes the transient life of a child of undocumented Mexican farmworkers, from dawn-to-dusk work to a series of shabby "homes" without electricity or running water. Modern languages professor Jiménez, who grew up reading books he found at the dump, follows up these autobiographical short stories with a collection about his teenage years, *Breaking Through,* that includes his family's deportation.

McCunn, Ruthanne Lum. *Thousand Pieces of Gold.* Boston: Beacon Press, 1989. Dramatizes the true life journey of Lalu Nathoy (known as Polly Bemis), sold into prostitution by her father during the 1871 famine in China and later transported to the American West as a slave. Eurasian writer McCunn writes often about Chinese Americans.

*Piña Ochoa, Annette, Betsy Franco, and Traci L. Gourdine, eds. *Night Is Gone, Day Is Still Coming: Stories and Poems by American Indian Teens and Young Adults.* Cambridge, Mass.: Candlewick Press, 2003. Anthologizes the work of 21 Native Americans reflecting on family, alcohol, discrimination, and identity.

*Strasser, Todd. *Can't Get There from Here.* New York: Simon & Schuster Children's Publishing, 2004. Exposes the despair of a group of runaway or thrown-away teens living on the New York streets. Novelist Strasser chooses Maybe to narrate the homeless kids' struggle with HIV, drugs, alcohol, and the basics of food and shelter.

POVERTY IN EUROPE

Books

Alesina, Alberto, and Edward Glaeser. *Fighting Poverty in the U.S. and Europe: A World of Difference.* New York: Oxford University Press, 2004. Probes why European states are more heavily involved in redistributing income. Harvard professors Alesina and Glaeser factor in race, law, and political history.

*Bartoletti, Susan Campbell. *Black Potatoes: The Story of the Great Irish Famine, 1845 to 1850.* New York: Houghton Mifflin, 2001. Chronicles the fungus that destroyed the main food source for 6 million people, providing historical, political, economic, and scientific background. Children's author Bartoletti includes primary sources in discussing the disaster that killed more than a million and created more than 2 million economic refugees.

*Greenfeld, Howard. *After the Holocaust.* New York: Greenwillow Books, 2002. Collects stories from eight Jewish survivors of World War II Nazi concentration camps who describe their struggles after liberation.

Guy, Will, ed. *The Roma of Central and Eastern Europe.* Hertfordshire, England: University of Hertfordshire Press, 2001. Presents academic studies that explain the mass unemployment and increasing discrimination that have followed the end of Communist rule. British sociologist Guy focuses on Roma studies, ethnic relations, and health inequalities.

Hitchcock, Tim. *Down and Out in Eighteenth-Century London.* London: Hambledon & London, 2004. Reveals poverty in the 1700s from court and workhouse records, memoirs, letters, and art. British history professor Hitchcock notes discrepancies between perception and reality; for example, while paintings depict men begging, most beggars were wives and children of soldiers.

*Lyons, Mary E., ed. *Feed the Children First: Irish Memories of the Great Hunger.* New York: Simon & Schuster Children's Publishing, 2002. Presents primary sources, along with artwork, about the 19th-century famine. Lyons draws on a book based on stories collected by the Irish Folklore Commission in the 1940s.

*Marrin, Albert. *Stalin: Russia's Man of Steel.* San Louis Obispo, Calif.: Beautiful Feet Books, 2002. Sets the stage for the Bolshevik Revolution and then documents the suffering—from famines to prisons—that Stalin inflicted on the people of the Soviet Union in the first half of the 20th century.

Ringold, Dena, Mitchell Orenstein, and Erika Wilkins. *Roma in Expanding Europe: Breaking the Poverty Cycle.* Washington, D.C.: World Bank Publications, 2004. Combines sociological research with the first household survey that compares Roma poverty from country to country—such as Bulgaria, where Roma are likely to be 10 times as poor as their compatriots elsewhere.

Rosenberg, Tina. *The Haunted Land: Facing Europe's Ghosts after Communism.* New York: Random House, 1995. Explores the legacy of Communist repression in Czechoslovakia, East Germany, and Poland. Journalist Rosenberg won both a Pulitzer Prize and National Book Award for this study of coercion and corruption that have stifled challenges to authoritarian rule.

Smith, George Davey, Daniel Dorling, and Mary Shaw. *Poverty, Inequality and Health in Britain: 1800–2000—a Reader.* Bristol, England: Policy Press, 2001. Excerpts classic texts, from "An Essay on the Principle of Population" (1798) by Thomas Malthus to "The condition of the working class in England" (1845) by Friedrich Engels to an "Independent Inquiry into Inequalities in Health," otherwise known as the Acheson Report (1998).

Articles, Reports, and Papers

Erlanger, Stephen. "On New Europe's Rim, Families Fear Ramparts." *New York Times,* March 7, 2001, A3. Travels to the frontier between relatively prosperous Hungary and relatively poor Ukraine, where borders seem arbitrary but mark stark differences in the legacy of Communist rule.

Rosenberg, Tina. "Albania: Habits of the Heart." *World Policy Journal* 11, no. 4 (Winter 1994): 85ff. Visits Albania in transition, where change has hardly loosened "the past's chokehold on a nation's throat." Journalist Rosenberg notes corruption and an impoverished justice system.

Taylor, Jeffrey. "Russia Is Finished." *Atlantic Monthly* 287, no. 5 (May 2001), pp. 16ff. Chronicles in detail the rise of the business mafia and bureaucratic corruption and the decline of living standards in postcommunist Russia

Vassilev, Rossen. "Bulgaria's Population Implosion." *East European Quarterly* 40, no. 1 (Spring 2006): 71ff. Attributes Bulgaria's shrinking population to a negative fertility rate (less than two children per couple), earlier deaths, and an increase in emigration—all fueled by the shock of transition to a market economy. Professor Vassilev calls the demographic trend "a national catastrophe."

Web Documents

Aassve, Arnstein, Maria Iacovou, and Letizia Mencarini. "Youth Poverty in Europe: What Do We Know?" Working paper 2005–2 of the Institute for

Social and Economic Research, University of Essex. January 2005. Available online. URL: http://www.iser.essex.ac.uk/pubs/workpaps/pdf/2005-02.pdf. Downloaded May 4, 2007. Reviews scholarly literature and presents statistics. The authors find that youth poverty generally mirrors the pattern across Europe but observe that in the United Kingdom it is worse among "younger youth" whereas in Scandinavia it peaks in the early 20s, as young people leave home.

Berry, Albert, and Karin Schelzig. "Economic Collapse, Poverty, and Inequality during Ukraine's Difficult Transition." Report for USAID. January 2005. Available online. URL: http://www.povertyfrontiers.org/ev_en.php?ID=1528_201&ID2=DO_TOPIC. Downloaded December 12, 2006. Probes the painful Ukrainian shift from central planning to a market economy and the apparent rebound since 1999. Professor Berry and development specialist Schelzig attribute the dramatic rise in inequality in the 1990s largely to the slow pace of reform and the collapse of governance, with corruption rampant.

"NGO: Migration Is Major Poverty Risk in Europe." Euractiv.com. June 20, 2006. Available online. URL: http://www.euractiv.com/en/socialeurope/ngo-migration-major-poverty-risk-europe/article-156240. Downloaded April 1, 2007. Summarizes Caritas Europa's third annual European poverty report, with links to the full report as well as EU documents.

"Poverty in Eastern Europe and the CIS." Chapter 7 of the United Nations Economic Commission for Europe's Economic Survey of Europe 2004, No. 1. Available online. URL: http://www.unece.org/ead/pub/041/041c7.pdf. Downloaded April 11, 2007. Documents the region's rough transition to market economies in the 1990s and modest rebound since the turn of the millennium.

United Nations Children's Fund. "Overview: Innocenti Social Monitor 2006: Understanding Child Poverty in South-Eastern Europe and the Commonwealth of Independent States." Florence, Italy: Innocenti Research Centre, 2006. Available online. URL: http://www.unicef-icdc.org/publications/pdf/ism06_overview_eng.pdf. Downloaded May 4, 2007. Summarizes a longer report that finds one in four children in the region living in extreme income poverty, particularly children in large or nonnuclear families and children in institutions, in rural areas, and in certain regions and smaller towns.

Other Media

The Children of Leningradsky. Produced and directed by Hanna Polak and Andrzej Celinski. 35 min. DVD, 2004. Available online. URL: http://www.childrenofleningradsky.com/index.php. Puts before the camera about a dozen homeless children in post-Soviet Russia. The Polish filmmakers filmed this Academy Award–nominated documentary in a Moscow train station.

7 Films from 7 Countries: 7 Testimonies about Women's Lives in Post-Soviet Space. DVD. New York: Open Society Institute, 2006. This collection of short films delves into poverty and social problems in Europe and Central Asia since the end of the cold war: *Return*, about domestic violence in Georgia; *Elechek*, about family gender discrimination in Kyrgyzstan; *Who Will Sing a Lullaby*, about changing parental roles in Ukraine; *Kristina and Christ*, about church discrimination in Lithuania; *New Penelope*, about the wives of emigrant laborers in Tajikistan; *There Are Women in Russian Villages*, about the feminization of poverty in rural Russia; and *Woman's Happiness or Man's Dignity*, about gender roles in Armenia.

Fiction

*Mead, Alice. *Adem's Cross*. New York: Farrar Straus Giroux, 1996. Plunges into ethnic conflict in Kosovo in the former Yugoslavia with a tale of an Albanian teen who defies Serbian occupiers. Children's novelist Mead traveled to the Balkans for firsthand information on war and "ethnic cleansing."

*Whelan, Gloria. *Angel on the Square*. New York: HarperCollins, 2001. Views the 1917 Russian Revolution through eyes of a downwardly mobile aristocratic girl who lives with the czar's family but cannot reconcile her personal friendship with the ruler's mistreatment of his people.

POVERTY IN THE MIDDLE EAST AND NORTH AFRICA

Books

Borneman, John. *Syrian Episodes: Sons, Fathers, and an Anthropologist in Aleppo*. Princeton, N. J.: Princeton University Press, 2007. Blends ethnography and travelog to present the everyday dilemmas of Syrians. Princeton anthropology professor Borneman draws these observations from a year living in the old city.

*Ellis, Deborah. *Three Wishes: Palestinian and Israeli Children Speak*. Toronto, Canada: Groundwood Books, 2006. Profiles 20 children between the ages of eight and 18, from the sister of a suicide bomber to a boy whose house was knocked down by soldiers. Activist and children's writer Ellis interviewed and photographed these Jewish, Christian, and Muslim children during a 2002 trip to Israel and Palestine.

El-Ghonemy, M. Riad. *Affluence and Poverty in the Middle East*. London: Routledge, 1998. Surveys inequality across the MENA region, from Morocco to Iran. An Egyptian-born economist, el-Ghonemy concludes that structural adjustment by and large has not helped the poor and that military spending should be redirected to social welfare.

*Marston, Elsa, and Ramsay Harik. *Women in the Middle East: Tradition and Change*. Rev. ed. New York: Franklin Watts, 2003. Surveys the diversity of women's experience with a focus on health, politics, and religion. Children's author Marston and son Harik also look at recent developments in Afghanistan.

Annotated Bibliography

Articles, Reports, and Papers

Anderson, Thorne. "Medical Mission to Baghdad." *Saudi Aramco World* 54, no. 3 (May–June 2003): 16–18. Follows the Saudi Field Hospital into strife-torn Iraq, where surgeons treat many children and reflect on poverty.

Antar, Elias. "A Day in the Life of Ibrahim Badran." *Saudi Aramco World* 20, no. 3 (May–June 1969): 34–40. Describes the life of a Palestinian farmer in a UNWRA-run refugee camp in Jordan.

Feeney, John. "Building for the 800 Million: An Interview." *Saudi Aramco World* 50; no. 4 (July–August 1999): 28–31. Records the Egyptian architect Hassan Fathy on the need for "barefoot architects" and other concepts in sustainable architecture.

Gillespie, Kristen. "The Poverty Trap." *Jerusalem Report,* December 1, 2003, 22. Examines poverty in Jordan, particularly among Palestinian refugees.

"The Greening of the Arab East." *Saudi Aramco World* 34, no. 5 (September–October 1983): 2–40. Explores agricultural development across the Middle East.

Kershner, Isabel. "Facing Up to the Harsh Reality of a Country in Steep Decline. *Jerusalem Report,* July 3, 2000, 28. Contrasts Syria's regional clout with its socioeconomic weakness.

"The Legacy of Hassan Fathy." *Saudi Aramco World* 50, no. 4 (July–August 1999): 54–63. Excerpts of a discussion from a conference at the University of Texas at Austin on the legacy of the Egyptian architect.

Mandaville, Jon. "Give to the Charity of Your Choice." *Aramco World* 24, no. 6 (November–December 1973): 2–5. Gives a historical overview of *waqfs*, Islamic charitable endowments.

Norton, Mary. "Sayat: The Town That Became a Family." *Aramco World* 23, no. 1 (January–February 1972): 2–5. Profiles a grass-roots social services organization in a Saudi Arabian town.

Rafeq, Abdul-Karim. "Making a Living or Making a Fortune in Ottoman Syria." In Nelly Hanna, ed. *Money, Land and Trade: An Economic History of the Muslim Mediterranean.* London: I. B. Tauris Publishers, 2002, 101–123. Discusses the tension between the poor majority and the rich minority in Syria from the 16th to 19th centuries. Rafeq touches upon European damage to local crafts guilds, widespread availability of loans and credit, and abuse of *waqf* lands held in trust.

Raghavan, Sudarsan. "War in Iraq Propelling a Massive Migration: Wave Creates Tension across the Middle East." *Washington Post,* February 4, 2007, A1ff. Reports on the difficulties of the nearly 2 million Iraqis who have fled the violence in their own country and sought refuge in neighboring countries, mostly Syria, Jordan, and Lebanon.

Watzman, Haim. "Israel's Arab Education Gap." *Chronicle of Higher Education* 50, no. 29 (March 26, 2004): A39. Attributes Israeli Arab underrepresentation at universities to poverty, isolation, and weak secondary schools.

Web Documents

Beinin, Joel. "The Working Class and Peasantry in the Middle East: From Economic Nationalism to Neoliberalism." *Midde East Report* (Spring 1999). Available online. URL: http://arabworld.nitle.org/texts.php?module_id=4&reading_id=19 &sequence=1. Downloaded March 20, 2007. Surveys, in scholarly language, the general trend away from development orchestrated by the state toward market economies, with much variation among individual countries.

Billeh, Victor. "Educational Reform in the Arab Region." *Newsletter of the Economic Research Forum, for the Arab Countries, Iran & Turkey* 9, no. 2 (Summer 2002): 30–32. Available online. URL: http://www.erf.org.eg/nletter/Newsletter_Sum02/ NewsletterSumIssue.Q30-32.pdf. Downloaded March 7, 2007. Sketches recent progress but blames problems with illiteracy, secondary schooling, and girls' enrollment across the region on a lack of "a system that governs education and sets measurable standards of performance."

Doraid, Moez. "Human Development and Poverty in the Arab States." Report by regional coordinator for United Nations Development Program. March 2000. Available online. URL: http://www.pogar.org/publications/other/undp/hdr/ 2000/arab/poverty2000.pdf. Downloaded April 4, 2007. Surveys the state of the region with references to colonialism, Islam, and poverty, and by international comparison. Includes bibliography and region-specific tables.

Fergany, Nader, et al. *Arab Human Development Report 2002: Creating Opportunities for Future Generations.* New York: United Nations Development Programme, Regional Bureau for Arab States, 2002. Available online. URL: http://www. undp-pogar.org/publications/other/ahdr/ahdr2002e.pdf. Downloaded March 24, 2007. Acknowledges regional progress in literacy, life expectancy, and reductions in child mortality while pointing out shortfalls in those areas as well as per-capita income. This groundbreaking first in a series of reports, assembled by Arab scholars, blames institutions for hindering development in three main areas: government, women's empowerment, and access to knowledge. The series continues with a focus on building a knowledge society (2003), better governance (2004), and empowering women (2005).

"Geography, Demographics, and Resources." National Institute for Technology and Liberal Education Arab World Project. Available online. URL: http://arabworld. nitle.org/introduction.php?module_id=4. Downloaded October 5, 2006. Explores the "material realities" that affect culture. Part of a comprehensive introduction to Arab civilization, this page links to scholarly articles about economics, population, water and oil supplies, and other natural resources.

Iqbal, Farrukh, and Mustapha Kamel Nabli. "Op-Ed: Poverty in the Middle East and North Africa: A Cause for Concern?" World Bank. Available online. URL: http:// siteresources.worldbank.org/INTMENA/Resources/Poverty_OpEd_06.pdf. Downloaded April 17, 2007. Debunks the myth of the oil-rich Middle East by pointing out the diversity (and stagnation) of regional economies. The World Bank economists argue that the region needs to improve the "return on education" and level the political and economic "playing field."

IRIN. "Syria: Interview with UNDP Resident Representative." United Nations Office for the Coordination of Humanitarian Affairs. March 15, 2005. Available online. URL: http://www.irinnews.org/report.aspx?reportid=41042. Downloaded January 7, 2007. Touches on the UNDP's three areas of concern in Syria: good governance, poverty alleviation, and sustainable energy and development.

El-Laithy, Heba, and Khalid Abu-Ismail. "Poverty in Syria: 1996–2004: Diagnosis and Pro-Poor Policy Considerations." United Nations Development Programme. June 2005. Available online. URL: http://www.undp.org.sy/publications/national/Poverty/Poverty_In_Syria_en.pdf. Downloaded September 12, 2006. Lays out the terrain for policy makers, government advisers, civil society, and Syria's development partners. A collaborative effort between the Syrian government, UNDP, and others, this report is based on the country's Household and Income and Expenditure survey.

Other Media

Educating Yaprak. Television Trust for the Environment series. Directed by Di Tatham. Series consultant Jenny Richards and series producer Luke Gawin. 26 min. DVD. Oley, Pa.: Bullfrog Films, 2005. Discusses Turkey's antipoverty campaign through education, especially targeting teenage girls in rural areas.

Interview with Marnia Lazreg. 47 min. National Institute for Technology and Liberal Education Arab World project, 2002. Available online. URL: http://arabworld.nitle.org/audiovisual.php?module_id=8&selected_feed=72. Sociologist Lazreg discusses the economic diversity of the Middle East and the impact of globalization, particularly on women.

The Miller's Tale: Bread for Life. Directed by Emily Marlow. 28 min. VHS. Oley, Pa.: Bullfrog Films, 2001. Documents attempts to introduce fortified bread flour to combat iron deficiency in Yemen and Egypt.

Waiting to Go. Directed by Charles Stewart and Di Tathem. 28 min. VHS. Oley, Pa.: Bullfrog Films, 2001. Shadows a Palestinian woman doctor on her hospital rounds in the Burj el-Baraineh refugee camp in Beirut, Lebanon.

Yemeni Futures. Television Trust for the Environment series. Directed by Ashley Bruce. Series consultant Jenny Richards and series producer Luke Gawin. 26 min. DVD. Oley, Pa.: Bullfrog Films, 2005. Assesses progress on the MDG in impoverished and mostly rural Yemen since the country's 1990 unification.

Fiction

*Hicyilmaz, Gaye. *Against the Storm.* Boston: Little Brown, 1992. Details urban poverty in Turkey. Based on a newspaper story, the novel follows a 12-year-old farm boy and his family from a drought-stricken village into debt in an Ankara shantytown.

*Laird, Elizabeth, with Sonia Nimr. *A Little Piece of Ground.* New York: Haymarket Books, 2006. Views the Israeli military occupation of Gaza through the eyes of a 12-year-old Palestinian boy and two friends, Muslim and Christian.

*Marston, Elsa. *Figs* and *Fate: Stories about Growing Up in the Arab World Today.* New York: George Brazilier, 2005. Offers a window on the Arab world through five short stories about teenagers. In "The Hand of Fatima," for instance, Aneesi works as a maid for a wealthy Lebanese family; in "In Line," Rania's city family adjusts to life in a rural village, where salaries are low.

*Schami, Rafik. *Hand Full of Stars.* Trans. by Rika Lesser. New York: Dutton, 1990. Reports through the fictional diary of a 14-year-old Syrian boy on the rippling effects of repression. In this autobiographical novel, the smart, ambitious hero chafes at working in his father's bakery and emulates his journalist hero by starting an underground newspaper.

POVERTY IN LATIN AMERICA AND THE CARIBBEAN

Books

Annis, Sheldon, and Peter Hakim. *Direct to the Poor: Grassroots Development in Latin America.* Boulder, Colo.: Lynne Rienner Publishers, 1988. Explores small-scale initiatives developed and controlled by locals.

*Bush, Jenna. *Ana's Story: A Journey of Hope.* New York: HarperCollins Children's Books, 2007. Recounts the tragedy and triumph of a 17-year-old Panamanian single mother with HIV. Daughter of President George W. Bush, the author met her subject while interning with UNICEF in Panama.

Dubois, Laurent, and John D. Garrigus. *Slave Revolution in the Caribbean, 1789–1804: A Brief History with Documents.* New York: Bedford/St. Martin's, 2006. Relates how the French Revolution inspired slaves in Saint-Domingue (later Haiti) to seize the island, resist Napoléon's troops, and achieve independence. Professors Dubois and Garrigus include many documents they have translated.

*Engle, Margarita. *The Poet Slave of Cuba: A Biography of Juan Francisco Manzano.* New York: Henry Holt, 2006. Describes the traumatic childhood of Manzano, born into slavery in 1797, who secretly learns to read. Cuban-American botanist and poet Engle writes Manzano's biography in verse.

*Franklin, Kristine L., and Nancy McGirr. *Out of the Dump: Writings and Photographs by Children from Guatemala.* New York : Lothrop, Lee & Shepard Books, 1995. Features poems and photograph by children who live in the municipal dump in Guatemala City.

Green, Duncan. *Hidden Lives: Voices of the Children in Latin America and the Caribbean.* London and Washington, D.C.: Cassell, 1998. Surveys the state of poor children. Aid analyst Green excerpts his personal conversations with children in Jamaica, Honduras, Nicaragua, Peru, Colombia, and Brazil.

Hooks, Margaret, ed. *Guatemalan Women Speak.* Washington, D.C.: Ecumenical Program on Central America and the Caribbean, 1993. Introduces primary sources talking frankly about work, racism, machismo, family, and activism.

Kidder, Tracy. *Mountains beyond Mountains: The Quest of Dr. Paul Farmer, a Man Who Would Cure the World.* New York: Random House, 2003. Chronicles the life of infectious-disease specialist Paul Farmer and his mission treating AIDS and drug-resistant tuberculosis in Peruvian slums, Russian prisons, and his first love, impoverished Haiti. Noted nonfiction journalist Kidder, who met Farmer by chance in Haiti, portrays the Harvard doctor-anthropologist as a profoundly driven and hopeful man.

Kozol, Jonathan. *Children of the Revolution: A Yankee Teacher in the Cuban Schools.* New York: Delacorte Press, 1978. Recalls Cuba's intensive and largely successful 1961 campaign to eradicate illiteracy. American muckraker Kozol visited Cuba briefly in 1976 and 1977 accompanied by a government translator.

Peabody, Sue, and Kelia Grinberg. *Slavery, Freedom, and the Law in the Atlantic World: A Brief History with Documents.* New York: Bedford/St. Martin's, 2007. Introduces and contextualizes primary sources from the French, British, Spanish, and Portuguese Empires. Professors Peabody and Grinberg include discussion questions and other points of entry into the material.

Poverty in Guatemala: A World Bank Country Study. Washington, D.C.: World Bank, 2004. Examines thoroughly the "high and deep" poverty in Guatemala and notes that the country has not met several targets set out in the 1996 peace accord.

Rosenberg, Tina. *Children of Cain: Violence and the Violent in Latin America.* New York: William Morrow, 1991. Profiles a Maoist guerrilla in Peru, a murdered judge in Colombia, a Chilean student leader, and other victims and perpetrators of political violence that has derailed the region's development. Rosenberg moved to the region for five years to collect this material. In 1996 she became an editorial writer at the *New York Times.*

Santiago, Esmeralda. *When I Was Puerto Rican.* New York: Vintage Books, 1994. Brings to life the author's warm but impoverished childhood between village and suburb in Puerto Rico. When Santiago turns 13, her unmarried mother moves to New York City, adding another layer to her cultural identity.

Articles, Reports, and Papers

Reel, Monte. "Bolivia's Rural Women Are Remaking Cities, Lives: For New Breadwinners, Transitions Can Be Trying." *Washington Post,* March 6, 2007, A1ff. Uses Bolivia as a case study of both difficulties and benefits for women in a global trend of rural-to-urban migration.

Roig-Franzia, Manuel. "Haiti's Lost Boys: Port-au-Prince Prison Reflects Overwhelming Problems Facing Country's Prison." *Washington Post,* March 3, 2007, A1ff. Listens to boys as young as six consigned to prison on charges both serious and vague. Activists are attempting to turn a warehouse for street children into a rehabilitation center in an impoverished country where "more than 200,000 children have lost one or both parents to AIDS and 300,000 more work as unpaid domestic servants."

Rosenberg, Tina. "Look at Brazil." *New York Times Magazine* (January 28, 2001), 26. Surveys the ravages of AIDS in developing nations before examining how Brazil managed to overcome health care distribution and drug-price barriers to deliver ARV drug therapy to the poor.

———. "The Taint of the Greased Palm." *New York Times Magazine* (August 10, 2003), 28–33. Considers the economic and social costs of official corruption with a close-up on Mexico and Chile, an exception. Foreign-policy editorialist Rosenberg blames history for a culture of corruption even though straightforward measures can fight graft effectively.

Web Documents

Deruyttere, Anne. "Indigenous Peoples and Sustainable Development: The Role of the Inter-American Development Bank." Washington, D.C.: Inter-American Development Bank, October 1997. Available online. URL: http://www.iadb.org/sds/doc/IND-97101E.PDF. Downloaded May 4, 2007. Highlights the main issues and demands of indigenous populations in Latin America, as well as the bank's targeted initiatives.

"Southern Voices." Resource Center of the Americas.org. Available online. URL: http://www.americas.org/southern_voices. Downloaded March 18, 2007. Publishes Spanish originals as well as English translations of newspaper editorials. An example: Orlando Nuñez Soto, "Helping the Rich Is Development, Helping the Poor Is Populism," which appeared in Nicaragua's *El Nuevo Diario* on July 21, 2006.

de Vylder, Stefan. "Poverty Reduction in South America: The Millennium Goal within or beyond Reach?" Swedish International Development Cooperation Agency. June 2002. Available online. URL: http://www.kus.uu.se/SAPoverty.pdf. Downloaded April 17, 2007. Surveys income poverty on the continent and attributes its entrenchment to unequal education and poor institutions. Economist de Vylder offers a clear perspective from a small-nation donor.

Other Media

Dalton, Scott, and Margarita Martínez. *La Sierra*. Produced and directed by Scott Dalton. 84 min. DVD. Brooklyn, N.Y.: First Run/Icarus Films, 2005. In Spanish with English subtitles. Profiles three young slumdwellers in Medellín, Colombia's second-largest city, infamous for unemployment, violence, and drug trafficking.

The Devil's Miner. Produced and directed by Kief Davidson and Richard Ladkani. DVD. 82 min. Los Angeles and New York: Urban Landscapes and La Mita Loca Films, 2005. Follows Bolivian children into the silver mines near Potosí, Bolivia. This award-winning documentary narrated by 14-year-old miner Basilio Vargas has helped raise more than a million dollars for the impoverished children of the region. Information about the film and child miners worldwide is available online from the Public Broadcasting System (http://www.pbs.org/independentlens/devilsminer/film.html).

Kincaid, Jamaica. *Life and Debt*. Produced and directed by Stephanie Black. 86 min. New York: New Yorker Video, 2003. Connects poverty in Jamaica, birthplace of noted writer Kincaid, with international lending practices.

Klein, Naomi. *The Take.* Directed by Avi Lewis and produced by Barna-Alper Productions and the National Film Board of Canada. 87 min. VHS. Brooklyn, N.Y.: First Run/Icarus Films, 2004. Captures antiglobalization sentiment as unemployed auto workers occupy their idled factory in Argentina.

Fiction

*Ellis, Deborah. *I Am a Taxi.* Toronto, Canada: Groundwood Books, 2006. Dramatizes the struggle of a Bolivian farm boy whose parents are mistakenly jailed and who falls prey to cocaine producers.

POVERTY IN ASIA

Books

Chayes, Sarah. *The Punishment of Virtue: Inside Afghanistan after the Taliban.* New York: Penguin Press, 2006. Gives a close-up view of corruption and warlord culture, abetted by American intervention, that have hindered Afghan development. Former National Public Radio reporter Chayes served as field director for Afghans for Civil Society, an NGO run by the president's brother, before turning to agribusiness.

Dobbin, Christine, ed. *Basic Documents in the Development of Modern India and Pakistan, 1835–1947.* London and New York: Van Nostrand Reinhold, 1970. Collects noteworthy primary material—speeches, writings, and documents—produced by British colonial administrators and Indian political and social activists.

Hayslip, Le Ly, and Charles Jay Wurts. *When Heaven and Earth Changed Places.* New York: Doubleday, 1989. Tells Hayslip's life story, from her childhood in a Vietnamese farming village torn apart by French colonialism and the Vietnam War to single motherhood in the city. Hayslip eventually married an American and started the East Meets West Foundation, which helps children and families living in poverty in Vietnam.

*Kuklin, Susan. *Iqbal Masih and the Crusaders against Child Slavery.* New York: Henry Holt, 1998. Profiles Pakistani activists Eshan Ullah Khan of the Bonded Labor Liberation Front and Iqbal Masih, who escaped from a carpet factory, drew outraged attention to child labor, and was shot to death on a return visit to his country in 1995.

Luce, Edward. *In Spite of the Gods: The Strange Rise of Modern India.* New York: Doubleday, 2007. Describes India's staggering social and economic changes around the turn of the millennium, exploring culture, development, unemployment, political corruption, and democracy. British journalist Luce, who is married to an Indian and works in New Delhi, compares the boom in the service and computer industries to an island "in a sea of indifferent farmland."

*Marrin, Albert. *Mao Tse-Tung and His China.* New York: Viking Kestrel, 1990. Covers the rise of the Communist peasant army from 1919 to 1949 and state surveillance in the People's Republic of China. Critics of the book fault history professor

Marrin for inconsistency in treating Mao as both hero and villain but find it to be a generally accurate look at a country undergoing tremendous change.

Pran, Dith, and Kim DePaul, eds. *Children of Cambodia's Killing Fields: Memoirs of Survivors.* New Haven, Conn.: Yale University Press, 1997. Assembles stories from 29 refugees who were mostly middle-class children when Pol Pot's regime wreaked terror on Cambodia at the end of the 1970s. *New York Times* photojournalist Pran, himself the subject of the movie *The Killing Fields,* tracks down genocide survivors who describe starvation, beatings, and misery.

Tenberken, Sabriye. *My Path Leads to Tibet: The Inspiring Story of How One Young Blind Woman Brought Hope to the Blind Children of Tibet.* New York: Arcade Publishing, 2003. Describes her quest to found a school to teach blind Tibetan children and to found an international mission, Braille without Borders. Blinded at 13 by retinal disease, Tenberken studied Tibetan in her native Germany but could not get a job. Once in Tibet, which has high rates of eye problems because its high altitude increases sun exposure, she discovers blind children hidden away in huts because of shame about their condition.

Ung, Loung. *First They Killed My Father: A Daughter of Cambodia Remembers.* New York: HarperCollins, 2000. Describes the destruction of a prosperous Cambodian family during the 1970s. Ung, now living in the United States and an anti-landmine activist, recalls her parents' killing, her training as a child soldier in a work camp for orphans, and finally her escape with an older brother to a refugee camp in Thailand at age 10. In the sequel, *Lucky Child: A Daughter of Cambodia Reunites with the Sister She Left Behind,* she juxtaposes her teen years as a poor refugee in Vermont with her sister's struggle to survive hunger and conflict in postwar Cambodia.

Zoya, with John Follain and Rita Cristofari. *Zoya's Story: An Afghan Woman's Battle for Freedom.* New York: Morrow, 2002. Describes a teenager's flight from Taliban-ruled Afghanistan after her parents, opposition activists, disappeared, presumably killed on the orders of fundamentalist warlords. Human-rights activist Zoya and journalists Follain and Cristofari discuss her mother's work with the Revolutionary Association of the Women of Afghanistan.

Articles, Reports, and Papers

Arnold, Wayne. "Hook Up Rural Asia, Some Say, and Ease Poverty." *New York Times,* January 19, 2001, C1. Presents debate on the value and the means of narrowing the "digital divide," with Indonesia as a case study. Should extending cell phone and Internet connections beyond the city be a priority in countries with extreme poverty?

Kapur, Akash. "Poor but Prosperous." *Atlantic Monthly* 282, no. 3 (November 1997), 40ff. Looks at the Indian state of Kerala, where income is low but literacy and other quality-of-life measures are high, and where pressures are building to add more industrial development to join the rest of the country's free-market transformation.

Lancaster, John. "Next Stop, Squalor." *Smithsonian* (March 2007), 96ff. Joins a tour of the Dharavi squatter settlement in Mumbai, perhaps the largest slum in Asia.

Lancaster, a *Washington Post* reporter, considers the ethics of poverty tourism—"poorism"—which he concludes can lead to understanding.

Lawton, John. "Rebuilding in Afghanistan." *Saudi Aramco World* 53, no. 6 (November–December 2002): 14–31. Surveys postwar reconstruction across Afghanistan with a sidebar on the work of Muslim agencies.

Rosenberg, Tina. "John Kamm's Third Way." *New York Times Magazine* (March 3, 2002), 58ff. Reports on a businessman's efforts to leverage political-prisoner releases in China. Journalist Rosenberg raises questions about the responsibility of international corporations, some of which operate factories in China that pay less than 20¢ an hour and require 15-hour work days.

Werner, Lewis. "Bangladesh Calling." *Saudi Aramco World* 50, no. 3 (May–June 1999): 44–51. Reports on the Grameen Bank's telecommunications initiatives in Bangladesh, with a mention of microcredit ventures in the Arab world.

Web Documents

Chayes, Sarah. "Days of Lies and Roses: Selling Out Afghanistan." *Boston Review* (March–April 2007). Available online. URL: http://bostonreview.net/BR32.2/chayes.html. Downloaded March 27, 2007. Critiques widespread corruption that has intensified since the U.S. "war on terror" in Afghanistan. Onetime radio reporter Chayes runs a soap-making cooperative that aims to give farmers an alternative to growing poppies, the raw ingredient of heroin.

Kremer, Michael, and David Clingingsmith. "Delivering Health Care." *Boston Review* (March–April 2007). Available online. URL: http://bostonreview.net/BR32.2/kremercling.html. Downloaded March 27, 2007. Explores weaknesses in developing countries' health care, from absenteeism in government clinics to weak preventative services among private practitioners. Economists Kremer and Clingingsmith report positive results from Cambodia's contracting private, nonprofit organizations to deliver health care in certain districts.

O'Connor, Rory. "India: Hole in the Wall." *Frontline*, October 2002. Public Broadcasting System. Available online. URL: http://www.pbs.org/frontlineworld/stories/india/thestory.html. Downloaded March 20, 2007. Reports on computer scientist Dr. Sugata Mitra's "Hole in the Wall" experiment to close the digital divide by giving children on the street access to computers with a high-speed Internet connection. Includes a video link to the segment.

Olken, Benjamin A. "The Problem of Corruption." *Boston Review* (March–April 2007). Available online. URL: http://bostonreview.net/BR32.2/olken.html. Downloaded March 27, 2007. Reports on experiments in Indonesia with auditing and community monitoring to curb corruption during the building of a road.

Other Media

Alpert, Jon. *To Have and Have Not.* Directed by Jon Alpert and produced by Matthew O'Neill. 75 min. VHS. New York: WNET, 2003. Contrasts wealth and poverty in contemporary China, touching on WTO policy and challenges of modernization.

Anonymously Yours. Produced and directed by Gayle Ferraro. 60 min. DVD. Berkeley, Calif.: Berkeley Media, 2003. Interviews four Burmese women forced into prostitution by poverty as part of an undercover exposé of the Southeast Asian sex trade.

Bruce, Ashley. *It Takes a Village*. Directed by Ashley Bruce and produced by TVE International and BBC Worldwide. 23 min. DVD. Oley, Pa.: Bullfrog Films, 2002. Features a new community health care center in Chakaria, Bangladesh, constructed after the devastating 1991 typhoon.

Feingold, David. *Trading Women*. Directed by David Feingold and produced by Feingold and Dean W. Slotar. 77 min. VHS. New York: Ophidian Films, 2002. Blames police corruption and poverty, landlessness, and exclusion for snaring Thailand's hill people in the sex trade.

Rice, Rodney. *India: Working to End Child Labor*. Directed by Ruth Meehan. 26 min. DVD. Princeton, N.J.: Films for the Humanities & Sciences, 2004. Documents the work of five children under age 12 as well as a rehabilitation program started by a political science professor.

Secret Nation. Produced by Mitchell Koss, Laura Ling, and Janet Choi. 19 min. DVD. Princeton, N.J.: Films for the Humanities & Sciences, 2003. Sneaks into food-starved North Korea for an undercover look at poverty and repression. Channel One journalist Janet Choi poses as a tourist for rare footage within the loner nation-state.

Seeds of Plenty, Seeds of Sorrow. Directed by Manjira Datta. 52 min. DVD. Oley, Pa.: Bullfrog Films, 2002. Dwells on the long-term disappointments of the Green Revolution, which increased food production but led to pesticide poisoning and a new serf class.

Small Change, Big Business: The Women's Bank of Bangladesh 10 Years Later. Produced and directed by Mark Aardenburg. 55 min. DVD. Princeton, N.J.: Films for the Humanities & Sciences, 2006. Revisits the Grameen Bank in the footsteps of an earlier documentary to explore the long-term impact of microcredit in a Muslim community. The film includes an interview with bank founder Muhammad Yunus.

Fiction

*Ellis, Deborah. *The Breadwinner*. Toronto, Canada: Groundwood Books, 2002. Describes through the eyes of a young girl repressive rule by the extremist Muslim Taliban in Afghanistan during the 1990s. Canadian activist and writer Ellis continues the tale of Parvana, who dresses as a boy to try to find her family, through two more novels, *Parvana's Journey* and *Mud City*, about a refugee camp. Ellis includes a map, glossary, and background note.

*McCormick, Patricia. *Sold*. New York: Hyperion Books, 2006. Describes the sale of a Nepalese village girl into prostitution as payment for a debt. Novelist McCormick bases this spare, first-person tale on interviews with sex-trade workers in India and Nepal.

*Whelan, Gloria. *Homeless Bird*. New York: HarperCollins, 2000. Lays out the predicament of a poor girl married—and widowed—at 13 and then abandoned by her in-laws. Critics questioned the upbeat ending although the novel won a National Book Award.

POVERTY IN SUB-SAHARAN AFRICA

Books

Asgedom, Mawi. *Of Beetles and Angels: A Boy's Remarkable Journey from a Refugee Camp to Harvard.* New York: Little, Brown and Company, 2002. Tells the story of the author and his family, who fled civil war in Ethiopia for a Sudanese refugee camp and eventually landed in Wheaton, Illinois, where the author grew up amidst poverty, prejudice, bewilderment, and "angels."

Beah, Ishmael. *A Long Way Gone: Memoirs of a Boy Soldier.* New York: Farrar Straus Giroux, 2007. Recalls a teenage boy's ordeal during the 1990s Sierra Leone civil war—from wandering with other orphans through the bush to killing rebels under the command of military officers who fed him drugs.

Berkeley, Bill. *The Graves Are Not Yet Full: Race, Tribe and Power in the Heart of Africa.* New York: Basic Books, 2001. Argues that tyranny has produced brutal ethnic conflict in such African countries as Liberia, the DRC, South Africa, Sudan, Uganda, and Rwanda. Journalist Berkeley, a *New York Times* editorial writer who covered Africa for prominent newspapers and magazines, ends with the conviction of a genocide perpetrator in Rwanda—a hopeful glimmer of justice.

*Engledorf, Laura, ed. *Africa: Opposing Viewpoints.* New York: Greenhaven Press, 2005. Presents divergent opinions about problems Africa faces, control of AIDS, preservation of wild lands, and beneficial policies.

French, Howard. *A Continent for the Taking: The Tragedy and Hope of Africa.* New York: Alfred A. Knopf, 2004. Follows the author's personal and professional sojourns in Ivory Coast, Mali, Nigeria, the DRC, and Liberia. *New York Times* reporter French, part of a strong African-American family and son of a public-health doctor, critiques Clinton administration policy as emblematic of Western indifference and misguided intervention.

Gourevitch, Philip. *We Wish to Inform You That Tomorrow We Will Be Killed with Our Families: Stories from Rwanda.* New York: Picador, 1998. Puts in context the 1994 genocide, including international indifference. A *New Yorker* writer, Gourevitch traveled to Rwanda shortly after the killings and interviewed many survivors.

Hochschild, Adam. *King Leopold's Ghost: A Story of Greed, Terror, and Heroism in Colonial Africa.* Boston: Houghton Mifflin, 1998. Unearths the atrocities against Africans in King Leopold II's personal colony, the Congo Free State, until the Belgian government took it over in 1908. Journalist Hochschild heroizes Edmund Morel and other antislavery activists.

Lewis, Stephen. *Race against Time.* Toronto, Canada: House of Anansi Press, 2005. Rails against Africa's mistreatment by colonial powers ("Cold Warriors") and international financial institutions. Canadian diplomat Lewis served as a UN special envoy for HIV/AIDS in Africa and wrote this series of passionate and conversational lectures upon his return home. He proposes dramatic change in current aid strategies.

Mathabane, Mark. *Kaffir Boy: The True Story of a Black Youth's Coming of Age in Apartheid South Africa*. New York: Macmillan, 1986. Describes the author's childhood in a black shantytown north of the capital, Johannesburg. Despite gangs and police raids, illiteracy and drunkenness, writer Mathabane taught himself to read and play tennis and won a tennis scholarship to an American university. His other memoirs, *African Women* and *Miriam's Song*, chronicle the struggle of his grandmother, mother, and sister.

Articles, Reports, and Papers

Goodwin, Jan. "Heart of Darkness." *Harper's Bazaar* 3,472 (March 2001): 450ff. Exposes the ravages of AIDS in Zambia before the push to expand treatment with ARV drugs.

Harford, Tim. "Why Countries Are Poor." *Reason* 37 (March 2006): 32ff. Blames bad governance for perpetuating poverty when other development pieces—new technology, infrastructure, and education—are available. Visiting Cameroon, financial journalist Harford attributes the African nation's dysfunction to official theft, waste, and "oppressive regulations."

Rosenberg, Tina. "When a Pill Is Not Enough." *New York Times Magazine* (August 6, 2006), 40ff. Takes South Africa as a case study to discuss how stigma and denial about AIDS render effective treatment useless.

Salopek, Paul. "Who Rules the Forest?" *National Geographic* 208 (September 2005), 74–95. Marvels at Pygmy lifestyle and alludes to the impact of civil war on their forests and culture.

Steinitz, Lucy Y. "Meeting the Challenge with God on Our Side: Churches and Faith-Based Organizations Confront the AIDS Pandemic in Namibia." *International Review of Mission* 95 (January–April 2006): 92ff. Considers churches' significant contribution to prevention, treatment, and orphan care in southern African countries. Steinitz, a Ph.D. aid worker in Namibia, draws eight lessons.

Web Documents

Commission for Africa. "Chapter 2—Lost Decades: Legacy and Causes," pp. 101–120. In *Our Common Interest: Report of the Commission for Africa.* March 11, 2005. Available online. URL: http://www.commissionforafrica.org/english/report/thereport/english/11-03-05_cr_chapter_2.pdf. Downloaded April 25, 2007. Sets out in clear language and graphics the multiple causes of African poverty.

GlobalSecurity.org. "Congo Civil War." Available online. URL: http://www.globalsecurity.org/military/world/war/congo.htm. Accessed December 12, 2006. Identifies the key players and events in the DRC's regional war.

Khonde, César Nkuku. "An Oral History of HIV/AIDS in the Congo." In Philippe Denis and Charles Becker, eds. *The HIV/AIDS Epidemic in Sub-Saharan Africa in a Historical Perspective*. October 2006. Available online. URL: http://www.refer.sn/rds/IMG/pdf/19NKUKUKONDE.pdf. Downloaded February 20, 2007. Charts the spread of disease and popular attitudes about it, quoting doctors, students, song lyrics, and other sources.

Mutume, Gumisai. "African Migration: From Tensions to Solutions." *Africa Renewal* 19, no. 4 (January 2006): 1. Available online. URL: http://www.un.org/ecosocdev/geninfo/afrec/vol19no4/194migration.html. Downloaded February 25, 2007. Considers what poor countries often see as a double standard: While industrialized countries promote easing barriers on goods, services, and capital (which they mostly supply), they are also restricting the flow of labor (which most often comes from developing countries).

Pouilly, Cécile. "Huge Country, Huge Problems, Huge Potential: Can the DR Congo Turn the Page?" *Refugees* 145, no. 1 (January 2007): 4–14. UN High Commissioner for Refugees is available online. URL: http://www.unhcr.org/publ/PUBL/45b091dc2.pdf. Downloaded February 15, 2007. Surveys the DRC's "descent into anarchy," people's coping strategies, difficulties of delivering humanitarian aid to IDPs and refugees, and hope for the future. This cover story includes an interview with a Congolese custom officer who witnessed rapes and other war atrocities in the east.

Salopek, Paul. "Africa—the Ailing Continent," "CEOs of War Bleed Angola," "The River Congo." *Chicago Tribune*, January 9,–December 12, 2000. Available online. URL: http://www.pulitzer.org/year/2001/international-reporting/works/index2.html. Downloaded April 7, 2007. Covers Africas woes, including sleeping sickness, AIDS, environmental degradation, and civil wars. Foreign correspondent Salopek won the 2001 Pulitzer Prize for international reporting.

Other Media

Darwin's Nightmare. Directed by Hubert Sauper and produced by Edouard Mauriat, et al. 111 min. DVD. Collingwood, Australia: Madman Entertainment/Madman Films, 2006. Studies the ecological and economic impact of an invading fish species in Tanzania. Migrant laborers, many with AIDS, catch the Nile perch, a prized food in Europe.

Lax, Lisa, et al. *Emmanuel's Gift*. Directed and produced by Lisa Lax and Nancy Stern. 80 min. DVD. Los Angeles: First Look Pictures, 2005. Follows a Ghanaian with a deformed leg who biked across his West African country to raise awareness about the abilities and potential of the disabled.

Left Behind: Kenya's AIDS Orphans. Directed and produced by Christof Putzel. 34 min. DVD. Princeton, N.J.: Films for the Humanities & Sciences, 2002. Sees the epidemic through the eyes of HIV-infected children in an orphanage and on the streets of Nairobi.

Mauritius: An Island of Ingenuity. Directed and produced by Jeanine Isabel Butler for the Economic Development Institute of the World Bank. 30 min. VHS. Princeton, N.J.: Films for the Humanities & Sciences, 1998. Cheers the economic gains of this Indian Ocean island, which has diversified its economy from agriculture (mostly sugarcane) to tourism, industry, and finance.

Rice, Rodney. *Malawi: A Nation Going Hungry.* Directed by Ruth Meehan. 26 min. DVD. Princeton, N.J.: Films for the Humanities & Sciences, 2004. Critiques IMF and WTO pressure to end farm subsidies in a country where a quarter of the population lives in absolute poverty and AIDS and hunger have orphaned more than a million children.

Strasburg, Toni. *My Mother Built This House.* Directed by Toni Strasburg and produced by TVE. 28 min. VHS. Oley, Pa.: Bullfrog Films, 2001. Focuses on the women in the South African Homeless People's Federation who make the most of a government grant program for building houses.

"The Story of Africa." BBC World Service radio project. Available online. URL: http://www.bbc.co.uk/worldservice/africa/features/storyofafrica. Downloaded November 12, 2007. Enlists historians in presenting the continent's history from early origins through modern independence from an African perspective. Links to 12 hours of history programming, an hour of discussion on the study of history, and three hours of debates on topics such as slavery and colonialism.

Fiction

*Levitin, Sonia. *Dream Freedom.* New York: Harcourt, 2000. Alternates stories of Dinka slaves in Sudan with the efforts of U.S. schoolchildren to raise money for their release. Levitin bases this fictional account on real-life Colorado teacher Barbara Vogel and her fifth-grade students who founded S.T.O.P. (Slavery That Oppresses People).

*Mead, Alice. *Year of No Rain.* New York: Farrar, Straus, Giroux, 2003. Follows the trek of an 11-year-old boy caught between drought and Sudan's civil war.

*Naidoo, Beverley. *No Turning Back: A Novel of South Africa.* New York: HarperCollins, 1997. Describes a boy's life on the streets of Johannesburg after running away from an abusive home. South African–born children's author Naidoo writes often about African problems.

———. *Out of Bounds: Seven Stories of Conflict and Hope.* New York: HarperCollins, 2003. Portrays the injustice of South African apartheid in short stories set between 1948 and 2000. Includes a foreword by South African archbishop and Nobel Peace Prize winner Desmond Tutu.

Chronology

618 C.E.

- In China, the Tang dynasty ushers in an era of economic growth. Trade along the Silk Road expands the merchant class and brings contact with India and the West. Rice production increases, and peasants allowed a lifelong lease on land have means to feed themselves and pay taxes.

832

- In Baghdad, capital of the Muslim Abbasid caliphate, the Bayt al-Hikma (House of Wisdom) sponsors translation of ancient Greek, Persian, and Indian works of science and catalyzes a golden age of Arab astronomy, medicine, pharmacy, philosophy, and literature.

1114

- In India, astronomer-mathematician Bhaskaracharya (Bhaskara) is born. Head of an observatory, he writes works on arithmetic, algebra, and the planets that anticipate modern sciences.

1324

- Mali's Muslim king Mansa Musa makes a pilgrimage to Mecca. Stopping at cities such as Cairo, Egypt, on his way to the Arabian Peninsula, he showers the poor with gold. His vast caravan of slaves, servants, followers, and gold-bearing camels draws attention to the wealth of West Africa. Under Mansa Musa, Timbuktu becomes a cultural crossroads famous for its libraries and universities.

1348

- Spread along trade routes, a bubonic plague pandemic reaches Europe, killing perhaps 20 million—a third of the population.

1440

- In Mexico, Moctezuma I becomes the Aztec's "Great Speaker." During his almost three-decade reign, he enlarges the empire through conquest and negotiation and oversees construction of an aqueduct supplying freshwater to the capital city.

1453

- Ottoman Turks conquer Constantinople, blocking European access to a popular trade route and spurring European explorers to search for a water route rather than overland access to the East.

1482

- Portuguese navigator Diogo Cão enters the Congo River in West Africa.

1492

- Catholic monarchs Ferdinand and Isabella expel Muslims and Jews from the Iberian Peninsula and agree to finance Christopher Columbus's search for a western route to the Indies.
- Columbus stumbles into the Americas.

1494

- In the name of spreading Christianity, Spain and Portugal divide the world in two with the Treaty of Tordesillas. They draw a line down the middle of the Atlantic, with Spain getting the west—the Americas (except Brazil)—and Portugal the east, including Africa and India.

1510

- In the Spanish colonies in the Americas, the first shipment of slaves arrives.
- In India, the Portuguese colonize Goa.

1537

- Influenced by Bartolomé de Las Casas, Pope Paul III declares the Indians of the Americas rational beings with souls, worthy of protection. The Spanish continue to grab their land and compel their labor, however.

1556

- In China, an earthquake kills about 830,000 people.

Chronology

1619

- In the Virginia colony, Africans arrive—either as slaves or indentured servants. A Dutch ship captain, who captured them from a Spanish ship, exchanges them for food.

1693

- In France, famine kills roughly 2 million people.

1712

- In New York City, 23 slaves set fire to a building and shoot, stab, and beat to death about nine whites. The city executes the offenders and passes strict laws regulating slave conduct.

1732

- In Japan, a two-year famine follows an earthquake. Food and land policy contribute to shortages.

1739

- In South Carolina, the Stono Rebellion grows as runaway slaves murder whites on their march toward the promise of land and freedom in Spanish Florida. Afterward, the colony passes the Negro Act, which bars slaves from growing their own food, meeting in groups, earning money, and learning to read.

1740

- In Indonesia, under control of the Dutch East Indies Company, Dutch soldiers and citizens massacre more than 10,000 Chinese residents and later, to avert united rebellions, impose restrictions isolating the Chinese immigrants.

1757

- In India, Major-General Robert Clive of the British East India Company defeats the nawab of Bengal (a provincial governor backed by the French) at the Battle of Plassey, beginning British rule of the subcontinent.

1766

- In the Hudson Valley of New York, tenant farmers withhold rent and rise up against wealthy landlords.

1769

- In Bengal, India, a four-year famine coupled with diseases such as smallpox kills about 10 million people.

1776

- Fed up with "taxation without representation," American colonists break with the British Crown, asserting in the Declaration of Independence "that all men are created equal, that they are endowed by their Creator with certain unalienable Rights, that among these are Life, Liberty and the pursuit of Happiness." In the decades following, many states, particularly in the North, begin emancipating slaves and outlawing the slave trade. The seven-year Revolutionary War causes personal hardship and plunges the new nation into debt. In its wake, however, long-term economic opportunities improve.
- Scottish economist Adam Smith publishes *An Inquiry into the Nature and Causes of the Wealth of Nations*, an influential text arguing that government should keep its hands off commerce (laissez-faire).

1786

- In Massachusetts, impoverished farmers and Revolutionary War veterans join Shays's Rebellion to protest the fining and imprisoning of debtors.

1789

- In France, peasants riot, and in the midst of revolution, the new National Assembly issues a Declaration of the Rights of Man and of the Citizen, which include "liberty, property, security, and resistance to oppression."

1793

- Eli Whitney patents the cotton gin, which reduces the labor needed to pick seeds from cotton but increases demand for land and slaves in growing it.

1794

- France abolishes slavery—but revives it in 1802 before finally banning it throughout the empire in 1848.

1800

- In Virginia, the state militia thwarts a revolt of more than 1,000 slaves led by Gabriel Prosser.

1804

- Haiti declares its independence from France after more than a decade of slave revolt led by Toussaint-Louverture and others. Not until 1862, however, does the United States extend the island nation diplomatic recognition.

Chronology

1807

- Britain abolishes the Atlantic slave trade and pressures other nations to follow.
- The United States bars the importation of slaves.

1811

- Spain abolishes slavery at home and in its colonies.

1815

- In Indonesia, the volcanic eruption of Mount Tambora kills at least 10,000 people locally and perhaps 60,000 more worldwide over the next year ("the year without a summer") as ash blocks the sun and crops fail, especially in New England and Europe.

1826

- In Massachusetts, traveling lecturer Josiah Holbrook sets up the first lyceum, a local study group that grew into a movement for universal, free, and lifelong education.

1831

- In Virginia, slave preacher Nat Turner leads a briefly successful slave rebellion that provokes more repressive laws.

1832

- In New Orleans, 4,000 people die in October alone, part of a global cholera pandemic from Russia to the United States.

1833

- Britain outlaws slavery (gradually) in all its colonies.

1834

- Across the United States, riots reveal ethnic, racial, and economic tensions among the poor and working class. In New York City, unskilled workers attack the home, churches, and businesses of African Americans and abolitionists. In Philadelphia, a largely Irish mob targets blacks. President Andrew Jackson sends federal troops to subdue a fight among Irish workmen along the Chesapeake and Ohio Canal from Washington, D.C.

1837

- In the United States, a bank crisis and a decline in cotton prices sparks a panic that grows into a depression marked by food riots and widespread unemployment (about a third of workers).

1838

- In the United States, about 4,000 Cherokee die on the "Trail of Tears" as federal troops march them from Georgia to Oklahoma. Although the Cherokee have been challenging the Indian Removal Act for eight years, the Supreme Court rules against them.

1840

- In Guatemala, Rafael Carrera installs himself as dictator-president after leading an indigenous uprising. He restores the Catholic Church to power and promotes conservative, authoritarian governments across Central America.

1845

- In Europe, potato crops fail, leading to a famine that kills about 2 million people. Particularly hard hit is Ireland, and millions of tenant farmers strike out over the next few years for Canada, Australia, and the United States.

1847

- In the United States, New Hampshire becomes the first state to institute a 10-hour workday.
- In Britain, the "Ten Hours Bill" limits women and children to a 63-hour work week, with Saturday afternoons off.

1848

- In Europe, rising food prices and industrial slowdowns feed long-simmering discontent with aristocratic rule, and worker-peasant revolutions spread from Italy and France to Poland, Germany, and the Austrian Empire.
- Cholera travels from port to port in a global epidemic that killed possibly a million people in Russia alone and that prompts Britain's first public health act.

1852

- Harriet Beecher Stowe's antislavery novel, *Uncle Tom's Cabin*, sells 300,000 copies in its debut year.

1856

- In Nicaragua, adventurer William Walker—one of many North Americans competing for transportation routes from the Atlantic to the Pacific—takes over the country, declaring English the national language and legalizing slavery. A year later, Central American forces oust Walker, whom U.S. Marines evacuate.

1857

- In the United States, the collapse of a life insurance company triggers a panic that snowballs into an economic depression.
- In India, local troops (sepoys) mutiny against their employer, the British East India Company. After putting down widespread rebellion, the British transfer administration of the colony to the Crown and promise reform.
- The U.S. Supreme Court rules in the Dred Scott case that slaves, ex-slaves, and their descendants have no right to citizenship.

1861

- In the United States, the Civil War begins.
- Congress enacts the first income tax to pay war costs but repeals it in 1872.

1862

- In the United States, the Homestead Act offers western land to settlers who farm it, although many claims end up with land speculators.

1863

- U.S. president Abraham Lincoln issues the Emancipation Proclamation, which frees all slaves in rebel territory.

1865

- The United States bars slavery with the Thirteenth Amendment of the Constitution; Congress authorizes the Freedmen's Bureau to help former slaves.
- In London, evangelist William Booth founds the Salvation Army, which grows into a major relief organization.

1866

- In New York City alone, 2,000 people die in a cholera pandemic that spans from Europe to the United States.
- In Tennessee, Confederate veterans found the Ku Klux Klan to resist social reordering. It disbands within three years but revives around 1920, tapping anti-immigrant sentiment and rural unease with urbanization.

1870

- The United States ratifies the Fifteenth Amendment to the Constitution, forbidding states to deny the right to vote based on race, color, or previous condition of servitude. Southern states later violate the amendment and bar blacks from voting through grandfather clauses, poll taxes, literacy tests, and violence.

- In Algeria, the French colonial government makes local Jews citizens—but not Muslims, unless they renounce their religion.

1873

- In the United States, a bank failure triggers widespread bankruptcy and a stock exchange crash, while drought and grasshoppers cripple western farms. The depression lasts six years and guts most unions.

1876

- In China, drought leads to three years of famine that kills 9 million people.

1877

- In the United States, railroad workers' strikes over pay cuts halt commerce until governors call in militia. Violent confrontations result and foreshadow the labor-industry clashes of the next two decades.

1878

- In the United States, yellow fever kills about 14,000 along the southern Gulf Coast states, while smallpox ravages the Dakota Territory.

1879

- In the United States, printer Henry George publishes *Progress and Poverty*, a worldwide best seller that fueled debates about increasing economic inequality.
- In Pennsylvania, former cavalry officer Richard Pratt founds the military Carlisle Indian Industrial School to "kill the Indian, save the man." For the next 50 years, educators attempt to obliterate "uncivilized" Native American culture by sending children to off-reservation boarding schools.

1881

- In Alabama, educator Booker T. Washington founds Tuskegee Normal and Industrial Institute dedicated to vocational education for African Americans.
- In Russia, after a bomb kills his father, Czar Alexander III blames the Jews, unleashing pogroms that kill many and reduce others to poverty. More than 2 million Jews flee Russia between 1880 and 1920.

1882

- In the United States, the Chinese Exclusion Act bars Chinese laborers and denies citizenship to those residents who had flocked to America in the 1850s to escape poverty and join the gold rush. Renewals keep the act in force until 1943.

Chronology

1884

- The Berlin Conference on African Affairs greenlights the "scramble for Africa" by disguising imperialism as a move to end slavery and the slave trade.

1885

- In Saratoga, New York, young scholars such as John Bates Clark, Woodrow Wilson, and Henry C. Adams form the American Economics Association, which faults laissez-faire and argues for a government role in extending the benefits of progress to all citizens.
- Belgian king Leopold II begins milking his Congo Free State in a reign of terror that lasts more than two decades.

1886

- In Chicago, hotbed of labor activism, a bomb thrown at police during a rally in Haymarket Square touches off a riot, temporarily derailing the eight-hour-day movement and leading to the execution of political radicals.

1887

- In China, a Yellow River flood kills 900,000 people.

1889

- In Chicago, Jane Addams opens Hull-House.
- Upstream from Johnstown, Pennsylvania, a dam collapses, and flooc waters churning with debris crash through the steel town, killing 2,209 people and destroying homes. Relief pours in from around the world, but lawsuits fail against the dam's owner, the South Fork Fishing and Hunting Club, a resort for wealthy industrialists.
- In *The Gospel of Wealth*, moralistic iron-and-steel magnate Andrew Carnegie admonishes millionaires to invest in society and oversee their philanthropy.

1892

- In St. Louis, Missouri, the Populist Party casts itself as the voice of working folks, particularly farmers, and enters a candidate in the presidential race on a platform promising an eight-hour day, a graduated income tax, and government ownership of railroads. Although the party fades out after 1908, one of its planks—direct election of senators—becomes law in 1913.

1893

- A worldwide depression compounds falling farm prices and a slowdown in construction and railroad expansion in the United States to cause a profound depression: Unemployment tops 10 percent for at least five years, with a quarter of industrial workers out of jobs in some cities.

1894

- Ohio sandstone quarrier Jacob Coxey leads "Coxey's army," made up of about 400 unemployed, on a march on Washington, D.C., to demand that the government create jobs.
- The new U.S. Bureau of Entomology notes that the cotton-infesting boll weevil has crossed from Mexico into Texas. Crop damage across the South helps spur the Great Migration of African Americans to the North, which promises less discrimination and more jobs.

1896

- In the United States, the Supreme Court upholds segregation—"separate but equal"—in *Plessy v. Ferguson* despite a dissent from Justice John Marshall Harlan, who says that "the destinies of the two races, in this country, are indissolubly linked together."

1900

- In China, the Boxer Rebellion targets Christian missionaries and European diplomats to protest their presence and special privileges. Instead of driving out foreigners, the uprising gives them an excuse to send troops to Peking (Beijing) and extend their influence.

1902

- In the United States, the federal government mediates for the first time in a labor dispute as Theodore Roosevelt meets with the striking United Mine Workers union. The five-month standoff that threatened winter fuel supplies ends with a pay increase, a cut in hours, and public sympathy for the miners.

1903

- In Kensington, Pennsylvania, in the midst of a textile strike that includes 16,000 children, Mother Jones leads a march of child millworkers to the Long Island home of President Theodore Roosevelt.

1905

- In Russia, hard-pressed industrial workers and their families march peacefully to the Winter Palace to protest abusive working conditions and the war that has raised bread prices and brought hunger to serfs across the country. Troops fire into the crowd, killing more than 100, and "Bloody Sunday" leads to a nationwide rebellion.

Chronology

1906

- In California, an earthquake sparks a four-day fire in San Francisco that leaves 225,000—more than half the city—homeless.
- In Finland, women win the right to vote—the first in Europe.
- In South Africa, Indian lawyer Mohandas Gandi protests discrimination against Indians.

1907

- In the United States, as a record 1.25 million immigrants pass through Ellis Island, Congress passes an immigration act that levies a $4 tax on each person and bars "feebleminded persons, epileptics, . . . paupers; persons likely to become a public charge; professional beggars; persons afflicted with tuberculosis or with a loathsome or dangerous contagious disease; persons not comprehended within any of the foregoing excluded classes who are found to be and are certified by the examining surgeon as being mentally or physically defective . . . persons hereinafter called contract laborers, who have been induced or solicited to migrate to this country by offers or promises of employment . . . [and] any person whose ticket or passage is paid for with the money of another, or who is assisted by others to come."
- In China, famine kills about 20 million people.

1908

- In the Congo, the Belgian parliament replaces King Leopold II as colonial ruler.
- In Italy, an earthquake kills about 200,000 people and forces the resettlement or emigration of many survivors.

1909

- John D. Rockefeller—the first U.S. billionaire—establishes the Rockefeller Sanitary Commission for Eradication of Hook-worm Disease, which afflicted poor southern farmers. On the success of that, in 1913, he endows the Rockefeller Foundation, which has since given more than $14 billion worldwide.

1910

- In Mexico, revolutionary groups begin a decadelong fight to overturn dictatorship and land policies that favor foreign investors over small farmers.

1911

- In Honduras, American banana shipper Samuel Zemurray orchestrates a coup to reinstall a deposed president, who then grants Zemurray's Cuyamel Fruit company land and 25 years without taxes.

1912

- In Central America, U.S. troops land in Honduras, Cuba, Panama, and Nicaragua, the last of which U.S. Marines occupy for more than two decades to defend American business and political interests.

1913

- The Sixteenth Amendment of the Constitution establishes a permanent income tax.

1914

- World War I engulfs Europe and within three years causes severe food shortages.
- Mohandas Gandhi returns to India from South Africa to join the campaign against British rule.

1915

- In the Ottoman Empire, Turkic leaders evict Armenians, more than a million of whom die of starvation, disease, and mass killings during forced migration to the edge of the Syrian desert.

1916

- In Brooklyn, Margaret Sanger opens the first American birth-control clinic, which operates for 10 days until police close it and arrest Sanger and her associates.
- A polio epidemic kills more than 6,000 Americans. Summer epidemics continue, peaking in the early 1950s.

1917

- In Russia, the Bolshevik Revolution leads to civil war.

1918

- ***January 8:*** President Wilson presents his Fourteen Points proposal for peace in Europe, arguing for free trade, open agreements, nations' right to self-determination, a settlement of colonial claims that weighs local interests, and the creation of a League of Nations.
- A flu pandemic kills 20 million people worldwide.

1919

- In the United States, African-American veterans' call for civil rights provokes race riots in 29 cities, notably East St. Louis and Chicago.

Chronology

1920

- In the United States, ratification of the Nineteenth Amendment establishes women's right to vote.
- In Italy, representatives of the Allies meeting at San Remo continue to dismantle the Ottoman Empire and carve up the Middle East. The League of Nations awards France a mandate over Syria and Lebanon and Britain a mandate over Palestine and Iraq.

1921

- In the United States, polio paralyzes future president Franklin Delano Roosevelt.
- In Ukraine and nearby regions of the new Soviet Union, famine follows drought, killing perhaps 5 million people.

1922

- The USSR unites Eastern European states under Communist government.

1924

- In the United States, Congress passes the National Origins Act, imposing strict quotas that limit immigration, especially from central and southern Europe.

1929

- In the United States, 1 percent of the population holds more than 40 percent of the nation's wealth.
- ***October 29:*** the U.S. stock market crashes, a loss of $30 billion.

1930

- In the United States, the number of unemployed tops 3.2 million, double the pre-crash figure. In New York City, thousands try to sell apples on the street.

1931

- In China, the Yangtze River bursts a dam, killing 3.7 million people by drowning, disease, and starvation.

1932

- In the United States, 10,000 banks have failed since 1929, and income and farm prices have fallen by more than half. Congress raises the top-tier tax rate from 25 to 63 percent.
- In Michigan, police and Ford Motor Company staff fire on union organizers and about 3,000 laid-off auto workers on a "Ford Hunger March," killing five and wounding scores.

- In Alabama, the U.S. Public Health Service enrolls about 600 poor, African-American sharecroppers in the Tuskegee Syphilis Study, which ends up lasting about 40 years. Although intended to improve black health care, the study withholds information and later treatment from 399 men with the infectious and sometimes fatal disease.
- In India, jailed nationalist leader Mohandas Gandhi begins a "fast unto death" to protest British plans for separate electorates for "Untouchables," the Dalits.
- In Ukraine and beyond, a "man-made famine" kills up to 7 million peasants.

1933

- ***March 4:*** With a quarter of the workforce unemployed, newly inaugurated President Franklin Roosevelt assures Americans that "the only thing we have to fear is fear itself."
- In Germany, Adolf Hitler and his new regime send political opponents to a concentration camp and sanction forced sterilization of Roma, African Germans, the handicapped, and others.

1934

- In the United States, drought and dust storms—black blizzards—continue to devastate farms small and large from the Great Plains west. In May, wind whips up about 350 million tons of western topsoil, which rains down on Chicago and prompts several East Coast cities to turn on the lights during the darkened day.
- Congress creates the Federal Housing Administration, which backs long-term mortgage loans, allowing more Americans to buy homes.
- In Mexico, newly elected president Lázaro Cárdenas carries out the promises of the 1910 revolution, supporting unions and dividing large estates among poor farmers. Six years later, he steps down to allow a free election.

1935

- In the United States, the Social Security Act establishes Aid to Families with Dependent Children (AFDC), unemployment insurance, aid to the blind, and old-age benefits.
- The Works Progress Administration (WPA) begins employing millions of Americans.
- The National Labor Relations (Wagner) Act protects workers' right to form unions and bargain collectively with their employers.

1936

- In China, a famine kills about 5 million people.

Chronology

1937

- In the United States, the Wagner-Steagle Housing Act authorizes construction of public housing and links it to slum removal.
- In the Midwest, the "Little Steel" strike fails but prompts harsh criticism of police brutality and management union-busting from the La Follette Civil Liberties Committee.

1938

- In the United States, Congress passes the Fair Labor Standards Act, which sets a minimum wage.
- ***November 9:*** In Germany, government-sanctioned mobs destroy Jewish synagogues, homes, and shops, smashing so many windows the pogroms come to be called Kristallnacht, night of broken glass. Troops kill at least 90 Jews and arrest 30,000, sending them to concentration camps.

1941

- Photographer Walker Evans and writer James Agee publish *Let Us Now Praise Famous Men*, a little-read documentary about Alabama sharecroppers that two decades later becomes a classic about social responsibility and the dignity, and complexity, of the poor.
- The United States enters World War II after Japan bombs Pearl Harbor in Hawaii.

1942

- President Roosevelt orders the internment of 110,000 Japanese Americans.
- In India, a rice fungus touches off a famine that kills 1.6 million people.

1943

- Race riots explode in Harlem and 46 other U.S. cities; in Detroit, white mobs riot for 30 hours, killing 25 African Americans.

1944

- In the United States, Congress prepares to reintegrate returning World War II veterans by passing the G.I. Bill of Rights, which eventually expands the middle class by underwriting college and technical education and backing home mortgages.
- African leaders meet French president Charles de Gaulle in Brazzaville, capital of the Republic of Congo. They issue a declaration calling for more democracy in French colonies.

- At the July Bretton Woods Conference in New Hampshire, representatives from 44 countries create the International Monetary Fund (IMF) and the International Bank for Reconstruction and Development (IBRD), one of five institutions of the World Bank.
- In Holland, Nazis discover the hiding place of teenager Anne Frank and her family and send them to concentration camps. She dies of typhus, but her diary, later published, gives an inkling of the misery unleashed by the Holocaust, a systematic genocide that kills 6 million Jews and more than 200,000 Roma and others.

1945

- The United States drops two atomic bombs on Japan. World War II ends.

1946

- The Allies lead the founding of the United Nations.
- Jordan, Lebanon, and Syria win independence.

1947

- In the United States, the Taft-Hartley Act passes despite President Harry Truman's veto and limits the power of organized labor.
- U.S. secretary of state George Marshall announces the Marshall Plan to catalyze European recovery.
- Free-trade proponents such as the United States launch the General Agreement on Tariffs and Trade (GATT).
- As Britain prepares to withdraw from Palestine, the United Nations proposes dividing the territory into two states, one Jewish and one Arab, with Jerusalem an international city.
- As Britain withdraws from India, Viceroy Lord Mountbatten partitions the subcontinent into separate states of India and (East and West) Pakistan. Strife between Hindus and Muslims—and briefly war between the two new countries—kills and displaces hundreds of thousands.
- In Argentina, rags-to-riches First Lady Eva Perón sets up a welfare foundation that builds hospitals and schools and distributes money, food, and medicine to the needy. Beloved by the masses, she dies of cancer in 1952.

1948

- In India, a Hindu extremist assassinates Mohandas Gandhi.
- In Palestine, Jewish extremists assassinate UN mediator Count Folke Bernadotte. War breaks out between the newly declared state of Israel and Arab fighters, driving millions of Palestinians off their land.

Chronology

- In Britain, the National Assistance Act abolishes the Poor Law that had linked aid with workhouses. Mandatory insurance payments fund a variety of benefits, from unemployment compensation to old-age pensions to "free" care by the National Health Service.

1949

- In China, civil war ends in victory for the Workers' and Peasants' Red Army, led by Mao Zedong. As leader of the new People's Republic of China, Mao effects land reform with an iron hand and institutes repressive Communist government.

1950

- In the United States, President Harry Truman's Point Four program provides technical aid to developing countries, in part to counter the spread of communism.
- In South Africa, the National Party passes the Population Registration Act, which requires the recording of everyone's race, and the Group Areas Act, which divides races into separate living areas. These and other laws created a system of apartheid that cement the white minority's control of the black and "Coloured" majority.

1951

- In Kansas and Missouri, the costliest U.S. flood to date causes about $1 billion in damage.

1952

- In Kenya, the Kikuyu people contest British colonialism, particularly land policies restricting Africans to "native reserves." The violent Mau Mau rebellion provokes a massive and brutal British response and claims at least 13,000 and perhaps many more lives before Kenya gains independence in 1963.

1954

- In Guatemala, a CIA-organized coup deposes Guatemalan president Jacobo Arbenz, whose land reforms threaten the multinational United Fruit Company.
- The U.S. Supreme Court declares racial segregation unconstitutional in *Brown v. Board of Education of Topeka, Kansas.*

1955

- In the United States, church bells ring at the announcement of a successful vaccine for polio.

- In Indonesia, representatives from 29 African and Asian countries (with more than half the world's population) meeting in Bandung condemn "colonialism in all of its manifestations" and stake out a nonaligned position between the two cold war superpowers, the United States and the Soviet Union.

1956

- In Montgomery, Alabama, Martin Luther King, Jr., organizes a bus boycott in the wake of Rosa Parks's arrest for refusing to sit at the back of bus.
- In North Africa, Morocco and Tunisia win independence from French colonial rule.

1957

- The Treaty of Rome creates the European Economic Community, the common market.
- The Gold Coast renames itself Ghana as it becomes the first sub-Saharan African colony to win independence.

1958

- In the United States, economist John Kenneth Galbraith's *The Affluent Society,* a critique of American consumerism, becomes a best seller.
- Nigerian writer Chinua Achebe publishes his novel about colonialism, *Things Fall Apart,* which asserts the dignity of traditional African village culture.

1959

- In Cuba, rebels led by Fidel Castro, "Ernesto Che" Guevara, and others succeed in toppling dictator Fulgencio Batista. The revolutionaries redistribute land and begin free education and health care. Opposed by the United States, the Castro government allies with the Soviet Union.
- In China, Mao's Great Leap Forward, a push for rapid industrialization and collective farming, catalyzes a famine that kills between 16.5 and 40 million people by 1961.

1960

- In South Africa, police kill 56 civilian protesters and the government bans two major antiapartheid groups, the African National Congress and the Pan-Africanist Congress.

1961

- From the United States, the first Peace Corps volunteers depart for development assignments in Ghana and Tanzania.

- President John F. Kennedy sends military advisers to help the South Vietnamese government fight Communist guerrillas. Within a year, U.S. troops are joining combat missions. To expose guerrilla trails and destroy enemy crops, they spray deadly chemicals such as "Agent Orange," which causes health and environmental problems that linger even after most U.S. troops withdraw 12 years later.
- The Kennedy administration proposes the Alliance for Progress to increase per-capita income and reduce inequality in Latin America—and counter the appeal of communism. During the Vietnam War, however, the United States scales back its financial commitment, and regional governments balk at reform.
- In East Germany, Communist leaders build a wall in East Berlin to prevent escape to the West.

1962

- In the United States, Congress passes the Public Welfare Amendments bill to spur states to expand services to the needy, such as job training and day care, promoting "self-support" through a return to work.

1963

- In the United States, Martin Luther King, Jr., leads a civil rights march 200,000 strong in Washington, D.C. and delivers his "I Have a Dream" speech at the Lincoln Memorial.
- Congress passes a bill guaranteeing women equal pay for equal work.
- The Supreme Court rules in *Gideon v. Wainwright* that states must provide poor defendants with a lawyer.

1964

- In the United States, Congress passes the Economic Opportunity Act, the heart of President Lyndon Johnson's War on Poverty, and the Civil Rights Act, which outlaws discrimination in public facilities and on the job.

1965

- In the United States, Medicare and Medicaid insure health care for the elderly, disabled, and poor.
- In Alabama, police with billy clubs and tear gas attack 600 peaceful civil rights marchers, who return later with Martin Luther King, Jr., and other leaders. Less than five months later, Congress passes the Voting Rights Act outlawing literacy tests and targeting other barriers to political participation.
- In the Dominican Republic, U.S. troops invade to prevent a Communist takeover.

- In the Democratic Republic of the Congo, renamed Zaire, General Mobutu Sese Seko seizes power and begins three decades of one-party rule. Backed by the West for his anticommunist stance, flamboyant Mobutu amasses a fortune as his country falls deeper into poverty.
- In India, drought leads to 1.5 million deaths.

1966

- In the United States, feminists such as journalist Betty Friedan found the National Organization for Women (NOW) to pursue equal rights for women.

1967

- In the United States, racial "disturbances" roil more than 120 cities. Friction between African Americans and police sparks deadly July riots in Newark and Detroit, where the five-day rampage leaves 43 dead, 1,189 injured, and 7,000 under arrest. Although police misconduct is the flashpoint, many acknowledge economic inequality as the underlying cause, particularly the lack of decent, affordable housing.
- In the Middle East, Israel seizes the Sinai and the Gaza Strip from Egypt, the West Bank and Jerusalem from Jordan, and the Golan Heights from Syria in the Six-Day War.

1968

- In the United States, the Kerner Commission, appointed by President Lyndon Johnson to investigate the Detroit riot, reports, "Our nation is moving toward two societies, one black, one white—separate and unequal."
- In Memphis, Tennessee, James Earl Ray assassinates Martin Luther King, Jr. who has come to Memphis to lead a sanitation workers' strike. Riots erupt nationwide.
- In Washington, D.C., more than a thousand squatters build shanties—"Resurrection City"—on the National Mall as part of the Poor People's Campaign organized by the Southern Christian Leadership and National Welfare Rights Organization. The protest for economic justice fizzles, however, under heavy rains, bad news, and differing agendas.
- In Los Angeles, Sirhan Sirhan assassinates pro-poor presidential candidate Robert F. Kennedy.
- Pope Paul VI reaffirms the Catholic Church's opposition to all forms of birth control except the rhythm method.
- In France, a student strike in May expands into a national strike involving about two-thirds of the workforce. It forces a leadership change and feeds into student and worker protests worldwide.

Chronology

1969

- U.S. astronauts land on the Moon, sending back images of Earth that suggest the fragility and interdependence of life on this planet floating in space.
- In China, a famine begins taking the lives of about 20 million people.

1970

- In California, the five-year boycott organized by the United Farm Workers yields fruit as most grape growers sign contracts with the union.

1971

- In the United States, the Supreme Court upholds busing as a means to school integration.
- President Richard Nixon announces a "New Economic Policy" to combat rising inflation and unemployment. Among his interventions are freezing wages and prices for three months, taxing imports, and reducing foreign aid by 10 percent.
- In North Vietnam, floods from heavy rains kill about 100,000 people.
- In Chile, democratically elected Marxist president Salvador Allende begins nationalizing foreign-owned businesses, including U.S. copper mines. An all-out U.S.-led effort to discredit Allende helps undermine the Chilean economy, and two years later Allende dies in a CIA-backed coup.

1972

- In Washington, D.C., American Indian Movement activists occupy the Bureau of Indian Affairs and deliver a 20-point manifesto demanding a review of treaty commitments and violations, protection for Indian religion and culture, and "health, housing, employment, economic development, and education."

1973

- In India, village women circle trees to prevent loggers working on behalf of a sporting goods company from cutting them down. Chipko (embrace) protests spread across the northern Himalayan region, becoming an environmental movement.
- In midst of the Middle East Yom Kippur War, Arab oil producers embargo shipments to the West to protest U.S. support for Israel. A global energy crisis follows.

1974

- In Europe, the EU starts a redevelopment fund to build infrastructure in poor areas and attract investment and create jobs.

- The EU and African, Caribbean, and Pacific states sign the Lomé Convention, which governs aid and trade relations until the Cotonou Agreement replaces it in 2000.
- In Argentina, the Bariloche Foundation, a research institute, publishes "Limits to Poverty," a Socialist proposal for fulfilling basic needs worldwide. It counters the controversial, pessimistic 1972 report, "Limits to Growth," in which the NGO Club of Rome predicted that overpopulation would lead to global collapse.

1975

- In Cambodia, Khmer Rouge leader Pol Pot institutes extreme peasant communism, marching city residents into the countryside and killing intellectuals. Over the next four years, about 3 million Cambodians—a quarter of the population—die of starvation, overwork, and execution.
- In Lebanon, civil war erupts.
- In Mexico City, the United Nations holds the First World Conference on Women and within a year creates UNIFEM, a development fund promoting women's human rights, political participation, and economic security.

1977

- In the United States, the minimum wage rises to $2.65 per hour.
- Breast-feeding proponents launch a boycott against infant formula maker Nestlé, which they claim advertises misleadingly in developing countries.

1978

- In the United States, the Supreme Court delivers a divided opinion in the Bakke case, ruling that universities can consider race as a factor in admissions but cannot use strict numerical quotas, a cornerstone of affirmative action.

1979

- In Iran, the U.S.-backed shah flees the Islamic Revolution.
- In Afghanistan, the Soviet Union invades and begins a nine-year occupation marked by battles with anticommunist Muslim *mujahideen*.

1980

- In Poland, shipyard workers strike and form the independent Solidarity trade union. Although the Communist government imposes martial law a year later, Solidarity persists, and in 1990, Poles elect Solidarity founder and one-time electrician Lech Walesa as president.
- The Independent Commission on International Development Issues publishes the "Brandt Report" on world poverty and North-South inequality, which generates much debate.

Chronology

The World Health Organization declares smallpox eradicated as a result of worldwide vaccinations.

1981

- President Ronald Reagan instigates the largest tax cut in U.S. history.

1982

- Mexico stops making loan payments, revealing the debt crisis among developing nations.
- In Syria, government forces seeking to expunge the Muslim Brotherhood destroy the city of Hama, perhaps killing as many as 25,000 civilians.

1984

- In Ethiopia, famine kills perhaps a million people.
- In Mexico City, at the International Conference on Population, Reagan administration officials announce that the United States will not fund NGOs that perform or promote abortions for family planning. Although President Bill Clinton discontinues the "Mexico City policy" in 1993, President George W. Bush restores it in 2001.

1985

- Boomtown Rats singer-songwriter Bob Geldof organizes the Live Aid charity rock concert. Held in London and Philadelphia and broadcast to 1.9 billion TV viewers worldwide, it raises well more than $70 million for famine relief in Ethiopia.

1986

- In Ukraine, an explosion at the Chernobyl plant spews radioactive material across Europe.
- Falling oil prices create hardships for developing-nation exporters such as Mexico, Libya, and Indonesia.

1987

- In the United States, the Stewart B. McKinney Homeless Assistance Act establishes the first comprehensive program to shelter and rehouse the homeless.

1988

- In the United States, the Family Support Act launches Job Opportunities and Basic Skills (JOBS), a voluntary welfare-to-work program.

1989

- In Germany, the Berlin Wall—a symbolic cold war barrier—falls.

WORLD POVERTY

1990

- In Thailand, delegates from 155 countries at the World Education Forum commit to Education for All (EFA), including universal primary schooling within 15 years.
- In Lebanon, Syrian troops intervene in a 15-year civil war.

1991

- In Eastern Europe, the Soviet Union dissolves and former satellite republics form a loose Commonwealth of Independent States.
- In Bangladesh, a cyclone kills 130,000 people and leaves 9 million more homeless.
- In Croatia, Serbia, and Bosnia and Herzegovina, civil war follows the breakup of Yugoslavia.

1994

- In Cairo, Egypt, delegates from 179 countries at the International Conference on Population and Development (ICPD) set goals to improve maternal-child health and reduce HIV infection through universal access to reproductive health services and to primary education.
- In Rwanda, ethnic strife intensifies, leading to the death of 800,000 during a genocide of Tutsis and the flight of Hutus into neighboring countries.

1995

- The World Trade Organization forms to establish rules among its members, building upon GATT.
- In Copenhagen, Denmark, leaders of 117 nations at the World Summit on Social Development pledge to eradicate poverty, achieve gender equality, and put people at the center of development.
- In North Korea, floods ruin about 16 percent of farming land, exacerbating chronic food shortages and leading to famine that kills about 2 million people. Reluctantly, the secretive regime asks for help.

1996

- The World Bank and IMF inaugurate the Heavily Indebted Poor Countries (HIPC) Initiative, debt relief for the poorest loan-saddled nations that cooperate on a poverty reduction plan. Revisions in 1999 make relief faster, deeper, and broader.
- In the United States, the Personal Responsibility and Work Opportunity Reconciliation Act replaces cash aid as an entitlement program with limited Temporary Assistance for Needy Families.

Chronology

- The United Nations declares an International Decade for the Eradication of Poverty.
- In Zaire, soon to be renamed the Democratic Republic of the Congo, rebel leader Laurent Kabila drives out 32-year dictator Mobutu Sese Seko. Civil war follows.
- In Albania, one of Europe's poorest countries, armed revolt breaks out after a nationwide swindle robs as much as two-thirds of the population of their life savings and derails democratization.

1998

- In Asia, a stock and currency crash creates economic crisis.

1999

- In Turkey, an earthquake kills about 17,000 people and leaves thousands more homeless.

2000

- In Syria, longtime dictator-president Hafiz al-Assad dies and is succeeded by son Bashar.
- ***September:*** The United Nations hosts a three-day Millennium Summit, the largest gathering of world leaders in history.

2001

- ***January:*** In El Salvador, an earthquake and aftershock kills more than 800 people and leaves perhaps a million homeless as adobe houses crumble and other buildings sustain structural damage. The same month, an earthquake in Gujarat, India, kills more than 16,000 and leaves another million or so homeless.
- In Quebec City, Canada, police arrest more than 400 antiglobalization protesters outside the Summit of the Americas economic conference.
- In Afghanistan, the United States invades as part of a "global war on terror" after a terrorist attack demolishes the World Trade Center in New York City and hits the Pentagon outside Washington, D.C., killing almost 3,000 people.

2002

- The Group of 8 (G8) launches the Global Fund to Fight AIDS, Tuberculosis, and Malaria.

2003

- In Iraq, the United States invades to topple the regime of Saddam Hussein.

- At the Vatican, Pope John Paul II beatifies Mother Teresa for her work among the Indian poor—perhaps the first step in declaring her a Catholic saint.
- In the Darfur region of western Sudan, government forces battle rebels from the Sudan Liberation Army (SLA) and the Justice and Equality Movement (JEM). Within four years, this complex and brutal conflict creates an estimated 2 million IDPs and refugees.

2004

- In Florida, four hurricanes land, killing 99 people and causing about $26 billion in damage, raising prices and the difficulty of obtaining homeowners' insurance.
- In Asia, an undersea earthquake launches a tsunami that inundates coasts in Sri Lanka, India, Thailand, and Indonesia (the hardest hit), kills approximately 150,000 people and leaves more than 5 million homeless.
- In Ukraine, widespread perception of election fraud spurs an "Orange Revolution" and a second ballot in which voters choose Viktor Yushchenko for president.

2005

- In the United States, Hurricane Katrina swamps the Gulf Coast and New Orleans.
- The U.S. Census Bureau reports that a record 35.2 million foreign-born people live in the United States—well more than double the number at the immigration peak of the early 1900s. The bureau estimates that between 9 and 13 million are illegal immigrants.
- In Pakistan and northern India, an earthquake kills about 73,000 and leaves 3 million homeless.
- In Britain, a coalition of organizations launches Make Poverty History, a campaign to pressure world leaders for fairer trade and debt relief. Live 8 concerts around the world echo this theme, playing off the 20th anniversary of Live Aid and the simultaneous G8 summit.
- In Scotland, G8 leaders vow to increase African aid $25 billion by 2010.

2006

- The World Bank, IMF, and African Development Fund begin forgiving debt in deeply impoverished nations under the Multilateral Debt Relief Initiative.
- In Bangladesh, Muhammad Yunus and the Grameen Bank celebrate winning the Nobel Peace Prize.

Chronology

2007

- In Venezuela, President Hugo Chávez begins nationalizing utilities in a fiery assertion of socialism to defy "U.S. imperialism."
- President George W. Bush visits Uruguay, Colombia, Brazil, Guatemala, and Mexico to underscore U.S. assistance to Latin America.
- The U.S. Congress passes the Mortgage Forgiveness Debt Relief Act and considers other measures to stem the financial crisis caused by predatory lending and the subsequent rise in loan defaults and home foreclosures.
- On the 20th anniversary of International Day for the Eradication of Poverty, UN General Secretary Ban Ki-Moon reports uneven progress, noting, "some regions—particularly sub-Saharan Africa—are not on track to redeem even a single one of our grand promises [MDGs]."

2008

- At the World Economic Forum in Davos, Switzerland, former U.S. vice president and 2007 Nobel Peace Prize winner Al Gore and activist/musician Bono warn that global leaders are not doing enough to tackle the linked issues of global warming and global poverty.
- As Damascus kicks off a year as "cultural capital of the Arab world," studies reveal that many of the roughly 1.5 million Iraqi refugees in Syria are running out of money.

2015

- The Millennium Development Goals come due.

Glossary

absolute poverty insufficient income to secure enough food (2,124 calories per person per day) or other nonfood essentials such as clothing and shelter.

accountability responsibility for actions, decisions, and policies that includes informing anyone affected.

affirmative action programs to counter past exclusion by increasing the representation of women and minorities in education, business, and government. Affirmative action sometimes takes the controversial form of preferences in admissions and hiring—so-called positive discrimination.

antiretroviral (ARV) therapy a combination of prescription drugs that interfere with HIV replication and prolong better health.

apartheid policy of strict racial segregation and political and economic discrimination implemented by the white minority in South Africa from 1948 to 1994.

appropriation government spending set aside for a specific purpose.

asset an item of economic value such as property, land, or money.

asylum seeker a person claiming refugee status.

balance of trade a situation in which the value of a country's exports equals the value of its imports. A balance of trade *deficit* refers to a preponderance of imports.

basic education informal and formal schooling (primary and sometimes lower secondary) that equips people with necessary life skills.

bonded labor a pledge of labor (your own or a family member's) in return for a loan.

brain drain migration of educated and skilled people from developing to developed countries in anticipation of better economic and social opportunities.

Bretton Woods institutions the five institutions of the World Bank (WB) and the International Monetary Fund (IMF).

Glossary

capabilities approach a development vision based not on income but on people's freedom to choose the life they want.

capacity building investing in people, institutions, and practices in order to develop skills (such as leadership) that increase a country's independence in the development process.

carrying capacity maximum population that can live in an area without causing irreparable environmental damage.

child mortality rate number of deaths among children under five years old per 1,000 children in the same age group.

civil society nongovernment and nonbusiness institutions ranging from voluntary and nonprofit organizations to philanthropies to social movements.

consumption use of goods and services by a consumer or producer.

cost-benefit analysis an appraisal that weighs the actual and potential costs (both private and social) of an investment or a policy change against potential benefits.

culture of poverty a theory that attributes the persistence of poverty among a subset of the urban poor to a value system characterized by mistrust of social institutions and short-term thinking.

debt relief loan cancellation, rescheduling, refinancing, or reorganization.

debt service ratio a common debt assessment measure that calculates what a country owes (including interest payments) as a percentage of exports. Experts consider a ratio of more than 30 percent severe debt.

deficiency disease an illness caused by malnutrition such as scurvy (lack of vitamin C), beriberi (lack of thiamine), pellagra (lack of niacin), and osteoporosis (lack of calcium).

dependency theory a variety of theories that blame the Global South's underdevelopment on external factors, particularly on an unhealthy, dependent relationship with the North. Generally critical of capitalism, development theory argues that rich nations penalize poor nations that try to strike an independent course because these First World countries need the Third World as a source of cheap labor and natural resources and as a dumping ground for obsolete consumer goods and technology.

desertification transformation of land into desert because of overgrazing, deforestation, climate change, and/or harmful agricultural practices.

developing country a loose term identifying a poor nation, often a former colony in Asia, Africa, Latin America, or the South Pacific. Synonyms for *developing* include *low-income, underdeveloped, Global South, majority world,* and *Third World.*

development a process of economic and social transformation that may take different forms. Done well, development can raise people's standard of living, increase their self-esteem, and expand their choices.

digital divide the opportunity gap between individuals or communities that have access to the Internet and those that do not.

dual economy the coexistence of two different and usually unequal economic systems within the same country. Typically, developing nations with a dual economy have cities with a growing, industrialized market economy that contrasts with a more traditional rural economy.

economic growth wealth-producing improvement over time in the (monetary and nonmonetary) value of goods and services and the ability to produce them.

economic sanction a penalty such as denying loans or freezing aid in order to change the economic or political policy of another nation.

empowerment expanding the poor's freedom of choice and action by increasing assets and capabilities.

enclave economy a developing country with small pockets of development and prosperity, usually because of foreign mining or plantation agriculture.

encomienda a Spanish colonial institution in the Americas that granted conquistadores the right to exploit the indigenous population—but not the land—within a designated area.

entitlement program a government program guaranteeing benefits—such as Social Security or farm price supports—to as many individuals as meet the criteria under law.

failed state a nation with a shattered and undependable political and social structure.

fair trade equal and nonexploitative exchange between producers in developing countries and Western consumers. It avoids middlemen and offers producers stable prices.

fertility rate number of children born alive per year per 1,000 women of childbearing age (normally 15 to 49).

food insecurity limited or uncertain access to nutritious, safe foods necessary to lead a healthy life, as defined by the U.S. Department of Agriculture.

forced migration involuntary movement of people because of conflict, development policies and projects, and natural disasters.

foreign direct investment long-term investment by a foreign firm in local buildings, equipment, or companies—but not the local stock market.

free trade international trade free of add-on charges and restrictions such as taxes and quotas.

Gini coefficient a measure of inequality. It falls between 0 (perfect equality) and 1 (total inequality).

globalization the interaction and integration of people, economies, and governments, which has accelerated at the turn of the millennium because of technology.

Green Revolution a term for 1960s agricultural advances that included fertilizers, pesticides, irrigation, mechanization, and new hybrid, high-yield strains of wheat, corn, and rice.

gross domestic product (GDP) the total value of all goods and services produced by a country in a specified period (usually annually).

gross national product (GNP) a measure of national income that equals the GDP plus income from foreign investments.

Group of 8 (G8) a group of economically powerful countries—Canada, France, Germany, Great Britain, Italy, Japan, Russia, and the United States—that holds an annual summit meeting.

human capital people and especially their skills and abilities, which contribute to economic productivity and well-being.

human trafficking kidnapping or coercing people in order to exploit them, such as forcing women into prostitution.

informal economy the buying and selling of goods and services, from day care to the black market, under government radar and often avoiding taxation.

internally displaced person (IDP) someone who flees violence, disaster, or human-rights abuses and seeks safety within the same country.

laissez-faire an economic doctrine opposed to government interference (regulation) in the marketplace.

liberation theology a school of thought first articulated by Latin American Catholics that finds in Christ's teaching a mandate to fight poverty and oppression, even if that means challenging the ruling elite within the church and the government.

living wage the minimum hourly wage workers need to earn to cross above the poverty line and support a family.

local knowledge traditional wisdom woven into the fabric of a community that has shaped rituals, relationships, and common practices.

low-income country a country such as Haiti, India, or Yemen defined by the World Bank as having a gross national per-capita income of $875 or less in 2005.

macroeconomics study of the "big picture" of an economy, such as a country's total production, income, and employment.

maquiladora foreign-owned assembly plant in Latin America that imports materials and equipment duty free, uses local labor, and exports products worldwide. Maquiladoras originated along the U.S.-Mexican border in the 1960s and employ mostly women.

marginalization ostracism of the disadvantaged or "undesirable."

market economy an economic system in which private companies produce most goods and services, the price of which follows supply and demand.

median income the middle income of a given group, with half earning more and half earning less.

microeconomics study of the behavior of small economic units such as individual companies or households.

microfinance small loans extended to nontraditional borrowers—such as poor, rural women—usually to enable them to start small businesses.

minimum wage the least hourly rate a U.S. employer may pay most workers according to the Fair Labor Standard Act.

multinational corporation a company such as Coca-Cola headquartered in one (usually) Western country but operating throughout the world.

neoliberalism a philosophy associated with the West and with globalization that favors economic competition and expansion of the marketplace.

newly industrialized countries nations such as South Korea and Malaysia that have attracted auto, electric, and other manufacturing plants thanks to government incentives, relatively educated workers, low wages, and lax environmental regulations.

nongovernmental organization (NGO) any local, national, or international organization not sponsored by the state.

oral rehydration therapy effective, inexpensive treatment for childhood diarrhea.

paradigm a general conception, model, or worldview that may be influential in shaping thinking on a particular subject.

Paris Club an informal group of lending nations—including many European countries, Japan, and the United States—that coordinates such debt relief to developing nations as postponing or reducing payments.

peripheral poverty material deprivation combined with isolation, as in rural areas.

poverty material deprivation, or "a human condition characterized by the sustained or chronic deprivation of the resources, capabilities, choices, security and power necessary for the enjoyment of an adequate standard of living and other civil, cultural, economic, political and social rights," as defined by the United Nations Educational, Scientific and Cultural Organization.

poverty gap a measure of the depth of poverty, roughly the difference between the poverty line and the actual incomes of poor people, multiplied by the percentage of the extremely poor.

poverty line or **threshold** a measurement that varies across time and societies that marks the minimum level of income necessary to meet basic needs.

poverty map graphic that shows the geographic distribution of poverty within a region.

predatory lending abusive practices such as hidden fees and high interest rates that take advantage of borrowers' ignorance or vulnerability.

public health either the general health of a community or the science of improving it, with an emphasis on preventing disease through sanitation and education.

qualitative method research analyzing human behavior and the reasons behind it.

quantitative method research involving numerical measurements.

refugee a person unable or unwilling to return to his or her home country because of a well-grounded fear of persecution.

relative poverty a diminished state of well-being measured against the average for a given society.

remittance money that migrants working abroad send back to their home country.

satyagraha nonviolent resistance to oppression, as coined by Mohandas Gandhi from the Sanskrit roots, *satya,* "truth," and *agraha,* "persuasion."

settlement house neighborhood center where middle- and upper-middle-class reformers of the late 19th century lived and served the poor

social capital connections among people—trust, shared values, and the like—that nurture cooperation, "glue" together institutions, and contribute to development.

social exclusion a consequence of poverty resulting from repeated unemployment, neighborhood decline, family breakdown, and so on that prevents people from contributing to and participating fully in society.

social safety net collection of government programs and services that prevents people from falling into absolute poverty.

stakeholder a person or group that stands to gain or lose from a project or policy.

structural adjustment macroeconomic reform that liberalizes trade and investment policy.

subsidiarity a decentralization principle that holds that a large and complex organization (such as a central government) should only take on tasks and make decisions that a smaller, simpler organization (such as a state office) cannot handle.

subsidy public aid such as a tax break, price support, or cash payment to keep prices low or stable or to help businesses survive.

subsistence economy a largely self-contained economy that produces just basic necessities—food, shelter, and clothing.

sustainable development economic growth that considers short- and long-term consequences, improving well-being today without jeopardizing resources for future generations.

tied aid loans or grants that require the recipient country to use the funds to purchase goods and or services from the donor country.

tithe a Judeo-Christian tradition of giving one-tenth of income or harvest to the religious community, often to support charity.

trade liberalization removing tariffs, quotas, subsidies, and other regulations and barriers that interfere with free trade.

transitional economy a country's economy that is changing from central planning to a market orientation.

transparency sharing information, maintaining clear channels of communication, and acting in an open manner.

trickle-down theory the belief that the benefits of economic growth, so apparent for the rich, trickle down to the masses in the form of jobs and other opportunities.

underclass a negative term for the chronically disadvantaged somehow cut off from mainstream society.

underdevelopment poverty, often seen as caused by the harmful and selfish policies of more powerful nations.

vulnerability increased risk to shock or negative impacts because of poverty, gender, age, disability, ethnicity, or other criteria that may reduce people's coping ability and access to resources.

waqf an endowment of land or property established under Islamic law. The income from the trust usually benefits mosques, schools, hospitals, orphanages, or other charities.

Washington Consensus a formula that major financial institutions based in Washington, D.C., recommend to foreign governments to achieve a sound market economy. The U.S. Treasury, World Bank, and IMF often advise reforms such as privatizing public companies, eliminating trade barriers, inviting foreign investment, protecting property rights, and spending on basic services and infrastructure.

Women in Development (WID) an attention to women's economic contributions that evolved from 1970s recognition that development schemes often ignored and sometimes harmed women. The concept has given way to a broader Gender and Development (GAD) awareness of gender bias and barriers.

Index

Note: page numbers in **boldface** indicate major treatment of a subject. Page numbers followed by *f* indicate figures. Page numbers followed by *b* indicate biographical entries. Page numbers followed by *c* indicate chronology entries. Page numbers followed by *g* indicate glossary entries.

Index

Index

H

Index

Index

Index

T

Index